# Good Housekeeping

# STEP-BY-STEP VEGETARIAN COOK BOOK

# Good Housekeeping

# STEP-BY-STEP VEGETARIAN COOK BOOK

TED SMART

A TED SMART Publication 1999

First published 1997

This new edition published 1999



First published in the United Kingdom in 1997 by Ebury Press,
Random House, 20 Vauxhall Bridge Road, London SW1V 2SA

Random House Australia (Pty) Limited
20 Alfred Street, Milsons Point, Sydney,
New South Wales 2061, Australia

Random House New Zealand Limited
18 Poland Road, Glenfield,
Auckland 10, New Zealand

Random House South Africa (Pty) Limited
Endulini, 5A Jubilee Road,
Parktown 2193, South Africa

Random House UK Limited Reg. No. 954009

A CIP catalogue record for this book is available from the British Library.

MANAGING EDITOR: JANET ILLSLEY

DESIGN: Sara Kidd
SPECIAL PHOTOGRAPHY: Graham Kirk
FOOD STYLIST: Louise Pickford
PHOTOGRAPHIC STYLIST: Helen Payne
TECHNIQUES PHOTOGRAPHY: Karl Adamson
FOOD TECHNIQUES STYLIST: Angela Kingsbury
OTHER PHOTOGRAPHS: Gus Filgate, James Murphy, Laurie Evans,
Ken Field, Philip Webb, Peter Knab, Harry Cory-Wright, James Merrell, David Gill
COLOUR ILLUSTRATIONS: Lynne Robinson

MAIN CONTRIBUTING AUTHOR: Louise Pickford
OTHER RECIPES FROM: The Good Housekeeping Institute, Joanna Farrow, Maxine Clark,
Lyn Rutherford, Jacqueline Clarke, Janet Smith, Linda Fraser, Clare Gordon-Smith, Linda Yewdall
RECIPE TESTING: Emma-Lee Gow
ADDITIONAL EDITORIAL ASSISTANCE: Fiona Hunter, Helen Bonthrone, Hilary Bird
The publishers are also grateful to THE VEGETARIAN SOCIETY for their help and advice.

Printed and bound in Portugal by Printer Portuguesa

# Contents

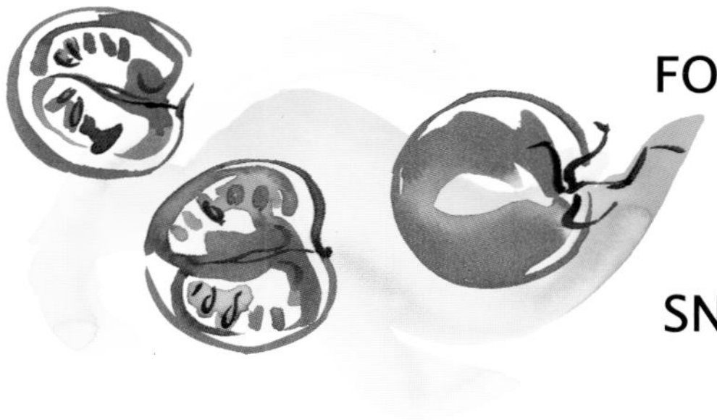

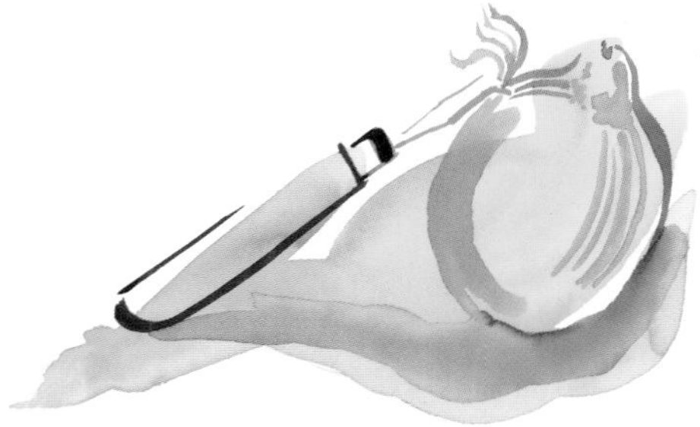

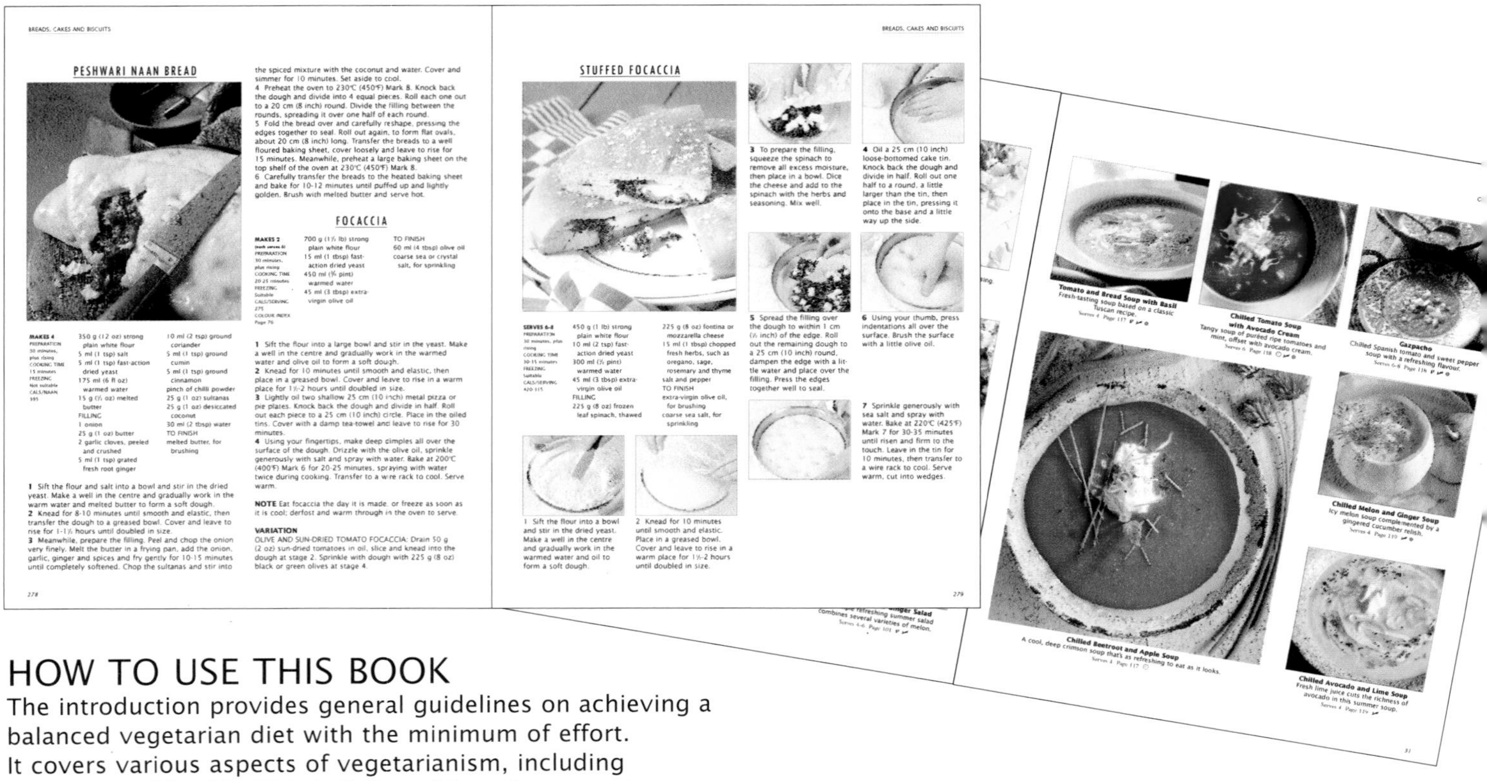


# HOW TO USE THIS BOOK

The introduction provides general guidelines on achieving a balanced vegetarian diet with the minimum of effort. It covers various aspects of vegetarianism, including nutrition and health. This is followed by a focus on those ingredients which feature strongly in a healthy vegetarian diet, with information on how to choose, prepare, cook and serve the food in question.

Your starting point for choosing recipes and planning a menu is the colour index. Here you will find a photograph of every recipe in the book, plus a brief description of the dish, the number it serves and reference to the page on which the recipe appears. In addition, you will find the following useful symbols:

❄ The 'freezer symbol' indicates that the recipe is suitable for freezing.

ν This denotes that the recipe is suitable for vegans (providing those non-vegan ingredients which are designated optional in the recipe are excluded).

✓ This symbol tells you that the recipe can be prepared ahead for convenience.

◷ The 'fast symbol' identifies those recipes which can be prepared and cooked in less than 30 minutes.

Step-by-step instructions and photographs make the recipes easy to follow. Alongside the ingredients of each recipe, you will also find the following information:

❑ Preparation and cooking times, including any additional time for marinating, soaking beans etc.

❑ Suitability of the dish for freezing. Where the dish should be frozen at the end of a certain stage of the method, this stage is indicated.

❑ Calorie counts are given per serving or appropriate portion of the dish. Where the calorie count ranges from a higher to a lower figure, this reflects that the number the recipe serves is variable. The lower calorie count will apply if you are serving the larger number, as the portion size will be smaller.

Refer to the basic reference section at the end of the book for clarification of any specific cookery terms, and for general information on food hygiene, storage and freezing.

COOKERY NOTES

❑ Both metric and imperial measures are given for the recipes. Follow either metric or imperial throughout as they are not interchangeable.

❑ All spoon measures are level unless otherwise stated. Sets of measuring spoons are available in metric and imperial for accurate measurement of small quantities.

❑ Ovens should be preheated to the specified temperature. Grills should also be preheated. The cooking times given in the recipes assume that this has been done.

❑ Where a stage is specified under freezing instructions, the dish should be frozen at the end of that stage.

❑ Large eggs should be used except where otherwise specified. Free-range eggs should be used.

❑ Use freshly ground black pepper and sea salt unless otherwise specified.

❑ Use fresh rather than dried herbs unless dried herbs are suggested in the recipe.

❑ Ideally stocks should be freshly made. Alternatively buy ready-made vegetarian stocks or good quality stock cubes.

# FOREWORD

When you love good food, it's a delight to find and enjoy a collection of really good recipes. Every week in the Good Housekeeping Institute – founded 75 years ago – we cook, taste and double-test dozens of new dishes for the pages of *Good Housekeeping* magazine and our books. And, thanks to your constant stream of letters and calls, we know we're winning you compliments from family and friends.

In response to current trends, we now produce as many vegetarian dishes as meat-based ones in the Good Housekeeping Institute. Gone are the days when vegetarian food was considered cranky and boring. And it's not only vegetarians who are enjoying meat-free dishes – more and more people are 'demi-veg' too.

In this exciting new cookbook, we offer no fewer than 500 recipe ideas and suggestions which show that vegetarian food can be creative, delicious and nourishing. And, as more and more ingredients have become available to the vegetarian cook, including exotic fruit and vegetables, nuts, pulses and grains, we have compiled a useful 'focus on ingredients' to highlight the wide choice. Finally, the complete colour index of all the recipes will help you to select at a glance the dishes you'd like to try.

**Moyra Fraser**
*Cookery Editor*
*Good Housekeeping*

# INTRODUCTION

These days being a vegetarian means enjoying a rich and varied diet of vegetables, pulses, fruit, spices, grains and herbs. Not surprising, then, that the proportion of vegetarians in the population as a whole has more than doubled in recent years – and numbers continue to rise. Furthermore, surveys have shown that many people who still consume meat eat far less than they used to.

Rejecting meat and fish allows you to draw on vegetarian dishes from some of the world's most exciting, flavourful and nutritious cuisines – southern India, the Far East, the Mediterranean and North Africa, for example. And with the wealth of choice in our markets and supermarkets, eating without meat need never be boring!

WHAT IS A VEGETARIAN?

A vegetarian is defined as 'someone who eats no fish, flesh or fowl'. Many vegetarians also avoid gelatine, animal fats such as lard and suet, and animal rennet in non-vegetarian cheeses. However the majority of vegetarians eat dairy produce, including milk, vegetarian cheeses and free-range eggs.

Vegans follow a more restrictive diet, which also excludes all dairy products, eggs, and even foods like honey.

WHY DO PEOPLE BECOME VEGETARIAN?

People become vegetarians for a variety of reasons. For many, it is a sense of compassion that causes a change in diet.

Several religions – including Hindu, Sikh and Seventh Day Adventists – advocate vegetarianism on the grounds that it is a more humane alternative to a diet which allows meat.

Some people decide to become vegetarian for health reasons. By its nature, a varied vegetarian diet is low in saturated fat and high in fibre. Studies have shown that obesity is less common in vegetarians – even when compared with health-conscious meat eaters, vegetarians have a lower incidence of obesity. Vegetarians are also less likely to suffer from heart disease, and are less vulnerable to cancer, diabetes, high blood pressure and gall stones. However, it is wrong to assume that all vegetarians have healthier diets than carnivores. For example, it is quite common for new vegetarians, in particular, to rely heavily on cheese and eggs which are high in saturated fat and cholesterol. A healthy vegetarian diet is a varied one.

HOW EASY IS IT TO BE A VEGETARIAN?

With the ever-increasing variety of fresh vegetables, fruit, nuts, seeds, spices and herbs, it is becoming much easier to cook a wide range of tasty, nutritious vegetarian meals. Supermarkets and healthfood shops also offer all kinds of pasta, rice and pulses.

To make shopping easier, many products suitable for vegetarians are now identified by the Ⓥ symbol. This endorsement by The Vegetarian Society ensures that the product has been thoroughly checked. Many supermarkets also have their own vegetarian symbol.

Food manufacturers are also responding to vegetarian demands. It is no longer difficult to obtain vegetarian cheeses or free-range eggs, for example. More and more ready meals are being developed to suit vegetarians, too.

Eating out is no longer the problem it used to be for vegetarians, as restaurant and hotel menus include increasingly imaginatively vegetarian options. If you are a strict vegetarian, you may wish to check that any stocks and cheeses used are vegetarian, and that cooking oils and fats are vegetable and not animal derived.

If you are just embarking on a vegetarian diet, you may find it difficult to exclude meat, fish and poultry all at once. Start by introducing two or three vegetarian meals each week then, as you and your family acquire the taste for vegetarian dishes, omit more animal protein from meals. The recipes in this book should provide plenty of ideas.

IS A VEGETARIAN DIET HEALTHY?

As with any kind of diet, variety is important. Provided a wide range of foods is eaten, a vegetarian diet is very unlikely to be lacking nutritionally. You do not need to be a nutritionist to ensure a healthy vegetarian diet, but a basic understanding of the value of certain foods is helpful. To maintain a healthy body, everyone needs protein, vitamins, minerals, fibre, carbohydrates and a little fat.

❑ PROTEIN is made up of smaller units (amino acids), which are an important part of every cell in the body. The body can manufacture some of these amino acids itself, but the 'essential amino acids' must be derived from food. Animal protein and soya protein contain almost all of these and are regarded as 'complete'. Other vegetable proteins are lacking in one or more of the essential amino acids. However by eating certain foods together, any deficiency is overcome. For example, the following combinations provide complete protein: cereals with milk or other dairy produce; pulses with rice or pasta; pulses or nuts with dairy produce; nuts with grains. This isn't as complicated as it sounds and tends to happen naturally in many vegetarian dishes, such as chilli with rice, and bean stews topped with yogurt or crème fraîche.

❑ VITAMINS are vital for a variety of body processes; a deficiency will result in illness. The fat-soluble vitamins A, D, E and K – as their name suggests – are largely derived from foods which contain fat, though the body acquires most of its vitamin D from the action of sunlight on the skin. These vitamins are stored in the liver. The water-soluble vitamins B and C cannot be stored, so a regular intake is important. Vegans need to ensure that they obtain sufficient vitamin B12, as this is only present in animal (including dairy) foods and foods which are fortified with the vitamin, such as yeast extracts, breakfast cereals and soya milk.

❑ MINERALS are needed in minute traces for a variety of essential body processes. Iron, calcium and zinc are especially important. Susceptibility to anaemia as a consequence of iron deficiency is often discussed in relation to a vegetarian diet, because meat is considered to be the most accessible source. However, iron is found in many vegetarian foods, especially leafy green vegetables, and the absorption of iron is greatly increased if some vitamin C rich food – even a glass of orange juice – is consumed at the same meal.

❑ FIBRE isn't a nutrient, but it is important for the proper functioning of the digestive system. Unrefined foods, such as wholemeal bread, brown rice, fruit, vegetables and pulses, are the best sources.

❑ CARBOHYDRATES provide the body with energy. They are found in all grains and cereals, pulses, dried fruits, potatoes, sugar and other foods.

❑ FATS are needed in small amounts for energy, heat and to assist the absorption of fat-soluble vitamins. They are present in fats, oils, cheeses and nuts.

## HOW TO BALANCE A VEGETARIAN DIET

Provided you eat some foods from each of the following groups every day, your diet should be nutritionally sound:-

❑ CEREALS AND GRAINS include bread, pasta, rice and breakfast cereals. These foods provide energy, fibre, B vitamins, calcium and iron.

❑ PULSES, NUTS AND SEEDS supply protein, energy, fibre, calcium, iron and zinc.

❑ FRUIT AND VEGETABLES are excellent sources of vitamins and minerals, especially vitamin C, vitamin A (in the form of Beta-carotene), iron and calcium. They also contain fibre.

❑ DAIRY AND SOYA PRODUCTS are valuable sources of protein, energy, calcium, minerals, vitamin B12 and vitamin D.

❑ In addition, you also need to include small quantities of plant oils, margarine or butter to provide essential fatty acids and vitamins A, D and E.

## WHAT ARE THE HIDDEN INGREDIENTS?

Avoiding meat and fish is fairly straightforward, but many of the most unlikely products contain animal ingredients.

The following list should help strict vegetarians who wish to avoid hidden animal ingredients:-

❑ ADDITIVES The E numbers on food packaging indicate which emulsifiers, stabilisers and colourings have been added to the food, but this information isn't sufficient to determine suitability for strict vegetarians, as in many cases the same additive can be derived from either a vegetarian or a non-vegetarian source. E120 and E542 are always non-vegetarian. For a comprehensive list of those additives which may be derived from animal, fish or vegetable sources, contact The Vegetarian Society.

❑ ANCHOVIES These small fish are frequently used as a flavouring ingredient, in some pizzas, certain brands of Worcestershire sauce and some ready-prepared olive pastes, for example.

❑ ANIMAL FATS These occur in a variety of foods. 'Fatty acids' and 'edible fats' may be of vegetable or animal origin. Look out for animal fats in biscuits, frozen chips, margarines, ice creams, ready-made pastries and fast-foods. It isn't uncommon to find fast-food chains selling vegetable burgers that have been fried in animal fat!

❑ CAVIAR Although these are the eggs of the sturgeon, the fish has to be killed for the eggs to be obtained.

❑ COCHINEAL This food colouring is made from crushed insects. It is often used in coloured sweets and cake icings.

❑ GELATINE This is found in a wide range of products, including jellies, sweets, canned soft drinks, ice creams and yogurts.

❑ GLYCERINE/GLYCEROL Sometimes produced from animal fats, though vegetarian sources are also used.

❑ ISINGLASS A fining agent derived from certain tropical fish, which is commonly used in wine and beer making.

❑ LACTOSE This is obtained from milk, but sometimes as a by-product of non-vegetarian cheese-making.

❑ LANOLIN Used to make vitamin D3, this is produced from wool – not always sheared from live sheep.

❑ WHEY Often obtained as a by-product of non-vegetarian cheese-making. Chocolate, crisps and ice creams often contain whey.

# Rice and Grains

Rice and grains are staple ingredients for most vegetarians, including vegans. These foods are important sources of energy; they also provide useful amounts of protein, fibre, B vitamins, calcium and iron.

TYPES OF RICE

❑ Brown rice is the whole rice grain with only the tough outer husk removed. Like other unrefined grains, it is richer in fibre, protein and B vitamins than refined alternatives. Because the bran is retained, it has a chewy texture and nutty flavour, and it takes longer to cook than white rice.

❑ Long grain white rice is universally popular, and there are many varieties, including Patna and Carolina. Once cooked the rice grains should be separate, dry and fluffy.

❑ Arborio is the classic Italian risotto rice with plump medium grains. It has the capacity to absorb plenty of liquid during cooking without turning mushy. Once cooked, Arborio has a wonderfully creamy texture, whilst still retaining a slight bite. Carnaroli is another excellent Italian risotto rice.

❑ Basmati rice is a superior variety of long-grain rice, originating from the foothills of The Himalayas. It has a characteristic, subtle fragrance and, once cooked, the grains are light, very fluffy, and quite separate. It is the perfect accompaniment to curries and other Indian dishes. Both white and brown varieties are available.

❑ Camargue rice from the south of France is an attractive russet red colour, with a flavour and texture similar to brown rice. It is less widely available than other varieties.

❑ Thai fragrant rice, as the name suggests, is distinctively aromatic, and is available from larger supermarkets. As long as it is correctly cooked, this rice has a soft, light, fluffy texture. It is the ideal accompaniment to Thai dishes.

❑ Glutinous, or 'sticky rice' as it is also known, is another Asian variety. This short-medium grain rice cooks to a sticky mass, rather than separate grains and is used in sweet and savoury dishes, including Japanese sushi.

❑ Pudding rice is short-grained and absorbs a lot of liquid during cooking. It is essential for creamy rice pudding.

RICE AND GRAINS
1 *Basmati rice*
2 *Bulghar wheat*
3 *Polenta*
4 *Potato flour*
5 *Buckwheat*
6 *Oatmeal*
7 *Wild rice*
8 *Arborio rice*
9 *Brown rice*
10 *Rye flour*
11 *Millet*
12 *Pearl barley*
13 *Couscous*

❑ Wild rice is not as the name suggests a rice at all, but the seed of an aquatic grass. It is dark brown in colour, highly nutritious and has a strong, nutty flavour. A little expensive, it is typically mixed with other grains or rice.

COOKING RICE

Some of the speciality rices are cooked in specific ways: liquid is added gradually to Arborio when making a risotto, for example; pudding rice is usually baked slowly in the oven; glutinous rice is steamed; but in general long-grain varieties can be treated in the same way. Check packet instructions for cooking times and specific directions.

❑ Most rice is bought pre-packed and does not require washing, but if you do buy it loose, wash thoroughly. With some varieties, such as Basmati, rinsing may be advisable to remove excess starch. To rinse rice, place in a sieve under cold running water until the water runs clear, picking out any tiny pieces of grit.

❑ To cook ordinary rice by the absorption method, place in a heavy-based saucepan with twice its volume of cold water. Add salt, bring to the boil, cover with a tight-fitting lid and turn down the heat to as low as possible. Cook until the water is absorbed and the rice is tender; white rice generally takes 15-20 minutes; brown rice usually cooks in 40-45 minutes. Resist the temptation to keep lifting the lid during cooking.

❑ If you prefer, simply add the rice to a large pan of fast boiling salted water, return to the boil, stir once and cook steadily, uncovered, until tender. White rice generally takes 10-12 minutes; brown rice usually cooks in 35-40 minutes. Drain the cooked rice in a sieve and rinse with a kettle of boiling water.

GRAINS

Grains such as wheat, barley, corn, oats and rye are the edible seeds of different grasses and are familiar sold ground into different flours. Many of these grains are also available in other forms which are valuable for vegetarians. These include:-

❑ Buckwheat is sold as a grain, although it is actually the seed of a plant related to rhubarb. It is processed into groats, which are often toasted, and milled into flour which is grey in colour.

❑ Bulghar wheat is partially processed cracked wheat which readily absorbs moisture and therefore cooks quickly. It has a mild, nutty taste and is used extensively in Middle Eastern cooking. Also known as pourgouri, bulghul and cracked wheat.

❑ Couscous is a form of processed semolina grains, pale yellow in colour, with a soft texture and mild flavour. It is a staple food in north African countries.

❑ Millet grains and flakes are available. Golden in colour, they have a chewy texture which works well in salads.

❑ Polenta is fine ground cornmeal, which forms the basis of the traditional Italian accompaniment of the same name.

❑ Pearl barley is the polished barley grain which is typically added to soups and stews.

# PASTA

Pasta is popular with most vegetarians. It is – after all – inexpensive, quick to cook and extremely versatile.

The range of dried and fresh pastas readily available from supermarkets and delicatessens today is seemingly endless and, of course, you can combine these with all manner of tasty sauces.

From a nutritional angle, pasta is essentially a carbohydrate food but, because it has a low fat content, pasta isn't particularly high in calories. Rich accompanying sauces are responsible for giving pasta dishes a high-calorie reputation. If you are watching your weight, keep the use of cream, olive oil, butter and full-fat cheese in sauces to a minimum. It is worth noting that some varieties of pasta, notably those made with eggs, may contain as much as 13 per cent protein, as well as some useful vitamins and minerals.

HOMEMADE PASTA
There is no real substitute for homemade pasta. It is surprisingly quick and rewarding to make, and has a wonderfully light texture and incomparable flavour – almost melting in the mouth. If you have never attempted to make your own pasta, do give it a try (using the recipe on page 122). You need very little basic equipment – a rolling pin, metal pastry cutters, a sharp knife and a pastry wheel will suffice – but, if you intend to make pasta regularly, invest in a pasta machine to take all of the hard work out of rolling and ensure a very thin, even dough. Once you have mastered the basic recipe, try your hand at some of the delicious flavoured pastas.

BOUGHT FRESH PASTA
If you prefer to buy fresh pasta rather than make your own or use dried, it is worth searching out a good supplier. Commercially produced fresh pasta can be unpleasantly thick and stodgy – quite unlike homemade pasta. However, some Italian delicatessens sell good quality pasta which has been freshly prepared on the premises – often in an interesting range of flavours.

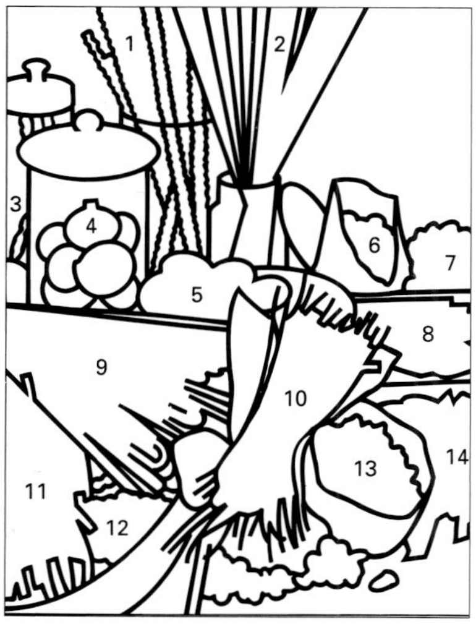


PASTA
1 *Mafaldini*
2 *Spaghetti*
3 *Pizzoccheri*
4 *Tagliatelle (buckwheat)*
5 *Vermicelli (nidi)*
6 *Orecchiette*
7 *Conchiglioni*
8 *Lasagne verde*
9 *Spaghettoni*
10 *Tagliolini verde*
11 *Tagliarelle*
12 *Conchligiette*
13 *Gigli del gargano*
14 *Penne tricolore*

DRIED PASTA
Dried pasta is available in an extensive range of shapes, sizes and flavours. The best are made from 100% durum wheat (*pasta di semola grano duro*); some include eggs (*all'uova*). With the exception of filled pastas, such as ravioli, dried pasta is suitable for the recipes in this book.
❑ The variety of dried pasta shapes is almost bewildering. Names of shapes often vary from one region of Italy to another, and new ones are constantly being introduced. A selection of dried pasta is shown opposite, and identified below for reference. Note that the suffix gives an indication of the size of the pasta. *Oni* denotes large, as in conchiglioni (large shells); *-ette* or *-etti* suggests small, as in spaghetti and cappelletti (small hats); while *-ine* or *-ini* means tiny, as in pastina (tiny soup pasta) and spaghettini, the finer version of spaghetti.
❑ The choice of pasta is largely a matter of personal taste, but you will find that some pasta shapes are more suited to particular recipes than others. Broad pappardelle noodles, for example, tend to work best in dishes where the other ingredients are chunky. Smoother-textured sauces are generally better served with finer pastas, such as spaghetti or linguine. Where a recipe includes a lot of sauce, shapes such as conchiglie (shells) and torchiette (torches) are ideal because they hold the sauce well.

QUANTITIES
It is difficult to give specific quantity guidelines for pasta, because there are so many factors, including the nature of the sauce and whether you are serving the pasta as a starter, lunch or main meal. Individual appetites for pasta seem to vary enormously too. As a very approximate guide, allow about 75-125 g (3-4 oz) uncooked weight per person.

COOKING PASTA
All pasta, fresh and dried, should be cooked until *al dente* – firm to the bite, definitely not soft, and without a hard, uncooked centre. Always add pasta to a large pan containing plenty of fast-boiling water; insufficient water will result in stodgy, unevenly cooked pasta. Fresh pasta needs only the briefest of cooking, so watch it carefully. Most dried pasta takes around 8-12 minutes. Manufacturers' recommended cooking times provide a rough guide, but the only way to determine when pasta is cooked is by tasting. Avoid overcooking at all costs!

SERVING SUGGESTIONS
Have warmed serving plates or bowls ready as pasta quickly loses its heat once it is drained. Toss the pasta with the chosen sauce, butter or olive oil as soon as it is cooked, or it may start to stick together. Parmesan cheese provides the finishing touch for many pasta dishes. Vegetarian Parmesan is available from healthfood shops; it may be expensive, but a little goes a long way, and a well-wrapped chunk of Parmesan will keep in the refrigerator for several weeks. Either grate the Parmesan over the finished dish or shave off thin flakes, using a swivel potato peeler.

# PULSES AND NUTS

The term pulse is used to describe all of the various beans, peas and lentils which have been preserved by drying. They are an important source of protein, energy and fibre in a vegetarian diet. In addition they are a useful source of B vitamins and minerals, especially iron. From a nutritional angle, eating pulses with grains is particularly advantageous as the combination constitutes a complete protein, as in *pasta e fagioli*, couscous, or any bean soup or stew served with rice or bread.

❑ Pulses should be stored in airtight containers in a cool, dry cupboard. They keep well, but after about 6 months their skins start to toughen and they take progressively longer to cook the longer they are stored.

❑ With the exception of lentils and split peas, pulses need to be soaked overnight in plenty of cold water. The following day, drain off the water prior to cooking.

❑ For some pulses, notably red kidney beans, aduki beans, black-eyed beans, black beans and borlotti beans, it is essential to cover with plenty of fresh cold water, bring to the boil and boil vigorously for 10 minutes to destroy any toxins present on the skins. Although pre-boiling isn't mandatory for other dried pulses, it does no harm and saves the need to remember which ones require it.

❑ After fast-boiling, lower the heat, cover and simmer until tender. To enhance the flavour a bouquet garni, a few bay leaves and/or 1 or 2 garlic cloves can be added to the cooking water. Salt should only be added 10-15 minutes before the end of the cooking time; if added at the start, it will toughen the skins.

❑ The cooking time is determined by the type of pulse, soaking time and, above all, by the length of time it has been stored. The following guide is therefore only approximate: lentils 30-45 minutes; split peas 45-60 minutes; aduki, black-eyed beans, borlotti beans, flageolets, haricot and pinto beans 1-1½ hours; black beans, butter beans and red kidney beans 1½-2 hours; chick peas 2-3 hours; soya beans 3-4 hours. (Note that soya beans must be pre-boiled for 1 hour, to destroy a substance they contain which prevents the body from absorbing protein.)

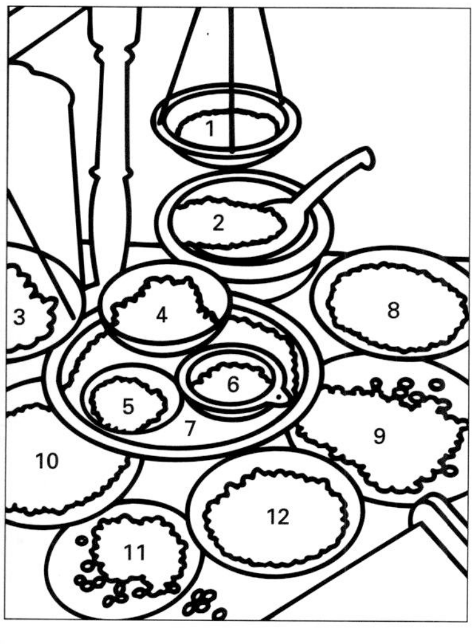


PULSES
1 *Mung beans*
2 *Aduki beans*
3 *Butter beans*
4 *Borlotti beans*
5 *Puy lentils*
6 *Green lentils*
7 *Red lentils*
8 *Flageolet beans*
9 *Yellow split peas*
10 *Soya beans*
11 *Haricot beans*
12 *Black-eyed beans*

❑ The weight of dried beans approximately doubles during soaking and cooking, so if a recipe calls for 225 g (8 oz) cooked beans, you would need to start with 125 g (4 oz) dried weight. Once cooked, pulses keep well in the refrigerator for 2-3 days.

❑ Most supermarkets now stock a wide range of cooked canned beans and pulses which provide a convenient, quick alternative to cooking your own. A 400 g (14 oz) can is roughly equivalent to 75 g (3 oz) dried beans and contains about 150 ml (¼ pint) liquid.

## SEEDS

Seeds are an excellent, highly nutritious vegetarian ingredient, adding texture, flavour and interest to a variety of foods, including breads, cakes and salads. Sunflower seeds, poppy seeds, sesame seeds and pumpkin seeds are especially popular. To enhance their flavour, dry-fry in a heavy-based pan until evenly toasted.

## SPROUTING BEANS AND SEEDS

These are rich in nutrients, containing substantial amounts of protein, fibre, minerals and vitamins, including vitamin C. Bean sprouts can be bought fresh from most supermarkets. Many beans and seeds can be sprouted in just a few days at home, though it is important to buy ones which are specifically produced for sprouting – from a healthfood shop or other reliable source. Mung beans, aduki beans, chick peas, alfafa seeds and fenugreek are all suitable. They add a nutty taste and crunchy texture to salads and stir-fries.

## NUTS

Nuts are the seeds or fruits of various trees; they have an edible kernel which is found inside a hard shell. Nuts are an excellent source of protein, carbohydrate and fat in a vegetarian diet, though anyone on a weight-reducing diet should be aware that their high fat content makes them high in calories too.

❑ Some nuts are available fresh or 'green' but most are sold dried and this is the form that we are most familiar with. Almonds, Brazil nuts, cashews, chestnuts, coconut in its various guises, hazelnuts, macadamias, peanuts, pecans, pine nuts, pistachios, walnuts and water chestnuts are all used to delicious effect in vegetarian dishes. Nuts can be bought in shells, shelled, or further processed into flakes or pieces, or ground.

❑ If buying nuts in their shells, make sure they feel heavy for their size and show no sign of mould. Store in a cool, dry place and consume well within the use-by date. Nuts do not keep particularly well as they soon lose flavour and turn rancid if stored too long.

❑ Toasting – either by grilling or oven-roasting – enhances the flavour of most nuts, especially almonds, cashews, hazelnuts, macadamias and pine nuts.

❑ Nuts, such as walnuts, hazelnuts, almonds and peanuts, are highly prized for their oil. A dash of walnut oil, for example, will add a superb flavour to a salad dressing.

# VEGETABLES

The variety of vegetables available in our markets, supermarkets and greengrocers today is almost overwhelming. Improvement in transportation methods means that alongside familiar homegrown produce, you will find an extraordinary array of exotic vegetables from all parts of the world, from christophenes to yams. In addition, genetic engineering brings us more and more hybrids and an abundance of baby vegetables, including miniature Savoy cabbages and succulent small fennel bulbs.

A growing awareness of possible health risks associated with the use of pesticides and artificial fertilisers has led to a high demand for organic produce. Most supermarkets now stock organic vegetables – grown without the use of chemicals – although they do tend to be more expensive.

This ever-increasing range of quality vegetables is, of course, good news for vegetarians, who can now rely on a constant source of inspiration for interesting meals. Imported produce gives us year-round availability of many varieties, but each season still brings new delights – purple sprouting broccoli in spring, fragrant homegrown asparagus in early summer, tender fresh peas and beans in pods during the summer...not to forget the wonderful fresh wild mushrooms which appear in the autumn.

From a nutritional angle, vegetables are invaluable in a vegetarian diet. In particular, they are an excellent source of some vitamins, such as vitamin C and carotenes, and certain minerals, for example iron and calcium; the exact content depending upon the variety. Low in fat and cholesterol, yet high in fibre, vegetables provide an important source of roughage. Starchy varieties, such as potatoes are also a good source of energy, but most vegetables are low in calories. Many varieties provide some protein too.

Vegetables can be classified into the following categories:-

❑ BRASSICAS Otherwise known as the cabbage family, this group includes brussels sprouts, cauliflower and curly kale, as well as the many different types of cabbage.

❑ ROOTS AND TUBERS are vegetables which grow underground, such as carrots, potatoes, parsnips, turnips, swede, Jerusalem artichokes, beetroot and the lesser-known salsify.

❑ PODS, PEAS AND BEANS This group takes in the many varieties of fresh beans, peas, okra and sweetcorn.

❑ STALKS AND SHOOTS Celery and prized delicacies, such as asparagus, globe artichokes and fennel belong here.

❑ THE ONION FAMILY comprises the various onions, as well as leeks, garlic, and shallots.

❑ MUSHROOMS are a type of fungus. Several cultivated varieties are now widely available, including shiitake, oyster, chestnut, cup, button and flat mushrooms. Seasonal fresh wild mushrooms, such as chanterelles and ceps, are now becoming easier to obtain.

❑ LEAFY VEGETABLES This group includes the exciting array of salad leaves. Choose from baby spinach, rocket, lamb's lettuce, frisée, radicchio, chicory and all kinds of lettuces.

❑ VEGETABLE FRUITS In this diverse category, the vegetables are more correctly the fruits of their plants. Aubergines, avocado, peppers, tomatoes, cucumbers, courgettes and squashes are all included.

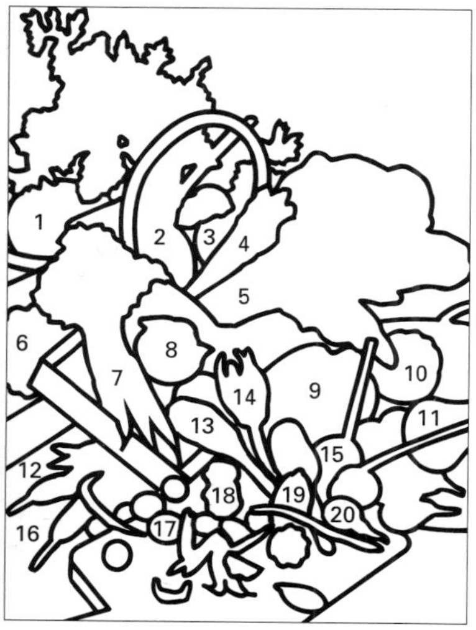


VEGETABLES
1 *Butterball squash*
2 *Celeriac* 3 *Kohlrabi*
4 *Asparagus* 5 *Pak Choi*
6 *Cauliflower (Romanesco)*
7 *Carrots*
8 *Savoy cabbage (baby)*
9 *Pumpkin*
10 *Acorn squash*
11 *Butternut squash*
12 *Chillies* 13 *Globe artichoke (baby)*
14 *Courgette flower*
15 *Garlic* 16 *Aubergine*
17 *Tomatoes*
18 *Patty pan squash*
20 *Aubergine (small, red)*

BUYING AND STORING

Look for bright, firm vegetables. Avoid any that look shrivelled or bruised. Don't buy potatoes with a green tinge, as these are unfit for eating.

❑ Don't buy the largest specimens, particularly when choosing roots. In general, the younger and smaller the vegetable, the sweeter and more tender it will be, but some baby vegetables lack flavour because they are so immature.

❑ To enjoy them at their best and most nutritious, vegetables should be eaten as soon as possible after picking or buying, but most will keep for a few days in a cool, dark place. Store green vegetables and salad ingredients in the salad drawer of the refrigerator. Roots can be stored in a cool, dark place, such as a wire rack in a cool larder, for up to 1 week. Exposure to light turns potatoes green, so they must be kept in the dark.

PREPARATION AND COOKING

Clean all vegetables thoroughly before cooking. Brush or shake off any loose dirt, then wash thoroughly (except mushrooms). The easiest way to clean leeks is to slit them lengthwise and rinse under cold running water to remove grit. Mushrooms are best wiped with damp kitchen paper.

❑ As soon as vegetables are peeled they begin to lose vitamins so, where possible, prepare at the last minute. Alternatively, if the produce is organic and the skins are edible, simply don't peel.

❑ Don't leave prepared vegetables immersed in cold water for long as water-soluble vitamins will be lost.

❑ Vegetables can be cooked by a variety of methods, including steaming, boiling, sautéeing, stir-frying, roasting, braising and grilling. To minimise the loss of water-soluble vitamins, cook in the minimum amount of water (if boiling), and use the cooking water as stock or to make a sauce. Avoid overcooking, whichever method you are using. In general, vegetables are at their best cooked until *al dente*, tender but still retaining some bite.

# FRUIT

Nowadays, there is a tremendous variety of fruit on sale in this country all year round. With the continuous development of cross-hybrids, new varieties are appearing on supermarket shelves all of the time. Take oranges, for example...in addition to the familiar navels, jaffas, satsumas etc, you can now buy navelinas, shamouti, minneolas and salustianas, to name but a few...

Imported produce gives us a host of exotic fruits from the tropics throughout the year, including paw-paws, guavas, physalis fruit and mangoes. As with vegetables, there is a current trend towards developing baby fruits, so we can now buy small, sweet pineapples and dwarf bananas, for example. However, there is still nothing to compare with the arrival of the first homegrown strawberries, raspberries and redcurrants in summer.

The demand for organic fruits continues to grow, and suppliers are responding. Most supermarkets stock a good range; some now display their organic fruit and vegetables together in one section, making it easier for consumers to shop entirely for organic produce if they so wish.

Fruit has always been regarded as a 'healthy' food. Most varieties are a good source of vitamin C; some also contain carotenes, notably apricots, mangoes and peaches. Useful minerals are present in many varieties. All fruits provide some energy, in the form of fructose (or fruit sugar), but most varieties are very low in fat and consequently low in calories. All fruits are an important source of dietary fibre. They can be classified as follows:-

❑ SOFT FRUITS These include strawberries, raspberries, red and blackcurrants, blueberries, cherries and gooseberries. Homegrown soft fruits have a superb flavour, but a relatively short season. Imported varieties are available at other times, though they often lack flavour and aroma.

❑ ORCHARD FRUITS Apples, pears, plums, peaches and greengages are in this category. Make the most of flavourful homegrown varieties during the autumn.

❑ CITRUS FRUITS These are imported, manly from the Mediterranean and South Africa. Popular varieties include lemons, limes, grapefruit, kumquats and oranges. They are all rich in vitamin C. Citrus zest is used to add flavour to sweet and savoury dishes, especially lemon zest. If you are likely to use the zest, buy unwaxed lemons.

❑ TROPICAL FRUITS Mangoes, guavas, passion fruit, persimmons and rambutans are just a few of the vast range of exotic fruits now imported throughout the year. Their unique flavours add variety to a vegetarian diet.

❑ VINE FRUITS Grapes are the most popular of the vine fruits. Imported chiefly from the Mediterranean and South Africa, they are available all year round. Muscat and Italia grapes are particularly good varieties.

❑ DRIED FRUITS These are an excellent nutritious vegetarian food, as they are high in dietary fibre, provide a ready source of energy and contain some minerals, such as iron and potassium, and some vitamins, such as carotenes. Apart from the familiar raisins, apricots, apples, dates, figs and prunes, you can also buy dried pears, peaches, bananas, mango and cranberries from healthfood shops and supermarkets. Check packet labels for additives. Sulphur dioxide and a certain mineral oil is used in the production of some varieties. Washing in warm water will help to remove these.

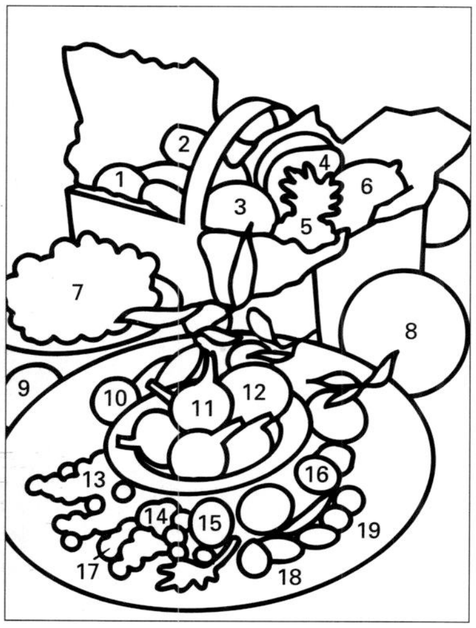


FRUIT
1 *Apple (Discovery)*
2 *Paw paw*
3 *Pomegranate* 4 *Pear*
5 *Pineapple* 6 *Mango*
7 *Grapes (white Italia)*
8 *Melon (Charentais)*
9 *Peach* 10 *Lime*
11 *Fig* 12 *Clementine*
13 *Redcurrants*
14 *Blueberries*
15 *Passion fruit*
16 *Strawberry*
17 *Raspberries*
18 *Blackberries*
19 *Cherries*

BUYING AND STORING

Choose fruits which look bright and fresh, avoiding any with bruised or shrivelled skins. In general, fruit should feel heavy for its size, as this is an indication of adequate moisture content. For the same reason, berries and other soft fruits should look plump; avoid any with signs of mould or seeping juices.

❑ Most unripe fruit will eventually ripen at home at room temperature but certain varieties, such as melons, will never do so if they have been picked too early. When choosing fragrant fruits, such as melons, mangoes, pineapple and peaches, make sure you can detect their distinctive aroma, as this is a good indication of ripeness. Melons and pineapples should yield to gentle pressure applied at the stem end.

❑ Soft fruits are best eaten within 1-2 days of purchase; transfer to a shallow dish, cover loosely and refrigerate. Most other ripe fruits, including peaches, apricots, plums and tropical fruits, are best kept in the refrigerator. Bananas and unripe fruits should be stored at room temperature. Citrus fruits keep at cool room temperature for up to 1 week.

PREPARATION AND COOKING

The majority of fresh, ripe fruits can be eaten raw. With the exception of soft berries, all fruit should be washed. Delicate berries should only be washed immediately before eating if they are sandy, as water encourages them to rot.

❑ Peel away inedible skins, and edible ones too, if the produce is non-organic and you are concerned about chemical residues.

❑ On peeling and cutting, fruits such as apples and pears quickly discolour as their flesh is exposed to air. Rubbing the cut surfaces with lemon or lime juice, or immersing in water acidulated with lemon juice helps to prevent this.

# Dairy Produce

Dairy foods are an important source of protein, energy, calcium, vitamins and minerals in a vegetarian diet, although they are not suitable for vegans who avoid animal products of all kinds. Animal-derived rennet is used in the manufacture of many cheeses, although cheeses made with vegetarian rennet are becoming increasingly available.

CHEESE

Cheese provides an excellent source of protein, calcium, zinc and some B vitamins, eg B12, for vegetarians. In general, cheese also has a high saturated fat content, which may contribute to a raised cholesterol level if eaten in too great a quantity. New vegetarians, in particular, should be cautious about eating too much cheese. Lower-fat varieties are available which can significantly reduce fat and calorie intake.

❑ In the cheese-making process, rennet is used to curdle milk and separate it into curds and whey. The curds are then processed, shaped and matured as necessary to create a wide range of cheeses. The method varies to some extent according to the type of cheese. Very hard cheeses, such as Parmesan, may take up to 3 years to develop their full flavour, while soft cheeses such as Brie and Camembert, are ready to eat within a month or two. Fresh soft goat's cheeses, mozzarella and cream cheeses are not matured in this way.

❑ Vegetarian plant-derived alternatives to animal rennet have been available for some time, but in the past these lacked the strength to be used on a commercial scale. However, the improved concentrated vegetarian rennets which are available today are considered to be as effective as their animal alternatives. As a consequence, the number of vegetarian cheeses produced is ever-increasing.

❑ Most supermarkets and cheese shops now stock an excellent range of vegetarian cheeses: as many as fifty or more lines in some larger stores. Look for a symbol which denotes suitability for vegetarians.

❑ For culinary purposes, cheeses can be divided roughly into four categories: hard cheeses, such as Parmesan; semi-hard cheeses, such as Cheddar, Gruyère and Stilton; soft ripened cheeses, such as Brie and Camembert; and fresh soft cheeses, such as mozzarella and goat's cheeses.

❑ There are no hard and fast rules as to which varieties are likely to be vegetarian; this depends upon the supplier.

❑ Of the cheeses most frequently used in cooking, vegetarian Parmesan is probably the most difficult to obtain, but it is available from some healthfood shops.

DAIRY PRODUCTS
1 *Stilton*
2 *Red Cheshire*
3 *Mozzarella*
4 *Free-range eggs*
5 *Cheddar*
6 *Fresh goat's cheese*
7 *Caerphilly*
8 *Waterloo*
9 *Ricotta*
10 *Fresh goat's cheese*
11 *Ragstone (goat's cheese)*
12 *Greek-style yogurt*

MILK, CREAM, YOGURT AND BUTTER

Milk is, of course, highly nutritious and forms the basis of the other dairy products which are so valuable to vegetarians – cheese, cream, yogurt and butter. Semi-skimmed milk tastes less rich than full-cream milk and is ideal for most general purposes.

❑ The variety of creams available today is extensive, ranging from single, pouring cream to extra-thick double cream and ultra-rich clotted cream, but these are broadly classified by their fat content. Crème fraîche is now widely available and, like soured cream, it lends a wonderful richness to vegetable and bean soups and stews.

❑ Yogurt is an excellent food in its own right, but it also has a wide variety of culinary uses. Greek-style yogurt is superbly rich and creamy, and it is used to enhance savoury and sweet dishes.

❑ Pure butter and some spreads are suitable for vegetarians, and many are labelled to this effect. Some spreads, however, contain animal fats or fish oils.

EGGS

Eggs are a valuable source of protein and some vitamins, such as A and D; they also contain iron. Eggs are not particularly high in fat or calories, but they are relatively high in dietary cholesterol and, for this reason, it is recommended that egg consumption is in moderation.

❑ Most supermarkets now stock a range of eggs produced by different farming methods, including free-range eggs, eggs from grain-only fed hens and battery eggs. Most of the eggs sold in this country are produced by 'battery hens' which are raised by intensive farming methods. Some vegetarians, therefore, choose to exclude battery eggs.

❑ Strict vegetarians need to be aware that manufactured products, such as pasta and noodles, may contain battery eggs. The ⓥ symbol is only applied to products which contain eggs if they are free-range.

❑ In cooking, the unique properties of eggs are rather taken for granted. In addition to being simply poached, boiled, scrambled or turned into tasty omelettes, eggs are used to lighten soufflés and cakes; thicken mousses; bind stuffings, set custards and emulsify sauces.

❑ Eggs are now graded into 4 categories according to weight: very large, large, medium and small. It is important to use the correct size of egg in a recipe. Unless otherwise stated, large eggs should be used for all Good Housekeeping recipes.

# Other Vegetarian Ingredients

In addition to the food groups detailed on the previous pages, certain ingredients are particularly significant in a vegetarian diet. These are described below.

## TOFU

Also known as bean curd, tofu is made from pressed soya beans in a process akin to cheese-making. It is a highly nutritious food, rich in some minerals, low in saturated fats, cholesterol-free and an excellent source of protein. Many vegetarians disregard tofu as it is vitually tasteless, but it readily absorbs other flavours on marinating and is worth experimenting with.

❑ Firm tofu can be cut into chunks, then immersed in tasty marinades and dressings prior to grilling, stir-frying, deep-frying or tossing raw into salads. It can also be chopped and made into burgers and roasts.

❑ Silken tofu is softer and creamier than firm tofu and is useful for sauces and dressings.

❑ Smoked tofu is also available, and can be used in the same way as firm tofu.

❑ Sold as a chilled product, tofu should be stored in the refrigerator. Once the packet is opened, the tofu should be kept in a bowl of water in the refrigerator and eaten within 4 days.

## TEXTURED VEGETABLE PROTEIN (TVP)

TVP forms the bulk of most ready-prepared veggie burgers, vegetarian sausages and vegetarian mince. It is made from a mixture of soya flour, flavourings and liquid, which is cooked, then extruded under pressure and cut into chunks or small pieces to resemble mince. Unlike tofu, it has a slightly chewy meat-like texture which makes it unappealing to some vegetarians and vegans, although for the same reason it may appeal to new vegetarians who miss the texture of meat. TVP is an excellent low-fat source of protein.

❑ TVP can be included in vegetable and bean stews, pies, curries and other dishes, rather as meat would be used by non-vegetarians.

❑ Sold in packets, TVP has a relatively long storage life. Vegans should note that some brands include egg albumen or whey and are therefore unsuitable for them.

## QUORN

Quorn is a product derived from a distant relative of the mushroom. It is a good source of complete protein, although it is is not suitable for vegans because it contains egg albumen. Strict vegetarians may also avoid using quorn because its egg content is not guaranteed to come from free-range eggs. Low in fat, yet high in fibre, quorn has a texture rather like chicken.

❑ Like tofu, it has a bland flavour and benefits from being marinated before cooking. It has the advantage that it cooks very quickly.

❑ Available from the chilled cabinet of supermarkets and health food shops, quorn should be stored in the refrigerator, where it will keep for up to 3 days.

## MARGARINE

Pure vegetable margarines are available from supermarkets and healthfood shops, as are hard pure vegetable fats, vegetarian suet and pure butters. However, some margarines and low-fat spreads contain fish oils, animal rennet and gelatine, so it is necessary to check the labels. Nut butters are available for vegans.

## GELATINE

Gelatine is produced from beef bones and is therefore unsuitable for vegetarians. Alternative gelling agents include agar-agar, which is derived from seaweed, and gelozone which contains carrageenan, guar gum and carob gum.

❑ Both are sold in powdered form and are used in a similar way to powdered gelatine, although agar-agar only dissolves when it is boiled.

❑ Agar-agar has other advantages for vegans; for example, it can be dissolved in a little water and used in place of egg white in royal icing.

❑ Vegetarians should be aware that gelatine is include in a number of commercial products, including some canned soft drinks, sweets and jellies.

## SOYA MILK

Soya milk can be used by vegans as a substitute for dairy milk. It does not have the same flavour as ordinary milk, but it is acceptable in most cooked dishes and is highly nutritious.

❑ Soya milk is available from larger supermarkets and healthfood shops; experiment with different brands to find out which one you prefer.

## NUT CREAM

Another vegan product, nut cream can be used in place of dairy cream as an accompaniment to desserts. It is available from healthfood shops.

# Colour Index

**Polenta Sandwiches with Fontina**
Delicious parcels of layered polenta and melting fontina cheese.
Serves 4–6 Page 82

**Tomato Bruschetta**
Classic Italian garlic toast spread with a fresh tomato and basil salsa.
Serves 4 Page 82

**Deep-Fried Potato Skins with Chilli Salsa**
More-ish deep-fried potato skins served with two contrasting tasty dips.
Serves 2–3 Page 83

**Filo Pies with Feta and Herb Filling**
Little triangular Greek-style filo pies with a tasty stuffing – best served warm.
Makes 20–24 Page 83

**Vegetable Samosas**
Tasty Indian snack, delicious served warm with a fresh-tasting coriander chutney.
Makes 24 Page 84

**Pakoras**
Spicy Indian fritters made with a variety of vegetables, served with cooling raita or chutney.
Serves 4 Page 85

**Spiced Pumpkin Fritters**
Deep-fried slices of pumpkin in a crisp spiced batter – ideal for Halloween!
Serves 4 Page 85

**Spring Rolls with Cucumber Relish**
A popular Thai snack which also makes a delicious starter.
Serves 4 Page 86

**Aubergine, Mushroom and Coriander Paté**
A rich, creamy pâté of smoky aubergine, dark mushrooms and fresh tangy coriander.
Serves 4-6 Page 89

**Falafel with Yogurt Dip**
Middle Eastern patties of pounded chick peas, garlic, herbs and spices.
Serves 4-6 Page 87

**Dips with Crudités**
Tasty homemade dips are the perfect way to start a casual meal. Serve these bowls of tzaziki, herbed cheese dip and hummus with crudités and warm pitta bread.
Each serves 6-8 Page 88

**Guacamole**
Fiery Mexican avocado dip flavoured with lime, fresh coriander and spices.
Serves 6-8 Page 88

**Aubergine Timbales with Roasted Pepper Salsa**
A stylish special occasion starter.
Serves 6 Page 86 ✓

**Butter Bean, Lemon and Sage Pâté**
A simple vegetarian pâté – delicious spread onto toasted ciabatta or pitta bread.
Serves 6 Page 89 V ◷ ✓

**Grilled Vegetable Terrine**
An eye-catching starter, vibrant with the colours of Mediterranean vegetables.
Serves 6 Page 90 V ✓

**Grilled Chicory, Stilton and Caramelised Walnut Salad**
Delicious grilled chicory, radicchio and sweet white onions tossed in a thyme and lemon dressing with spiced caramelised walnuts.
Serves 6 Page 92

**Roquefort and Walnut Soufflés**
Decadent individual hot soufflés which can be prepared ahead for convenience.
Serves 6 Page 91 ✓

**Roasted Mushrooms with Lemon and Garlic Oil**
Buy flavourful field mushrooms for this and prepare the oil infusion 3 days ahead.
Serves 4 Page 91 V

**Ricotta Quenelles with Fresh Tomato Sauce**
Creamy ricotta flavoured with Parmesan and herbs, served on a fresh-tasting tomato sauce.
Serves 4  Page 93 ✔

**Squash Gnocchi with Sage**
Tasty little butternut squash dumplings, served with sage butter.
Serves 4  Page 94 ✔

**Potato and Celeriac Crêpe with Beetroot Dressing**
A thick, yet light crêpe made with equal quantities of celeriac and potato.
Serves 4  Page 95 ✔

**Mushroom and Parmesan Wafers with Champagne Sauce**
Wild mushrooms in a rich sauce sandwiched between Parmesan puff pastry.
Serves 8  Page 92

**Summer Melon Salad with Roquefort Dressing**
Sweet, refreshing melon and pear slices, tossed with a piquant dressing.
Serves 4  Page 93 ⊙

**Piadina with Grilled Pepper, Mint and Feta**
Italian-style flat bread topped with grilled peppers, feta and chopped mint.
Serves 6  Page 95 ✔

**Cherry Tomato and Mozzarella Salad on Bruschetta**
A classic salad served on garlic-scented toast surrounded by rocket and basil leaves.
Serves 4 Page 97 ◷

**Moroccan Aubergine Salad with Flat Bread**
Flavoured with coriander and lemon, this salad is served with unleavened bread.
Serves 6 Page 98 V

**Sweet Roast Onion Salad**
Sweet roasted onions tossed in a lime and caper dressing.
Serves 6 Page 98 V ✓

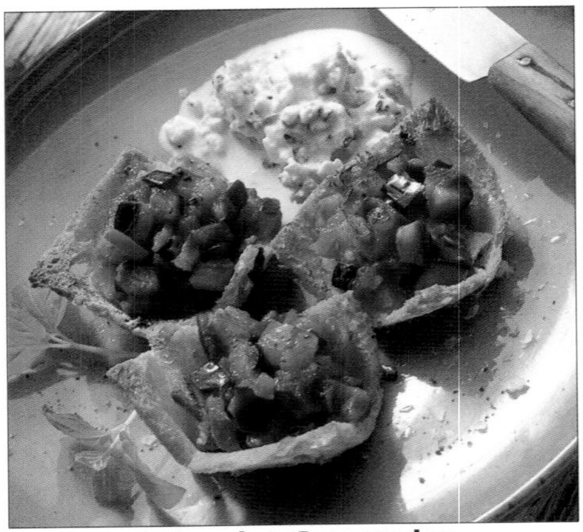

**Aubergine Croustades with Minted Yogurt and Feta**
Ciabatta cases filled with hot, garlicky aubergines, contrasted by a cool, minty sauce.
Serves 4 Page 96

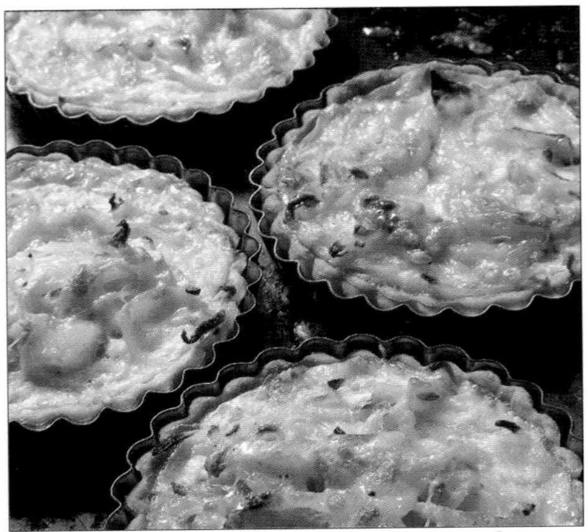

**Fennel, Onion and Gruyère Tartlets**
Delicious cheese pastry tartlets with an aromatic, creamy fennel and onion filling.
Serves 4 Page 97 ❄

**Fennel Carpaccio**
Thinly sliced fennel marinated in a piquant dressing to delicious effect.
Serves 4 Page 99 V ✓

**Roasted Asparagus Salad**
Asparagus is roasted to enhance its flavour, then served cool in a lemony dressing.
Serves 4–6 Page 99

**Grilled Stuffed Pepper Salad**
Smoky grilled peppers, filled with fennel and garlic, with a sweet balsamic dressing.
Serves 6 Page 101

**Broad Bean and Pecorino Salad**
Delectable salad of fresh broad beans, red chicory, roasted hazelnuts and Pecorino cheese.
Serves 4 Page 100

**Roasted Greek Salad**
Thyme and garlic scented roasted vegetables with baked feta cheese and black olives.
Serves 4 Page 100

**Chilled Melon and Ginger Salad**
This simple refreshing summer salad combines several varieties of melon.
Serves 4–6 Page 101

**Mexican Bean Soup with Lime Butter**
A hearty bean soup that makes the most of canned beans.
Serves 6 Page 104 ✔ ❄

**Leek and Potato Soup**
A satisfying Portuguese-style soup that requires no stock.
Serves 4 Page 104 𝓥 🕑

**Jerusalem Artichoke and Parmesan Soup**
Artichoke soup with a hint of spice and the nutty taste of Parmesan.
Serves 6 Page 105 ✔ ❄

**Tomato and Harissa Soup with Coriander Cream**
Smooth tomato soup spiced with harissa, cumin, ginger and garlic. Served topped with coriander flavoured cream.
Serves 8 Page 106 ✔ ❄

**Curried Carrot and Split Pea Soup**
A tangy coriander and lime butter complements this really thick, tasty soup.
Serves 6 Page 106 ✔ ❄

**Tuscan Bean Soup with Garlic and Olive Oil**
A substantial white bean soup from Tuscany topped with garlic fried in olive oil.
Serves 6 Page 105 𝓥 ✔ ❄

**Squash and Haricot Bean Soup**
Sustaining winter soup made with butternut squash or pumpkin, enhanced with olive pesto.
Serves 4–6 Page 107

**Sweet Potato and Cumin Soup**
Orange-fleshed sweet potatoes give this potato soup an exotic flavour.
Serves 6–8 Page 107

**Chick Pea Soup**
Hearty and warming, this spiced soup is topped with garlic croûtons.
Serves 6 Page 108

**Spinach and Pea Soup with Lemon**
Quick and easy vibrant soup with a refreshing tang.
Serves 4 Page 108

**Miso Soup with Noodles**
Japanese-style soup with miso, tofu and spinach.
Serves 4–6 Page 109

**Baked Red Onion Soup**
A variation of classic French onion soup – cooked completely in the oven.
Serves 4–6 Page 110

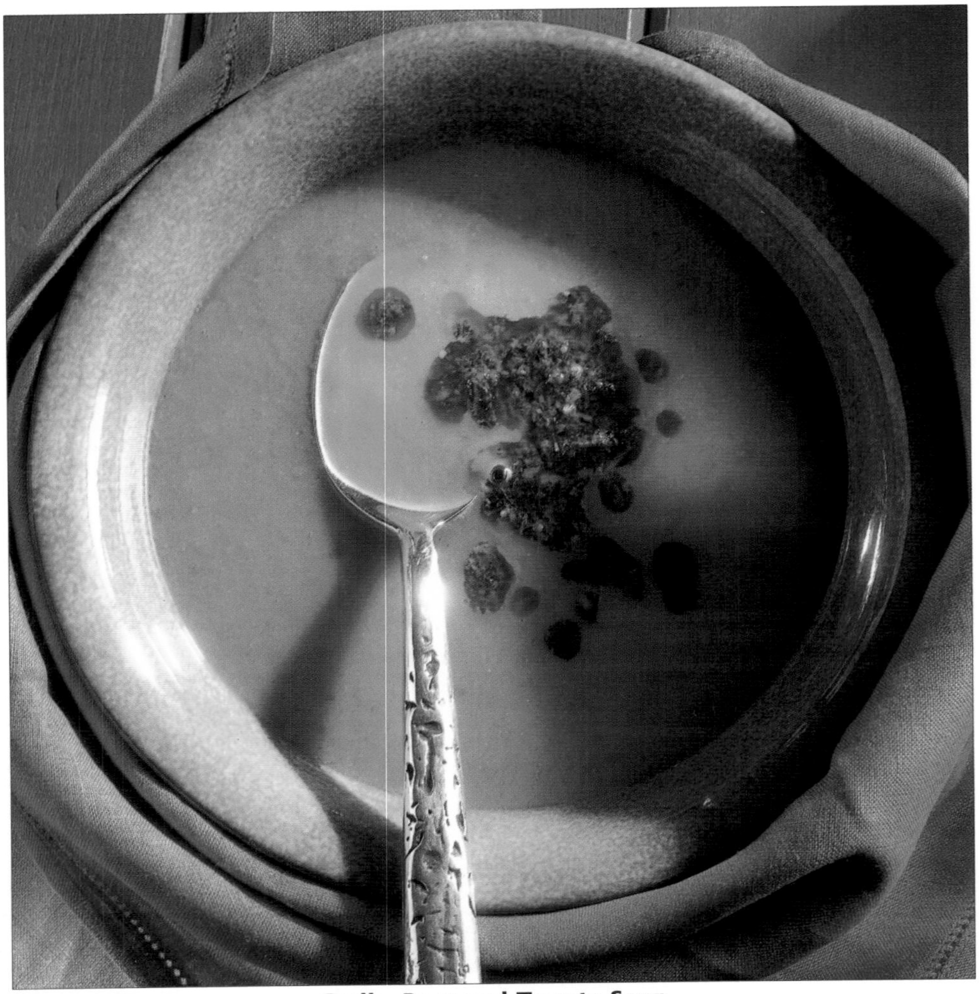

**Garlic, Bean and Tomato Soup**
This sustaining soup is one for confirmed garlic lovers!
Serves 4 Page 110

**Grilled Pepper and Aubergine Soup**
An intensely flavoured soup topped with a delicious saffron cream.
Serves 4–6 Page 111

**Walnut Soup with Charmoula**
A richly flavoured soup featuring toasted walnuts and a North African spice mix.
Serves 4 Page 111

**Soup au Pistou**
Colourful sustaining vegetable soup from Provence enlivened with garlic, basil and olive oil.
Serves 6–8 Page 113

**Spinach and Rice Soup**
Tasty soup which works well with fresh or frozen spinach.
Serves 4–6 Page 112

**Cauliflower and Coconut Soup**
Thai-style coconut soup with lemon grass, lime leaves and galangal.
Serves 6 Page 112

**Lettuce and Sorrel Soup**
Delicately flavoured summer soup with thyme and chives – served hot.
Serves 4 Page 113 ʋ ❄

**Potato and Garlic Soup with Watercress**
Delicious Californian soup with a wonderfully smooth texture.
Serves 4–6 Page 116 ʋ ✔ ❄

**Vichyssoise with Lemon Grass**
Creamy, velvety classic – with the added fragrance of lemon grass.
Serves 6 Page 116 ✔ ❄

**Mushroom Tom Yam**
A fragrant Thai broth, flavoured with dried shiitake mushrooms.
Serves 4 Page 114 ʋ ❄

**Creamy Pea and Flageolet Soup with Mint Cream**
Fresh-tasting summer soup – especially good made with fresh peas.
Serves 6 Page 115 ✔ ❄

**Mushroom and Artichoke Soup with Walnuts**
A rich mushroom stock enhanced with Jerusalem artichokes and toasted walnuts.
Serves 4 Page 114 ʋ ✔ ❄

**Tomato and Bread Soup with Basil**
Fresh-tasting soup based on a classic
Tuscan recipe.
Serves 4  Page 117  ⓥ ✔ ❋

**Chilled Tomato Soup
with Avocado Cream**
Tangy soup of puréed ripe tomatoes and
mint, offset with avocado cream.
Serves 6  Page 118  🕐 ✔ ❋

**Gazpacho**
Chilled Spanish tomato and sweet pepper
soup with a refreshing flavour.
Serves 6-8  Page 118  ⓥ ✔ ❋

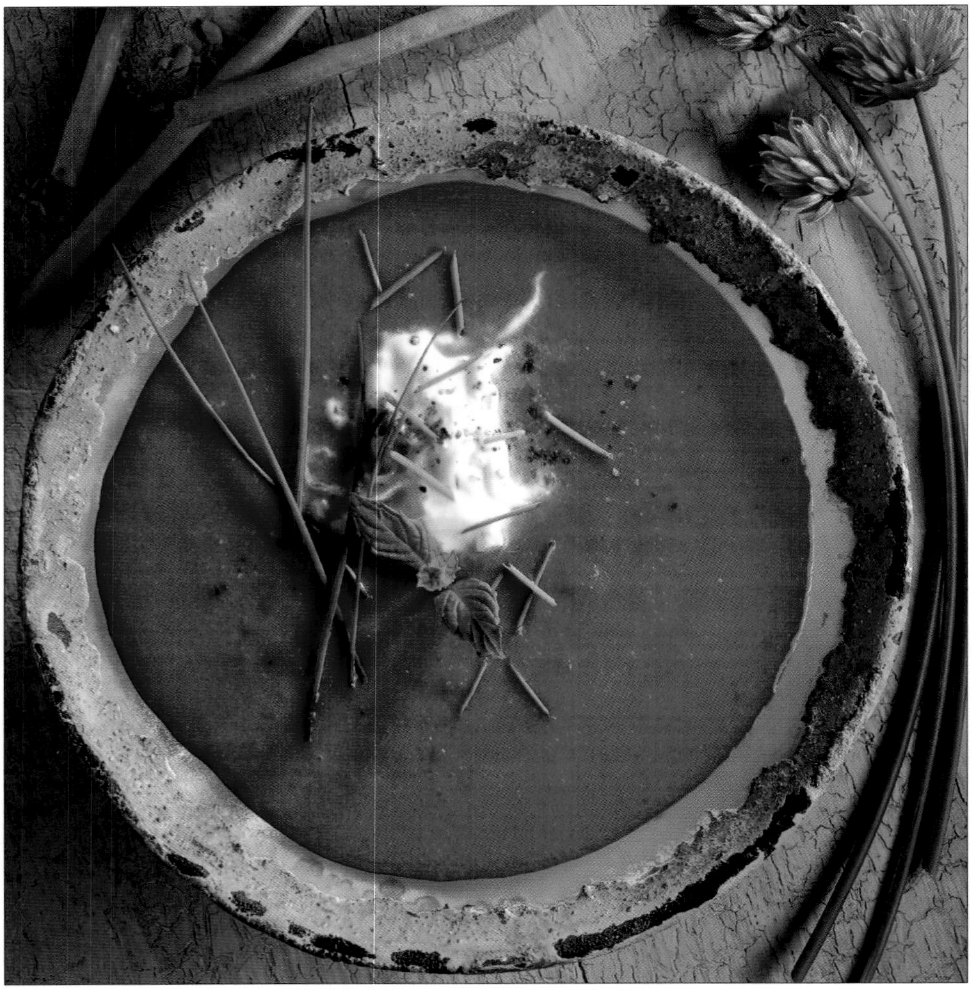

**Chilled Beetroot and Apple Soup**
A cool, deep crimson soup that's as refreshing to eat as it looks.
Serves 4  Page 117  🕐

**Chilled Melon and Ginger Soup**
Icy melon soup complemented by a
gingered cucumber relish.
Serves 4  Page 119  ✔ ❋

**Chilled Avocado and Lime Soup**
Fresh lime juice cuts the richness of
avocado in this summer soup.
Serves 4  Page 119  ✔

**Sicilian Aubergine and Ricotta Pasta**
Delicious combination of pasta, creamy ricotta, tomato, aubergine and basil.
Serves 4–6 Page 126

**Fettucine with Gorgonzola and Spinach**
Rich, creamy pasta dish – best served with a salad and flavoured bread.
Serves 4–6 Page 125

**Tagliatelle with Broad Beans, Chicory and Cream**
Tagliatelle tossed with broad beans and chicory in a creamy sauce with herbs.
Serves 4–6 Page 126

**Penne with Broccoli Pesto**
Pasta tossed with an original broccoli pesto, enriched with cream.
Serves 4 Page 124

**Spaghetti with Courgettes, Lemon and Pistachio Nuts**
This simple spaghetti dish with pistachios has a refreshing lemon tang.
Serves 4 Page 125 v

**Pasta Primavera**
Ribbon pasta perfectly offsets colourful spring vegetables or 'primavera'.
Serves 4–6 Page 126

**Pasta with Grilled Asparagus and Broad Beans**
Light, summery pasta dish which makes the most of homegrown asparagus.
Serves 4 Page 127

**Pasta with Caper Sauce and Grilled Halloumi Cheese**
Pasta and grilled peppers in a caper sauce topped with grilled halloumi.
Serves 4–6 Page 128

**Lasagnette with Courgettes and Sun-dried Tomatoes**
Pretty pasta dish accompanied by a piquant tomato sauce.
Serves 4 Page 129

**Spaghetti with Leeks, Peas and Saffron Cream**
Saffron imparts a distinctive flavour to this creamy pasta dish.
Serves 4–6 Page 127 ◷

**Orecchiette with Rocket and Cherry Tomatoes**
Quick, fresh-tasting pasta dish which relies on peppery rocket leaves.
Serves 4 Page 128 ◷

**Tagliatelle with Summer Vegetables and Herb Sauce**
Vibrant, fresh-tasting pasta dish – perfect for a summer supper.
Serves 4–6 Page 129

**Buckwheat Pasta with Grilled Radicchio**
Smoky grilled radicchio and sweet-sour caramelised onions tossed with pasta.
Serves 4 Page 130 *v*

**Calabrian Pasta**
Pasta tossed with broccoli, pine nuts, sultanas, garlic and breadcrumbs.
Serves 4-6 Page 131 *v* ⌚

**Spaghetti with Wild Mushrooms and Sage**
Dried porcini add a superb depth of flavour to this dish.
Serves 4-6 Page 133 *v*

**Fusilli with Asparagus and Parmesan**
Quick and easy dish of pasta and asparagus in a creamy sauce.
Serves 4-6 Page 132 ⌚

**Tagliatelle with Pumpkin and Blue Cheese Sauce**
Rich combination of pumpkin, cream and dolcelatte with pasta ribbons.
Serves 4-6 Page 130 ⌚

**Tagliatelle with Sage, Pimento and Garlic**
Canned pimentos lend a mellow flavour to this quick and easy dish.
Serves 4-6 Page 131 ⌚

**Pasta with Mediterranean Vegetables and Walnut Paste**
Taglietelle tossed in walnut paste and topped with grilled vegetables.
Serves 4–6 Page 132

**Mushroom and Pasta Gratin**
Quick gratin of pasta shells and mushrooms under a rich cream sauce.
Serves 4 Page 133

**Spinach and Ricotta Ravioli**
Delicately flavoured ravioli, served tossed in melted butter and Parmesan.
Serves 4 Page 134 ✓ ❄

**Herbed Mushroom Ravioli**
Pretty green herb-speckled ravioli filled with wild mushrooms.
Serves 4 (or 6 as a starter) Page 134 ✓ ❄

**Lasagne with Goat's Cheese Topping**
Lasagne with a rich vegetable filling and a custard-like cheesy topping.
Serves 6 Page 135 ✓ ❄

**Artichoke and Mushroom Lasagne**
Fresh lasagne with a filling of mushrooms, artichoke hearts and cherry tomatoes.
Serves 4 Page 135 ✓

**Tortelloni with Roasted Squash and Sage Butter**
Irresistible little pasta parcels – perfect for a special occasion.
Serves 4 (or 6 as a starter) Page 136 ✓ ❄

**Simple Oriental Noodles**
East meets West in this oriental pasta dish – perfect as a quick snack.
Serves 4 Page 137 ◷

**Pad Thai**
Thai snack of rice noodles, eggs and vegetables in a tangy peanut sauce.
Serves 4 Page 137 ◷

**Pumpkin and Barley Risotto**
Pearl barley replaces rice in this variation of a classic Italian risotto.
Serves 4 Page 141

**Spinach Risotto**
Tasty, colourful risotto – ideal for a quick and easy midweek supper.
Serves 4 Page 142 ◷

**Risotto Galette with Melted Taleggio**
Risotto transformed into a substantial galette with a melted cheese filling.
Serves 6–8 Page 143

**Summer Vegetable Risotto**
Easy risotto that can be made with any green vegetables in season.
Serves 4 Page 141 ♥ ◷

**Mushroom and Aubergine Risotto**
Full-flavoured Italian risotto with a wonderfully creamy texture.
Serves 4 Page 142

**Wild Mushroom Risotto**
Exquisite Italian risotto flavoured with a mixture of dried and fresh mushrooms.
Serves 4 Page 140

**Baby Onion and Fresh Pea Risotto**
Sweet caramelised baby onions add a rich depth of flavour to this risotto.
Serves 4 Page 144

**Vegetable Pilau**
Versatile pilau which can be served as a main meal or an accompaniment.
Serves 4-6 Page 145 v

**Vegetable and Rice Tian**
Tasty rice, tomato and vegetable bake topped with breadcrumbs, almonds, and grated Parmesan if wished.
Serves 4 Page 144 v

**Catalan Red Peppers**
Spanish-style stuffed peppers with a garlicky rice stuffing.
Serves 4 Page 145 v ✓

**Courgette and Cheese Pilaf**
Delicious Middle Eastern-style bulghar dish with typical sweet and savoury flavours.
Serves 4 Page 146

**Puy Lentil and Rice Pilaf**
Deliciously spicy supper dish, best served with toasted pitta and yogurt.
Serves 4-6 Page 146 v

**Vegetarian Paella**
Colourful vegetarian adaptation of the popular Spanish classic.
Serves 4 Page 147

**Mozzarella-stuffed Rice Balls**
Irresistible crisp golden balls, stuffed with melting mozzarella and basil leaves.
Serves 4 Page 149

**Couscous-stuffed Peppers**
Fresh mint and raisins lend a Middle Eastern flavour to these peppers.
Serves 4-6 Page 150

**Spanish Rice with Aioli**
Tasty supper dish – cooked like a paella and served with a fiery aioli.
Serves 4-6 Page 148

**Rice Cakes with Sage Butter**
Saffron risotto cakes enriched with ricotta, served with a fragrant sage butter.
Serves 6-8 Page 148

**Vegetable Biryani**
Spectacular Indian celebration dish – served as a meal in itself.
Serves 4 Page 147

**Vegetable Couscous with Harissa**
North African dish of couscous with a tasty vegetable stew and fiery harissa.
Serves 4–6 Page 150

**Couscous-filled Aubergines with a Coriander Dressing**
Aubergines stuffed with couscous, sun-dried tomatoes, dried apricots and pine nuts.
Serves 2 (or 4 as a starter) Page 151

**Tamale Pie**
Cornmeal-thickened stew with Caribbean and South American origins.
Serves 4–6 Page 152

**Baked Cabbage with Fruited Bulghar Wheat Stuffing**
Cabbage leaves rolled around a deliciously savoury stuffing.
Serves 4 Page 152

**Bulghar Wheat and Walnut Patties with Tomato Sauce**
Unlike most veggie burgers these are a real delight!
Serves 4 Page 153

**White Bean Stew with Tapenade**
Lemon and rosemary scented stew,
perfectly offset by homemade tapenade.
Serves 4  Page 156  ❂ ✔ ❄

**Quick Vegetable and Bean Mole**
Based on a traditional Mexican dish, this
stew is enriched with a little chocolate.
Serves 4-6  Page 158  ❂ ✔ ❄

**Boston Baked Beans**
Serve this tasty version of the classic
American favourite with garlic bread and
plenty of salad.
Serves 4  Page 158  ❂ ✔ ❄

**Mixed Bean Chilli**
Vegetarian version of popular Mexican
chilli – served with tortillas or rice.
Serves 6  Page 157  ❂ ✔ ❄

**Crusted Bean and Pesto Bake**
Quick and easy bean stew with a delicious
crumb, cheese and almond topping.
Serves 4  Page 157  ✔ ❄

**Clay Pot Stew**
Full-flavoured one-pot stew based on an authentic Greek dish.
Serves 6  Page 159  ❂ ✔ ❄

**Vegetable and Bean Stew with Rouille**
Colourful mixed vegetable and bean stew, served with a fiery pepper sauce.
Serves 4 Page 159 *v*

**Cauliflower and Lentil Dhal with Coconut**
Vegetable dhal deliciously enriched and mellowed by coconut cream.
Serves 4 Page 162 *v*

**Egyptian-style Lentils**
Middle-eastern spiced lentil dish, with caramelised onions and hard-boiled eggs.
Serves 4 Page 162

**Oriental-style Bean Stew**
Soy bean and arame seaweed stew with tomatoes, leek and coriander.
Serves 4 Page 160 *v*

**Root Vegetable and Lentil Casserole**
Spicy combination of mixed root vegetables and assorted lentils – an ideal winter supper.
Serves 6 Page 160 *v*

**Pasta e Fagioli**
Somewhere between a stew and a hearty soup this pasta and bean dish is an Italian institution!
Serves 6 Page 161

**Nut Roast with Onion and Port Gravy**
Tasty roast well flavoured with nuts and cheese, enhanced with a rich gravy.
Serves 8 Page 161

**Spring Green, Lentil and Red Pepper Stir-fry**
Quick and easy stir-fry spiked with ginger, chilli and soy sauce.
Serves 4 Page 163

**Chick Peas with Ginger and Tomato**
Serve these curried chick peas as part of an Indian meal, or with jacket potatoes.
Serves 4 Page 163

**Massaman Curry**
Superb authentic mixed vegetable and nut curry, prepared with homemade curry paste.
Serves 4-6 Page 164

**Stir-fried Cabbage with Cashews**
A tasty stir-fry of Savoy cabbage, French beans, cashew nuts and red chillies, with a hint of lime.
Serves 4 Page 166

**Spinach and Chick Pea Sauté**
Richly flavoured with spices, raisins and pine nuts, this dish is best served with warm bread.
Serves 4 Page 166

**Chick Pea, Aubergine and
Mushroom Tagine**
Spicy sweet and sour stew from North
Africa – served with couscous.
Serves 4  Page 165  *V* ❋

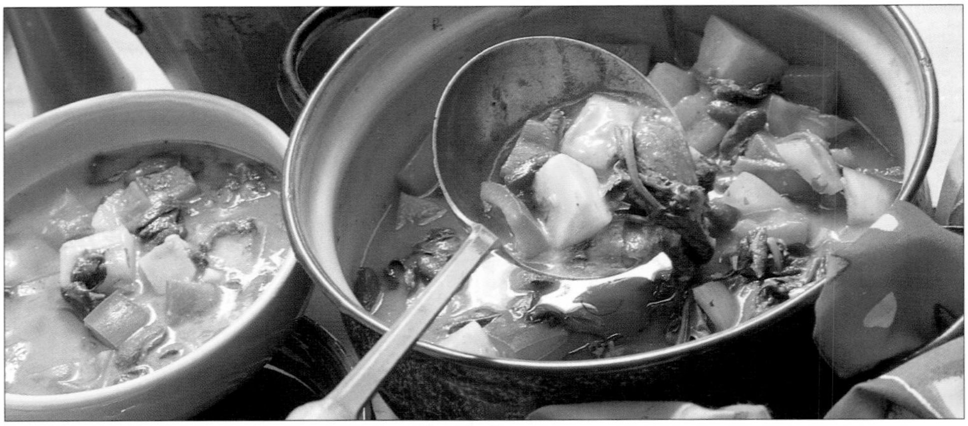

**Carib Stew**
Caribbean hot pot of vegetables, beans and spices cooked in a tomato broth.
Serves 4-6  Page 165  *V* ✔ ❋

**Spiced Chick Pea, Rice and Carrot Pilaf**
Richly spiced North African dish – serve on
its own or with a mild curry.
Serves 4  Page 167  *V*

**African Sweet Potato Stew**
Based on a typical African dish, this stew is
richly flavoured with spinach, mushrooms,
spices and peanuts.
Serves 4-6  Page 167  *V* ✔ ❋

**Nutty Bean Burgers with a
Mango and Ginger Relish**
Moist, tasty burgers, with a crisp crust and
a spicy relish.
Serves 6  Page 168  *V* ✔ ❋

**Festive Nut and Cranberry Terrine**
Hot watercrust pie, encasing a vegetable, walnut and herb filling, topped with cranberries
or redcurrants.
Serves 8-10  Page 169  ✔

**Vegetable Grill with Walnut Sauce**
Colourful grilled vegetables served with a
delicious walnut dipping sauce.
Serves 4  Page 169  *V*

**Fritto Misto with Almond Aioli**
Crisp deep-fried vegetables coated in a light batter, served with a wickedly delicious dipping sauce.
Serves 4–6 Page 172

**Potato Gnocchi with Red Pesto**
Classic Italian potato dumplings topped with a delicious spicy red pesto.
Serves 4 Page 173

**Vegetables à la Grecque**
Poached baby vegetables subtly flavoured with herbs, spices and aromatics – served at room temperature.
Serves 4 Page 173

**Herb Gnocchi with Grilled Tomato Sauce**
Rosemary-flavoured gnocchi served with a grilled tomato sauce.
Serves 4 Page 174

**Barbecued Aubergine Baguette**
Grilled aubergine slices in a tangy sauce are used in this vegetarian version of a steak sandwich!
Serves 4 Page 174

**Thai Grilled Vegetables**
Char-grilled asparagus, courgettes and spring onions with Thai-flavoured noodles.
Serves 4 Page 175

**Roasted Red Onions with Mushroom and Thyme Sauce**
Flavoured with port, these tasty onions are perfect with spinach and a potato gratin.
Serves 6  Page 175  ♥ ✔

**Provençal Vegetable Pie**
Typical Provençal vegetables cooked in a tomato sauce, then baked under a delicious crust.
Serves 4–6  Page 178  ✔ ❀

**Veggie Crumble**
A creamy medley of winter vegetables topped with a walnut and Cheddar crumble.
Serves 4–6  Page 178  ✔ ❀

**Roasted Vegetables with Salsa Verde**
Oven-roasted Mediterranean vegetables served with a delicious garlic and herb sauce.
Serves 4  Page 176  ♥ ✔

**Goulash with Tarragon and Horseradish Dumplings**
Warming winter casserole – the light, herby dumplings can be omitted if you prefer.
Serves 6  Page 177  ♥ ✔ ❀

**Spring Vegetable Stew**
A fresh-tasting stew of baby vegetables, peas, broad beans and spring herbs.
Serves 4  Page 177

**Summer Vegetable Pie with a Herby Cheese Crust**
A rich leek, courgette and tomato stew, baked with a cheesy herb scone topping.
Serves 4–6 Page 179 ✔

**Vegetable and Chick Pea Balti**
French beans, butternut squash and tomatoes are included in this wonderfully fragrant balti. Serve with plenty of naan bread and poppadoms.
Serves 6 Page 181 V ✔ ❄

**Aubergine Cannelloni**
Char-grilled aubergine slices rolled around mozzarella slices and pesto, then baked under a tomato sauce.
Serves 6 Page 180 ✔ ❄

**Roasted Vegetable Ratatouille**
Delicious thyme and garlic scented vegetables with a goat's cheese topping.
Serves 6 Page 180 ✔

**Red Cabbage Timbales with Mushroom Stuffing**
An impressive dish, ideal as an alternative Christmas lunch.
Serves 6 Page 181

**Mixed Vegetable Curry**
Grind your own spices for this Indian curry and vary the vegetables as you like.
Serves 4–6 Page 182 V ✔ ❄

**Vegetable Pasanda**
Rich, creamy Indian curry, flavoured with nuts and dry-fried spices.
Serves 6 Page 182 ✓

**Spiced Vegetables with Coconut**
Fresh coconut gives this spicy Indian dish a superior texture and flavour.
Serves 4 Page 183 V ✓

**Spiced Potatoes and Cauliflower**
Known as aloo gobi, this curry is always a great favourite.
Serves 4 Page 183 V ◷

**Mattar Paneer**
Make the paneer the day before you intend to serve this authentic Indian dish.
Serves 4 Page 184 ✓ ❄

**African Vegetable and Fruit Curry**
This superb South African curry includes vegetables, dried fruit and cashew nuts.
Serves 4 Page 184 V ✓ ❄

**Stir-fried Vegetables with Hoisin and Tofu**
Tofu roasted in a spicy glaze, then tossed with stir-fried vegetables.
Serves 4 Page 185 V

**Grilled Polenta with Mushrooms**
Herby mushroom and polenta terrine – sliced and grilled until crisp.
Serves 6-8 Page 186

**Smoked Tofu, Aubergine and Shiitake Mushroom Kebabs**
Oriental-style kebabs enhanced by a soy sauce and sesame marinade.
Serves 4 Page 186

**Spicy Vegetable and Tofu Kebabs**
Tasty kebabs marinated in a piquant dressing before grilling – served with a coriander yogurt sauce.
Serves 6 Page 187

**Okra Tagine**
Spicy Moroccan vegetable stew of okra, baby courgettes, fennel and tomatoes.
Serves 4-6 Page 188

**Baked Jacket Potatoes**
Topped with a cheesy carrot filling, or mixed bean chilli, these jacket potatoes make a sustaining supper.
Serves 8 Page 188

**Roast Peppers Stuffed with Mushrooms**
Tasty peppers filled with tomatoes, pine nuts, marjoram and mushrooms – best served with warm crusty bread and a leafy salad.
Serves 4 Page 189

**Baked Stuffed Pumpkin**
A whole stuffed pumpkin looks particularly grand carried to the table!
Serves 4–6 Page 191 ✓

**Oven-roasted Spaghetti Squash with Herb Butter**
Spaghetti squash is easy to prepare and makes an unusual supper dish.
Serves 4 Page 189 ✓

**Baked Beef Tomatoes stuffed with Pesto Rice**
Pesto, mozzarella and a crisp topping give stuffed tomatoes a new lease of life!
Serves 4 Page 190 ✓

**Turkish Aubergines**
Aubergines with a tasty tomato, garlic and parsley stuffing – served chilled.
Serves 6 Page 191 V ✓

**Mushroom, Spinach and Roasted Potato Bake**
Mushrooms, spinach and small potatoes baked in a rich creamy cheese sauce.
Serves 6 Page 190 ✓ ❄

**Vegetable Cheese Pie with Potato Crust**
A medley of vegetables cooked in a cheesy sauce under a crisp potato pastry lid.
Serves 4 Page 195

**Mediterranean Vegetable Flan**
A vibrant arrangement of Mediterranean vegetables set in a ricotta custard.
Serves 4–6 Page 197

**Roasted Vegetable Tatin**
Roasted root vegetables, shallots and leeks cooked under a layer of puff pastry and inverted to serve.
Serves 4 Page 197

**Creamy Cauliflower Pie**
Cauliflower in a creamy sauce flavoured with mustard and herbs, topped with puff pastry.
Serves 4 Page 195

**Chestnut and Vegetable Pie with Herb Stuffing**
Tasty stuffing balls add a festive touch to this sustaining pie.
Serves 6–8 Page 196

**Onion and Potato Tart**
A tasty cheese-topped flan, flavoured with capers, olive pesto and fresh herbs.
Serves 4 Page 198

**Saffron Tart with Wild Mushrooms**
Saffron flavoured pastry with an exquisite garlicky wild mushroom filling.
Serves 4–6 Page 199 ✓ ❄

**Creamy Leek Tart**
A deliciously creamy flan with a filling of soft, melting leeks and a hint of nutmeg.
Serves 6 Page 200 ✓

**Courgette, Feta and Thyme Tart**
Thin, crisp pastry and fresh summer flavours make this tart ideal for a light supper.
Serves 6 Page 199 ✓ ❄

**Tarte au Roquefort**
A superb creamy blue cheese tart with a tasty garlic and walnut topping.
Serves 6–8 Page 200 ✓

**Oatmeal and Courgette Quiche**
Short, crumbly oatmeal pastry case with a creamy courgette filling.
Serves 6 Page 201 ✓ ❄

**Spring Vegetable Strudel**
Layers of buttery filo pastry rolled around a tasty filling of spring vegetables.
Serves 6 Page 201 ✓ ❄

**Spanakopitta Strudel**
Classic Greek minted feta and spinach filo
strudel, served with a tomato sauce.
Serves 4-6  Page 202 ✔ ❉

**Crusty Vegetable Parcels**
Roasted vegetables topped with a cheesy
sauce and encased in puff pastry.
Serves 8  Page 205 ✔ ❉

**Mediterranean Cheese Puffs**
Puff pastry parcels filled with ricotta,
halloumi, pine nuts, olives and fresh
coriander.
Makes 8  Page 205 ✔

**Onion, Feta and Pine Nut Tarts**
Caramelised onions, olives, sun-dried
tomatoes and pine nuts in puff pastry.
Serves 4  Page 203 ✔ ❉

**Moroccan Filo Pie**
Spicy spinach, lentil and cheese pie –
scented with garlic and herbs.
Serves 6-8  Page 204 ✔ ❉

**Filo Mushroom Tarlets**
Individual tarts filled with tasty mushrooms, topped with an egg, then baked to perfection.
Serves 6  Page 203

**Tomato and Garlic Pizza**
Thin, crispy pizza with a topping of tomatoes, black olives, garlic and feta cheese.
Serves 2  Page 208  ✔ ⏲

**Roasted Onion and Olive Calzone**
A folded pizza with a creamy cheese and roasted onion filling.
Serves 4  Page 209  ✔ ❄

**Artichoke and Dolcelatte Pizza**
Superb rich pizza, topped with sun-dried tomato pesto, artichoke hearts and dolcelatte cheese.
Serves 2-4  Page 207  ✔ ⏲

**Four-cheese Pizza**
Tasty pizza with a rich topping of mozzarella, dolcelatte, ricotta and Parmesan.
Serves 4  Page 208  ✔

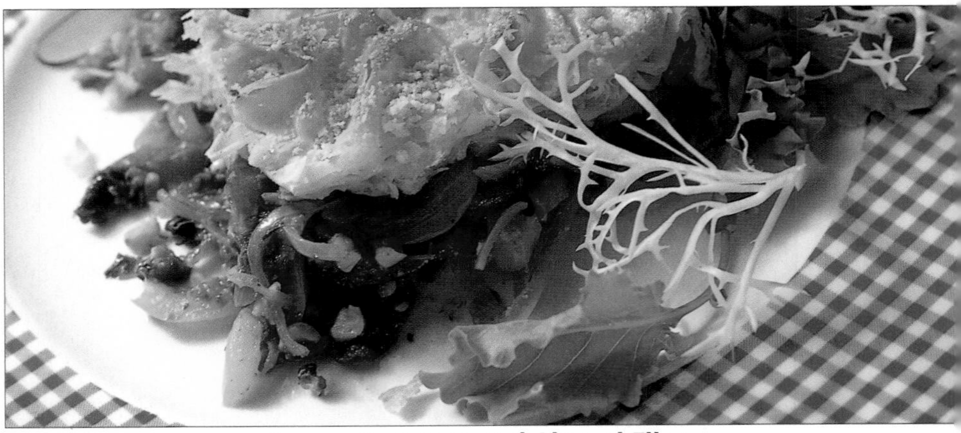

**Pepper, Parmesan and Almond Filos**
A medley of peppers, tomatoes, nuts and herbs sandwiched between cheesy filo layers.
Serves 6  Page 206  ✔ ❄

**Classic French Omelette**
The perfect folded omelette – with a variety of fillings to choose from.
Serves 1 Page 212

**Broccoli, Olive and Goat's Cheese Frittata**
Quick and easy Italian-style omelette, flavoured with tarragon and parsley.
Serves 4 Page 214

**Asparagus, Broad Bean and Parmesan Frittata**
This superb frittata includes a variety of summer vegetables and herbs.
Serves 2-4 Page 214

**Omelette Cannelloni with Mushroom Stuffing**
Omelettes rolled around a mushroom filling, then baked under a cheese sauce.
Serves 4 Page 213

**Egg and Roasted Pepper Stew**
Baked eggs nestling in tomato halves on a bed of roasted vegetables.
Serves 2-3 Page 213

**Thai-style Stuffed Omelette**
Stir-fried vegetables tossed in a coriander pesto make a tasty stuffing for this omelette.
Serves 2 Page 212

**Spanish Tortilla**
Heavy on the potato and light on the egg, this is as a Spanish tortilla should be!
Serves 6–8 Page 215 ✔

**Sweet Potato and Leek Tortilla**
Tasty variation of a Spanish tortilla – equally good served hot or cold.
Serves 4 Page 215 ◷

**Crunchy Chick Pea Eggs with Aioli**
Vegetarian version of Scotch eggs, served with garlic mayonnaise.
Serves 6 Page 216 ✔

**Savoury Pancakes**
Plain, wholewheat, buckwheat and spiced chick pea pancakes, and a variety of fillings to choose from.
Makes 8 Page 216 ◷ ✔ ❄

**Bruschetta of Field Mushrooms with Poached Eggs**
This excellent combination makes a great brunch, lunch or supper dish.
Serves 4 Page 218 ◷

**Curried Eggs on Toast**
Scrambled eggs enhanced with Indian spices – served on toasted naan or pitta bread.
Serves 2 Page 218 ◷

**Oven-baked Mushroom Pancake**
Vegetarian 'toad in the hole', served with a rich tomato sauce.
Serves 6–8 Page 217

**Herby Cheese and Vegetables with Spicy Carrot Salsa**
Roasted vegetables with grilled halloumi or feta and a spicy carrot salsa.
Serves 4 Page 221

**Macaroni Cheese**
Ever-popular supper dish, with a luxury three-cheese variation.
Serves 4 Page 219

**Pasticcio with Spinach and Feta**
Pasta, feta cheese and spinach in a tomato sauce, baked under a creamy sauce.
Serves 4–6 Page 219

**Spinach and Potato Mascarpone Gratin**
An excellent supper dish, best served with a green salad and crusty bread.
Serves 4 Page 220

**Marinated Baked Goat's Cheese
with Chilli Dressing**
Prepare-ahead dish – delicious served
warm with salad and focaccia bread.
Serves 4  Page 220  ✔

**Caponata with Cheesy Potato Crust**
Sicilian aubergine, tomato and celery stew,
with a mashed potato and cheese topping.
Serves 4-6  Page 221  ✔ ❄

**Summer Vegetable Soufflé**
Lovely, light two-layered soufflé – perfect
for a summer lunch.
Serves 6  Page 222  ✔

**Cheese Soufflé**
An impressive classic hot cheese soufflé,
with variations.
Serves 4  Page 223  ✔

**Aubergine and Pepper Parmigiana**
Oven-baked layers of aubergine, grilled
peppers, tomato and cheese.
Serves 6  Page 223  ✔

**Parsnip, Potato and Cheese Rosti**
A deliciously deep rosti with a layer of
melting cheese through the middle.
Serves 4  Page 225  ⏱

**Spinach and Ricotta Gnocchi**
Light, tasty version of gnocchi – served with melted butter and chopped sage leaves.
Serves 4  Page 224  ✔

**Cheese Sausages on Apple
and Watercress Salad**
Based on a Welsh recipe, these vegetarian
sausages fry to a deep golden crust.
Serves 4  Page 225  ⏱ ✔ ❄

**Tomato and Roasted Bread Salad**
Colourful, gutsy Mediterranean salad full of interesting flavours and textures – best served *al fresco* with a glass of chilled white wine.
Serves 4 Page 230

**Roasted Vegetable Salad**
Fontina cheese imparts a delectable creamy texture to these roasted Mediterranean vegetables.
Serves 8 Page 228

**Indonesian Vegetable Salad**
Based on a classic Indonesian recipe, this version is topped with toasted peanuts.
Serves 4-6 Page 229

**Mediterranean Salad with a Spicy Dressing**
This hearty main course salad is best served with olive or sun-dried tomato bread.
Serves 4-6 Page 230

**Mediterranean Pasta Salad**
Pasta, sun-dried and cherry tomatoes, basil and olives tossed in a tomato vinaigrette.
Serves 4 Page 231

**Thai Vegetable Salad with Crispy Noodles**
Crisp, colourful salad tossed in a spicy dressing and topped with deep-fried noodles.
Serves 4-6 Page 229

**Spinach and Feta Cheese Salad**
Dark green leafy salad offset with slivers of red pepper and cubes of feta cheese.
Serves 4 Page 232 ◷

**Salad of Haricot Beans and Summer Vegetables**
A fresh-tasting, delicately flavoured warm salad – perfect for a summer's lunch.
Serves 6-8 Page 231 ♥

**Yellow Pepper Caesar Salad**
Hot buttery croûtons and smoky grilled pepper strips tossed with lettuce in a garlic and Parmesan flavoured mayonnaise.
Serves 4-6 Page 232

**Rocket and Goat's Cheese Salad with Roasted Pepper Salsa**
A delicious juicy pepper salsa is the perfect partner for crumbly goat's cheese.
Serves 4 Page 233

**Green Pea, Potato and Walnut Salad**
Minted baby new potatoes, sugar snaps and freshly podded peas tossed in a walnut dressing.
Serves 4 Page 233 ♥

**Lentil Salad with Green Vegetables and Goat's Cheese**
Puy lentils, mangetout, asparagus tips and French beans in a lemony dressing, with goat's cheese.
Serves 4–6 Page 234

**Bulghar Wheat Salad with Dried Fruit and Pine Nuts**
A tangy salad, generously flavoured with lemon, coriander and dried fruit.
Serves 4 Page 234

**Ciabatta, Plum Tomato and Mozzarella Salad**
A colourful peasant-style salad tossed in a basil-flavoured dressing.
Serves 4–6 Page 235

**Millet Salad with Grilled Peppers**
A tasty salad of grilled peppers, tomatoes, chilli and cooked millet in a balsamic dressing.
Serves 4 Page 235

**Mesclun with Toasted Seeds**
Assorted salad leaves and herbs enhanced with toasted seeds and a few edible flowers – if available.
Serves 4 Page 236

**Mixed Leaf Salad with Croûtons**
A crisp, colourful salad featuring peppery rocket, watercress, radishes and crunchy croûtons.
Serves 6–8 Page 236

**Three Tomato Salad with Capers and Olives**
Flavourful plum, cherry and beef tomatoes marinated in a lemon vinaigrette.
Serves 4–6 Page 237 ν ✓ ◷

**Courgette and Lemon Salad**
Mixed yellow and green courgettes marinated in a lemony dressing, flavoured with oregano.
Serves 6 Page 236 ν ✓ ◷

**Three Bean Salad**
Colourful mixed bean and grilled pepper salad tossed in a spicy dressing with fresh coriander.
Serves 6 Page 237 ν ✓ ◷

**Red Cabbage Slaw**
A deliciously rich and creamy homemade coleslaw – best prepared in advance.
Serves 4–6 Page 238 ✓ ◷

**Fennel and Orange Salad**
Here rocket leaves and slivers of red onion are added to the classic combination of fennel and orange – and the salad is enhanced with an olive dressing.
Serves 4 Page 238 ν ◷

**Potato Salad with Basil Dressing**
A quick and easy potato salad speckled with toasted pine nuts. Serve either warm or cold as you prefer.
Serves 4 Page 239 V ✓ ◷

**New Potato and Dill Salad**
New potatoes tossed with fresh dill in a creamy mustardy dressing.
Serves 6 Page 239 ✓ ◷

**Wild Rice and Thyme Salad**
A pretty rice salad flecked with broad beans, French beans and mushrooms.
Serves 6–8 Page 239 V ✓

**Orzo Salad with Pesto Sauce**
Tiny rice-shaped orzo pasta works particularly well in this tangy salad.
Serves 4 Page 240 V ✓ ◷

**Gingered Rice Salad**
Nutty brown rice salad liberally flavoured with coriander and mint in a ginger, soy and sesame dressing.
Serves 6 Page 240 V ✓

**Classic Tabbouleh**
A simple, classic version of the Middle Eastern bulghar wheat salad – best served with a selection of other dishes.
Serves 4 Page 241 V ✓

**Roast Sweet Peppers with Sage**
Roast peppers flavoured with frazzled sage leaves, garlic and pine nuts.
Serves 4 Page 246

**Crunchy-topped Asparagus and Courgettes**
A breadcrumb and Parmesan topping is the perfect foil for these vegetables.
Serves 4-6 Page 244

**Grilled Chicory and Radicchio with Orange**
Grilling chicory and radicchio caramelises their juices – to delicious effect!
Serves 4 Page 244

**Stir-fried Summer Vegetables**
Balsamic vinegar brings out the earthy sweetness of the vegetables in this colourful stir-fry.
Serves 4-6 Page 245

**Fennel Gratin**
Deliciously rich creamy accompaniment to serve on special occasions.
Serves 6 Page 245

**Baked Fennel with Lemon and Olives**
Fennel bulbs braised to tender sweetness with smoky black olives and lemon juice.
Serves 4 Page 244

**Broad Beans in a Cream Herb Sauce**
Tender, young broad beans in a creamy sauce flavoured with chervil and parsley.
Serves 4-6 Page 246

**Runner Beans with Hazelnut Butter**
An original, tasty manner to serve this popular homegrown vegetable.
Serves 4-6 Page 247

**Spicy Grilled Aubergines**
Aubergine halves are drizzled with a chilli and herb topping, then grilled until tender.
Serves 4 Page 247

**Minted Peas with Cucumber and Spring Onions**
Peas tossed with sautéed spring onions and cucumber in a creamy sauce, spiked with vermouth. An excellent way to bring out the full flavour of fresh peas.
Serves 4-6 Page 247

**Honey-glazed Shallots**
Sweet shallots are braised in a piquant dressing until meltingly tender and glazed.
Serves 4 Page 247

**Roast Tomatoes with a Garlic Crust**
Flavourful cherry tomatoes are baked whole under a garlicky breadcrumb crust.
Serves 6 Page 246

**Okra with Onion and Tomato**
Tasty Indian-style side dish flavoured with a homemade masala spice mix.
Serves 4 Page 249

**Potato Parsnip Galette**
Golden cake of butter-basted potatoes and sweet parsnips with a hint of honey and lemon.
Serves 6 Page 252

**Red Cabbage with Pine Nuts**
Braised red cabbage enhanced with ginger, balsamic vinegar and pine nuts.
Serves 8 Page 249

**Sweet Potato and Chestnut Cakes with Spring Onions**
Chestnuts and sweet potatoes complement each other perfectly in these crisp-fried patties.
Serves 4–6 Page 250

**Baby Carrots with Basil**
Sweet, baby carrots in a creamy sauce liberally flavoured with freshly torn basil.
Serves 6 Page 251

**Parsnips in a Lime Glaze**
Tender young parsnips braised in a sweet glaze, enhanced with the tang of lime.
Serves 4 Page 251

**Roasted Winter Vegetables with Cardamom**
Cardamoms add a hint of aroma to this roast medley of winter vegetables.
Serves 6–8 Page 251 v ✓

**Potato Gratin**
Deliciously creamy gratin of potatoes flavoured with garlic, herbs and a hint of saffron.
Serves 4–6 Page 253 ✓ ❄

**Sage Hackle Backs**
Crisp, baked potatoes spiked with garlic, fresh sage and lemon zest.
Serves 6 Page 253 v ✓

**Rösti with Garlic and Thyme**
Thin potato sticks tossed with garlic and thyme, then pan-fried to a crisp golden cake.
Serves 6 Page 252

**New Potatoes with Peas and Broad Beans**
Freshly shelled peas and broad beans tossed with new potatoes and parsley.
Serves 4 Page 254 ◷

**Creamy Baked Potatoes with Mustard Seeds**
Jacket potatoes with a creamy garlic and mustard flavoured filling.
Serves 6 Page 254 ✓ ❄

**Steamed Basil and Mustard Seed Rice**
Fragrant rice dish, flavoured with black mustard seeds and fresh basil.
Serves 4 Page 254 v

**Soft Polenta with Sage Butter**
This classic Italian accompaniment makes a welcome change from mashed potatoes!
Serves 4 Page 255 ◷

**Summer Vegetable Couscous**
Couscous tossed with a medley of green vegetables in a lemony dressing.
Serves 8 Page 255 v ◷

**Golden Croissant Pudding**
For this gourmet version of bread and butter pudding light, flaky croissants and plump sultanas are baked in a creamy custard until softly set.
Serves 6 Page 259

**Apple Fritters with Honey Cream**
Apple slices coated in a light batter and crisp-fried until golden – served with flavoured cream.
Serves 4 Page 258

**Tropical Fruits with Sabayon**
Wonderfully fragrant fruit salad topped with sabayon and grilled to perfection.
Serves 4 Page 258

**Frangipane Baked Pears**
Whole pears, stuffed with a delicious filling and baked in frangipane.
Serves 6 Page 259

**Individual Sticky Toffee Puddings**
Irresistibly wicked, these make an excellent winter pudding.
Serves 4 Page 260

**Christmas Pudding**
Traditional festive plum pudding served with a light sabayon sauce.
Serves 8 Page 260

**Apple and Pecan Tart with Spiced Caramel**
Pan-fried apples piled high in a pecan pastry case, topped with caramel.
Serves 8 Page 262

**Plum Tart with Cinnamon Cream**
Tempting sticky plum tart served warm with cinnamon-flavoured whipped cream.
Serves 6 Page 262 ✓

**Spiced Nut Strudel**
Assorted nuts, glacé cherries and raisins flavoured with spices and enveloped in buttery layers of filo pastry.
Serves 8 Page 263 ✓ ❄

**Glazed Brandied Prune Tart**
Sweet plump prunes are steeped overnight in brandy, then baked in a sweet flan pastry – enveloped in a rich, creamy custard.
Serves 8 Page 261 ✓ ❄

**Apricot, Pistachio and Honey Slices**
Plump apricots and pistachios set in a creamy custard within flaky layers of filo pastry.
Serves 8 Page 264 ✓

**Traditional Mince Pies**
Rich shortcrust mince pies – with a delicious homemade apricot mincemeat.
Makes 12 Page 264 ✓ ❄

**Peach Cinnamon Tartlets**
Fresh, ripe peach halves baked on puff pastry rounds flavoured with cinnamon butter.
Serves 4 Page 265 ◷

**Syllabub with Poached Plums**
Ripe plums poached in dessert wine, then topped with a fragrant creamy syllabub.
Serves 8 Page 265 ✓

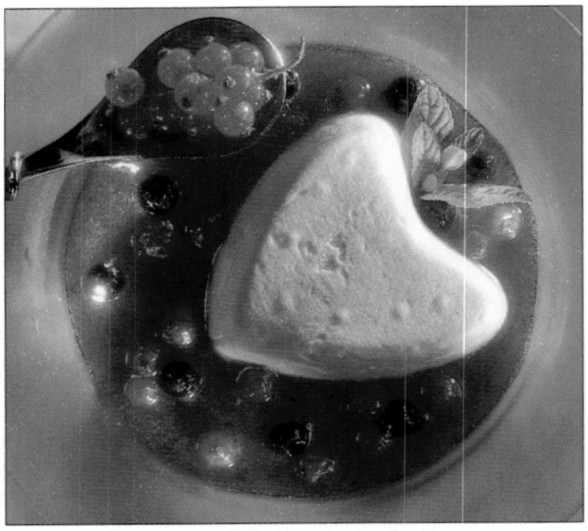

**Crèmets with Red Fruit Sauce**
Delicate creamy dessert served with a tart redcurrant and raspberry sauce.
Serves 6 Page 266 ✓

**Pineapple, Date and Kumquat Salad**
Pretty winter fruit salad of oranges, kumquats, pineapple, dates and walnuts.
Serves 6 Page 265 v ✓

**Petits Pots de Crème au Chocolat**
Deliciously rich smooth chocolate creams set in individual pots.
Serves 6-8 Page 266 ✓

**Berry Trifle with Praline**
Sumptuous creamy trifle, packed with berry fruits and topped with a contrasting crunchy praline.
Serves 10 Page 267 ✓

**Summer Fruit Brûlée**
A medley of summer berries, concealed under whipped cream and yogurt with a crisp caramelised sugar topping. An excellent quick and easy dessert to round off a dinner party.
Serves 4 Page 267 ◷

**Summer Pudding**
This quintessential British pudding is best made the day before it is to be served.
Serves 6–8 Page 268 V ✓ ❄

**Chocolate and Orange Cheesecake**
Baked layered cheesecake with an impressive caraque and orange topping.
Serves 8 Page 269 ✓ ❄

**Pistachio Praline Floating Islands**
Soft pillows of poached meringue flecked with pistachio praline sit atop a delicate custard.
Serves 4–6 Page 268 ✓

**Hazelnut Meringue Gateau**
Tiers of lightly spiced meringue,
laced with chocolate and sandwiched with
cream and hazelnut praline.
Serves 8–10 Page 269 ✔

**Almond and Apricot Roulade**
Irresistibly moist roulade with a superb almondy flavour rolled around a fresh apricot and
crème fraîche filling.
Serves 8 Page 270 ✔

**Chocolate Cinnamon Mousse Cake**
An appealing crusted surface to this cake conceals a heavenly mousse-like texture within.
Serves 8 Page 271 ✔

**Orange Sorbet**
Sicilian sorbet delicately flavoured
with orange flower water and freshly
squeezed orange juice.
Serves 4–6 Page 271 ✔

**Strawberry Sorbet**
A hint of balsamic vinegar brings out
the full flavour of the strawberries
in this sorbet.
Serves 4–6 Page 271 ✔

**Rustic Loaf**
Country-style bread with a good flavour
and texture.
Makes 1  Page 274  𝐯 ✔ ❊

**Multigrain Loaf**
Enriched with sunflower, poppy and
sesame seeds, this moist granary bread
has a delicious nutty taste.
Makes 2  Page 274  𝐯 ✔ ❊

**Cornbread**
Golden close-textured loaf with a
distinctive flavour.
Makes 1  Page 275  𝐯 ✔ ❊

**Parmesan and Chive Rolls**
These tasty cheese and herb rolls are great
served with soups.
Makes 8  Page 275  ✔ ❊

**Griddled Flat Breads**
Gram flour and spicy cumin give these homemade pitta breads a delicious flavour.
Makes 12  Page 276  𝐯 ✔ ❊

**Soda Bread**
Classic Irish bread which relies on baking
soda to both raise and flavour the dough.
Makes 1  Page 275  ✔ ❊

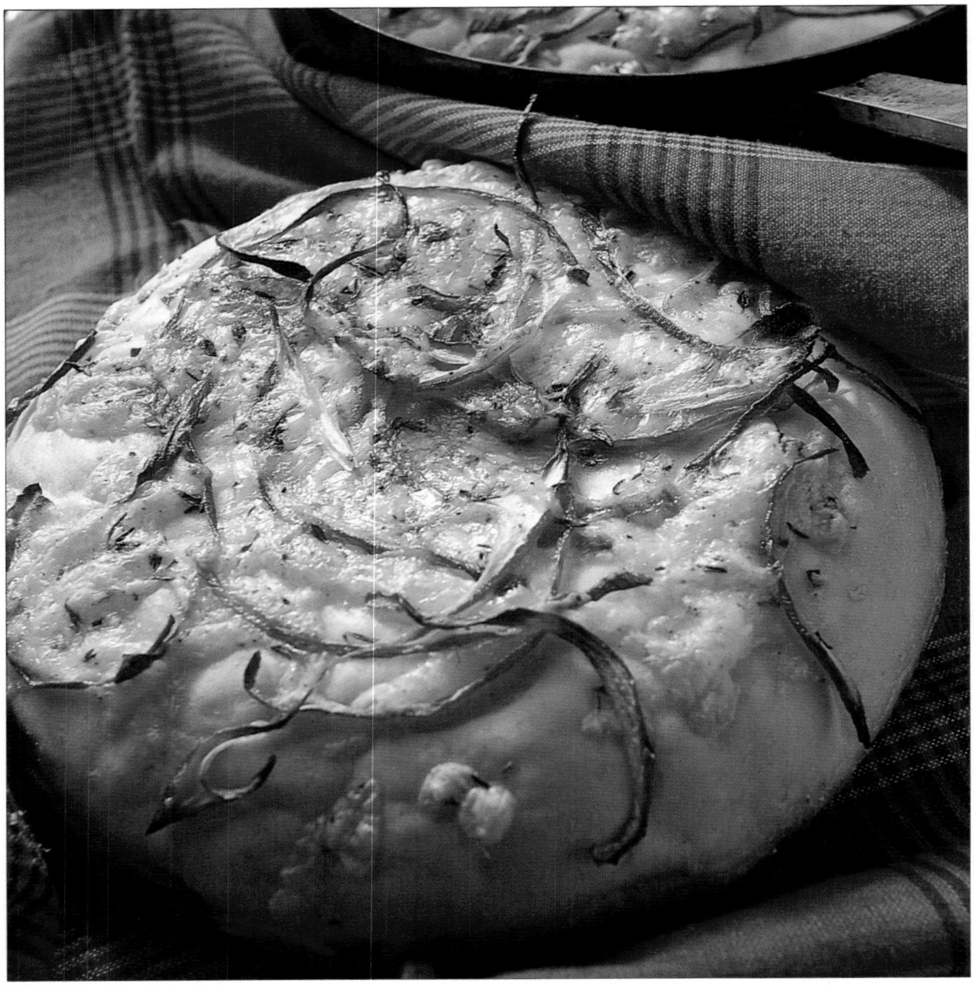

**Focaccia**
Popular Italian bread – served as an
accompaniment to salads, soups, stews
and other hearty dishes.
Makes 2  Page 278  𝓥 ✔ ❉

**Fried Onion Bread**
Based on a Greek recipe, this bread is first pan-fried, then baked in the oven with a
cheesy onion and thyme topping.
Makes 2  Page 276  ✔

**Stuffed Focaccia**
Irresistible focaccia with a melting cheese
and spinach stuffing.
Makes 1  Page 279  ✔ ❉

**Peshwari Naan Bread**
Surprisingly easy to make, this is a tasty
variation of Indian stuffed naan.
Makes 4  Page 278  𝓥 ❉

**Pesto-stuffed Breads**
Italian-style flat breads folded around a
tasty pesto filling.
Makes 4  Page 277  ✔ ❉

**Schiacciata**
Delicious Italian flat pizza-style bread with
a garlic, sage and olive oil topping.
Makes 2  Page 277  𝓥 ✔ ❉

**Apricot and Hazelnut Bread**
This flavoured granary bread has a superb moist texture and an excellent flavour.
Makes 2 Page 280

**Hinny Cakes with Blueberries**
Moist spiced teatime cakes with a topping of sugared blackberries.
Makes 10 Page 280

**Shortbread**
Melt-in-the-mouth Scottish shortbread with a rich, buttery taste.
Makes 18-20 Page 280

**Double Chocolate Cookies**
American-style cookies – chunky, crumbly and rich with dark and white chocolate.
Makes 18 Page 281

**Almond Fudge Crumbles**
Easy-to-make cookies enriched with crushed almond flakes and nibs of chewy fudge.
Makes 24 Page 281

**Double Chocolate Muffins**
Rich, dark chocolate muffins with a wonderfully light texture.
Makes 12-15 Page 282

**Sticky Gingerbread**
Superb adaptation of an all-time favourite – enhanced with syrupy stem ginger.
12 slices Page 282

**Syrupy Semolina Halva**
Tangy sponge moistened with orange juice and topped with slices of citrus fruit.
10 slices Page 283

**Apple, Sultana and Cider Slices**
Mouth-watering sponge – richly filled with apples and sultanas – baked on a puff pastry base.
12 slices Page 283

**Sticky Orange Flapjacks**
Nutty sunflower seeds and orange zest add
a new twist to this irresistible traybake.
Makes 18  Page 284  ✔ ❄

**Rippled Date and Banana Loaf**
Homely teabread with a distinctive banana
flavour, rippled with puréed dates.
8–10 slices  Page 285  ✔ ❄

**Christmas Cake**
Superb cake, best made 4-5 weeks ahead
to allow to mature. For optimum flavour,
feed weekly with 30 ml (2 tbsp) rum.
16 slices  Page 288  ✔ ❄

**Chocolate Pecan Fudge Cake**
Layers of dark chocolate cake sandwiched
together with cream, toasted pecans and
maple syrup – topped with fudge icing.
16 slices  Page 286  ✔ ❄

**Crumbly Apple and Cheese Cake**
Light, crumbly apple cake with
a hidden layer of Caerphilly cheese – best
served warm.
10 slices  Page 286  ✔ ❄

**Carrot Cake with Mascarpone Topping**
Moist cake with a creamy mascarpone
frosting and an unusual decoration of
crisp-fried carrot shavings.
8–10 slices  Page 287  ✔ ❄

**Raspberry and Pistachio
Sandwich Cake**
All-in-one sponge flavoured with
pistachios and sandwiched with fresh
raspberries and cream.
8–10 slices  Page 287  ✔ ❄

**White Chocolate Brownies**
Laden with generous chunks of white chocolate and hazelnuts, and crusted in a glossy
coat of sugar, these enticing teatime treats are deliciously moist.
Makes 12  Page 285  ✔ ❄

# RECIPES

# SNACKS AND STARTERS

## POLENTA SANDWICHES WITH FONTINA

**SERVES 4-6**
PREPARATION
20 minutes, plus chilling
COOKING TIME
10-15 minutes
FREEZING
Not suitable
CALS/SERVING
535-355

900 ml (1½ pints) water
15 g (½ oz) butter
2.5 ml (½ tsp) salt
175 g (6 oz) quick-cook polenta
25 g (1 oz) Parmesan cheese, freshly grated
pepper
175 g (6 oz) fontina or mozzarella cheese
seasoned flour, for coating
2 eggs, beaten
75 g (3 oz) fresh white breadcrumbs
oil, for deep-frying

**1** Bring the water to a rolling boil in a saucepan. Add the butter and salt. With the water at a steady simmer, gradually whisk in the polenta. Cook gently, stirring from time to time, for 6-8 minutes until the polenta is thickened and comes away from the sides of the pan.
**2** Remove from the heat and beat in the Parmesan and plenty of black pepper. Pour the mixture into a greased 23 x 25 cm (9 x 11 inch) shallow tin and level the surface with a palette knife. Leave until cold.
**3** Turn the set polenta out onto a board. Using a plain 5 cm (2 inch) cutter, stamp out 12 rounds, then halve each one horizontally to give 24 rounds. Cut the cheese into thin slices, then cut out 12 rounds, using the same cutter. Sandwich each disc of cheese between 2 polenta rounds.
**4** Dip the sandwiches into the seasoned flour to coat on all sides, then carefully dip into the beaten egg and finally in the breadcrumbs to coat thoroughly. Chill for 30 minutes.
**5** Heat a 10-12 cm (4-5 inch) depth of vegetable oil in a deep heavy-based saucepan to 180°C (350°F), or until a cube of bread dropped into the oil crisps in 30 seconds.
**6** Fry the polenta and fontina sandwiches in the hot oil, three at a time, for about 1-2 minutes until crisp and golden. Drain on kitchen paper and keep warm in a low oven whilst cooking the rest. Serve immediately.

## TOMATO BRUSCHETTA

**SERVES 4**
PREPARATION
20 minutes, plus infusing
COOKING TIME
1-2 minutes
FREEZING
Not suitable
CALS/SERVING
180

6 ripe plum tomatoes, peeled
1.25 ml (¼ tsp) caster sugar
15 ml (1 tbsp) chopped fresh basil
60 ml (2 fl oz) extra-virgin olive oil
4 slices day-old white bread
1 garlic clove, peeled and halved
salt and pepper
basil sprigs, to garnish

**1** Roughly dice the tomatoes and place in a bowl. Add the sugar, chopped basil and half of the olive oil. Cover and set aside for 30 minutes to allow the flavours to mingle.
**2** Preheat the grill. Toast the bread on both sides until crisp and golden, then rub all over with the cut garlic clove.
**3** Spoon the tomato mixture over the toasted bread, pressing it firmly into the bread. Drizzle over the remaining olive oil and season generously with salt and pepper. Garnish with basil leaves to serve.

# DEEP-FRIED POTATO SKINS WITH CHILLI SALSA

**SERVES 2-3**
PREPARATION
15 minutes
COOKING TIME
1 hour
FREEZING
Not suitable
CALS/SERVING
720-480
COLOUR INDEX
Page 24

8 potatoes, each about 125 g (4 oz)
30 ml (2 tbsp) oil
salt and pepper
oil, for deep-frying
CHILLI SALSA
350 g (12 oz) juicy ripe tomatoes
2 spring onions
15 ml (1 tbsp) chilli sauce
SOURED CREAM AND CHIVE DIP
150 ml (¼ pint) soured cream
30 ml (2 tbsp) chopped fresh chives
TO GARNISH
spring onions
coriander sprigs

**1** Scrub the potatoes and pat dry with kitchen paper. Push a skewer through each one, then brush with the oil and sprinkle with salt. Place directly on the oven shelf and bake in the oven at 200°C (400°F) Mark 6 for 45-55 minutes or until the potatoes feel soft when squeezed.
**2** Meanwhile, make the chilli salsa and soured cream dips. Finely chop the tomatoes and spring onions and mix with the chilli sauce; season with salt and pepper. Mix the soured cream with the chives and season with salt and pepper. Cover both dips and chilli in the refrigerator.
**3** Halve the baked potatoes lengthwise and scoop out the flesh, leaving a layer of potato about 1 cm (½ inch) thick on the skin. Cut each potato skin in half lenthwise.
**4** Heat the oil in a deep-fat fryer to 190°C (375°F) or until a cube of bread dropped into the oil browns within 30 seconds. Deep-fry the potato skins, a few at a time, for ½-1 minute until crisp. Remove with a slotted spoon and drain on kitchen paper.
**5** Once all the potato skins are fried, sprinkle them with a little salt. Serve immediately, garnished with spring onions and coriander and accompanied by the dips.

**NOTE** For added colour and crunch, serve a few vegetable crudités as well, if you like.

# FILO PIES WITH FETA AND HERB FILLING

**MAKES 20-24**
PREPARATION
30 minutes
COOKING TIME
20-25 minutes
FREEZING
Not suitable
CALS/PIE
100-75

225 g (8 oz) packet filo pastry
olive oil, for brushing
FILLING
300 g (10 oz) feta cheese
60 ml (4 tbsp) pine nuts, toasted
30 ml (2 tbsp) chopped fresh parsley or coriander
15 ml (1 tbsp) chopped fresh dill
½ egg, lightly beaten
pinch of freshly grated nutmeg
pepper

**1** First prepare the filling. Crumble the cheese into a bowl and add the pine nuts, herbs, egg, nutmeg and pepper to taste. Mix well.
**2** Cut the filo pastry sheets into strips, measuring about 10 x 25 cm (4 x 10 inches). Keep covered with a damp cloth while not in use to prevent them drying out.
**3** Working with 3 or 4 filo strips at a time, brush with oil and place a heaped teaspoonful of filling at the top right-hand corner of each strip. Fold the corner down to make a triangle and continue to flip the filled triangle down the length of the filo strip to wrap in the pastry. Place the filo triangles on a greased baking sheet and brush with a little more oil. Repeat to use all of the filo strips and filling.
**4** Bake the filo pies in the oven at 190°C (375°F) Mark 5 for 20-25 minutes until crisp and deep golden in colour. Serve hot or warm.

**VARIATION** For the filling, mix 3 chopped hard-boiled eggs with 50 g (2 oz) finely chopped olives, 3 finely chopped sun-dried tomatoes, 30 ml (2 tbsp) chopped walnuts and 30 ml (2 tbsp) chopped basil. Season generously.

# VEGETABLE SAMOSAS

**MAKES 24**
PREPARATION
45 minutes
COOKING TIME
About 15 minutes
FREEZING
Suitable
CALS/SAMOSA
150

450 g (1 lb) potatoes
salt and pepper
1 onion, peeled
1-2 hot green chillies
15 ml (1 tbsp) oil
1 garlic clove, peeled and crushed
10 ml (2 tsp) ground coriander
10 ml (2 tsp) cumin seeds
5 ml (1 tsp) ground fenugreek
1 large ripe tomato
50 g (2 oz) frozen peas
30 ml (2 tbsp) chopped fresh coriander
15 ml (1 tbsp) chopped fresh mint

PASTRY
450 g (1 lb) plain white flour
45 ml (3 tbsp) chopped fresh coriander
60 ml (4 tbsp) oil, melted ghee or butter
200 ml (7 fl oz) warm water (approx)

TO FINISH
oil, for deep-frying
mint sprigs and lime halves, to garnish
chutney (see note), to serve

**1** Peel and halve the potatoes. Cook in salted water until just tender. Drain thoroughly and chop into fairly small pieces.

**2** Finely chop onion and chilli(es), discarding seeds if preferred. Heat the oil in a frying pan. Add the onion and garlic and cook until softened. Add the spices and cook, stirring for 2 minutes.

**3** Chop the tomato, add to the pan and simmer until softened. Add the potatoes and stir to coat in the spice mixture. Add the peas and cook for 1-2 minutes until thawed. Add the herbs and plenty of seasoning. Take off the heat; let cool.

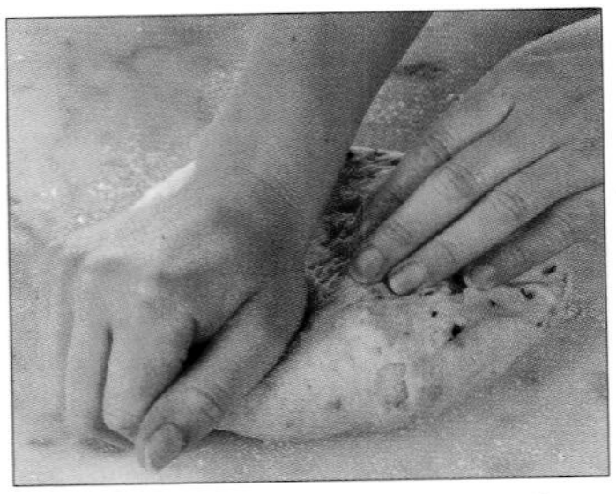

**4** To make the pastry, mix the flour, 5 ml (1 tsp) salt, and coriander in a bowl. Add the oil or melted fat and enough warm water to make a soft dough – about 200 ml (7 fl oz). Turn onto a lightly floured surface and knead for about 5 minutes.

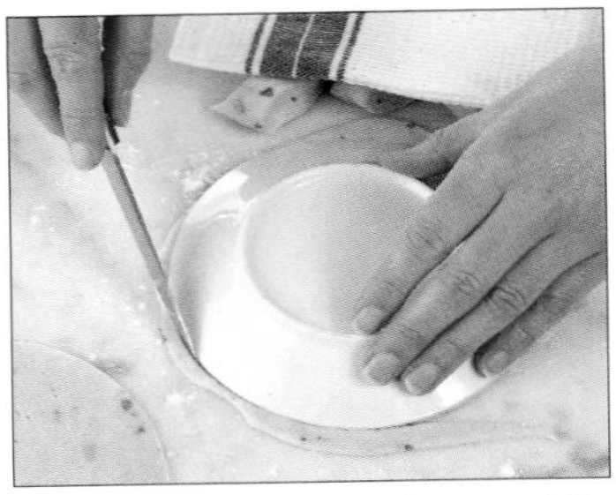

**5** Divide the dough into 12 pieces; keep covered with a damp cloth to prevent drying out. Roll one piece out to a 15 cm (6 inch) round, using a plate as a guide to trim the edges. Cut in half to make 2 semi-circles.

**6** Put a heaped teaspoon of filling on each semicircle. Dampen the edges, fold over the filling and press together firmly to seal. Repeat with the remaining pastry and filling.

**7** Heat the oil in a deep-fat fryer to 180°C (350°F) or until a small piece of pastry dropped into the oil sizzles immediately on contact and rises to the surface.

**8** Deep-fry the samosas, two or three at a time, for 3-5 minutes until golden. Drain on kitchen paper. Serve warm, garnished with mint and lime halves.

**NOTE** For a quick, fresh-tasting chutney to accompany these samosas, toss a few sliced spring onions with freshly torn mint and coriander leaves, crushed garlic, a splash of lemon juice, a dash of oil and plenty of seasoning.

# PAKORAS

**SERVES 4**
PREPARATION
30 minutes
COOKING TIME
12-15 minutes
FREEZING
Suitable
CALS/SERVING
225
COLOUR INDEX
Page 24

about 550 g (1¼ lb) mixed vegetables, such as courgettes, onion, potato, okra, aubergine, red or yellow pepper, spinach leaves

BATTER

1 garlic clove, peeled and crushed
5 ml (1 tsp) ground cumin
5 ml (1 tsp) ground coriander
10 ml (2 tsp) garam masala
5 ml (1 tsp) chilli powder
5 ml (1 tsp) turmeric
175 g (6 oz) gram flour or plain wholemeal flour
5 ml (1 tsp) salt
30 ml (2 tbsp) oil
200 ml (7 fl oz) water (approximately)
large handful of fresh mint leaves
large handful of fresh coriander leaves
15 ml (1 tbsp) black poppy seeds

TO FINISH

oil, for deep-frying
coriander sprigs, to garnish
Raita (see page 88) or chutney, to serve

**1** First make the batter. Mix the garlic, cumin, coriander, garam masala, chilli powder, turmeric, flour and salt together in a bowl. Add the oil, then gradually stir in approximately 200 ml (7 fl oz) cold water to make a thick batter. Beat vigorously to remove any lumps. Leave to stand for about 30 minutes.

**2** Prepare the vegetables as necessary. Cut the courgettes into thick slices or chunks. Peel and thickly slice the onion. Peel the potato, cut into thick slices and blanch in boiling salted water for 2 minutes; drain and pat dry with kitchen paper. Trim the okra. Trim the aubergine and cut into thick slices; cut each slice into 3 fingers. Halve, core and deseed the pepper, then cut the flesh into chunks. Wash and thoroughly dry the spinach leaves.

**3** Shred the mint and coriander leaves and beat into the batter, together with the poppy seeds.

**4** Heat the oil in a deep-fat fryer to 190°C (375°F), or until a teaspoonful of the batter dropped into the oil sizzles immediately on contact and rises to the surface.

**5** When the oil is ready, cook the pakoras in batches. Dip a few vegetable pieces into the batter. Remove one piece at a time, carefully drop into the hot oil and cook for about 4-5 minutes or until golden brown and crisp on all sides.

**6** Drain the pakoras on crumpled kitchen paper and keep warm while cooking the remaining vegetables in batches. Don't try to cook too many pieces together or they will stick together. Serve warm, garnished with coriander and accompanied by raita, and/or chutney if desired.

**NOTE** Gram flour is obtainable from Indian food stores and healthfood shops. It is made from ground chick peas.

# SPICED PUMPKIN FRITTERS

**SERVES 4**
PREPARATION
15 minutes
COOKING TIME
About 15 minutes
FREEZING
Not suitable
CALS/SERVING
355

700 g (1½ lb) peeled, deseeded pumpkin

BATTER

175 g (6 oz) wholemeal plain flour
2.5-5 ml (½-1 tsp) salt
1.25 ml (¼ tsp) baking powder
5 ml (1 tsp) cumin seeds
2.5 ml (½ tsp) ground cumin
1 egg, separated
175 ml (6 fl oz) water (approximately)
1 small onion, peeled
1-2 garlic cloves, peeled and crushed
7.5 ml (1½ tsp) chilli sauce
30 ml (2 tbsp) chopped fresh coriander

TO FINISH

oil, for deep-frying
coarse salt, to serve

**1** Cut the pumpkin flesh into thick slices, about 12 cm (5 inches) long and 1 cm (½ inch) wide. Steam for 8-10 minutes or until only just tender. Remove from the steamer and allow to cool.

**2** To make the batter, place the flour, salt, baking powder, cumin seeds and ground cumin in a bowl and mix well. Make a well in the centre, add the egg yolk and gradually stir in the water to form a smooth batter, adding a little extra if necessary. Finely chop the onion and stir into the batter with the garlic, chilli sauce and chopped coriander. Stiffly whisk the egg white and fold lightly into the batter.

**3** Heat the oil in a deep-fat fryer to 180°C (350°F) or until a cube of bread dropped into the oil browns in 30 seconds. Deep-fry the pumpkin in batches. Using two forks, dip a few slices of pumpkin into the batter to coat evenly, then lower into the hot oil and deep-fry for 1-1½ minutes, turning frequently, until crisp, golden brown and cooked through.

**4** Drain on crumpled kitchen paper and keep warm while cooking the remaining pumpkin. Serve the fritters piping hot, sprinkled with coarse salt.

# SPRING ROLLS WITH CUCUMBER RELISH

**SERVES 4**
PREPARATION
30 minutes
COOKING TIME
8-10 minutes
FREEZING
Suitable: Uncooked rolls only
CALS/SERVING
270
COLOUR INDEX

25 g (1 oz) rice vermicelli noodles
50 g (2 oz) carrot
50 g (2 oz) mangetout
15 ml (1 tbsp) sunflower oil
5 ml (1 tsp) grated fresh galangal or root ginger
grated zest and juice of 1 lime
25 g (1 oz) spinach leaves
30 ml (2 tbsp) light soy sauce
15 ml (1 tbsp) chopped fresh mint
15 ml (1 tbsp) chopped fresh coriander
pepper, to taste
6 sheets filo pastry
1 egg white, lightly beaten
oil, for deep-frying

CUCUMBER RELISH
1 small red chilli, seeded
50 g (2 oz) caster sugar
60 ml (2 fl oz) rice vinegar
2.5 ml (½ tsp) salt
30 ml (2 tbsp) water
1 small tomato
50 g (2 oz) cucumber

**1** Soak the noodles according to the packet instructions; drain, refresh under cold water and shake dry. Using scissors, snip the noodles into 2.5 cm (1 inch) lengths.
**2** Cut the carrot and mangetout into matchstick strips. Heat the oil in a wok or large frying pan. Add the galangal or ginger, lime zest, carrot and mangetout and stir-fry for 3 minutes. Add the lime juice, spinach, soy sauce, herbs and pepper together with the noodles, and stir-fry for 1 minute. Remove from the heat; set aside to cool.
**3** Meanwhile make the relish. Place the chilli, sugar, vinegar, salt and water in a small pan. Stir slowly until the sugar is dissolved and the mixture boils. Remove from the heat. Peel, deseed and dice the tomato; halve, deseed and slice the cucumber. Stir the tomato and cucumber into the relish and set aside.
**4** Cut the filo pastry into 18 cm (7 inch) squares, then halve each square diagonally to make 2 triangles. Take one triangle, brush with a little egg white and place a spoonful of the noodle mixture at the point opposite the longest side. Roll up the pastry from this point over the filling, folding the sides in as you go, to form a small spring roll. Press the seam together well and repeat to make 12 rolls.
**5** Heat a 10 cm (4 inch) depth of oil in a deep heavy-based saucepan to 180°C (350°F), or until a cube of bread dropped into the oil browns in 30 seconds. Deep-fry the rolls in batches for 2-3 minutes, until crisp and golden. Drain on kitchen paper and serve hot with the cucumber relish.

**NOTE** When using filo pastry always work with one sheet at a time. Keep the rest covered with a lightly dampened tea-towel to stop it from drying out.

# AUBERGINE TIMBALES WITH ROASTED RED PEPPER SALSA

**SERVES 6**
PREPARATION
40 minutes
COOKING TIME
1 hour 30 minutes, plus cooling
FREEZING
Not suitable
CALS/SERVING
205
COLOUR INDEX
Page 26

4 garlic cloves
60 ml (4 tbsp) olive oil, plus extra for brushing
two 400 g cans chopped plum tomatoes
150 ml (¼ pint) dry white wine
2 fresh thyme sprigs
15 ml (1 tbsp) sun-dried tomato paste
5 ml (1 tsp) caster sugar
salt and pepper
4 long, thin aubergines
90 ml (6 tbsp) Greek-style yogurt

RED PEPPER SALSA
1 large red pepper
45 ml (3 tbsp) olive oil
10 ml (2 tsp) balsamic vinegar

TO SERVE
thyme sprigs
rocket leaves

**1** Peel and finely chop the garlic. Heat the olive oil in a large saucepan, add the garlic and fry for 30 seconds. Add the chopped tomatoes, wine, thyme sprigs, sun-dried tomato paste, sugar, salt and pepper. Bring to the boil and simmer, uncovered, for about 45 minutes until thick, stirring occasionally. Discard the thyme sprigs and set the mixture aside to cool.
**2** To make the salsa, roast the red pepper in the oven at 220°C (425°F) Mark 7 for 30 minutes or until the skin is charred. Leave to cool, then remove the skin, core and seeds. Cut the pepper flesh into strips or dice and place in a bowl with the olive oil, balsamic vinegar, salt and pepper. Mix well, then cover and refrigerate until ready to serve.
**3** Meanwhile, trim off the ends of the aubergines, then slice off 6 thin rounds. Cut the remaining aubergines lengthways into 5 mm (¼ inch) thick slices. Brush both sides of the aubergine slices with olive oil and chargrill on a hot griddle or grill for 4-5 minutes, turning once, until brown.
**4** Lightly oil six 175 ml (6 fl oz) timbales, large ramekins or other ovenproof moulds. Place an aubergine round in the bottom of each mould and use the long strips of aubergine to line the sides, making sure there are no gaps. Leave the excess aubergine overhanging the top edge of the moulds.
**5** Spoon 15 ml (1 tbsp) yogurt into each mould, then add 45 ml (3 tbsp) of the tomato mixture. Trim the excess aubergine and cover the tops with foil.
**6** Place the moulds in a roasting tin half-filled with hot water. Cook at 180°C (350°F) Mark 4 for about 30-35 minutes. Allow to cool.
**7** Turn the aubergine timbales out on to serving plates. Garnish with thyme sprigs and serve with the red pepper salsa and a rocket salad.

# FALAFEL WITH YOGURT DIP

**ERVES 4-6**
REPARATION
0-25 minutes,
lus overnight
oaking and
nfusing
COOKING TIME
-10 minutes
REEZING
Not suitable
CALS/SERVING
50-240

225 g (8 oz) dried chick peas, soaked overnight in cold water
15 ml (1 tbsp) tahini paste
1 garlic clove, peeled and crushed
5 ml (1 tsp) sea salt
5 ml (1 tsp) turmeric
5 ml (1 tsp) ground cumin
1.25 ml (¼ tsp) cayenne pepper
30 ml (2 tbsp) chopped fresh coriander
15 ml (1 tbsp) chopped fresh mint
15 ml (1 tbsp) lemon juice
a little seasoned flour
YOGURT SAUCE
150 ml (¼ pint) Greek-style yogurt
1-2 garlic cloves, peeled and crushed
15 ml (1 tbsp) olive oil
30 ml (2 tbsp) chopped fresh mint
salt and pepper
TO FINISH
oil, for shallow-frying

1 Drain the soaked chick peas. Place in a food processor and process until airly smooth paste; the mixture will be quite stiff.

**2** Transfer to a bowl and add the tahini paste, garlic, salt, spices, herbs and lemon juice. Cover and leave to stand for at least 30 minutes to allow the flavours to develop.

**3** Meanwhile, mix all the ingredients for the yogurt dip together in a bowl and season with salt and pepper to taste. Cover and set aside until required.

**4** With floured hands, shape the chick pea mixture into 2.5 cm (1 inch) balls. Flatten slightly and dust with the seasoned flour.

**5** Heat a 1 cm (½ inch) depth of oil in a frying pan. When hot, fry the patties in batches for 1-2 minutes on each side until evenly browned.

**6** Drain on crumpled kitchen paper and keep warm while cooking the rest. Serve warm, with the yogurt dip and some warm pitta bread. Alternatively allow the falafel to cool before serving.

**NOTE** Falafel are always made with dried chick peas which need to be soaked – but not pre-cooked. The flavour improves as the mixture stands, so make it well in advance if possible for optimum results.

## DIPS WITH CRUDITÉS

Serve an assortment of colourful crudités and warm pitta bread with these dips. Baby vegetables, such as carrots, tiny courgettes, cherry tomatoes and button mushrooms can be served whole. Celery, fennel, cucumber, courgettes, peppers and carrots need to be cut into strips or trimmed to a manageable size. Radishes, spring onions and cauliflower florets can also be used.

Sliced fresh fruit, such as apples, pears, nectarines, grapes, mangoes, papaya, star fruit and fresh dates, make good crudités too.

## HERBED CHEESE DIP

**SERVES 6-8**
PREPARATION
5 minutes
FREEZING
Not suitable
CALS/SERVING
230-170

300 g (10 oz) carton full-fat soft cheese with garlic and parsley
60 ml (4 tbsp) mayonnaise
30 ml (2 tbsp) chopped fresh parsley
30 ml (2 tbsp) chopped fresh chives
salt and pepper
chives, to garnish
crudités, to serve

**1** In a small bowl, beat the soft cheese with the mayonnaise, parsley and chives until evenly mixed. Season with salt and pepper to taste. Cover and chill in the refrigerator until ready to serve.
**2** Transfer to a serving dish and garnish with chives. Serve with a colourful selection of crudités.

## TZAZIKI

**SERVES 8**
PREPARATION
10 minutes
FREEZING
Not suitable
CALS/SERVING
45

1 cucumber
300 ml (½ pint) Greek-style yogurt
10 ml (2 tsp) olive oil
30 ml (2 tbsp) chopped fresh mint
1 large garlic clove, peeled and crushed
salt and pepper
TO SERVE
warm pitta bread
crudités

**1** Halve, deseed and dice the cucumber; place in a bowl.
**2** Add the yogurt and olive oil. Stir in the chopped mint and garlic, seasoning with salt and pepper to taste. Cover and chill in the refrigerator until ready to serve. Accompany with warm pitta bread and crudités.

**RAITA** This cooling Indian accompaniment is similar to tzaziki. Make as above, using ¼ cucumber, increasing the mint to 45 ml (3 tbsp) and omitting the oil.

## HUMMUS

**SERVES 8**
PREPARATION
10 minutes
FREEZING
Not suitable
CALS/SERVING
290

two 400 g (14 oz) cans chick peas, drained
juice of 2 large lemons
150 ml (½ pint) light tahini paste
60 ml (4 tbsp) olive oil
2 garlic cloves, peeled and crushed
salt and pepper
TO SERVE
black olives and chopped parsley, to garnish
warm pitta bread

**1** Put the chick peas in a blender or food processor with the lemon juice and work to a smooth purée.
**2** Add the tahini paste, all but 10 ml (2 tsp) of the oil, the garlic and seasoning. Blend until smooth.
**3** Spoon into a serving dish and sprinkle with the reserved oil. Garnish with olives and chopped parsley. Serve with warm pitta bread.

## GUACAMOLE

**SERVES 6-8**
PREPARATION
10 minutes
FREEZING
Not suitable
CALS/SERVING
140-85
COLOUR INDEX
Page 25

1 small onion, peeled
2-3 garlic cloves, peeled
2.5 cm (1 inch) piece fresh root ginger, peeled
4 large ripe avocados
finely grated zest and juice of 2 small limes
60 ml (4 tbsp) chopped fresh coriander
10 ml (2 tsp) ground coriander
10 ml (2 tsp) ground cumin
5 ml (1 tsp) chilli powder
2 ripe tomatoes
salt and pepper
crudités, to serve

**1** Put the onion, garlic and ginger in a food processor and process until finely chopped.
**2** Halve, stone and peel the avocados, then chop roughly.

3 Add the chopped avocados to the onion mixture in the processor, with the lime zest and juice, chopped coriander and spices. Process until almost smooth. Transfer to a bowl.
4 Halve, deseed and roughly chop the tomatoes. Stir into the guacamole and season with salt and pepper to taste. Cover and chill in the refrigerator for 30 minutes. Serve with crudités.

## AUBERGINE, MUSHROOM AND CORIANDER PATÉ

**SERVES 4-6**
PREPARATION
20 minutes
COOKING TIME
1 hour
FREEZING
Suitable
CALS/SERVING
140-95
COLOUR INDEX
Page 25

2 medium aubergines
2 shallots
225 g (8 oz) large flat mushrooms
45 ml (3 tbsp) olive oil
10-15 ml (2-3 tsp) crushed coriander seeds
45 ml (3 tbsp) dry white wine
60 ml (4 tbsp) chopped fresh coriander
salt and pepper
TO SERVE
coriander sprigs, to garnish
warm toasted bread

**1** Place the aubergines on a baking sheet and bake in the oven at 200°C (400°F) Mark 6 for about 45 minutes or until soft and beginning to char.
**2** Meanwhile, peel and finely chop the shallots. Wipe the mushrooms clean with a damp cloth, then chop finely.
**3** Heat the oil in a saucepan, add the shallots with the coriander seeds and cook gently for 5 minutes until soft and golden. Stir in the mushrooms and wine and cook over a high heat for 10 minutes or until all the liquid has evaporated, stirring occasionally.
**4** When the aubergines are cooked, split them open and scoop out the flesh. Chop the aubergine flesh roughly, then beat into the mushroom mixture. Stir in the chopped coriander and season well with salt and pepper. Either serve warm or allow to cool, then chill.
**5** Serve the pâté garnished with coriander sprigs and accompanied by hot toast.

**NOTE** Toasted walnut bread is particularly good served with this tasty pâté.

**VARIATION** For a milder flavour, stir 125 g (4 oz) fromage frais into the cold pâté.

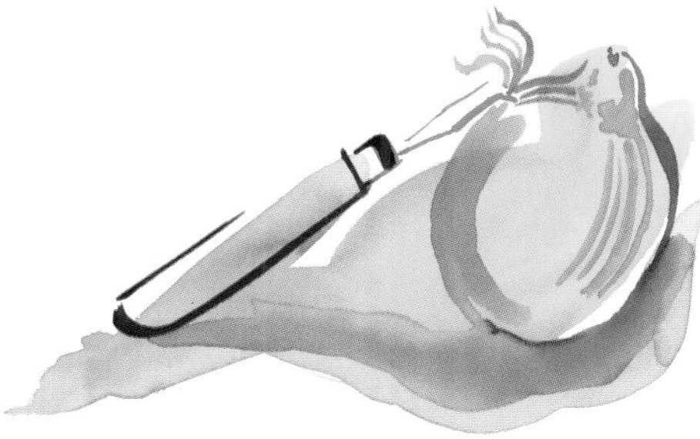

## BUTTER BEAN, LEMON AND SAGE PATÉ

**SERVES 6**
PREPARATION
10 minutes
COOKING TIME
10 minutes
FREEZING
Not suitable
CALS/SERVING
215

4 shallots, peeled
70 ml (4½ tbsp) extra-virgin olive oil (approximately)
2 large garlic cloves, peeled and crushed
30 ml (2 tbsp) chopped fresh sage
grated zest and juice of 1 small lemon
two 400 g (14 oz) cans butter beans or cannellini beans
salt and pepper
TO SERVE
toasted ciabatta or pitta bread
crudités

**1** Finely chop the shallots. Heat 60 ml (4 tbsp) of the oil in a frying pan, add the shallots, garlic, sage and lemon zest and fry gently for 5 minutes until softened.
**2** Meanwhile, drain the beans, reserving 120 ml (4 fl oz) of the liquid. Add the beans and reserved liquid to the frying pan. Bring to the boil, cover and simmer gently for 5 minutes.
**3** Transfer the mixture to a bowl and mash well, to a fairly smooth paste. Stir in the lemon juice and seasoning to taste, then gradually beat in a little extra oil.
**4** Leave until cold. Serve with crudités and toasted ciabatta or pitta bread.

**NOTE** If preferred, you can serve this pâté straight from the pan whilst still warm. Alternatively it can be served chilled as a dip with a selection of crudités.

# GRILLED VEGETABLE TERRINE

**SERVES 6**
PREPARATION
35 minutes, plus cooling
COOKING TIME
About 15 minutes
FREEZING
Not suitable
CALS/SERVING
250

3 large red peppers
2 large yellow peppers
2 large courgettes
1 long aubergine
75 ml (5 tbsp) olive oil
450 ml (¾ pint) tomato juice
15 g (½ oz) gelozone
60 ml (4 tbsp) chopped mixed fresh herbs, such as chervil, parsley and basil

DRESSING
90 ml (3 fl oz) virgin olive oil
30 ml (2 tbsp) red wine vinegar
salt and pepper

TO GARNISH
basil leaves
chervil sprigs
few chives

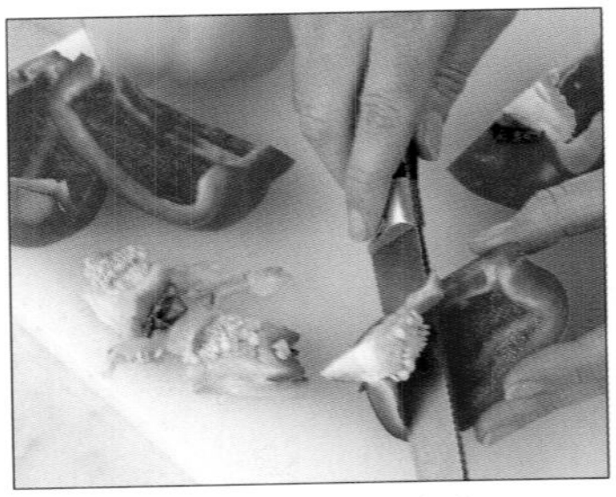

**1** Quarter, core and de-seed the peppers, then place skin-side up under a hot grill until the skins are blackened. Transfer to a bowl, cover and leave to cool. When the peppers are cool enough to handle, remove the skins.

**2** Slice the courgettes and aubergine lengthwise, brush with oil and cook under the grill, turning occasionally, until tender and golden. (You may need to do this in two batches, depending on the size of your grill pan.)

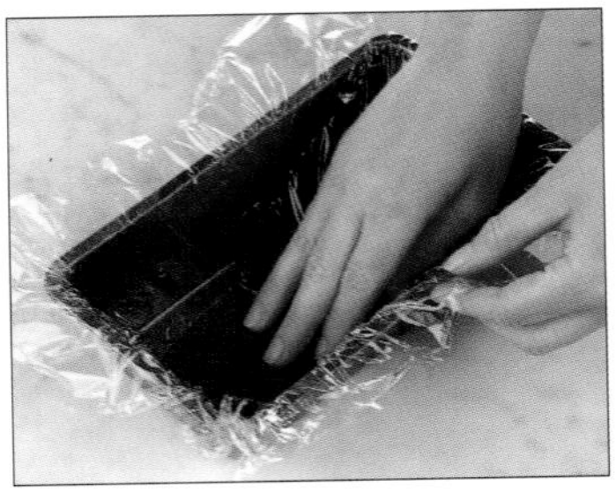

**3** Lightly oil a 1.5 litre (2½ pint) loaf tin or terrine and line with cling film, allowing it to overhang the sides.

**4** Put 60 ml (4 tbsp) of the tomato juice in a small bowl and sprinkle with the gelozone. Leave to soften for about 10 minutes, then place the bowl over a pan of simmering water until the gelozone is dissolved. Add to the remaining tomato juice, stirring well.

**5** Place a layer of red peppers in the bottom of the terrine and pour in enough tomato juice to cover. Add a layer of aubergine slices, followed by courgette, yellow pepper and a sprinkling of herbs, pouring tomato juice onto each layer. Repeat the layers, finishing with red pepper.

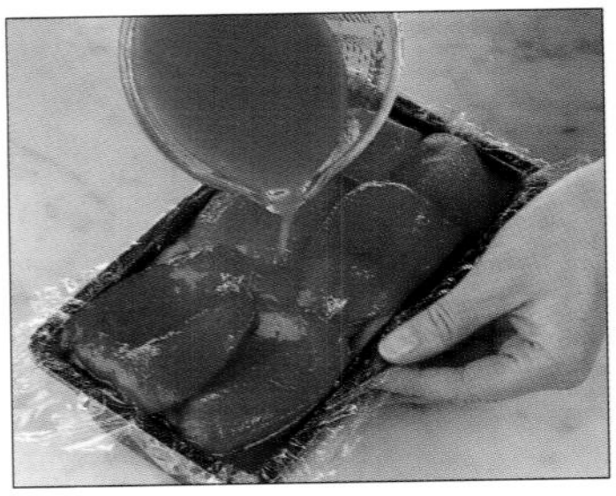

**6** Add the rest of the tomato juice to fill the loaf tin or terrine. Give the tin a sharp tap to encourage the juice to disperse through the vegetables. Cover and refrigerate until set.

**7** To make the dressing, whisk together the oil, vinegar and seasoning.

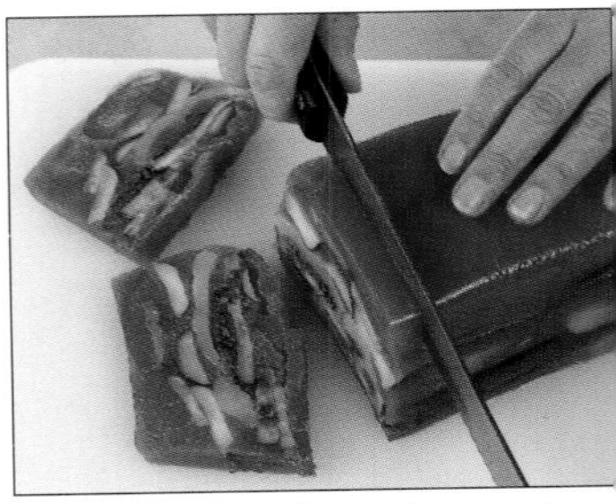

**8** To serve, slice the terrine using a serrated knife. Place on individual serving plates and drizzle with the dressing. Garnish with herbs and serve with flavoured bread.

# ROQUEFORT AND WALNUT SOUFFLÉS

**SERVES 6**
PREPARATION
30 minutes, plus cooling
COOKING TIME
20 minutes
FREEZING
Not suitable
CALS/SERVING
175
COLOUR INDEX
Page 26

15 g (½ oz) walnuts
15 ml (1 tbsp) fresh white breadcrumbs
15 ml (1 tbsp) freshly grated Parmesan cheese
25 g (1 oz) plain white flour
150 ml (¼ pint) semi-skimmed milk
2 whole eggs, separated, plus 2 egg whites
125 g (4 oz) Roquefort cheese, crumbled
salt and pepper
TO SERVE
salad leaves
toasted walnuts, to garnish

**1** Grease and base-line six 150 ml (¼ pint) ramekin dishes. Toast and finely chop the walnuts. Mix the nuts with the breadcrumbs and Parmesan cheese. Coat the sides of the ramekins with about two thirds of this mixture; reserve the rest for the topping.
**2** Put the flour into a saucepan, whisk in the milk to form a smooth paste and slowly bring to the boil, stirring continuously. Reduce the heat and cook gently for 1 minute until thick. Remove from the heat and allow to cool slightly.
**3** Beat the egg yolks and Roquefort cheese into the sauce. Season generously with pepper and a little salt. In a separate bowl, whisk the 4 egg whites until they form soft peaks. Using a large metal spoon, carefully fold the egg whites into the cheese sauce.
**4** Divide the soufflé mixture between the ramekins, then top with the reserved breadcrumbs. Stand the ramekins in a roasting tin and half-fill the tin with boiling water. Bake in the oven at 190°C (375°F) Mark 5 for 15-20 minutes or until just firm to the touch.
**5** Leave the soufflés in the ramekins for 10 minutes, then turn out, remove the paper and invert on to an oiled baking tray. Place under a hot grill for about 1 minute to brown the tops. Serve on individual plates surrounded by salad leaves drizzled with a little olive oil. Garnish with toasted walnuts.

**NOTE** These soufflés can be prepared ahead. Turn out, cool, cover and leave in a cool place for up to 4 hours. Reheat in the oven at 180°C (350°F) Mark 4 for 15-20 minutes, then brown under a preheated grill.

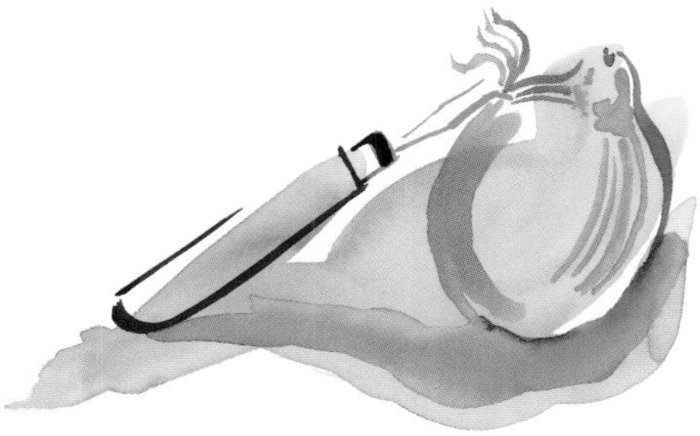

# ROASTED MUSHROOMS WITH LEMON AND GARLIC OIL

**SERVES 4**
PREPARATION
5 minutes, plus 3 days infusing
COOKING TIME
20-25 minutes
FREEZING
Not suitable
CALS/SERVING
350

2 garlic cloves, peeled
2.5 ml (½ tsp) sea salt
finely pared zest of 1 lemon
150 ml (¼ pint) olive oil
8 large flat field mushrooms, about 12 cm (5 inches) in diameter
30 ml (2 tbsp) chopped fresh parsley
salt and pepper
lemon wedges, to serve

**1** Crush the garlic and salt together with a pestle and mortar or on a chopping board and place in a jar. Add the lemon rind and oil. Shake well, ensuring that the garlic and lemon are covered by the oil. Seal and refrigerate for 3 days.
**2** Place the mushrooms, stalk-side up, in a shallow roasting tin in which they fit closely together. Drizzle liberally with two thirds of the infused oil. Bake in the oven at 220°C (425°F) Mark 7 for 15 minutes. Turn the mushrooms over and baste with more oil. Bake for a further 5-10 minutes until the mushrooms are tender and browned, basting occasionally.
**3** Transfer to a warmed serving platter and scatter over the chopped parsley. Season with salt and pepper. Serve at once, with lemon wedges and any remaining infused oil.

**NOTE** To barbecue the mushrooms, place, stalk-side up, on a double piece of foil, pour over the infused oil and seal the foil. Cook over the coals for 20 minutes and serve straight from the parcels.

# GRILLED CHICORY, STILTON AND CARAMELISED WALNUT SALAD

**SERVES 6**
PREPARATION
25 minutes
COOKING TIME
20 minutes, plus infusing
FREEZING
Not suitable
CALS/SERVING
360

2 white onions, peeled
1 head of chicory
1 head of radicchio
2 red chillies
5 ml (1 tsp) caster sugar
salt and pepper
125 g (4 oz) blue Stilton cheese, crumbled
DRESSING
100 ml (3½ fl oz) olive oil
2 fresh thyme sprigs
grated zest of 1 lemon
2 garlic cloves, peeled and bruised
30 ml (2 tbsp) lemon juice
CARAMELISED NUTS
75 g (3 oz) walnuts
5 ml (1 tsp) paprika
5 ml (1 tsp) icing sugar
45 ml (3 tbsp) oil
TO GARNISH
flat-leafed parsley

**1** First make the dressing. Put the olive oil in a small pan with the thyme sprigs, lemon zest and garlic cloves. Warm gently; do not boil. Set aside to infuse for 30 minutes.
**2** For the caramelised nuts, cook the walnuts in boiling water for 5 minutes; drain and dry on kitchen paper. Mix together the paprika and icing sugar. Toss the walnuts in this mixture to coat. Heat the oil in a frying pan, add the nuts and cook for 1-2 minutes until brown. Drain and cool.
**3** For the salad, quarter the onions, chicory and radicchio; separate the onions into 'petals'. Halve and deseed chillies. Brush all of the vegetables with half of the infused oil.
**4** Place onions in grill pan, sprinkle with sugar and cook under a hot grill for 5-10 minutes, turning once, until soft and slightly charred. Add the chicory and chillies and cook for 5 minutes, then add the radicchio, cook for 1 minute.
**5** Allow the vegetables to cool slightly. Cut the chicory and radicchio into pieces if preferred; finely slice the chillies.
**6** Whisk the lemon juice into the remaining infused oil and season with salt and pepper. Combine all of the vegetables and gently toss together with the dressing, cheese and caramelised walnuts. Arrange on individual plates and serve garnished with parsley.

# MUSHROOM AND PARMESAN WAFERS WITH CHAMPAGNE SAUCE

**SERVES 8**
PREPARATION
35 minutes, plus chilling
COOKING TIME
1 hour
FREEZING
Not suitable
CALS/SERVING
480
COLOUR INDEX
Page 27

75 g (3 oz) butter
450 g (1 lb) mixed wild mushrooms, such as ceps morels, chanterelles
225 g (8 oz) shallots, peeled
350 g (12 oz) ready-made puff pastry
75 g (3 oz) Parmesan cheese, freshly grated
salt and pepper
300 ml (½ pint) Champagne or sparkling dry white wine
300 ml (½ pint) vegetable stock
300 ml (½ pint) double cream
thyme sprigs, to garnish

**1** Melt 25 g (1 oz) of the butter. Rinse and quarter the mushrooms (see note). Finely chop the shallots.
**2** Roll the pastry out on a lightly floured surface to a 23 x 33 cm (9 x 13 inch) rectangle and cut across into three even-sized pieces. Brush with the melted butter, sprinkle with half the grated Parmesan and season with pepper. Stack the pieces of pastry on top of one another, then re-roll the pastry stack out to the same dimensions. Cover with cling film and chill in the refrigerator for 15 minutes.
**3** Cut out eight 10 cm (4 inch) rounds from the pastry and place on a greased baking sheet. Sprinkle with the remaining grated Parmesan, season with pepper and refrigerate for 30 minutes.
**4** Bake the pastry rounds in the oven at 200°C (400°F) Mark 6 for 15 minutes. Set aside to cool, then carefully split each round in two horizontally.
**5** Heat the remaining butter in a large frying pan, add the shallots and cook, stirring, for 10 minutes or until soft. Add the mushrooms and cook for 5 minutes, stirring, then add the Champagne and stock. Bring to the boil and simmer for 5 minutes. Drain the mushrooms, reserving the liquor; set aside.
**6** Return the liquor to the pan and stir in the cream. Bring to the boil and let bubble for 20 minutes or until syrupy. Season to taste and stir in the reserved mushrooms.
**7** To serve, place a pastry base on each plate, then spoon the mushrooms and sauce on top. Cover with a pastry lid and garnish with thyme.

**NOTE** Most supermarkets now sell selections of wild mushroom. Make sure you rinse them thoroughly under cold running water; fine soil is often trapped in the gills.

# RICOTTA QUENELLES WITH FRESH TOMATO SAUCE

**SERVES 4**
PREPARATION
35 minutes, plus chilling
COOKING TIME
45 minutes
FREEZING
Suitable: Tomato sauce only
CALS/SERVING
505
COLOUR INDEX
Page 27

TOMATO SAUCE
900 g (2 lb) ripe tomatoes
120 ml (4 fl oz) olive oil
finely grated zest of 1 lemon
5 ml (1 tsp) salt
pinch of sugar
30 ml (2 tbsp) chopped fresh basil
15 ml (1 tbsp) balsamic vinegar
RICOTTA QUENELLES
350 g (12 oz) ricotta cheese
45 ml (3 tbsp) freshly grated Parmesan cheese
30 ml (2 tbsp) chopped fresh chives
15 ml (1 tbsp) chopped fresh chervil or parsley
5 ml (1 tsp) celery salt
1.25 ml (¼ tsp) freshly grated nutmeg
salt and pepper
TO GARNISH
chives
chervil or parsley sprigs

**1** For the tomato sauce, immerse the tomatoes in a bowl of boiling water for 10 seconds, then remove with a slotted spoon and peel away the skins. Halve, deseed, then dice the tomato flesh.

**2** Place the tomatoes, oil, lemon zest, salt, sugar and a little pepper in a small pan. Bring to the boil, cover and simmer over a low heat for 30 minutes. Remove the lid and simmer, uncovered, for a further 15 minutes to reduce and thicken. Leave to cool, then stir in the basil and vinegar. Cover and chill in the refrigerator.

**3** To make the quenelles, place the ricotta in a bowl and beat for several minutes until light and fluffy. Fold in the grated Parmesan, herbs, celery salt, nutmeg and seasoning to taste. Chill in the refrigerator for at least 1 hour.

**4** Using 2 dessertspoons, form the chilled ricotta mixture into 12 quenelles, by passing each heaped spoonful of the mixture between the spoons to form an oval.

**5** Spoon the tomato sauce onto serving plates and arrange the ricotta quenelles on top. Garnish with chives and chervil or parsley. Serve accompanied by toasted ciabatta or French bread.

**NOTE** When fresh tomatoes are not at their best use canned ones instead: you will need two 400 g (14 oz) cans chopped tomatoes. Prepare the tomato sauce as above, omitting the final uncovered simmering stage.

# SUMMER MELON SALAD WITH ROQUEFORT DRESSING

**SERVES 4**
PREPARATION
15 minutes
COOKING TIME
2 minutes
FREEZING
Not suitable
CALS/SERVING
435

225 g (8 oz) sugar snap peas
salt and pepper
½ charentais melon, about 700 g (1½ lb)
1 pear
juice of ½ lemon
125 g (4 oz) Roquefort cheese
DRESSING
30 ml (2 tbsp) white wine vinegar
60 ml (4 tbsp) walnut oil
60 ml (4 tbsp) olive oil
TO GARNISH
25 g (1 oz) walnuts, roughly chopped and toasted

**1** Halve the sugar snap peas on the diagonal and cook in boiling salted water for 2 minutes. Drain, refresh in cold water and drain thoroughly.

**2** Deseed, peel and slice the melon. Peel, quarter, core and slice the pear. Toss the pear and melon together with the lemon juice in a bowl. Crumble in the Roquefort cheese, then season with pepper and a little salt.

**3** For the dressing, shake the vinegar, walnut oil, olive oil and seasoning together in a screw-top jar until amalgamated.

**4** Arrange the pear, melon and Roquefort on a plate and top with the sugar snap peas. Drizzle the dressing over the salad and sprinkle with the toasted walnuts to serve.

# SQUASH GNOCCHI WITH SAGE

**SERVES 4**
PREPARATION
40 minutes
COOKING TIME
20 minutes
FREEZING
Not suitable
CALS/SERVING
455

GNOCCHI
- 350 g (12 oz) peeled butternut squash
- 225 g (8 oz) peeled potatoes
- 1 egg yolk
- 125 g (4 oz) plain white flour
- salt and pepper

SAGE BUTTER
- 125 g (4 oz) unsalted butter
- 30 ml (2 tbsp) fresh sage leaves

TO SERVE
- 25 g (1 oz) Parmesan cheese, freshly grated
- lemon wedges

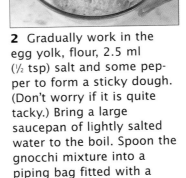

**1** To make the gnocchi, cut the squash and potatoes into 2.5 cm (1 inch) cubes and steam over gently simmering water for 10-15 minutes until tender. Pass through a vegetable mouli or mash with a potato masher into a clean pan. Place over a low heat for a few seconds to dry out. Transfer to a bowl and allow to cool slightly.

**2** Gradually work in the egg yolk, flour, 2.5 ml (½ tsp) salt and some pepper to form a sticky dough. (Don't worry if it is quite tacky.) Bring a large saucepan of lightly salted water to the boil. Spoon the gnocchi mixture into a piping bag fitted with a large plain nozzle.

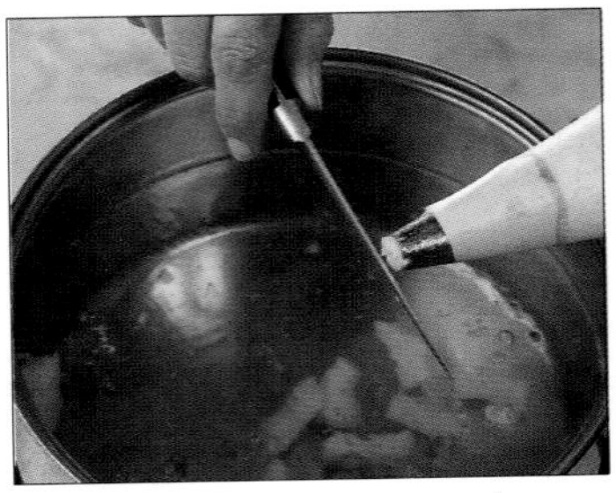

**3** When the water reaches a rolling boil cook the gnocchi in batches. Quickly pipe about 12 short lengths of gnocchi, directly into the water, using a sharp knife to cut them at the nozzle.

**4** Once the water returns to the boil, simmer fast for about 1½ minutes until the gnocchi have risen to the surface and are softening slightly around the edges. Remove with a slotted spoon and drain on kitchen paper. Repeat with the remaining mixture.

**5** To prepare the sage butter, melt the butter in a large frying pan, add the sage leaves and fry gently for 1-2 minutes until the butter starts to turn golden.

**6** Immediately add the gnocchi and stir over a low heat for 30 seconds or so, until heated through. Spoon into warmed individual bowls and sprinkle generously with Parmesan and pepper. Serve at once, with lemon wedges.

**NOTE** These little dumplings can be cooked ahead of time and reheated later. Cook in boiling water as above; drain and refresh under cold water; dry and toss with a little oil to prevent them sticking. To serve, add the gnocchi to the sage butter, cover and heat through for 3-4 minutes.

## POTATO AND CELERIAC CRÊPE WITH BEETROOT DRESSING

ERVES 4
EPARATION
minutes
OOKING TIME
out 15 minutes
EEZING
ot suitable
ALS/SERVING
5

CREPES
125 g (4 oz) peeled potatoes
125 g (4 oz) peeled celeriac
30 ml (2 tbsp) plain white flour
2 eggs, beaten
2 egg whites
25 ml (1 fl oz) double cream
25 ml (1 fl oz) milk
a little oil, for frying

BEETROOT DRESSING
225 g (8 oz) cooked beetroot
125 g (4 oz) crème fraîche
15 ml (1 tbsp) creamed horseradish
salt and pepper
30 ml (2 tbsp) chopped fresh chives
TO GARNISH
chives

First make the beetroot dressing. Peel the beetroot if ecessary and cut into small dice. Place in a bowl and stir the crème fraîche, horseradish and salt and pepper to aste. Cover and set aside until required.

For the crêpes, cut the potatoes and celeriac into cubes, ace in a steamer and cook over boiling water for 12-15 inutes until both are tender. Pass through a vegetable ouli or mash with a potato masher until smooth. Place in clean pan over a low heat for a few seconds to dry out. llow to cool slightly.

Add the flour, whole eggs, egg whites, cream and milk, nd beat thoroughly until smooth. Season the crêpe mixure with plenty of salt and pepper.

**4** Lightly oil a blini pan (see note). When smoking, pour in a quarter of the batter and immediately reduce the heat to its lowest setting. Cook for 3-4 minutes until bubbles appear over the surface and the batter is almost set.
**5** Carefully flip the crêpe over and cook the second side for about 10 seconds until firm to the touch. Keep warm in a low oven while making 3 more crêpes.
**6** Transfer the crêpes to warmed serving plates. Add the chives to the beetroot dressing and spoon on top of the crêpes. Serve immediately, garnished with chives.

**NOTE** A blini pan is a small individual serving pancake pan, available from good cook shops. If unavailable, use an oiled 10 cm (4 inch) metal ring set in a frying pan. Alternatively you can use a crêpe pan to make thinner crêpes.

## PIADINA WITH GRILLED PEPPER, MINT AND FETA

**SERVES 6**
PREPARATION
20 minutes, plus resting
COOKING TIME
20-25 minutes
FREEZING
Not suitable
CALS/SERVING
305
COLOUR INDEX
Page 27

PIADINA
225 g (8 oz) plain flour
2.5 ml (½ tsp) salt
15 g (½ oz) butter, softened
150 ml (¼ pint) tepid water
TOPPING
4 red peppers
60 ml (4 tbsp) extra-virgin olive oil
15 ml (1 tbsp) balsamic vinegar
1 small garlic clove, peeled and crushed
salt and pepper
150 g (5 oz) feta cheese
15 ml (1 tbsp) chopped fresh mint
TO GARNISH
mint sprigs

**1** First start preparing the topping. Cook the peppers under the grill, turning frequently, for 15-20 minutes, until evenly charred and softened. Transfer to a bowl, cover tightly and set aside until cool enough to handle.
**2** Meanwhile, prepare the bread. Sift the flour and salt into a bowl and make a well in the centre. Add the butter and water and work together to form a soft dough. Knead for 10 minutes until smooth, then wrap in cling film and leave to rest for 30 minutes.
**3** Peel away the skin from the peppers, holding them over a bowl to catch the juices. Slice each pepper into strips, discarding the core and seeds. Place in a bowl with their juices and add the oil, vinegar, garlic and salt and pepper. Set aside until required.
**4** Divide the dough into 6 equal pieces and roll each one out to an 18 cm (7 inch) circle, about 3 mm (⅛ inch) thick. Preheat a griddle or heavy-based frying pan until really hot, add a dough round and cook for 1 minute until the base is cooked and flecked with brown. Flip over and cook the other side for 30 seconds. Remove and keep warm wrapped in a tea-towel while making five more piadina.
**5** Lay the piadina on individual serving plates and top with the pepper mixture. Crumble over the feta and scatter with the chopped mint. Serve immediately, garnished with mint.

# AUBERGINE CROUSTADES WITH MINTED YOGURT AND FETA

**SERVES 4**
PREPARATION
35 minutes
COOKING TIME
20 minutes
FREEZING
Not suitable
CALS/SERVING
400

CIABATTA CASES
1 olive ciabatta loaf
30 ml (2 tbsp) olive oil
SAUCE
1 spring onion
125 g (4 oz) feta cheese
150 ml (¼ pint) Greek yogurt
large pinch of caster sugar
30 ml (2 tbsp) chopped fresh mint
salt and pepper
FILLING
1 small aubergine
1 red onion, peeled
1 beefsteak tomato
½ red chilli
60 ml (4 tbsp) olive oil
5 cloves garlic, peeled and crushed
30 ml (2 tbsp) tomato paste
TO GARNISH
mint sprigs

**1** Using a sharp knife, cut 12 wafer-thin 7.5 cm (3 inch) square slices from the bread. (Because of the open texture of the bread you may need several extra attempts to get enough good thin squares.)

**2** Make a cut from one edge of each square to the centre. Lightly brush both sides of the bread with the olive oil. Press into muffin or Yorkshire pudding tins, overlapping the cut edges to form 8 baskets.

**3** To make the sauce, finely chop the spring onion. Crumble the feta into a bowl. Add the onion, yogurt, sugar, mint and seasoning; stir lightly. Chill in the refrigerator until required.

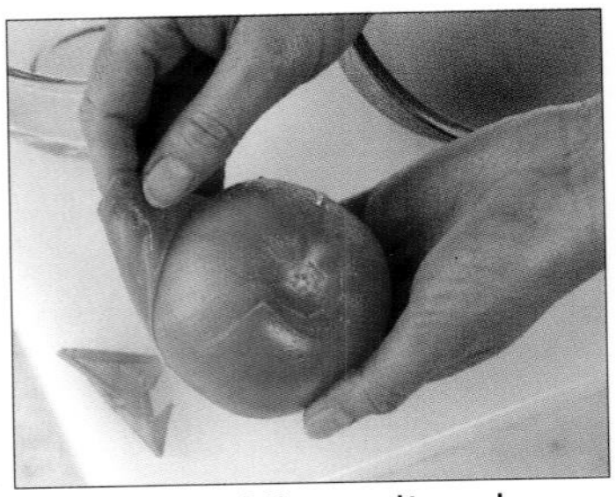

**4** For the filling, dice the aubergine; roughly chop the onion. Immerse the tomato in a small bowl of boiling water for 1 minute, then drain and peel away the skin. Roughly chop the tomato flesh. Deseed and chop the chilli.

**5** Heat the oil in a saucepan. Add the aubergine, onion and garlic and fry for 5 minutes until golden. Stir in the chilli and tomato. Let cool slightly, then transfer to a food processor and process briefly until pulpy but not puréed. Stir in the tomato paste and season.

**6** Spoon the aubergine mixture into the ciabatta cases. Bake in the oven at 190°C (375°F) Mark 5 for about 15 minutes until the cases are golden. Transfer to serving plates and spoon a little of the yogurt sauce beside each one. Serve garnished with mint.

**VARIATION** Use 350 g (12 oz) open mushrooms instead of the aubergine, and chopped coriander for the sauce in place of the mint.

## FENNEL, ONION AND GRUYERE TARTLETS

**SERVES 4**
PREPARATION
5 minutes,
plus chilling
COOKING TIME
0 minutes
FREEZING
Suitable
CALS/SERVING
70

CHEESE PASTRY
175 g (6 oz) plain white flour
75 g (3 oz) lightly salted butter, in pieces
50 g (2 oz) gruyère cheese, grated
1 egg yolk
30 ml (2 tbsp) cold water
FILLING
225 g (8 oz) onion, peeled
225 g (8 oz) fennel bulb
45 ml (3 tbsp) olive oil
5 ml (1 tsp) fennel seeds
1 egg
150 ml (¼ pint) double cream
salt and pepper
25 g (1 oz) gruyère cheese, grated

To make the pastry, sift the flour into a bowl. Rub in the butter, using your fingertips, then stir in the cheese. Add the egg yolk and cold water and mix to a firm dough. Knead lightly until smooth, then wrap in cling film and chill in the refrigerator for 30 minutes.
Roll out the pastry thinly on a lightly floured surface and use to line four individual flan tins, 10 cm (4 inches) in diameter and 2 cm (¾ inch) deep.
Line with greaseproof paper and baking beans and bake blind at 200°C (400°F) Mark 6 for 10 minutes until beginning to colour around the edges. Remove the paper and beans and bake for a further 5 minutes.
**4** For the filling, slice the onion and fennel as thinly as possible. Heat the oil in a large frying pan and add the onion and fennel, with the fennel seeds. Fry very gently for 10 minutes or until softened. Allow to cool slightly.
**5** In a bowl, beat together the egg, cream and a little seasoning. Divide the fennel mixture between the pastry cases and pack down lightly. Pour on the egg mixture and sprinkle with the cheese. Bake for about 20-25 minutes until the custard is just set. Serve warm.

**VARIATION** For classic onion tarts, omit the fennel and fennel seeds and double the quantity of onion.

## CHERRY TOMATO AND MOZZARELLA SALAD ON BRUSCHETTA

**SERVES 4**
PREPARATION
15 minutes
FREEZING
Not suitable
CALS/SERVING
590
COLOUR INDEX
Page 28

12 boconcini (baby mozzarelle) or 375 g (12 oz) mozzarella
20 cherry tomatoes
45 ml (3 tbsp) olive oil
5 ml (1 tsp) balsamic vinegar
salt and pepper
4 thick slices of Italian country bread
1 garlic clove, peeled and halved
125 g (4 oz) rocket or watercress
extra olive oil, to serve
basil leaves, to garnish

**1** Halve baby mozzarelle if using, or cut whole mozzarella into large cubes; place in a bowl. Halve the cherry tomatoes and add to the cheese.
**2** Whisk together the olive oil and balsamic vinegar. Season with salt and pepper, then pour over the cheese and tomatoes. Stir well.
**3** Toast the slices of bread under the grill until golden on both sides, then rub with the cut garlic clove.
**4** Place a slice of toast on each serving plate and surround with the rocket or watercress. Pile the mozzarella and tomato salad onto the toast and drizzle the olive oil over the rocket. Garnish with basil leaves and serve at once.

**NOTE** Baby mozzarelle are sold in tubs, immersed in water. They look very pretty in this salad, but ordinary mozzarella will do. Use the round-shaped cheese in preference to mozzarella 'bricks' which are best reserved for pizzas.

**VARIATION** Replace the mozzarella with chopped avocado.

# MOROCCAN AUBERGINE SALAD WITH FLAT BREAD

**SERVES 4**
PREPARATION
30 minutes, plus standing
COOKING TIME
55 minutes
FREEZING
Not suitable
CALS/SERVING
265

- 2 large aubergines, each about 350 g (12 oz)
- salt and pepper
- 60 ml (4 tbsp) olive oil
- 2 garlic cloves, peeled
- 1 onion, peeled
- 4 ripe plum tomatoes
- 1.25 ml (¼ tsp) turmeric
- 2.5 ml (½ tsp) ground coriander
- pinch of ground cinnamon
- pinch of cayenne pepper
- grated zest and juice of ½ lemon, or to taste
- 15-30 ml (1-2 tbsp) chopped fresh coriander

BREAD
- 25 g (1 oz) strong plain white flour
- 25 g (1 oz) plain white flour
- 15 g (½ oz) fine cornmeal
- 1.25 ml (¼ tsp) salt
- 45 ml (3 tbsp) warm water
- sesame and cumin seeds, for sprinkling
- olive oil, for brushing

TO GARNISH
- coriander sprigs

**1** Halve the aubergines lengthwise, then score a criss-cross pattern over the cut surfaces. Sprinkle with 10 ml (2 tsp) salt and set aside for 30 minutes. Rinse thoroughly and pat dry with kitchen paper.
**2** Place the aubergines in a roasting tin and brush the cut surfaces liberally with 30 ml (2 tbsp) of the oil. Roast in the oven at 230°C (450°F) Mark 8 for 45-50 minutes until browned and soft, brushing occasionally with more oil. Allow to cool slightly, then cut the aubergine flesh into small cubes.
**3** Meanwhile, finely chop the garlic and onion. Immerse the tomatoes in boiling water for 30 seconds, then remove and peel; dice the flesh. Heat the remaining oil in a frying pan, add the garlic and onion and fry for 5 minutes. Add the tomatoes, spices and lemon zest and fry for 1 minute, then cover and simmer for 5 minutes. Stir in the aubergine, coriander and lemon juice to taste. Remove from the heat and set aside to cool.
**4** To make the bread, sift the flours, cornmeal and salt into a bowl and gradually work in the warm water to form a firm dough. Knead lightly, divide into 4 equal pieces and place on a floured plate. Cover with cling film and leave to rest for 30 minutes.
**5** Brush a griddle or heavy-based frying pan liberally with oil. Roll out each piece of dough thinly on a floured surface to a round, about 3 mm (⅛ inch) thick. Sprinkle with sesame and cumin seeds and roll firmly to incorporate them.
**6** Place one bread on the heated griddle and cook for 1 minute until the underside is speckled brown. Flip over and cook the other side for 40 seconds - 1 minute. Remove and keep warm wrapped in a tea-towel while cooking the remaining bread.
**7** Serve the aubergine salad garnished with coriander and accompanied by the warm bread.

**NOTE** If you haven't time to make your own bread, serve the salad with warm pitta bread and top with a spoonful of Greek yogurt.

# SWEET ROAST ONION SALAD

**SERVES 6**
PREPARATION
10 minutes
COOKING TIME
About 2 hours
FREEZING
Not suitable
CALS/SERVING
340
COLOUR INDEX
Page 28

- 6 even-sized onions, about 700 g (1½ lb) total weight
- 50 ml (2 fl oz) oil

DRESSING
- 45 ml (3 tbsp) capers
- finely pared zest and juice of 1 large lime
- 2.5 ml (½ tsp) caster sugar
- 150 ml (¼ pint) olive oil
- 30 ml (2 tbsp) chopped fresh flat-leaf parsley
- salt and pepper

TO SERVE
- salad leaves, such as rocket or baby spinach

**1** Peel the onions, if wished, and stand them in an oven-proof dish in which they fit snugly. Pour over the oil and cook in the oven at 200°C (400°F) Mark 6 for 1½ hours or until beginning to colour. Cover the dish with foil and bake for a further 20 minutes or until the onions are soft in the centre.
**2** For the dressing, roughly chop the capers and mix together with the lime zest and juice, sugar, olive oil, parsley and seasoning. Cover and set aside.
**3** To serve, add any cooking juices from the onions to the dressing and adjust the seasoning. Halve each onion and place on a serving plate. Garnish with salad leaves, spoon over the dressing and serve warm or at room temperature.

## FENNEL CARPACCIO

**SERVES 4**
PREPARATION
15-20 minutes, plus marinating
FREEZING
Not suitable
CALS/SERVING
220

2 heads of fennel, about 700 g (1½ lb) total weight
120 ml (4 fl oz) extra-virgin olive oil
shredded zest and juice of ½ lemon
1 garlic clove, peeled and crushed
pinch of sugar
5 ml (1 tsp) coriander seeds, crushed
2 fresh thyme sprigs, bruised
2 fresh rosemary sprigs, bruised
salt and pepper
15 ml (1 tbsp) chopped fresh fennel fronds or dill

TO SERVE
handful of rocket leaves (optional)
Parmesan cheese shavings (optional)
fennel flowers (optional)

**1** Trim the fennel and slice the bulbs crosswise into wafer-thin slices, using a sharp knife. Place in a large shallow dish.
**2** Combine the oil, lemon zest and juice, garlic, sugar, coriander seeds, thyme, rosemary and salt and pepper. Pour over the fennel and stir well until the fennel is evenly coated. Cover and leave to marinate at room temperature for at least 1 hour.
**3** Drain the fennel, reserving the juices. Divide the fennel between individual serving plates and top each serving with a few rocket leaves, if desired.
**4** Taste the marinade and adjust the seasoning if necessary. Stir in the fennel fronds or dill and drizzle liberally over the fennel and rocket. Top with plenty of fresh Parmesan shavings and garnish with fennel flowers if available. Serve with walnut or olive bread.

**NOTE** The easiest way to shave wafer-thin slivers of Parmesan is to use a swivel potato peeler on a large wedge of cheese at room temperature (ie not hard from the refrigerator).

## ROASTED ASPARAGUS SALAD

**SERVES 4-6**
PREPARATION
10 minutes
COOKING TIME
20 minutes
FREEZING
Not suitable
CALS/SERVING
275-180
COLOUR INDEX
Page 29

700 g (1½ lb) asparagus spears
90 ml (6 tbsp) olive oil
45 ml (3 tbsp) lemon juice
coarse sea salt and pepper

TO SERVE
rocket leaves
lemon wedges
Parmesan cheese shavings (optional)

**1** Trim the asparagus spears and use a potato peeler to peel the bottom 5 cm (2 inches) of each stalk.
**2** Lay the asparagus in a shallow roasting tin and spoon over 60 ml (4 tbsp) of the olive oil. Shake lightly to mix. Roast in the oven at 200°C (400°F) Mark 6 for about 20 minutes until just tender, turning the asparagus spears once during cooking. Allow to cool.
**3** To serve, spoon the remaining olive oil over the asparagus and sprinkle with the lemon juice. Season with coarse sea salt and freshly ground black pepper and toss lightly. Serve with rocket leaves and lemon wedges. Sprinkle with finely pared shavings of Parmesan, if liked.

**NOTE** The cooking time applies to stalks of medium thickness and should be increased if you are using fatter asparagus stems.

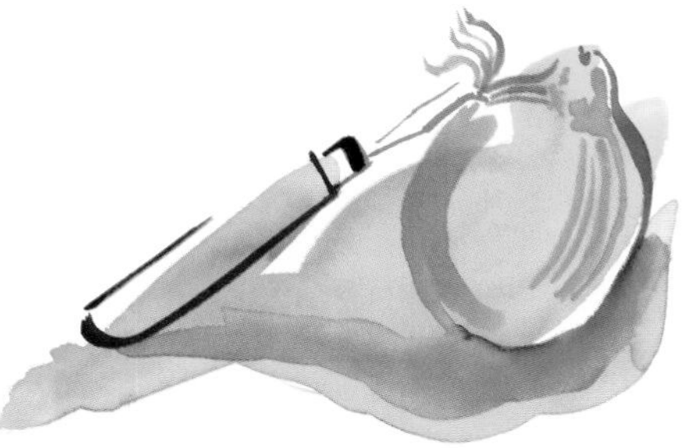

# BROAD BEAN AND PECORINO SALAD

**SERVES 4**
PREPARATION
30 minutes
COOKING TIME
1 minute
FREEZING
Not suitable
CALS/SERVING
310

2.5 kg (4 lb) broad beans
3-4 heads of red chicory, trimmed
50 g (2 oz) hard Pecorino cheese (see note)
½ small red onion, peeled
25 g (1 oz) hazelnuts, toasted

DRESSING
10 ml (2 tsp) raspberry vinegar
2.5 ml (½ tsp) thin honey
salt and pepper
60 ml (4 tbsp) hazelnut oil

**1** Shell the broad beans: you should have about 450 g (1 lb) shelled weight. Bring a large pan of lightly salted water to a rolling boil, add the broad beans, return to the boil and cook for 1 minute. Drain and immediately refresh under cold water. Drain and pat dry.
**2** Slip the broad beans out of their tough outer skins by pinching them at one end, then place in a large bowl.
**3** Separate the chicory into leaves and add to the beans. Using a swivel vegetable peeler, finely pare the cheese. Thinly slice the onion. Roughly chop the hazelnuts.
**4** To make the dressing, place the vinegar, honey and seasoning in a small jug and gradually whisk in the oil until blended. Pour half of the dressing over the beans and chicory and toss until well coated.
**5** Arrange the beans and chicory on individual serving plates, top with the cheese, onion and nuts and drizzle over the remaining dressing. Serve at once.

**NOTE** Pecorino is a ewes' milk cheese which hardens as it ages, in a similar way to Parmesan. A young, softer Pecorino or Parmesan cheese can be substituted if preferred.

# ROASTED GREEK SALAD

**SERVES 4**
PREPARATION
10 minutes, plus marinating
COOKING TIME
45 minutes
FREEZING
Not suitable
CALS/SERVING
290
COLOUR INDEX
Page 29

225 g (8 oz) feta cheese
30 ml (2 tbsp) olive oil
2.5 ml (½ tsp) balsamic or red wine vinegar
15 ml (1 tbsp) lemon juice
30 ml (2 tbsp) chopped fresh thyme
pepper
700 g (1½ lb) tomatoes
900 g (2 lb) courgettes
4 garlic cloves, peeled
225 g (8 oz) small red onions, peeled
50 g (2 oz) pitted black olives

**1** Cut the feta cheese into 1 cm (½ inch) thick slices and place in a shallow dish. Mix together 15 ml (1 tbsp) olive oil, the balsamic vinegar, lemon juice and half of the chopped thyme. Season with plenty of black pepper. Pour over the feta and leave to marinate for at least 1 hour.
**2** Halve or quarter the tomatoes; thickly slice the courgettes; thinly slice the garlic cloves; quarter the onions. Place the courgettes, garlic and onions in a roasting tin and drizzle over the remaining olive oil. Cook in the oven at 230°C (450°F) Mark 8 for 30 minutes, turning occasionally. Add the tomatoes, olives, remaining thyme and pepper to taste. Cook for 10 minutes or until the vegetables are tender.
**3** About 5-7 minutes before the end of the cooking time, remove the cheese from the marinade with a fish slice and place on a baking sheet below the vegetables until bubbling and slightly browned.
**4** Transfer the roasted vegetables to individual serving plates and spoon over the remaining marinade. Top with the feta cheese and serve with crusty bread.

**NOTE** As feta cheese is very salty, season the salad with black pepper only.

# GRILLED STUFFED PEPPER SALAD

**SERVES 6**
PREPARATION
20 minutes
COOKING TIME
About 20 minutes
FREEZING
Not suitable
CALS/SERVING
200

- 3 small onions
- 3 red peppers
- 3 yellow peppers
- 3 garlic cloves, peeled
- 45 ml (3 tbsp) capers
- 25 ml (1½ tbsp) fennel seeds
- 90 ml (6 tbsp) extra-virgin olive oil
- 30 ml (2 tbsp) balsamic vinegar
- 45 ml (3 tbsp) roughly torn fresh flat-leaf parsley
- coarse sea salt and pepper

**1** Peel the onions, leaving the root end intact, and cut into quarters. Drop them into a pan of boiling water and cook for 1 minute; drain well.

**2** Halve the peppers lengthwise cutting through the stems, then core and deseed them. Arrange on the grill rack, skin-side up, in a single layer with the onions and garlic. Grill until the pepper skins are blistered and well charred. Turn the onions and garlic as necessary, but let them char slightly too.

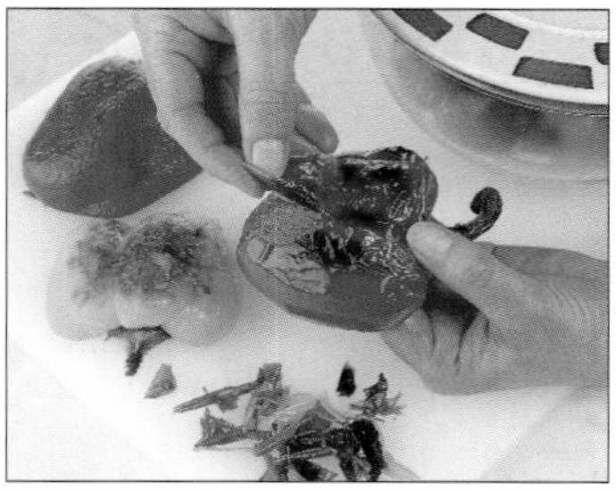

**3** Place the peppers in a bowl, cover with a plate and allow to cool slightly, then peel away their skins. Arrange the peppers on a serving platter. Fill the cavities with the grilled onions and capers.

**4** Put the fennel seeds in a dry frying pan and toast over a moderate heat for a few minutes until they begin to pop and release their aroma. Transfer to a mortar and grind using a pestle. Add the grilled garlic and grind to a paste.

**5** Transfer the garlic paste to a small bowl and whisk in the oil and vinegar. Sprinkle the parsley, sea salt and pepper over the salad and spoon on the dressing. Serve at room temperature.

**NOTE** If you have a small grill, it may be necessary to grill the peppers in two batches.

# CHILLED MELON AND GINGER SALAD

**SERVES 4-6**
PREPARATION
15 minutes, plus chilling
COOKING TIME
10 minutes
FREEZING
Not suitable
CALS/SERVING
105-70
COLOUR INDEX
page 29

- 1 small charantais or cantaloupe melon
- 1 small ogen or galia melon
- ½ large honeydew melon
- 350 g (12 oz) water melon

DRESSING
- 15 ml (2 tbsp) caster sugar
- 15 ml (1 tbsp) chopped preserved stem ginger in syrup
- 120 ml (4 fl oz) water
- 30 ml (2 tbsp) orange juice
- 10 ml (2 tsp) lemon juice

**1** First make the dressing. Place the sugar and ginger in a small saucepan with the water. Heat gently to dissolve the sugar, then bring to the boil and simmer for 10 minutes. Transfer to a bowl and stir in the orange and lemon juices. Set aside to cool.
**2** Peel each melon and discard the seeds. Cut the flesh into thin wedges and mix together in a large bowl.
**3** Pour the cooled dressing over the melon and toss gently to mix. Cover and chill in the refrigerator for about 1 hour before serving.

# SOUPS

## MEXICAN BEAN SOUP WITH LIME BUTTER

**SERVES 6**
PREPARATION
15 minutes
COOKING TIME
25 minutes
FREEZING
Suitable
CALS/SERVING
630

1 onion
2 garlic cloves
60 ml (4 tbsp) extra-virgin olive oil
pinch of crushed dried red chillies
5 ml (1 tsp) ground coriander
5 ml (1 tsp) ground cumin
2.5 ml (½ tsp) ground cinnamon
900 ml (1½ pints) vegetable stock
300 ml (½ pint) tomato juice
5-10 (1-2 tsp) chilli sauce
two 400 g (14 oz) cans red kidney beans
30 ml (2 tbsp) chopped fresh coriander
salt and pepper
LIME BUTTER
50 g (2 oz) unsalted butter, softened
grated zest and juice of ½ lime
TO GARNISH
1 small avocado
few tortilla chips
coriander sprigs

**1** First prepare the lime butter. Beat the butter with the lime zest and juice, and seasoning. Shape into a log, wrap in cling film and chill.

**2** Peel and chop the onion and garlic. Heat the oil in a large pan, add the onion, garlic, chilli and spices and fry gently for 5 minutes.

**3** Add the stock, tomato juice, chilli sauce and beans, with their liquid. Bring to the boil, cover and simmer gently, for 20 minutes. Let cool slightly.

**4** Purée the soup in a blender or food processor until smooth, then return to the pan. Stir in the coriander and heat through. Check the seasoning.

**5** Unwrap the lime butter and slice thinly. Peel, stone and chop the avocado. Pour the soup into warmed bowls. Top each serving with a slice of lime butter, some avocado and a few tortilla chips. Serve garnished with coriander.

**VARIATIONS**
❑ Use aduki beans instead of red kidney beans.
❑ Flavour the butter with lemon or orange, instead of lime.

## LEEK AND POTATO SOUP

**SERVES 4**
PREPARATION
10 minutes
COOKING TIME
15 minutes
FREEZING
Not suitable
CALS/SERVING
260
COLOUR INDEX
Page 30

575 g (1¼ lb) floury potatoes
2-3 garlic cloves
salt and pepper
350 g (12 oz) trimmed leeks
celery salt (optional)
60 ml (4 tbsp) coarsely chopped fresh parsley
60 ml (4 tbsp) extra-virgin olive oil
TO SERVE
sun-dried tomato or olive bread

**1** Peel and thinly slice the potatoes and garlic. Place in a saucepan and cover with 1.2 litres (2 pints) cold water. Bring to the boil and add salt. Cover and simmer for about 10 minutes until the potatoes are soft.
**2** Meanwhile, slice the leeks. Add them to the potatoes and simmer for a further 5 minutes or so to soften the leeks.
**3** Roughly mash the potatoes into the soup, using a potato masher. Correct the seasoning with celery salt (or ordinary salt) and pepper to taste. Stir in the chopped parsley.
**4** Ladle the soup into warmed bowls and drizzle 15 ml (1 tbsp) olive oil over each portion. Serve immediately, with chunks of flavoured bread.

**VARIATION** Replace parsley with roughly chopped watercress.

# TUSCAN BEAN SOUP WITH GARLIC AND OLIVE OIL

**ERVES 6**
REPARATION
0 minutes,
lus soaking
OOKING TIME
¼ hours
REEZING
uitable
ALS/SERVING
30

225 g (8 oz) dried haricot or cannellini beans, soaked overnight in cold water
4 garlic cloves, peeled
150 ml (¼ pint) olive oil
salt and pepper
15-30 ml (1-2 tbsp) chopped fresh parsley (optional)

Drain the beans, place in a flameproof casserole and add ufficient cold water to cover by 5 cm (2 inches). Bring to he boil, cover tightly and bake in the oven at 170°C (325°F) Mark 3 for about 1 hour or until tender (see note).
Meanwhile, finely chop half the garlic and thinly slice the emainder.
Transfer half of the beans and cooking liquid to a food processor or blender and process until smooth. Add this purée to the beans in the casserole and stir well.
Heat half the olive oil in a frying pan, add the chopped garlic and fry gently until soft and golden. Stir into the oup and reheat until boiling. Simmer gently for about 0 minutes. Taste and season well with salt and pepper. Pour into a warmed tureen or individual soup bowls.
Heat the remaining olive oil in the frying pan and fry the liced garlic until golden. Spoon over the soup and serve at once, sprinkled with chopped parsley if preferred.

**IOTE** The cooking time depends on the freshness of the eans. Older beans will take longer to cook. Begin testing hem after 45 minutes.

**VARIATIONS**

❑ Stir 4 skinned, deseeded and chopped tomatoes into the soup as it is reheated.

❑ Stir 30 ml (2 tbsp) chopped fresh sage or rosemary into the soup with the puréed beans.

# JERUSALEM ARTICHOKE AND PARMESAN SOUP

**SERVES 6**
PREPARATION
15 minutes
COOKING TIME
25 minutes
FREEZING
Suitable
CALS/SERVING
190
COLOUR INDEX
Page 30

450 g (1 lb) Jerusalem artichokes
2 shallots
50 g (2 oz) butter
5 ml (1 tsp) mild curry paste
900 ml (1½ pints) vegetable stock
150 ml (¼ pint) single cream (or milk for a less rich soup)
freshly grated nutmeg, to taste
pinch of cayenne pepper
60 ml (4 tbsp) freshly grated Parmesan cheese
salt and pepper
MELBA TOAST
3-4 slices day-old soft grain white bread
a little freshly grated Parmesan cheese, for sprinkling
pinch of paprika

**1** Scrub the Jerusalem artichokes thoroughly, pat dry, then slice thinly. Peel and dice the shallots.

**2** Melt the butter in a large saucepan, add the shallots and cook gently for 5 minutes until soft and golden. Stir in the curry paste and cook for 1 minute. Add the artichokes and stock; stir well. Bring to the boil, cover and simmer for about 15 minutes until the artichokes are tender.

**3** Meanwhile, make the Melba toast. Toast the bread lightly on both sides. Quickly cut off the crusts and split each slice in two. Scrape off any doughy bits, then sprinkle with Parmesan and paprika. Place on a baking sheet and bake in the oven at 180°C (350°F) Mark 4 for 10-15 minutes or until uniformly golden.

**4** Add the cream, nutmeg and cayenne to the soup. Transfer to a blender or food processor and work until smooth, then pass through a sieve into a clean saucepan. Reheat the soup and stir in the Parmesan cheese. Taste and adjust the seasoning. Serve at once, with the Melba toast.

**NOTE** If preferred the Melba toast can be prepared ahead, allowed to cool, then stored in an airtight tin. Warm through in the oven before serving.

**VARIATION** Replace the artichokes with 1 large cauliflower, divided into florets. Add to the shallots with the stock and bring to the boil. Simmer for about 10 minutes or until very soft, then continue as in step 4.

## CURRIED CARROT AND SPLIT PEA SOUP

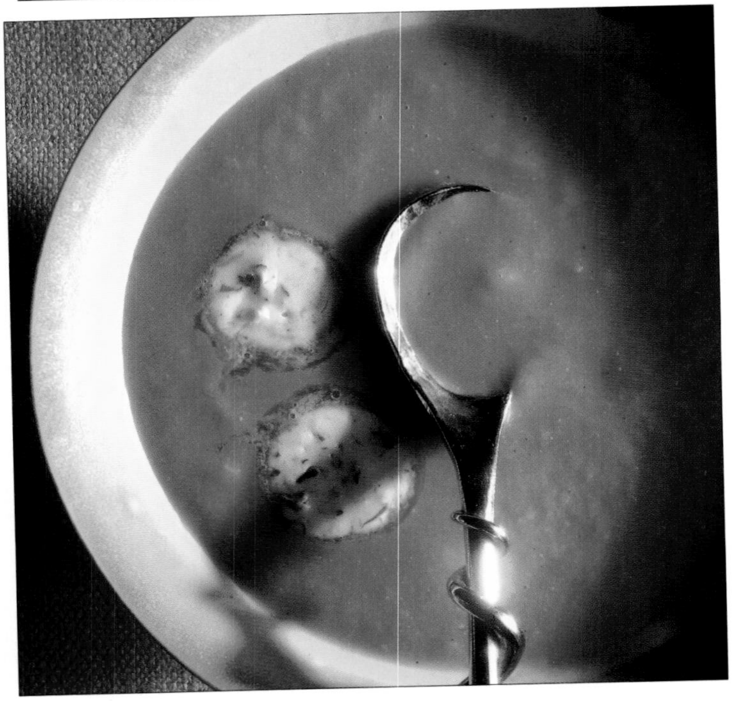

**SERVES 4**
PREPARATION
35 minutes, plus overnight soaking
COOKING TIME
1-1¼ hours
FREEZING
Suitable: Stage 4
CALS/SERVING
260

50 g (2 oz) split yellow peas, soaked overnight in cold water
1 small onion
1 garlic clove
225 g (8 oz) carrots
1 potato
1 red chilli
15 ml (1 tbsp) sunflower oil
5 ml (1 tsp) grated fresh root ginger
7.5 ml (1½ tsp) hot curry paste
salt and pepper
CORIANDER AND LIME BUTTER
50 g (2 oz) butter, softened
grated zest and juice of 1 lime
7.5 ml (1½ tsp) chopped fresh coriander

**1** Drain the split peas, rinse well and place in a large saucepan with 1.5 litres (2½ pints) cold water. Bring to the boil and boil steadily for 10 minutes. Reduce the heat, cover and simmer gently for 30 minutes.
**2** Meanwhile, make the coriander and lime butter. In a bowl, cream the butter with the lime juice and zest, coriander and a little pepper, until evenly combined. Form into a log shape on a piece of greaseproof paper, overwrap in foil and chill in the refrigerator until required.
**3** Peel and chop the onion, garlic, carrots and potato. Halve, deseed and chop the chilli. Heat the oil in a pan, add the onion, garlic, ginger and chilli and fry, stirring, for 10 minutes until evenly browned. Stir in the curry paste, carrots and potato and fry for a further 5 minutes.
**4** Add the curried vegetable mixture to the split peas. Return to the boil, cover and simmer for a further 35 minutes until the vegetables and peas are tender. Transfer to a blender or food processor and work until fairly smooth. Return to the pan, season with salt and pepper to taste and heat through.
**5** Unwrap the butter and cut into thin slices. Pour the soup into warmed serving bowls and serve each portion topped with two slices of the flavoured butter.

**VARIATION** Replace the split peas with red lentils, which do not require pre-soaking. Add 125 g (4 oz) red lentils to the fried curried vegetables, together with 1.2 litres (2 pints) vegetable stock. Cook for 30 minutes until the vegetables and lentils are cooked. Continue as above.

## TOMATO AND HARISSA SOUP WITH CORIANDER CREAM

**SERVES 8**
PREPARATION
20 minutes
COOKING TIME
30 minutes
FREEZING
Suitable
CALS/SERVING
215
COLOUR INDEX
Page 30

450 g (1 lb) onions, peeled
90 ml (6 tbsp) oil
4 garlic cloves, peeled and crushed
20 ml (4 tsp) ground cumin
10 ml (2 tsp) harissa
30 ml (2 tbsp) tomato paste
two 400 g cans chopped plum tomatoes
10 ml (2 tsp) sugar
2.5 cm (1 inch) fresh root ginger, grated
2 litres (3½ pints) light vegetable stock
salt and pepper
CORIANDER CREAM
200 ml (7 fl oz) double cream
90 ml (6 tbsp) roughly chopped fresh coriander
TO GARNISH
coriander sprigs

**1** Finely chop the onions. Heat the oil in a saucepan, add the onions and cook gently for 5 minutes or until soft but not coloured. Add the garlic and cumin; cook for 30 seconds. Add the harissa and tomato paste and fry for 1 minute. Stir in the tomatoes, sugar, ginger and stock. Season and bring to the boil, then simmer gently for 20 minutes. Allow to cool slightly.
**2** Purée the mixture in a blender until smooth. Pass through a sieve, then return the soup to the pan. Bring to the boil and check the seasoning.
**3** For the coriander cream, lightly whip the cream in a bowl, season and fold in the chopped coriander.
**4** To serve, spoon the soup into warmed bowls. Top each portion with a spoonful of the coriander cream, garnish with coriander and accompany with warm naan bread.

## SQUASH AND HARICOT BEAN SOUP

RVES 4-6
EPARATION
minutes
OOKING TIME
minutes
EEZING
itable
LS/SERVING
0-235

1 onion
2 garlic cloves
900 g (2 lb) butternut squash
60 ml (4 tbsp) olive oil
30 ml (2 tbsp) chopped fresh sage
2.5 ml (½ tsp) paprika
pinch of cayenne pepper
1.2 litres (2 pints) vegetable stock
400 g (14 oz) can haricot beans, drained
salt and pepper
TO SERVE
60 ml (4 tbsp) Olive Pesto (see note)

Peel and chop the onion and garlic. Peel and deseed the uash: you should have about 700 g (1½ lb) flesh; cut into cm (½ inch) cubes.
Heat the oil in a large saucepan. Add the onion, garlic, uash, sage and spices, and fry gently for 10 minutes until ghtly golden.
Add the stock and bring to the boil. Cover and simmer ntly for 15 minutes. Transfer half of the soup to a ender or food processor and work until very smooth.
Return the puréed soup to the pan, stir in the haricot ans and return to a steady simmer. Cook gently for minutes until the beans are heated through. Check the asoning. Serve the soup in warmed bowls topped with a oonful of olive pesto.

**OTE** Olive pesto is available from some supermarkets and licatessens, but strict vegetarians will need to check the bel – as some brands contain anchovies. If you have time ake your own (see page 292).

## SWEET POTATO AND CUMIN SOUP

**SERVES 6-8**
PREPARATION
25 minutes
COOKING TIME
50 minutes
FREEZING
Suitable
CALS/SERVING
165-125

30 ml (2 tbsp) olive oil
1 onion, chopped
2 garlic cloves, peeled and crushed
10 ml (2 tsp) ground cumin
575 g (1¼ lb) peeled potatoes
350 g (12 oz) peeled sweet potatoes
1.2 litres (2 pints) hot vegetable stock
45-60 ml (3-4 tbsp) chopped fresh coriander
15 ml (1 tbsp) lemon juice
salt and pepper
a little extra-virgin olive oil, to serve

**1** Heat the oil in a saucepan, add the onion, garlic and cumin and fry gently for 10 minutes.
**2** Meanwhile, dice all of the potatoes. Add them to the pan and fry for a further 5 minutes, stirring occasionally to prevent sticking, until the potatoes are lightly browned.
**3** Add the stock, bring to the boil, cover and simmer for 30 minutes. Transfer the soup to a blender or food processor and blend briefly until smooth.
**4** Pour the soup into a clean pan and return to the boil. Stir in the coriander and simmer gently for 2-3 minutes.
**5** Add the lemon juice and season with salt and pepper to taste. Serve the soup at once, drizzled with olive oil.

**NOTE** This soup is best made with the orange-fleshed sweet potatoes which are available during the winter.

**VARIATION** Instead of olive oil, add a drizzle of walnut or hazelnut oil for a change.

## CHICK PEA SOUP

**SERVES 6**
PREPARATION
20 minutes, plus soaking
COOKING TIME
1½ hours
FREEZING
Suitable
CALS/SERVING
390
COLOUR INDEX
Page 31

225 g (8 oz) dried chick peas, soaked overnight in cold water
1 onion
60 ml (4 tbsp) olive oil
2 garlic cloves, peeled and crushed
15 ml (1 tbsp) ground coriander
15 ml (1 tbsp) paprika
10 ml (2 tsp) ground cumin
2 fresh thyme sprigs
1.5 litres (2½ pints) vegetable stock
1 large potato, about 175 g (6 oz)
2 carrots
3 tomatoes
30 ml (2 tbsp) chopped fresh coriander
salt and pepper
15 ml (1 tbsp) tahini paste

GARLIC CROUTONS
50 g (2 oz) butter, or margarine, softened
2 garlic cloves, crushed
4 thick slices white bread

TO GARNISH
coriander sprigs

**1** Drain the chick peas, place in a saucepan and add sufficient water to cover by 5 cm (2 inches). Bring to the boil, cover and boil rapidly for 15 minutes, then drain.
**2** Meanwhile, peel and chop the onion. Heat the olive oil in a large saucepan, add the onion and sauté over a medium heat for 5 minutes, until softened. Add the garlic and spices and cook for a further 3 minutes.
**3** Add the chick peas to the saucepan with the thyme and stock. Bring to the boil, then lower the heat, cover and cook for 40 minutes.
**4** Meanwhile, peel and chop the potato; peel and slice the carrots. Immerse the tomatoes in a bowl of boiling water for 30 seconds, then drain and refresh under cold running water. Peel away the skins and roughly chop the flesh.
**5** Add the potato, carrots and tomatoes to the pan. Stir in the chopped coriander and season with salt and pepper. Bring back to the boil, then lower the heat and simmer for a further 30-40 minutes until the chick peas and vegetables are tender. Stir in the tahini paste.
**6** Using a food processor or blender, purée the soup, in batches if necessary, until fairly smooth. Taste and adjust the seasoning.
**7** Shortly before serving, prepare the croûtons. In a small bowl, mix the butter and garlic together until evenly blended. Remove the crusts from the bread, then spread with the garlic butter. Cut into squares and place on a baking sheet. Bake in the oven at 200°C (400°F) Mark 6 for 8-10 minutes until crisp and golden. Sprinkle with salt.
**8** Reheat the soup before serving. Ladle into warmed bowls, garnish with coriander and serve accompanied by the hot croûtons.

**VARIATION** Use two 400 g (14 oz) cans chick peas, rinsed and drained. At stage 3, add the stock and thyme to the soup with the vegetables and simmer for 30 minutes, then add the chick peas and cook for a further 10 minutes.

## SPINACH AND PEA SOUP WITH LEMON

**SERVES 4**
PREPARATION
10 minutes
COOKING TIME
30 minutes
FREEZING
Suitable
CALS/SERVING
300

1 onion
1 garlic clove
30 ml (2 tbsp) olive oil
2.5 ml (½ tsp) ground cumin
450 g (1 lb) spinach leaves
225 g (8 oz) shelled peas (thawed if frozen)
30 ml (2 tbsp) chopped fresh mint
900 ml (1½ pints) vegetable stock
1.25 ml (¼ tsp) freshly grated nutmeg
salt and pepper

TO GARNISH
60 ml (4 tbsp) extra-virgin olive oil blended with 30 ml (2 tbsp) lemon juice
Parmesan cheese shavings (optional)

**1** Peel and chop the onion and garlic. Heat the oil in a saucepan, add the onion, garlic and cumin and fry gently for 10 minutes until lightly golden.
**2** Wash and dry the spinach leaves and cut away the thick central stalks. Shred the leaves roughly and add to the pan with the peas, mint and stock.
**3** Bring slowly to the boil, cover and simmer over a very gentle heat for 15 minutes.
**4** Transfer the soup to a blender or food processor and blend until very smooth. Return to the pan and heat gently until the soup just reaches the boil. Add the nutmeg and season with salt and pepper to taste.
**5** Spoon into warmed serving bowls and drizzle over the lemon oil. Scatter the cheese on top and serve at once.

**VARIATION** For a more substantial soup, add 225 g (8 oz) peeled, diced potatoes with the onion. Increase the stock to 1.2 litres (2 pints); add to the potatoes and onion and simmer for 15 minutes before stirring in the spinach etc.

# MISO SOUP WITH NOODLES

**SERVES 4-6**
PREPARATION
15 minutes
COOKING TIME
25 minutes
FREEZING
Not suitable
CALS/SERVING
335-225

- 125 g (4 oz) Japanese noodles (udon) or tagliatelle
- 10 ml (2 tsp) oil
- 1.2 litres (2 pints) vegetable stock
- 60 ml (2 fl oz) sake or Japanese rice wine
- 5 ml (1 tsp) sugar
- 5 ml (1 tsp) dark soy sauce
- 2 carrots, peeled
- 2 spring onions, trimmed
- 125 g (4 oz) plain tofu
- 50 g (2 oz) spinach leaves, trimmed
- 30 ml (2 tbsp) barley miso paste

**1** Cook the noodles according to the packet instructions until just tender. Drain, refresh immediately under cold water and drain again. Toss with the oil to prevent sticking and set aside.

**2** Meanwhile, pour the stock into a saucepan and add the sake or rice wine, sugar and soy sauce. Bring to the boil, cover and simmer for 10 minutes.

**3** Meanwhile, prepare the vegetables and tofu. Cut the carrots into matchsticks, the spring onions into thin slices and the tofu into small thin batons.

**4** Add the carrots and spring onions to the broth and simmer for 10 minutes. Finely shred the spinach leaves.

**5** Put the miso paste in a bowl and mix with a little of the hot stock until blended.

**6** Stir the miso into the soup and add the tofu and spinach. Heat gently, without boiling, for 5 minutes. Add the noodles to heat through. Serve immediately.

**NOTE** You can use any form of miso paste for this soup according to preference. Alternatively, stir in a sachet of instant miso soup, available from larger supermarkets.

## BAKED RED ONION SOUP

**SERVES 4-6**
PREPARATION
20-25 minutes
COOKING TIME
$1^{1}/_{4}$-$1^{1}/_{2}$ hours
FREEZING
Not suitable
CALS/SERVING
575-385
COLOUR INDEX
Page 31

4 large red onions, each about 300 g (10 oz)
60 ml (4 tbsp) olive oil
1 garlic clove, peeled and crushed
10 ml (2 tsp) chopped fresh sage
salt and pepper
8 slices ciabatta, 1 cm (½ inch) thick (cut on the diagonal)
900 ml (1½ pints) hot vegetable stock
175 g (6 oz) gruyère or Cheddar cheese, grated
50 g (2 oz) Parmesan cheese, freshly grated

**1** Peel the onions and cut each one into 8 wedges; place in a deep ovenproof dish. Combine the olive oil, garlic and sage, add to the onions and toss well. Roast in the oven at 200°C (400°F) Mark 6 for 1 hour, stirring occasionally to ensure the onions brown evenly. Season generously with salt and pepper.

**2** Divide about half of the roasted onions between 4-6 individual ovenproof soup bowls. Toast the ciabatta slices on both sides under the grill. Place one slice in each soup bowl. Add sufficient stock to cover, then scatter over half the gruyère or Cheddar and half the Parmesan.

**3** Sprinkle with the remaining onions, then repeat the layers of toasted ciabatta, stock and grated cheese.

**4** Stand the bowls in a large shallow baking tin and bake in the oven for about 20 minutes until the cheese is melted and browned. Let stand for 5-10 minutes before serving.

## GARLIC, BEAN AND TOMATO SOUP

**SERVES 4**
PREPARATION
15 minutes, plus overnight soaking
COOKING TIME
1 hour
FREEZING
Suitable
CALS/SERVING
530

125 g (4 oz) dried borlotti beans, soaked overnight in cold water (see note)
1.2 litres (2 pints) vegetable stock
1 garlic bulb
30 ml (2 tbsp) olive oil
450 g (1 lb) ripe tomatoes
15 ml (1 tbsp) lemon juice
salt and pepper
TO SERVE
60 ml (4 tbsp) Pesto or Olive Pesto (see page 292)

**1** Drain and rinse the beans and place in a saucepan with the stock. Bring to the boil and boil rapidly for 10 minutes. Reduce the heat, cover and simmer for 40-45 minutes until the beans are tender.
**2** Meanwhile, separate and peel the garlic cloves. Place them in a roasting tin, drizzle with the oil and bake near the top of the oven at 200°C (400°F) Mark 6 for 15 minutes. Meanwhile, roughly chop the tomatoes. Add to the garlic, stir to mix and bake for a further 10-15 minutes until the garlic is lightly browned and the tomatoes are soft.
**3** Transfer the cooked beans and their liquid to a blender or food processor, then add the tomato and garlic mixture, salt and pepper. Purée until fairly smooth, then return to the pan. Add the lemon juice and check the seasoning. Heat through for 5 minutes.
**4** Ladle the soup into warmed bowls and top each serving with a spoonful of pesto.

**NOTE** To save time, you can use a 400 g (14 oz) can borlotti or haricot beans rather than dried beans. Reduce stock to 900 ml (1½ pints). Rinse the beans before puréeing them with the stock and tomato mixture at stage 3.

**'ARIATION** Add 225 g (8 oz) button mushrooms to the omato and garlic mixture with an extra 15 ml (1 tbsp) live oil. Bake as above, stir into the cooked beans and add 25 g (4 oz) each of peas, broad beans and diced broccoli. 'ook until tender and serve topped with pesto.

## GRILLED PEPPER AND AUBERGINE SOUP

**ERVES 4-6**
EPARATION
5 minutes
OOKING TIME
5 minutes
EEZING
itable: Without ffron cream
ALS/SERVING
0-300
OLOUR INDEX
ge 32

2 large red peppers
1 large aubergine
90 ml (3 fl oz) olive oil
1 large onion
2 garlic cloves
5 ml (1 tsp) grated lemon zest
15 ml (1 tbsp) chopped fresh thyme
5 ml (1 tsp) dried oregano
400 g (14 oz) can chopped tomatoes
900 ml (1½ pints) vegetable stock
1 bay leaf
30 ml (2 tbsp) chopped fresh basil
salt and pepper

SAFFRON CREAM
small pinch of saffron strands
15 ml (1 tbsp) boiling water
1 egg yolk
1 garlic clove, peeled and crushed
2.5 ml (½ tsp) cayenne pepper
10 ml (2 tsp) lemon juice
150-175 ml (5-6 fl oz) olive oil

TO GARNISH
basil leaves

Quarter, core and deseed the red peppers. Brush with a tle olive oil and grill, skin-side up, for 3-4 minutes each de until charred and tender. Transfer to a plate, cover with cloth and leave until cool enough to handle. Peel the eppers and roughly chop the flesh.

Thinly slice the aubergine lengthwise. Brush with oil and ill for 4-5 minutes on each side until charred and tender. ave until cool enough to handle, then chop roughly.

Peel and chop the onion and garlic. Heat the remaining l in a large pan, add the onion, garlic, lemon zest, thyme d oregano and fry, stirring, for 10 minutes until browned. dd the peppers, aubergine, tomatoes, stock and bay leaf. ing to the boil, cover and simmer for 20 minutes. Discard e bay leaf.

Meanwhile, make the saffron cream. Soak the saffron in e boiling water for 5 minutes. In a bowl, whisk the egg lk with the garlic, cayenne, lemon juice and seasoning til pale and slightly thickened. Gradually whisk in the ve oil, until thick. Stir in the saffron liquid and check the asoning.

Transfer the soup to a blender or food processor. Add e basil and work until smooth. Return the soup to the pan d heat through. Adjust the seasoning.

Pour into warmed soup bowls. Spoon a little saffron eam on top of each portion, garnish with basil leaves and rve at once.

**RIATION** Replace the aubergine with 2 yellow peppers d grill as above.

## WALNUT SOUP WITH CHARMOULA

**SERVES 4**
PREPARATION
30 minutes
COOKING TIME
30 minutes
FREEZING
Suitable
CALS/SERVING
510

175 g (6 oz) walnuts, toasted
1 onion
30 ml (2 tbsp) walnut oil
5 ml (1 tsp) ground cinnamon
50 g (2 oz) fresh breadcrumbs
15 ml (1 tbsp) red wine vinegar
900 ml (1½ pints) vegetable stock
salt and pepper

CHARMOULA
5 ml (1 tsp) paprika
2.5 ml (½ tsp) ground cumin
2.5 ml (½ tsp) turmeric
1.25 ml (¼ tsp) cayenne pepper
2 garlic cloves, peeled and chopped
30 ml (2 tbsp) chopped fresh coriander
15 ml (1 tbsp) lime juice
60 ml (4 tbsp) olive oil

TO SERVE
Greek-style yogurt (optional)
flat-leaf parsley

**1** First make the charmoula. Place all the ingredients except the olive oil in a spice grinder or blender and work until smooth. Transfer to a bowl and stir in the oil. Season with salt and pepper to taste.

**2** For the soup, roughly chop the walnuts. Peel and finely chop the onion. Heat the walnut oil in a saucepan and add the onion, cinnamon and 30 ml (2 tbsp) of the charmoula. Fry gently for 5 minutes until golden. Add the walnuts and breadcrumbs and fry for a further 5 minutes, stirring occasionally to prevent sticking.

**3** Transfer the mixture to a blender or food processor, add the vinegar and 15-30 ml (1-2 tbsp) of the stock and work to a paste. Return to the pan, add remaining stock and bring to the boil. Cover and simmer for 15 minutes. Adjust the seasoning.

**4** Divide the soup between warmed bowls. Serve each portion topped with a spoonful of yogurt if desired, a sprinkling of parsley and a little charmoula.

## SPINACH AND RICE SOUP

**SERVES 4-6**
PREPARATION
10 minutes
COOKING TIME
25-30 minutes
FREEZING
Not suitable
CALS/SERVING
305-205

- 1 onion
- 60 ml (4 tbsp) extra-virgin olive oil
- 2 garlic cloves, peeled and crushed
- 10 ml (2 tsp) chopped fresh thyme
- 10 ml (2 tsp) chopped fresh rosemary (optional)
- grated zest of ½ lemon
- 10 ml (2 tsp) ground coriander
- 1.25 ml (¼ tsp) cayenne pepper, or to taste
- 125 g (4 oz) Arborio rice
- 1.2 litres (2 pints) vegetable stock
- 225 g (8 oz) spinach leaves (see note), or chopped frozen spinach
- 60 ml (4 tbsp) Pesto (see page 292)
- salt and pepper

TO SERVE
- extra-virgin olive oil
- freshly grated Parmesan cheese

**1** Peel and finely chop the onion. Heat half the oil in a large saucepan. Add the onion, garlic, herbs, lemon zest and spices and fry gently for 5 minutes until softened.
**2** Add the remaining oil, then add the rice and cook, stirring, for 1 minute until all the grains are glossy. Add the stock, bring to the boil and simmer gently for 20 minutes until the rice is tender.
**3** Meanwhile, remove any thick stalks from the spinach and shred the leaves. Stir the spinach into the soup with the pesto and cook for a further 2 minutes. Season with salt and pepper to taste.
**4** Serve the soup drizzled with a little olive oil and topped with a generous spoonful of Parmesan.

**NOTE** If using frozen spinach, defrost and drain thoroughly before stirring into the soup.

## CAULIFLOWER AND COCONUT SOUP

**SERVES 6**
PREPARATION
25 minutes
COOKING TIME
35-40 minutes
FREEZING
Suitable
CALS/SERVING
540

- two 400 g (14 oz) cans coconut milk
- 750 ml (1¼ pints) vegetable stock
- 4 garlic cloves
- 5 cm (2 inch) piece fresh galangal or root ginger
- 4 lemon grass stalks, roughly chopped
- 4 kaffir lime leaves, shredded (see note)
- 4 red chillies
- 1 large onion
- 30 ml (2 tbsp) groundnut oil
- 10 ml (2 tsp) sesame oil
- 10 ml (2 tsp) turmeric
- 10 ml (2 tsp) sugar
- 900 g (2 lb) cauliflower florets
- 30 ml (2 tbsp) lime juice
- 30 ml (2 tbsp) light soy sauce
- 4 spring onions, trimmed
- 60 ml (4 tbsp) chopped fresh coriander
- a little chilli or sesame oil, to serve

**1** Put the coconut milk and vegetable stock into a saucepan. Peel and finely chop the garlic and galangal or ginger. Add to the pan with the lemon grass, lime leaves and whole chillies. Bring to the boil, cover and simmer for 15 minutes. Strain and reserve the liquid.
**2** Peel and thinly slice the onion. Heat the groundnut and sesame oils in a clean saucepan. Add the onion, turmeric and sugar and fry gently for 5 minutes. Cut the cauliflower into pieces. Add to the pan and stir-fry for 5 minutes until lightly golden.
**3** Add the coconut stock, lime juice and soy sauce. Bring to the boil, cover and simmer gently for 10-15 minutes until the cauliflower is tender. Check the seasoning. Shred the spring onion and add to the soup with the coriander.
**4** Ladle into warmed soup bowls, drizzle over a little chilli or sesame oil and serve immediately.

**NOTE** If kaffir lime leaves are unobtainable, use the grated zest of 1 lime instead.

**VARIATION** Instead of the cauliflower, use 900 g (2 lb) mixed vegetables – such as carrots, potatoes and peas.

## SOUPE AU PISTOU

**SERVES 6-8**
PREPARATION
30 minutes, plus overnight soaking
COOKING TIME
About 1¾ hours
FREEZING
Not suitable
CALS/SERVING
480-360
COLOUR INDEX
Page 32

125 g (4 oz) dried haricot or black-eyed beans, soaked overnight in cold water
1 onion
1 leek, trimmed
2 carrots
175 g (6 oz) potatoes
350 g (12 oz) courgettes
450 g (1 lb) ripe tomatoes
125 g (4 oz) green beans
125 g (4 oz) fresh shelled peas (optional)
45 ml (3 tbsp) olive oil
few fresh thyme sprigs
2 bay leaves
75 g (3 oz) dried vermicelli
salt and pepper
PISTOU
25 g (1 oz) fresh basil leaves
4 garlic cloves, peeled
50 g (2 oz) Parmesan cheese, freshly grated
150 ml (¼ pint) extra-virgin olive oil
TO SERVE
freshly grated Parmesan or gruyère cheese

**1** Drain the beans and place in a saucepan. Cover with cold water and bring to the boil. Boil steadily for 10 minutes, then lower the heat, cover and simmer for about 45 minutes to 1 hour until almost tender. Drain.
**2** Peel and slice the onion; thinly slice the leek. Peel and finely dice the carrots and potatoes; dice the courgettes. Plunge the tomatoes into boiling water for 30 seconds, then remove, peel away the skins and dice the flesh. Cut the green beans into short lengths.
**3** Heat the oil in a large pan, add the onion and leek and cook gently for 10 minutes until beginning to soften. Add the cooked dried beans, carrots, potatoes and herbs. Pour in enough water to cover, about 1.2 litres (2 pints). Bring to the boil, cover and simmer for 30 minutes until the white beans begin to disintegrate.
**4** Meanwhile, make the pistou. Pound the basil, garlic and Parmesan in a pestle and mortar until paste-like, then gradually work in the olive oil, until amalgamated. Add salt and pepper to taste. (Alternatively, work the basil, garlic and Parmesan in a food processor until smooth then, with the motor running, add the olive oil in a steady stream through the feeder tube.) Transfer to a bowl.
**5** Add the green beans, courgettes, peas if using, tomatoes and broken vermicelli to the soup. Season with salt and pepper. Cook for a further 10-15 minutes, until all of the vegetables and the vermicella are very tender. Check the seasoning.
**6** Ladle the soup into warmed bowls and serve piping hot, accompanied by the pistou and cheese. Each guest adds pistou and cheese to their soup, according to taste.

## LETTUCE AND SORREL SOUP

**SERVES 4**
PREPARATION
15 minutes
COOKING TIME
20-25 minutes
FREEZING
Suitable
CALS/SERVING
205

6 spring onions, trimmed
450 g (1 lb) Cos lettuce, trimmed
125 g (4 oz) sorrel, trimmed
60 ml (4 tbsp) extra-virgin olive oil
1 garlic clove, peeled and crushed
5 ml (1 tsp) chopped fresh thyme (preferably lemon)
50 g (2 oz) long-grain rice
1.2 litres (2 pints) vegetable stock
30 ml (2 tbsp) chopped fresh chives
pinch of freshly grated nutmeg
salt and pepper
TO SERVE
Parmesan cheese shavings (optional)

**1** Slice the spring onions. Shred the lettuce and sorrel.
**2** Heat 15 ml (1 tbsp) of the oil in a saucepan, add the spring onions, garlic and thyme and fry gently for 5 minutes until softened but not coloured. Add the rice and stir-fry for 1 minute.
**3** Stir in the lettuce and sorrel, then pour in the stock. Bring to the boil, cover and simmer gently for 15 minutes until the rice is cooked.
**4** Transfer to a blender or food processor, add the chives and nutmeg and purée until smooth. Return the soup to the pan.
**5** Heat through, whisking in the remaining oil and seasoning with salt and pepper to taste. Serve hot, topped with a little Parmesan if preferred.

**VARIATIONS**
❑ For a more substantial soup, replace the rice with 225 g (8 oz) peeled, diced potatoes. Use 225 g (8 oz) lettuce.
❑ If sorrel is unobtainable, use spinach instead.

# MUSHROOM AND ARTICHOKE SOUP WITH WALNUTS

**SERVES 4**
PREPARATION
20 minutes, plus soaking
COOKING TIME
1½ hours
FREEZING
Suitable
CALS/SERVING
250
COLOUR INDEX
Page 33

15 g (½ oz) dried ceps
150 ml (¼ pint) boiling water
1 small onion, peeled
450 g (1 lb) chestnut mushrooms
25 g (1 oz) butter or margarine
15 ml (1 tbsp) chopped fresh thyme
90 ml (3 fl oz) dry sherry
1.2 litres (2 pints) vegetable stock
450 g (1 lb) Jerusalem artichokes
1 garlic clove
30 ml (2 tbsp) walnut oil
salt and pepper
TO SERVE
25 g (1 oz) walnuts, chopped and toasted
a little extra walnut oil
thyme sprigs, to garnish

**1** Put the dried ceps into a bowl, pour over the boiling water and let soak for 30 minutes. Drain, reserving the liquid, and chop finely.
**2** Chop the onion and chestnut mushrooms. Melt the butter in a saucepan, add the onion and thyme and fry gently for 10 minutes until soft but not browned. Increase the heat, add the chestnut mushrooms and ceps and stir-fry for 2 minutes. Add the sherry and boil rapidly until well reduced.
**3** Add the vegetable stock and reserved cep stock and bring to the boil. Cover and simmer gently for 20 minutes until the stock is rich tasting and the mushrooms have lost all their flavour.
**4** Meanwhile, scrub the artichokes thoroughly. Peel, then dice the flesh. Peel and chop the garlic. Heat the oil in a large pan, add the artichokes and garlic and fry for 10 minutes, stirring, until evenly browned.
**5** Strain the mushroom liquid through a fine sieve and add to the artichokes. Bring to the boil, cover and simmer for 35-40 minutes until the artichokes are cooked. Transfer to a blender or food processor and purée until very smooth.
**6** Return the soup to the pan and heat through. Season with salt and pepper to taste and spoon into warmed soup bowls. Scatter the toasted nuts over the soup and drizzle with walnut oil. Serve at once, garnished with thyme.

**NOTE** It is essential that the mushrooms impart their full flavour to the stock. Before straining the stock, check that they are quite tasteless.

**VARIATION** Stir 150 ml (¼ pint) single cream into the puréed artichokes at the end of stage 5. Finish as above.

# MUSHROOM TOM YAM

**SERVES 4**
PREPARATION
35 minutes
COOKING TIME
35-40 minutes
FREEZING
Suitable
CALS/SERVING
80

25 g (1 oz) dried shiitake mushrooms
150 ml (¼ pint) boiling water
2 shallots
2 small red chillies
30 ml (2 tbsp) groundnut oil
2 garlic cloves, peeled and crushed
2 ripe tomatoes
30 ml (2 tbsp) lemon juice
5 ml (1 tsp) sugar
1.2 litres (2 pints) vegetable stock
1 lemon grass stalk, finely diced
4 kaffir lime leaves, finely shredded or grated zest of 1 lime
225 g (8 oz) oyster or button mushrooms, sliced
15 ml (1 tbsp) light soy sauce
30 ml (2 tbsp) chopped fresh coriander

**1** Put the dried mushrooms in a bowl, pour on the boiling water and set aside to soak for 20 minutes. Strain and reserve the liquid; chop and reserve the mushrooms.
**2** Meanwhile, peel and finely chop the shallots. Deseed and chop the chillies. Heat the oil in a saucepan, add the shallots, chillies and garlic and fry gently for 5 minutes. Chop the tomatoes and add to the pan with the lemon juice and sugar. Fry for a further 5 minutes until the tomatoes are soft and pulpy.
**3** Pour in the stock and reserved mushroom liquid, then add the lemon grass and lime leaves. Bring to the boil, cover and simmer for 20 minutes.
**4** Add the soaked shiitake, fresh mushrooms and soy sauce. Return to the boil and simmer gently for a further 5-10 minutes until the mushrooms are tender. Stir in the coriander and serve at once.

# CREAMY PEA AND FLAGEOLET SOUP WITH MINT CREAM

**SERVES 6**
PREPARATION
20 minutes
COOKING TIME
35 minutes
FREEZING
Suitable
CALS/SERVING
245

2 leeks, trimmed
2 celery sticks, trimmed
1 large potato
30 ml (2 tbsp) olive oil
2 garlic cloves, peeled and crushed
15 ml (1 tbsp) chopped fresh thyme
1.2 litres (2 pints) vegetable stock
225 g (8 oz) fresh or frozen peas (see note)
400 g (14 oz) can flageolet beans
salt and pepper
MINT CREAM
30 ml (2 tbsp) chopped fresh mint
15 ml (1 tbsp) boiling water
120 ml (4 fl oz) double cream
TO GARNISH
mint sprigs

**1** First make the mint cream. Put the mint in a bowl, pour on the boiling water and set aside until cool. Drain the mint and mix with the cream. Season with salt and pepper to taste. Cover and set aside.

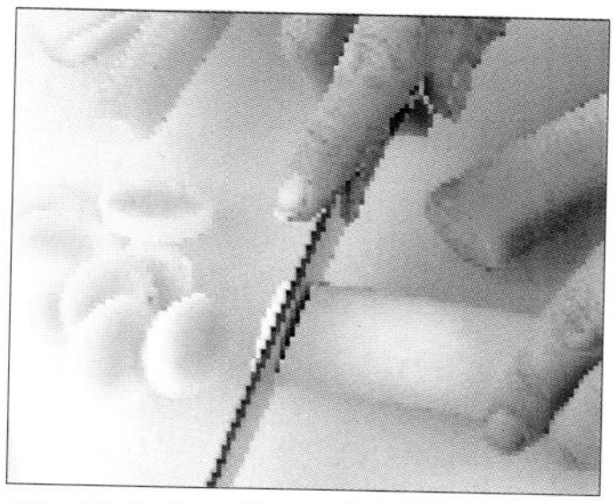

**2** Thinly slice the leeks and celery; peel and dice the potato. Heat the oil in a large saucepan, add the leeks, celery and garlic and fry gently for 5 minutes until softened.

**3** Stir in the potato and thyme and fry for a further 5 minutes until beginning to colour. Add the stock and bring to the boil. Cover and simmer for 15 minutes.

**4** Stir in the peas and flageolet beans together with their liquid. Return to the boil and cook, covered, for a further 10 minutes.

**5** Let cool slightly, then purée the soup in a blender or food processor until very smooth.

**6** Return the soup to the pan and heat through gently. Check the seasoning. Serve topped with a swirl of mint cream and garnish with mint sprigs.

**NOTE** If using fresh peas in the pod you will need about 675 g (1½ lb) to give this podded weight.

**VARIATION** Replace the peas with fresh or frozen broad beans. Substitute the mint with chopped fresh dill.

# POTATO AND GARLIC SOUP WITH WATERCRESS

**SERVES 4-6**
PREPARATION
30 minutes
COOKING TIME
30 minutes
FREEZING
Suitable
CALS/SERVING
195-130

- 1 onion, peeled
- 1 leek, trimmed
- 2 celery sticks, trimmed
- 1 small garlic bulb
- 350 g (12 oz) new potatoes
- 60 ml (4 tbsp) extra-virgin olive oil
- 15 ml (1 tbsp) chopped fresh sage
- 1.2 litres (2 pints) vegetable stock
- 125 g (4 oz) watercress, trimmed
- 15 ml (1 tbsp) lemon juice
- 30 ml (2 tbsp) chopped mixed fresh herbs, such as chervil, basil, chives and parsley

TO SERVE
- 4-6 slices French bread, toasted
- mayonnaise (optional)
- chives, to garnish

**1** Roughly chop the onion, leek and celery. Separate and peel the garlic cloves. Scrub and dice the new potatoes.

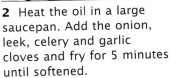

**2** Heat the oil in a large saucepan. Add the onion, leek, celery and garlic cloves and fry for 5 minutes until softened.

**3** Add the potatoes and sage and fry gently for a further 5 minutes. Add the stock and bring to the boil. Cover and simmer for 20 minutes until the vegetables are cooked.

**4** Meanwhile, remove and discard any thick stalks from the watercress, then roughly chop the leaves.

**5** Transfer the soup to a blender or food processor. Add the watercress, lemon juice and mixed herbs and blend until very smooth.

**6** Return to the pan, season with salt and pepper to taste and heat through.
Ladle into warmed bowls and top each serving with a slice of toast and a spoonful of mayonnaise if desired. Garnish with chives.

**VARIATION** To transform this into a delightful winter soup use orange-fleshed sweet potatoes; alternatively ordinary winter potatoes will suffice.

# VICHYSSOISE WITH LEMON GRASS

**SERVES 6**
PREPARATION
15 minutes
COOKING TIME
30 minutes
FREEZING
Suitable: Stage 4
CALS/SERVING
225
COLOUR INDEX
Page 33

- 2 onions
- 450 g (1 lb) leeks (white part only), trimmed
- 175 g (6 oz) floury potatoes
- 1 lemon grass stalk (preferably fresh)
- 75 g (3 oz) butter
- 1.35 litres (2¼ pints) vegetable stock
- 300 ml (½ pint) milk
- 150 ml (¼ pint) crème fraîche
- salt and white pepper

TO SERVE
- extra crème fraîche
- chives, to garnish

**1** Peel and thinly slice the onions. Slice the leeks. Peel and dice the potatoes. Bruise the lemon grass by striking it firmly with the end of a rolling pin to release the flavour.
**2** Melt the butter in a large saucepan and add the onions and leeks. Stir well, add 45 ml (3 tbsp) water, cover tightly

nd sweat over a gentle heat for 10 minutes until soft and olden.

Stir in the potatoes, lemon grass, stock and milk. Bring ɔ the boil, lower the heat, cover and simmer for about 0 minutes until the potatoes are tender.

Discard the lemon grass. Allow the soup to cool slightly, nen transfer to a blender or food processor and work until mooth. Pass through a sieve and return to the pan if erving hot.

Stir in the crème fraîche and seasoning to taste. Either ool and chill (in this case season really well) or reheat and our into warmed soup bowls. Serve topped with a dollop f crème fraîche and chives.

**IOTE** Fresh lemon grass is sold in the herb section of ome supermarkets. Alternatively use dried lemon grass.

**'ARIATION** Replace the leeks with a bunch of spring nions, and add a bunch of trimmed and chopped vatercress to the soup just before liquidising.

## CHILLED BEETROOT AND APPLE SOUP

**ERVES 4**
REPARATION
0 minutes
REEZING
ot suitable
ALS/SERVING
50
OLOUR INDEX
age 34

350 g (12 oz) cooked, peeled beetroot
juice of ½ lemon
600 ml (1 pint) unsweetened apple juice, chilled
200 g (7 oz) Greek-style yogurt, chilled
cayenne pepper, to taste
salt and pepper
10 cm (4 inch) piece cucumber
6 fresh mint leaves
6-8 fresh chives
TO SERVE
chives and mint sprigs, to garnish
grissini bread sticks

Slice the beetroot and place in a food processor or lender. Add the lemon juice, half the apple juice and half ne yogurt. Process for 1-2 minutes until smooth.

Pour the beetroot mixture into a mixing bowl, stir in the est of the apple juice and season with cayenne, salt and epper to taste. Chill until ready to serve, then pour into ndividual soup bowls.

To make the cucumber cream, grate the cucumber and tir into the remaining yogurt. Chop the mint and stir into ne mixture. Spoon some cucumber cream into the middle f each serving and sprinkle with a little cayenne pepper. nip some chives over the top and garnish with mint. Serve t once, accompanied by the bread sticks.

**'ARIATION** For the cucumber cream, use crème fraîche nstead of yogurt.

## TOMATO AND BREAD SOUP WITH BASIL

**SERVES 4**
PREPARATION
15 minutes
COOKING TIME
25 minutes
FREEZING
Suitable
CALS/SERVING
325

1 large onion
3 garlic cloves
900 g (2 lb) ripe tomatoes
90 ml (6 tbsp) extra-virgin olive oil
600 ml (1 pint) vegetable stock
5 ml (1 tsp) sugar
175 g (6 oz) day-old country-style Italian or French bread
15-30 ml (1-2 tbsp) balsamic or red wine vinegar
120 ml (4 fl oz) water
30 ml (2 tbsp) chopped fresh basil
salt and pepper
TO SERVE
extra-virgin olive oil
Parmesan cheese shavings (optional)
basil sprigs

**1** Peel and finely chop the onion and garlic; roughly chop the tomatoes. Heat half the oil in a saucepan, add the onion and garlic and fry for 5 minutes until softened.
**2** Add the tomatoes, stir-fry for 1 minute, then add the stock and sugar. Bring to the boil, cover and simmer for 20 minutes.
**3** Meanwhile, cut the bread into cubes and place in a large bowl. Mix the vinegar with the water and remaining oil. Pour over the bread and toss well until all the bread is slightly moistened.
**4** Using a blender or food processor, purée the soup with the bread, in 2-3 batches, until smooth. Return the soup to the pan. Add the chopped basil and seasoning to taste. Heat through; the soup should be thick.
**5** To serve, divide the soup between warmed bowls and top each portion with a drizzle of olive oil, shavings of Parmesan if wished, and a basil sprig.

**NOTE** This soup is best made during the summer months when good ripe tomatoes are plentiful and cheap. In the winter use canned plum tomatoes rather than flavourless fresh ones: you will need two 400 g (14 oz) cans.

# CHILLED TOMATO SOUP WITH AVOCADO CREAM

**SERVES 6**
PREPARATION
20 minutes, plus chilling
FREEZING
Suitable: Soup only
CALS/SERVING
145

1.4 kg (3 lb) ripe red tomatoes
750 ml (1¼ pints) tomato juice
pinch of sugar
dash of Tabasco
15 ml (1 tbsp) lemon juice
30 ml (2 tbsp) chopped fresh mint
salt and pepper

AVOCADO CREAM
1 large ripe avocado
10-15 ml (2-3 tsp) lemon juice
½ small onion
30 ml (2 tbsp) chopped fresh mint
90 ml (6 tbsp) soured cream
TO GARNISH
mint sprigs

**1** Halve the tomatoes, then squeeze out the seeds into a bowl. Reserve 4 tomato halves and cut into fine dice; cover and refrigerate. Strain the tomato seeds through a small sieve to extract any juices; discard the seeds.
**2** Place the remaining tomatoes in a blender or food processor with the tomato juice, sugar, Tabasco, lemon juice, chopped mint and salt and pepper to taste. Process until smooth, then pass through a sieve into a clean bowl. Taste and adjust the seasoning.
**3** Cover and chill in the refrigerator for at least 2 hours.
**4** About 20 minutes before serving, halve the avocado, remove the stone, then peel. Mash the avocado flesh in a bowl, using a fork, adding lemon juice to taste. Peel and finely grate the onion and mix into the avocado with the chopped mint and soured cream.
**5** Stir the reserved diced tomato into the chilled soup. Ladle the soup into serving bowls and add a dollop of the avocado cream to each one. Garnish with mint to serve.

**VARIATION** Substitute fresh basil for the mint. Dice the avocado and stir into the soup, leaving out the grated onion. Serve topped with spoonfuls of soured cream.

# GAZPACHO

**SERVES 6-8**
PREPARATION
25 minutes, plus chilling time
FREEZING
Suitable: Stage 4
CALS/SERVING
310-230
COLOUR INDEX
Page 34

700 g (1½ lb) flavourful ripe tomatoes
1 cucumber
1 red pepper
1 green pepper
1 red chilli
3 garlic cloves
225 g (8 oz) fresh wholemeal bread crumbs
15 ml (1 tbsp) tomato paste
60 ml (4 tbsp) wine vinegar
90 ml (6 tbsp) olive oil
10 ml (2 tsp) salt
pepper
600 ml (1 pint) water
TO SERVE
chopped cucumber
red and green pepper slices
chopped hard-boiled egg (optional)
chopped red or mild onion
ice cubes
croûtons (see below)

**1** Immerse the tomatoes in a bowl of boiling water, then drain, refresh under cold running water and peel away the skins. Roughly chop the tomato flesh. Peel the cucumber and chop the flesh.
**2** Halve, core and deseed the peppers and chilli, then chop roughly. Peel and chop the garlic.
**3** Put the prepared vegetables and garlic into a large bowl. Add the breadcrumbs, tomato paste, wine vinegar, olive oil, salt and pepper to taste. Stir thoroughly.
**4** Transfer half of the soup to a blender or food processor. Add about 300 ml (½ pint) water and process until fairly smooth. Transfer to a large serving bowl. Purée the remaining half of the soup mixture with another 300 ml (½ pint) water. Add to the puréed soup and stir well. Adjust the seasoning to taste. Cover and chill in the refrigerator for at least 2 hours.
**5** To serve, put the garnishes in separate small bowls. Add a little ice to the gazpacho and serve accompanied by the garnishes.

**CROUTONS** Cut 3-4 thick slices of day-old white bread into 2.5 cm (1 inch) squares. Fry in butter and/or oil, turning constantly, until crisp and golden. Drain on kitchen paper.

# CHILLED MELON AND GINGER SOUP

**ERVES 4**
REPARATION
5 minutes,
lus chilling
REEZING
uitable:
ithout relish
ALS/SERVING
85

4 small Charentais or Cantaloupe melons
4 spring onions, trimmed
60 ml (2 fl oz) ginger wine
15 ml (1 tbsp) chopped fresh dill
150 ml (¼ pint) crème fraîche
salt and pepper
lime juice, to taste

CUCUMBER RELISH
125 g (4 oz) cucumber
15 ml (1 tbsp) extra-virgin olive oil
5 ml (1 tsp) lime juice
15 ml (1 tbsp) chopped fresh dill
5-10 ml (1-2 tsp) chopped stem ginger in syrup
TO GARNISH
extra-virgin olive oil
dill sprigs

Cut a sliver from the ase of each melon so it vill stand upright, then cut slice off the top. Scoop ut and discard the seeds ver a sieve, reserving the uices. Scoop out the flesh. eep the melon shells for erving, if wished.

**2** Purée the melon flesh in a blender or food processor with the spring onions, ginger wine, dill and crème fraîche, then blend in enough of the reserved melon juice to give a good consistency. Season and add a little lime juice to taste. Chill for 1 hour.

**3** Meanwhile, make the cucumber relish. Peel and halve the cucumber, scoop out the seeds and very thinly slice the flesh. Sprinkle with salt and set aside for 30 minutes.

**4** Wash the cucumber to remove the salt and pat dry on kitchen paper. Place in a bowl and stir in the remaining ingredients, seasoning with pepper to taste.

**5** Divide the soup between the reserved melon shells or soup bowls and top each portion with a little of the cucumber relish. Drizzle over a little extra-virgin olive oil and serve garnished with dill.

# CHILLED AVOCADO AND LIME SOUP

**SERVES 4**
PREPARATION
5-10 minutes, plus chilling
COOKING TIME
20 minutes
FREEZING
Not suitable
CALS/SERVING
235
COLOUR INDEX
Page 34

1 bunch of spring onions, trimmed
15 ml (1 tbsp) extra-virgin olive oil
225 g (8 oz) potato
900 ml (1½ pints) vegetable stock
2 ripe avocados
juice of 1-2 limes
salt and pepper
30 ml (2 tbsp) crème fraîche
TO SERVE
60 ml (4 tbsp) crème fraîche
few snipped chives
shredded lemon zest, to garnish

**1** Finely slice the spring onions. Heat the oil in a large saucepan, add the spring onions and fry gently until softened.
**2** Meanwhile, peel and dice the potato. Add to the spring onions and fry, stirring, for 2 minutes. Add the stock and bring to the boil. Cover and simmer for 15-20 minutes.
**3** Halve, stone and peel the avocados, then chop roughly. Add to the soup with the juice of 1 lime. Check the seasoning, adding extra lime juice if required.
**4** Let the soup cool slightly, then transfer to a blender or food processor and work until smooth. Transfer to a bowl, then stir in the crème fraîche. Cover and chill in the refrigerator for 3-4 hours; the soup will thicken as it chills.
**5** To serve, pour into soup bowls and add a swirl of crème fraîche. Sprinkle with pepper and garnish with snipped chives and lime zest. Serve with Melba toast or bread rolls.

# PASTA

# BASIC PASTA DOUGH

Pasta dough can either be made by hand, in a food processor with a dough attachment, or in a large mixer with a dough hook. Initially it is probably best to make the dough by hand to learn how the dough should feel at each stage. The more you make fresh pasta the easier it will be to judge the correct texture of the dough – it should be soft, not at all sticky, and with a good elasticity.

The best type of flour to use for making pasta is a very fine-textured soft wheat flour "type 00" or *"farino tipo 00"*, available from Italian delicatessens and some larger supermarkets. Strong plain flour can be used as a substitute if necessary, but you may need to adjust the water slightly.

This recipe makes sufficient pasta to serve 4 as a main course, accompanied by a side salad and bread.

**SERVES 4**
PREPARATION
5 minutes, plus kneading
COOKING TIME
1-2 minutes
CALS/SERVING
285

225 g (8 oz) type "00" pasta flour, plus extra for dusting
5 ml (1 tsp) salt
2 medium eggs, plus 1 egg yolk, beaten
15 ml (1 tbsp) extra-virgin olive oil
15-30 ml (1-2 tbsp) cold water

**1** Sift the flour and salt into a mound on a clean work surface. Make a well in the centre and add the eggs, egg yolk, oil and 15 ml (1 tbsp) water.

**2** Using a fork, gently beat the eggs together, then gradually work in the flour, adding a little extra water if necessary to form a soft but not sticky dough.

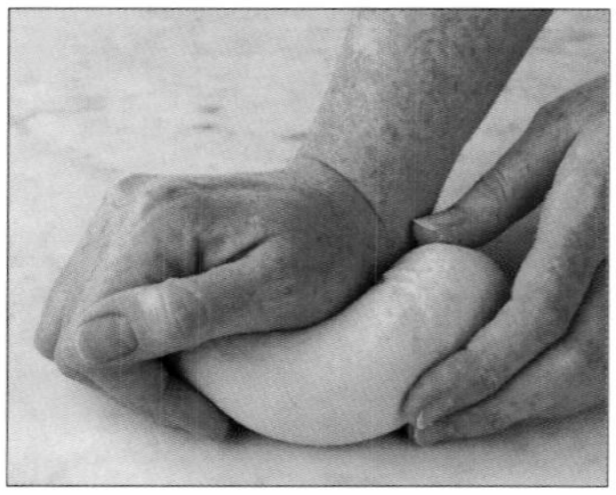

**3** Transfer to a lightly floured surface and knead for about 5 minutes until the dough is firm, smooth and elastic. Form into a flattish ball, wrap in cling film and leave to rest in the refrigerator for at least 30 minutes.

USING A FOOD PROCESSOR Sift the flour and salt into the processor bowl and add the eggs, egg yolk, oil and 15 ml (1 tbsp) water (together with any flavourings). Process just until the dough begins to come together, adding the extra water if necessary to form a soft but not sticky dough. Wrap in cling film and rest (as above).

**VARIATIONS** The choice of flavoured pastas is endless. Fresh herbs such as basil, rosemary and dill are particularly good. Vegetable purées, such as beetroot and spinach, and flavoured pastes, like sun-dried tomato and olive, produce vibrant coloured pastas which have a delicious flavour. Note that some of the colour will be lost during cooking, without detriment to the flavour.

FRESH HERB PASTA Sift the flour and salt into the bowl and stir in 45 ml (3 tbsp) freshly chopped mixed herbs, such as tarragon, marjoram and parsley. Continue as above.

GARLIC AND BASIL PASTA Sift the flour and salt into a bowl, stir in 15 g (½ oz) freshly chopped basil and 1 small crushed garlic clove. Continue as above.

LEMON PASTA Sift the flour and salt into a bowl, then stir in the grated zest of 2 unwaxed lemons. Continue as above, replacing the water with 30 ml (2 tbsp) lemon juice.

SAFFRON PASTA Sift the flour and salt into a bowl and stir in 5 ml (1 tsp) saffron strands. Continue as above.

OLIVE PASTA Beat the eggs with 30 ml (2 tbsp) black olive paste before adding to the flour. Reduce the water to about 10 ml (2 tsp).

SUN-DRIED TOMATO PASTA Beat the eggs with 30 ml (2 tbsp) sun-dried tomato paste before adding to the flour. Reduce the water to about 10 ml (2 tsp).

BLACK PEPPERCORN PASTA Sift the flour and salt into a bowl. Roughly grind 10 ml (2 tsp) black peppercorns using a pestle and mortar or spice grinder. Stir into the flour and continue as above.

BUCKWHEAT PASTA Sift 150 g (5 oz) "00" pasta flour and the salt into a bowl, then stir in 75 g (3 oz) buckwheat flour. Increase the amount of water to 30-45 ml (2-3 tbsp) and continue to work in the remaining ingredients, as above.

SPINACH PASTA Blanch 50 g (2 oz) spinach leaves until wilted. Refresh under cold water, drain and squeeze out all excess water, then chop finely. Add to the flour and salt, together with the remaining ingredients. Continue as above.

## ROLLING OUT USING A PASTA MACHINE

Aost pasta machines work in the same way and this nethod should therefore apply, but do refer to the nanufacturer's instructions for your particular model.

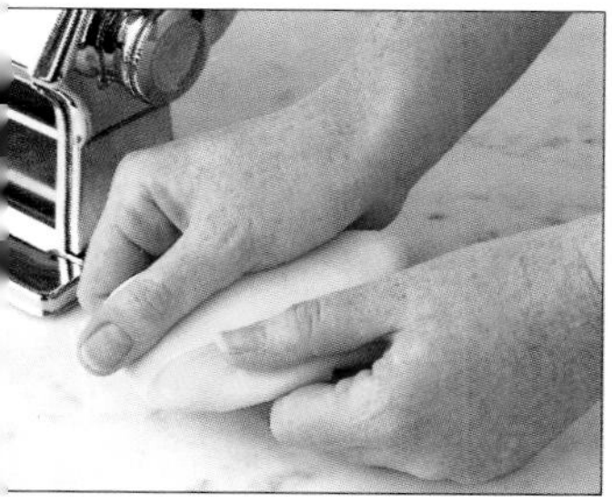

Divide the rested dough nto 4 equal pieces; re-wrap ll but one in cling film to revent it from drying out. latten the piece slightly, so hat it will fit through the asta machine. With the ollers at the widest setting, ass the pasta through.

**2** Fold the strip of dough in three, rotate and pass through the machine on this widest setting once more. The dough should now be smooth and of an even thickness.

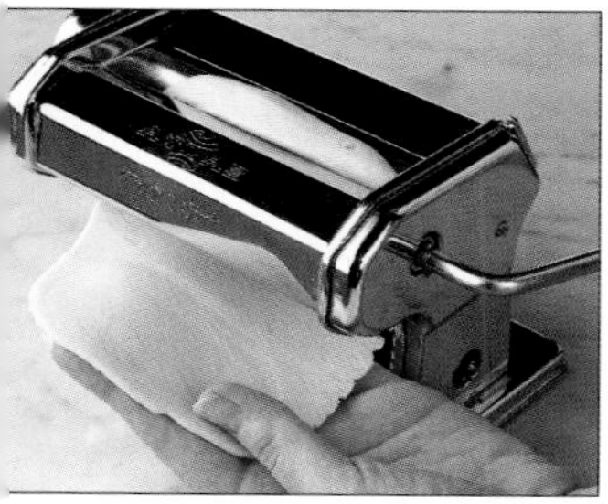

Continue to pass the asta through the machine n this way, narrowing the oller setting by one notch ach time, and flouring the ough a little if it starts to eel sticky. Guide it through ne machine with your ands; do not pull or the ough may drag and tear.

**4** Pass the dough just once through the final setting to form a long thin sheet. For spaghetti and tagliatelle, the last but one setting is generally used. For filled pastas, such as ravioli, use the finest setting. Repeat process with remaining dough to form 4 sheets.

## ALLOWING PASTA TO DRY

making filled pasta, the dough should be used straight way, while it is a little sticky – to enable it to adhere.

Otherwise, drape the sheet of pasta over a wooden pole or pasta dryer and leave to dry slightly, for 3-5 minutes; this makes it easier to cut and prevents the pasta from sticking together. Alternatively, lay on a clean tea-towel for 5-10 minutes.

## ROLLING PASTA DOUGH BY HAND

**1** Divide the dough into 4 equal pieces; re-wrap all except one piece in cling film to prevent it from drying out. Roll out on a clean surface to a 5 mm (¼ inch) thickness.

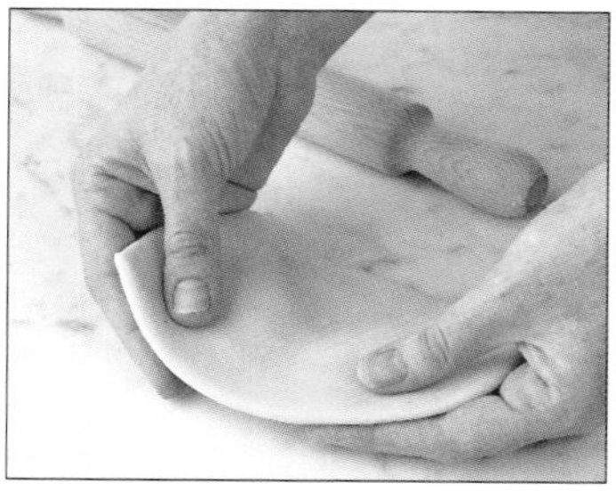

**2** Lift the dough from the surface and rotate 45°. The dough should cling slightly (not stick) to the surface; this helps the stretching process.

**3** Continue rolling, lifting and rotating until the dough is very thin, about 30 cm (12 inches) square. The dough should be so thin that you could almost read print through it!
Repeat process with remaining dough to form 4 sheets. Leave to dry if necessary (see left).

## SHAPING PASTA

For lasagne, simply trim the pasta sheets to neaten and cut into lengths according to the size of your lasagne dish. For instructions on shaping ravioli and tortellini see individual recipes.

## CUTTING NOODLES BY MACHINE

If using a pasta machine, fit the tagliatelle or linguine cutters, as required.

Pass one sheet of dough through the cutters. Transfer to a floured tea-towel or hang the noodles over a pole or pasta dryer. Repeat with the remaining pasta sheets. The noodles are now ready to cook.

## CUTTING NOODLES BY HAND

Broad pappardelle can be cut directly from the flat square of pasta, using a pasta wheel. Alternatively you will find the following technique very easy.

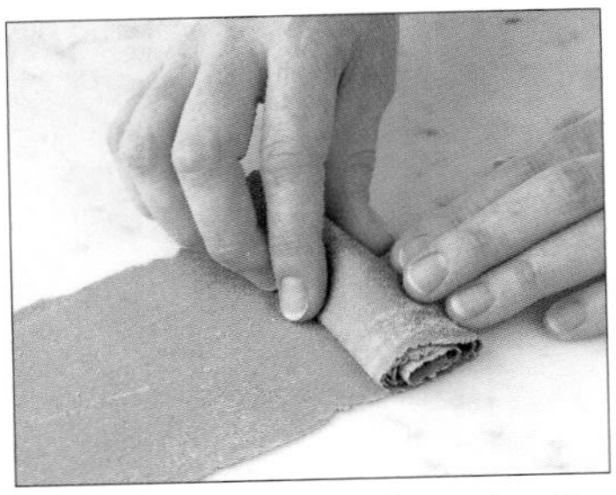

**1** Flour the dough and roll up loosely into a Swiss roll.

**2** Using a sharp knife, cut into slices, the thickness depending on the noodles required. For linguine, cut 5 mm (¼ inch) slices; for tagliatelle cut 8 mm (⅓ inch) slices; for pappardelle, cut 2 cm (¾ inch) slices.

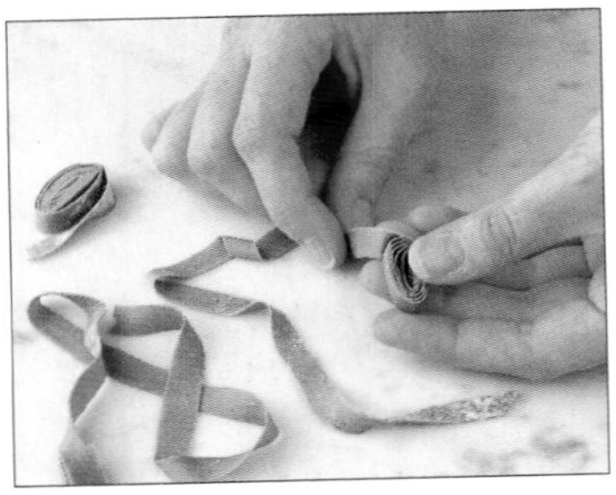

**3** Unravel the noodles and curl into 'nests' onto a floured tea towel.

## COOKING FRESH PASTA

It is essential to cook pasta in plenty of boiling water to ensure that the pasta has room to move around in the water and doesn't stick together. For the quantity of pasta in the basic recipe you will need at least 2.5 litres (4 pints) water. Add 10 ml (2 tsp) sea salt to the water, bring to a rolling boil, add the pasta, return to the boil and cook, with the water at a fast simmer. Fresh pasta is so thin that it will only take about 1-2 minutes to cook. Stuffed pasta shapes such as ravioli need about 3 minutes to enable the filling to cook through.

As soon as the pasta is cooked, turn into a colander or large strainer over the sink, shake off excess water, then immediately add to the sauce or vegetables. When serving pasta with an oily sauce, hold back a few tablespoons of the cooking water to add to the sauce with the noodles; this transforms the oiliness into a glossy coating sauce.

# PENNE WITH BROCCOLI PESTO

**SERVES 4**
PREPARATION
10 minutes
COOKING TIME
30 minutes
FREEZING
Not suitable
CALS/SERVING
535

- 700 g (1½ lb) broccoli
- 2 garlic cloves
- salt and pepper
- 60 ml (4 tbsp) olive oil
- 350 g (12 oz) dried penne or other pasta shapes
- 45 ml (3 tbsp) lemon juice
- 150 ml (¼ pint) double cream
- 15 g (½ oz) Parmesan cheese, freshly grated

TO SERVE
- Pesto (see page 292)
- basil leaves, to garnish
- pickled red chillies (optional)

**1** Trim the thick base of the broccoli stalks, then slice the stalks and divide the tops into small florets. Peel and chop the garlic.
**2** Cook the broccoli in a pan of boiling salted water for 5-6 minutes until tender. Drain, reserving 50 ml (2 fl oz) cooking liquor. Refresh the broccoli in cold water; drain well.
**3** Heat the olive oil in a medium pan, add the chopped garlic and cook for 1-2 minutes until softened. Stir in the broccoli and cook over a medium heat for about 15 minutes, stirring all the time, until the broccoli is reduced to a thick pulp.
**4** Meanwhile, cook the pasta in a large pan of boiling salted water until *al dente*. Drain well.

Stir the lemon juice and cream into the broccoli mixture d simmer gently for a further 3-4 minutes. Thin the sauce the consistency of single cream with some of the served cooking liquor. Stir in the Parmesan and season nerously.
Toss the pasta with the broccoli pesto. Serve mediately, with a little classic pesto spooned over. rnish with basil leaves and pickled chillies if using.

## SPAGHETTI WITH COURGETTES, LEMON AND PISTACHIO NUTS

**RVES 4**
PARATION
minutes
OKING TIME
minutes
EZING
suitable
S/SERVING
)
OUR INDEX
e 35

600 g (1¼ lb) courgettes (preferably mixed green and yellow ones), trimmed
2 garlic cloves, peeled
1 small red chilli
350 g (12 oz) dried spaghetti
90 ml (6 tbsp) extra-virgin olive oil
grated zest and juice of 2 lemons
30 ml (2 tbsp) chopped fresh chives
salt and pepper
TO SERVE
50 g (2 oz) toasted pistachio nuts, finely chopped
Parmesan cheese shavings (optional)
extra-virgin olive oil (optional)

Thinly slice the courgettes and garlic; deseed and finely op the chilli.
Cook the spaghetti in a large saucepan of boiling salted ater until *al dente*.
Meanwhile, heat the oil in a large frying pan. Add the urgettes, garlic, chilli and lemon zest and stir-fry over a gh heat for 4-5 minutes until the courgettes are golden. move from the heat and add the lemon juice.
Drain the pasta and add to the courgettes with the ives. Season with salt and pepper and toss over a low at for 30 seconds.
Divide the spaghetti between warmed serving plates and p each portion with toasted pistachios. Top with Parmesan avings and drizzle with a little olive oil if wished.

**OTE** During the summer months look out for vibrant llow courgettes. They have the same flavour as the miliar green ones, and the two colours combine to make is a stunning dish.

**ARIATION** Replace the pistachios with pine nuts.

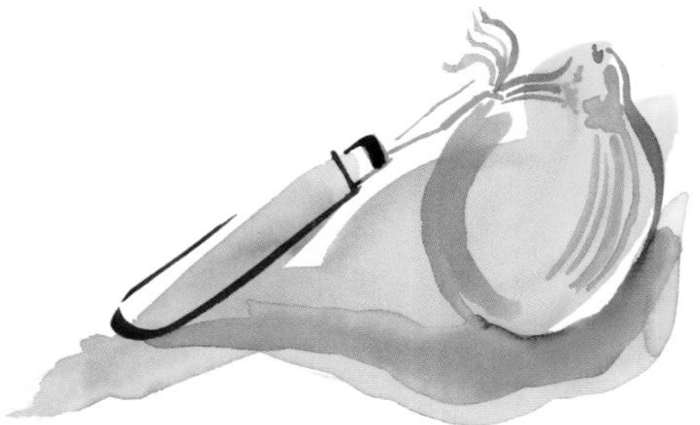

## FETTUCINE WITH GORGONZOLA AND SPINACH

**SERVES 4-6**
PREPARATION
15 minutes
COOKING TIME
2-10 minutes
FREEZING
Not suitable
CALS/SERVING
630-420

350 g (12 oz) young leaf spinach, trimmed
400 g (14 oz) fresh or dried fettucine, tagliatelle or long fusilli
salt and pepper
225 g (8 oz) gorgonzola cheese
90 ml (3 fl oz) milk
25 g (1 oz) butter
freshly grated nutmeg, to taste

**1** Place the spinach in a saucepan with just the water clinging to the leaves after washing and cook, stirring, over a medium high heat for 2-3 minutes until wilted. Drain well in a colander or sieve, pressing out any excess liquid.
**2** Cook the pasta in a large pan of boiling salted water until *al dente*.
**3** Meanwhile, dice the gorgonzola and place in a clean pan with the milk and butter. Heat gently, stirring, until melted to a creamy sauce. Stir in the drained spinach. Season to taste with pepper; it shouldn't be necessary to add salt.
**4** Drain the pasta and add to the sauce. Toss well to mix. Serve at once, sprinkled with a little nutmeg.

**VARIATION** For a milder alternative, use dolcelatte rather than gorgonzola cheese.

## TAGLIATELLE WITH BROAD BEANS, CHICORY AND CREAM

**SERVES 4-6**
PREPARATION
25 minutes
COOKING TIME
10 minutes
FREEZING
Not suitable
CALS/SERVING
880-590
COLOUR INDEX
Page 35

350 g (12 oz) frozen broad beans, thawed
1 onion
40 g (1½ oz) butter
400 g (14 oz) dried tagliatelle
2 heads of chicory, total weight about 200 g (7 oz)
45 ml (3 tbsp) chopped fresh parsley or chervil
300 ml (½ pint) extra-thick double cream
60 ml (4 tbsp) freshly grated Parmesan cheese
salt and pepper
TO SERVE
chervil or parsley sprigs
Parmesan cheese shavings

**1** Squeeze the broad beans out of their waxy skins and put into a bowl; set aside. Peel and finely chop the onion.
**2** Melt the butter in a large frying pan. Add the onion and cook over a medium heat for 5-6 minutes until soft.
**3** Cook the pasta in a large pan of boiling salted water until *al dente.*
**4** Meanwhile slice the chicory. Add the broad beans to the onion in the frying pan and continue cooking for 2 minutes, then stir in the chicory slices and parsley or chervil. Cook for a further 2 minutes, then stir in the cream. Bring to the boil and add the Parmesan and seasoning to taste.
**5** Drain the pasta and transfer to a warmed serving dish. Add the sauce and toss to mix. Serve at once, sprinkled with herbs and shavings of Parmesan.

## SICILIAN AUBERGINE AND RICOTTA PASTA

**SERVES 4-6**
PREPARATION
15 minutes
COOKING TIME
35 minutes
FREEZING
Not suitable
CALS/SERVING
870-580
COLOUR INDEX
Page 35

2 medium thin aubergines
450 g (1 lb) dried penne or pasta shells
salt and pepper
light olive oil, for shallow-frying
600 ml (1 pint) Tomato Sauce (see page 291)
30-45 ml (2-3 tbsp) shredded fresh basil leaves
225 g (8 oz) ricotta cheese, crumbled
basil leaves, to garnish

**1** Slice the aubergines thinly.
**2** Cook the pasta in a large pan of boiling salted water until *al dente.*
**3** Meanwhile, heat the oil in a deep frying pan. When hot, shallow-fry the aubergines in batches until golden. Drain well on kitchen paper. Reheat the tomato sauce.
**4** Drain the pasta, then add the tomato sauce, basil and half of the ricotta. Toss well and transfer to a warmed serving bowl. Arrange the aubergine slices on top, sprinkle over the remaining ricotta and serve, garnished with basil.

## PASTA PRIMAVERA

**SERVES 4-6**
PREPARATION
25 minutes
COOKING TIME
About 25 minutes
FREEZING
Not suitable
CALS/SERVING
950-635
COLOUR INDEX
Page 35

1 red pepper
175 g (6 oz) thin asparagus
salt and pepper
125 g (4 oz) sugar snap peas, trimmed
225 g (8 oz) carrots (preferably baby ones)
1 small onion
2 celery stalks
2 courgettes
6-8 spring onions (white part only)
50 g (2 oz) butter
400 g (14 oz) dried tagliatelle or pappardelle
300 ml (½ pint) double cream
60 ml (4 tbsp) freshly grated Parmesan cheese
15 ml (1 tbsp) oil
20 ml (4 tsp) snipped chives
20 ml (4 tsp) chopped fresh chervil
20 ml (4 tsp) chopped fresh dill

**1** Grill the pepper, turning occasionally, until the skin is blistered all over. Place in a covered dish until cool enough to handle, then skin, core, deseed and dice.
**2** Halve the asparagus spears and cook in boiling salted water for 3-4 minutes, adding the sugar snaps after 2 minutes so that both are cooked until just tender. Drain, refresh with cold water and drain again; set aside.
**3** If the carrots are tiny baby ones, leave whole; otherwise peel and cut into matchsticks. Peel and chop the onion; trim and dice the celery, courgettes and spring onions.
**4** Melt the butter in a large frying pan. Add the onion and sauté over a medium heat for 7-8 minutes until soft and golden. Add the red pepper and celery and cook for 5 minutes. Stir in the courgettes, carrots and spring onions and cook for 12-15 minutes, stirring frequently, until the vegetables are tender and beginning to colour.
**5** Cook the pasta in a large pan of boiling salted water until *al dente.*
**6** Meanwhile, stir the cream into the vegetables and bring to the boil. Allow to bubble, stirring frequently, for a few minutes until it is reduced by about one third. Stir in the asparagus and sugar snaps. Add the Parmesan and heat gently. Season with salt and pepper to taste.
**7** Drain the pasta thoroughly and toss with the oil to prevent sticking. Pour the sauce over the pasta and sprinkle with the herbs. Toss well and serve at once.

**VARIATIONS**

❑ Vary the vegetables according to availability; fennel, broccoli florets, fresh peas and fine beans are suitable options.
❑ Replace one of the herbs with 40 g (1½ oz) chopped walnuts.

# PASTA WITH GRILLED ASPARAGUS AND BROAD BEANS

**ERVES 4**
REPARATION
0 minutes
OOKING TIME
2-15 minutes
REEZING
ot suitable
ALS/SERVING
55

225 g (8 oz) shelled broad beans
salt and pepper
350 g (12 oz) dried pasta
450 g (1 lb) asparagus, trimmed
90 ml (6 tbsp) extra-virgin olive oil
2 garlic cloves, peeled and crushed
grated or shredded zest and juice of 1 lemon
45 ml (3 tbsp) chopped fresh mint
60 ml (4 tbsp) single cream
60 ml (4 tbsp) grated pecorino or Parmesan cheese

 Blanch the broad beans n a large saucepan of light-y salted water for 2 min-tes, then drain, reserving he water. Refresh the eans under cold running vater, then slip out of their ough outer skins.

**2** Bring the reserved water to a rolling boil, add the pasta, return to the boil and cook for 10 minutes until *al dente.*

**3** Meanwhile, halve the asparagus spears and place on the grill rack. Brush with a little oil and grill for 3-4 minutes on each side until charred and tender.

**4** At the same time, heat 30 ml (2 tbsp) oil in a pan, add the garlic and lemon zest and fry gently for 3 minutes. Add the beans, mint and cream; heat gently.

**5** Drain the cooked pasta and immediately toss with the remaining oil. Add the asparagus and bean sauce, cheese and lemon juice. Toss to mix and season with salt and pepper to taste. Serve at once.

# SPAGHETTI WITH LEEKS, PEAS AND SAFFRON CREAM

**SERVES 4-6**
PREPARATION
10 minutes
COOKING TIME
15 minutes
FREEZING
Not suitable
CALS/SERVING
925-615
COLOUR INDEX
Page 36

1.25 ml (¼ tsp) saffron strands, crumbled
350 g (12 oz) leeks, trimmed
50 g (2 oz) butter
150 g (5 oz) frozen peas, thawed
400 g (14 oz) dried spaghetti or paglia e fieno
300 ml (½ pint) extra-thick double cream
90 ml (6 tbsp) freshly grated Parmesan cheese
salt and pepper
chervil or parsley sprigs, to garnish

**1** Put the saffron in a small bowl, cover with 60 ml (4 tbsp) boiling water and leave to stand.
**2** Thinly slice the leeks. Melt the butter in a large frying pan. Add the leeks and cook, stirring, over a medium heat for 7-8 minutes to soften. Add the peas and continue cooking for a further 3 minutes.
**3** Meanwhile, cook the pasta in a large pan of boiling salted water until *al dente.*
**4** Add the saffron liquid and cream to the leeks and peas. Heat gently until simmering. Stir in half of the Parmesan and remove from the heat. Season with salt and pepper.
**5** Drain the pasta thoroughly and return to the pan. Add the sauce and toss lightly to mix. Add the remaining Parmesan cheese and toss again. Serve at once, garnished with chervil or parsley.

## ORECCHIETTE WITH ROCKET AND CHERRY TOMATOES

**SERVES 4**
PREPARATION
10 minutes
COOKING TIME
About 10 minutes
FREEZING
Not suitable
CALS/SERVING
580

400 g (14 oz) dried orecchiette or other pasta shapes
salt and pepper
45 ml (3 tbsp) extra-virgin olive oil
30 ml (2 tbsp) pine nuts
450 g (1 lb) very ripe cherry tomatoes, halved
75 g (3 oz) rocket leaves
TO SERVE
50 g (2 oz) Parmesan cheese shavings

**1** Cook the pasta in a large pan of boiling salted water until *al dente*.
**2** A few minutes before the pasta will be ready, heat 30 ml (2 tbsp) of the oil in a large saucepan. Add the pine nuts and cook for 1-2 minutes until golden. Add the tomatoes and cook for barely 1 minute until only just heated through, not disintegrated.
**3** Drain the pasta and toss with the remaining olive oil. Add the pasta to the tomatoes, then add the rocket. Carefully stir to mix and heat through. Season generously with salt and pepper.
**4** Serve immediately, topped with plenty of Parmesan shavings and accompanied by a crisp leafy salad and warm crusty bread.

**VARIATIONS**
- Use young spinach leaves in place of the rocket.
- Use a mixture of red cherry and yellow pear tomatoes.

## PASTA WITH CAPER SAUCE AND GRILLED HALLOUMI CHEESE

**SERVES 4-6**
PREPARATION
30 minutes
COOKING TIME
15 minutes
FREEZING
Not suitable
CALS/SERVING
755-505
COLOUR INDEX
Page 36

2 red peppers
2 onions
2 garlic cloves
90 ml (6 tbsp) extra-virgin olive oil
45 ml (3 tbsp) chopped fresh parsley
50 g (2 oz) capers in wine vinegar, rinsed and drained
salt and pepper
400 g (14 oz) dried penne, rigatoni or tagliatelle
225 g (8 oz) halloumi cheese

**1** Grill the red peppers, turning occasionally until the skin is blistered and blackened all over; this will take about 20 minutes. Place in a bowl, cover and let cool slightly then, over a bowl to catch the juices, peel away the charred skin and remove the seeds. Cut the flesh into strips and add to the bowl; set aside.
**2** Meanwhile, peel and chop the onions and garlic. Heat 75 ml (5 tbsp) olive oil in a large frying pan. Add the onions and cook over a medium heat, stirring frequently, for 7-8 minutes until soft. Stir in the garlic and continue cooking for 2-3 minutes, then stir in the parsley.
**3** Transfer the mixture to a food processor and add the capers and seasoning. Process briefly to chop coarsely.
**4** Cook the pasta in a large pan of boiling salted water until *al dente*.
**5** Meanwhile, cut the halloumi into 1 cm (½ inch) cubes. Place in a baking tin large enough to take them in one layer. Sprinkle with the remaining 15 ml (1 tbsp) olive oil and plenty of pepper; toss to coat the cheese. Grill, turning occasionally, for about 8 minutes until evenly golden on all sides.
**6** Drain the pasta and return to the pan. Add the caper sauce and reserved pepper strips. Toss to mix. Serve at once, topped with the grilled cheese cubes.

**NOTE** Firm-textured Cypriot halloumi is a wonderful cheese for grilling as it softens, rather than melts, developing a lovely golden crust. Many supermarkets now sell halloumi, or it can be obtained from Cypriot food stores. If unobtainable, use a firm goat's cheese, cut into slices.

# TAGLIATELLE WITH SUMMER VEGETABLES AND HERB SAUCE

**ERVES 4-6**
REPARATION
5 minutes,
lus standing
COOKING TIME
0 minutes
REEZING
Not suitable
CALS/SERVING
15-475

25 g (1 oz) mixed fresh herbs, such as basil, chervil, chives, dill, parsley, roughly chopped
5 ml (1 tsp) dried oregano
120 ml (4 fl oz) extra-virgin olive oil
700 g (1½ lb) mixed summer vegetables, such as courgettes, asparagus tips, French beans, shelled broad beans and/or peas, baby carrots, cherry tomatoes
2 shallots
1 garlic clove, peeled and crushed
1 quantity fresh lemon tagliatelle (see page 122), or 400 g (14 oz) dried plain tagliatelle
salt and pepper
90 ml (6 tbsp) single cream
Parmesan cheese shavings, to serve (optional)

Place the fresh herbs and dried oregano in a bowl. Add ll but 30 ml (2 tbsp) of the olive oil. Stir well and set aside or a few hours if possible, to infuse.

Prepare the vegetables. Thinly slice the courgettes; trim he asparagus spears and French beans; peel the carrots nd halve lengthwise if large.

Blanch all the vegetables, except the cherry tomatoes, eparately, in a large pan of lightly salted boiling water for -3 minutes depending on size and vegetable (see note). Drain and immediately refresh under cold water. Pat dry.

**4** Peel and finely chop the shallots. Heat the remaining oil in a large frying pan, add the shallots and garlic and sauté for 5 minutes. Add the vegetables to the pan, stir-fry over a gentle heat and add the herb mixture.

**5** Meanwhile cook the tagliatelle in a large pan of boiling salted water until *al dente*; fresh pasta will only take 1-2 minutes.

**6** Drain the pasta, reserving 60 ml (4 tbsp) of the cooking water. Add the pasta and water to the frying pan and toss with the vegetables and sauce. Stir in the cream and heat through briefly. Serve at once, seasoned with salt and pepper, and scattered liberally with Parmesan shavings.

**NOTE** The vegetables are listed in order of blanching time required: courgette slices take the shortest time; baby carrots the longest.

# LASAGNETTE WITH COURGETTES AND SUN-DRIED TOMATOES

**SERVES 4**
PREPARATION
25 minutes
COOKING TIME
About 10 minutes
FREEZING
Not suitable
CALS/SERVING
625
COLOUR INDEX
Page 36

250 g (9 oz) dried lasagnette
8 small, thin courgettes
salt and pepper
15 ml (1 tbsp) olive oil
8 sun-dried tomatoes in oil, cut into strips
shredded zest of 1 lemon
6 large basil leaves, shredded

SAUCE
50 g (2 oz) sun-dried tomatoes in oil
1 tomato
2 garlic cloves, peeled
50 g (2 oz) pine nuts
50 g (2 oz) Parmesan cheese, freshly grated
30 ml (2 tbsp) olive oil
juice of 1 lemon
10 ml (2 tsp) grated horseradish (optional)
5-10 ml (1-2 tsp) soft brown sugar, to taste
30 ml (2 tbsp) water

TO GARNISH
basil leaves

**1** Break the lasagnette in half. Pare the courgettes into long ribbons, using a swivel vegetable peeler or mandolin.

**2** To make the sauce, drain the sun-dried tomatoes, reserving 30 ml (2 tbsp) oil. Place in a blender or food processor with the fresh tomato and garlic and work to a purée. Add the remaining ingredients and work until evenly blended. Season to taste and add a little more sugar if required. If the sauce is too thick, thin with a little more water. Transfer to a serving bowl.

**3** Cook the lasagnette in a large saucepan of boiling salted water until *al dente*.

**4** Meanwhile, heat the oil in a frying pan and quickly stir-fry the courgette ribbons, in batches, for 2-3 minutes or until just *al dente*. Remove from the heat and add the sun-dried tomatoes and lemon zest.

**5** Drain the pasta well and toss with the courgette mixture and shredded basil. Transfer to a warmed serving bowl and garnish with basil. Serve accompanied by the sauce at room temperature, and warm focaccia or flavoured bread.

# BUCKWHEAT PASTA WITH GRILLED RADICCHIO

**SERVES 4**
PREPARATION
25 minutes
COOKING TIME
15 minutes
FREEZING
Not suitable
CALS/SERVING
575

2 small red onions
60 ml (4 tbsp) extra-virgin olive oil, plus extra for brushing
1 garlic clove, peeled and crushed
15 ml (1 tbsp) chopped fresh thyme
pinch of sugar
2 heads of radicchio
1 quantity fresh buckwheat tagliatelle (see page 122), or 400 g (14 oz) dried
salt and pepper
30 ml (2 tbsp) balsamic vinegar
25 g (1 oz) capers in wine vinegar, drained
50 g (2 oz) pine nuts, toasted
30 ml (2 tbsp) chopped fresh basil
freshly grated Parmesan cheese, to serve (optional)

**1** Peel and thinly slice the onions. Heat the 60 ml (4 tbsp) oil in a deep frying pan. Add the onions, garlic, thyme and sugar and fry for 10-15 minutes until golden and tender.

**2** Meanwhile, cut the radicchio into wedges and lay on the grill rack. Brush with a little oil and grill for 2-3 minutes. Turn, brush with oil and grill for a further 2-3 minutes until charred and tender; keep warm.

**3** Cook the buckwheat pasta in a large pan of boiling salted water until *al dente*; fresh pasta will only take 1-2 minutes.

**4** Add the balsamic vinegar, capers, nuts and basil to the onions and stir well; keep warm.

**5** Drain the pasta, reserving 60 ml (4 tbsp) cooking water. Add both to the caramelised onions with the radicchio. Stir briefly over a medium heat, then season with salt and pepper and serve at once, with Parmesan, if wished.

# TAGLIATELLE WITH PUMPKIN AND BLUE CHEESE SAUCE

**SERVES 4-6**
PREPARATION
15 minutes
COOKING TIME
About 12 minutes
FREEZING
Not suitable
CALS/SERVING
930-620
COLOUR INDEX
Page 37

350 g (12 oz) wedge of pumpkin, peeled and deseeded
25 g (1 oz) butter
1 garlic clove, peeled and crushed
30 ml (2 tbsp) chopped fresh parsley
300 ml (½ pint) extra-thick double cream
1.25 ml (¼ tsp) freshly grated nutmeg
400 g (14 oz) dried tagliatelle, pappardelle or fusilli
175 g (6 oz) dolcelatte cheese
salt and pepper
TO GARNISH
30 ml (2 tbsp) pine nuts, toasted
15 ml (1 tbsp) chopped fresh parsley

**1** Grate the pumpkin flesh, using a food processor with a grating attachment, or by hand.
**2** Melt the butter in a large frying pan. Add the pumpkin and garlic and cook, stirring, over a medium heat for about 5 minutes, until softened. Stir in the parsley, cream and nutmeg and cook for a further 2 minutes.
**3** Cook the pasta in a large pan of boiling salted water until *al dente*.
**4** Cut the dolcelatte into small pieces and add to the sauce. Heat gently, stirring until melted. Season with salt and pepper to taste.
**5** Drain the pasta thoroughly and return to the pan. Add the sauce and toss well to mix. Serve at once, sprinkled with toasted pine nuts and chopped parsley.

**NOTE** Other firm-fleshed squashes, such as butternut or acorn squash, can be used with equally good results when pumpkin is out of season.

**VARIATION** Replace the dolcelatte with 175 g (6 oz) Boursin or other garlic and herb-flavoured cheese.

## TAGLIATELLE WITH SAGE, PIMENTO AND GARLIC

**SERVES 4-6**
PREPARATION
10 minutes
COOKING TIME
About 10 minutes
FREEZING
Not suitable
CALS/SERVING
775-520
COLOUR INDEX
Page 37

- 1 small onion
- 2 garlic cloves
- 60 ml (4 tbsp) extra-virgin olive oil
- 400 g (14 oz) can pimentos in brine, drained and rinsed
- 30 ml (2 tbsp) chopped fresh sage
- 150 ml (¼ pint) extra-thick double cream
- 75 ml (5 tbsp) freshly grated Parmesan cheese
- salt and pepper
- 400 g (14 oz) green and plain tagliatelle
- sage sprigs, to garnish

**1** Peel and finely chop the onion and garlic. Heat the oil in a large frying pan. Add the onion and garlic and cook over a medium heat for about 5 minutes until softened; do not allow to brown.
**2** Dice the pimentos and add to the pan with the sage. Continue cooking for 3 minutes. Stir in the cream and bring to a simmer, then stir in all but 15 ml (1 tbsp) of the grated Parmesan. Season with salt and pepper to taste.
**3** Meanwhile, cook the pasta in a large pan of boiling salted water until *al dente.* (Fresh pasta will require only 2-3 minutes cooking time.)
**4** To serve, drain the pasta thoroughly and add to the sauce. Toss well to mix. Serve sprinkled with the remaining Parmesan and garnished with sage leaves.

**NOTE** Extra-thick double cream is used here and in other creamy pasta sauces as it lends the correct consistency. If you prefer to use ordinary double cream, increase the quantity by about one third and reduce the creamy sauce slightly by simmering to the desired consistency.

**VARIATION** Use rigatoni or penne in place of tagliatelle and add 175 g (6 oz) diced mozzarella cheese to the sauce at the end of cooking. The cheese cubes should melt softly when tossed with the hot pasta but not disappear completely into the sauce.

## CALABRIAN PASTA

**SERVES 4-6**
PREPARATION
10 minutes
COOKING TIME
12-15 minutes
FREEZING
Not suitable
CALS/SERVING
695-465

- 50 g (2 oz) sultanas
- 150 g (5 oz) broccoli
- 300-350 g (10-12 oz) ziti, long fusilli or spaghetti
- salt and pepper
- 125 ml (4 fl oz) olive oil
- 75 g (3 oz) white breadcrumbs
- 2 garlic cloves, peeled and finely chopped
- 25 g (1 oz) pine nuts
- 15 ml (1 tbsp) sun-dried tomato paste
- 45 ml (3 tbsp) chopped fresh parsley
- cayenne pepper, to taste

**1** Put the sultanas in a bowl, pour on a little boiling water and leave to soak. Break the broccoli into small florets, cutting the stems into similar sized pieces. Add the broccoli to a pan of boiling water, return to the boil and simmer for 30 seconds; drain.
**2** Cook the pasta in a large pan of boiling salted water until *al dente.*
**3** In the meantime, heat the oil in a frying pan, add the breadcrumbs and fry, stirring until they begin to crisp. Add the garlic and pine nuts and continue to fry, stirring, until the pine nuts begin to colour. Add the broccoli and stir over the heat until it is thoroughly heated through.
**4** Drain the pasta in a colander, setting it back on top of the saucepan to catch the last 15 ml (1 tbsp) cooking water. Stir the sun-dried tomato paste and drained sultanas into this liquid, then return the pasta to the pan. Toss with a generous grinding of black pepper and half of the chopped parsley. Transfer to a heated serving bowl.
**5** Mix the remaining parsley with the broccoli and crumb mixture. Add to the pasta and toss to mix. Sprinkle with cayenne pepper to serve.

# PASTA WITH MEDITERRANEAN VEGETABLES AND WALNUT PASTE

**SERVES 4-6**
PREPARATION
25 minutes
COOKING TIME
20 minutes
FREEZING
Not suitable
CALS/SERVING
950-630

1 fennel bulb, trimmed
2 small red onions, peeled
2 courgettes
1 large red pepper
6 small tomatoes
45 ml (3 tbsp) extra-virgin olive oil
15 ml (1 tbsp) chopped fresh thyme
5 ml (1 tsp) finely grated lemon zest
coarse sea salt and pepper
400 g (14 oz) dried tagliatelle

WALNUT PASTE
150 g (5 oz) walnuts
1 garlic clove, peeled
45 ml (3 tbsp) chopped fresh parsley
75 ml (5 tbsp) extra-virgin olive oil
50 g (2 oz) ricotta or other soft cheese

TO GARNISH
thyme sprigs

**1** Cut the fennel and onions into wedges. Halve the courgettes, then thinly slice lengthwise. Halve, core and deseed the red pepper, then cut into broad strips. Halve the tomatoes.
**2** Add the fennel and onions to a large pan of boiling water, bring back to the boil and cook for 2 minutes. Add the courgette strips and cook for a further 1 minute. Drain in a colander and refresh under cold running water. Drain and set aside.
**3** Preheat the grill to high. Put the blanched vegetables in a bowl with the red pepper and tomatoes. Add the olive oil, thyme, lemon zest and seasoning; toss to coat.
**4** Transfer the vegetables to the foil-lined grill pan and grill for 15-20 minutes, turning occasionally until they are tender and patched with brown.
**5** Meanwhile, cook the pasta in a large pan of boiling salted water until *al dente.*
**6** Meanwhile, prepare the walnut paste. Put the walnuts and garlic into a food processor and process briefly to chop finely. Add the parsley and process for 1 second. Add the oil and work to a coarse paste. Transfer to a bowl and stir in the ricotta and seasoning.
**7** Drain the pasta thoroughly in a colander. Meanwhile, gently heat the walnut paste in the large pasta pan for a few seconds, then remove from the heat, add the pasta and toss to mix. Serve at once, topped with the grilled vegetables, drizzling over any oil and juices from the grill pan. Garnish with thyme sprigs.

**VARIATION** Use olive paste rather than walnut paste. Buy ready-made paste or make your own, by processing stoned olives with a chopped garlic clove, olive oil and herbs.

# FUSILLI WITH ASPARAGUS AND PARMESAN

**SERVES 4-6**
PREPARATION
5 minutes
COOKING TIME
12 minutes
FREEZING
Not suitable
CALS/SERVING
875-585
COLOUR INDEX
Page 37

400 g (14 oz) thin, trimmed asparagus
salt and pepper
1 onion
50 g (2 oz) butter
90 ml (3 fl oz) dry white wine
400 g (14 oz) dried long fusilli, tagliatelle or penne
300 ml (½ pint) extra-thick double cream
50 g (2 oz) Parmesan cheese, freshly grated
30 ml (2 tbsp) chopped fresh chervil or parsley (optional)

**1** Pour sufficient water into a frying pan to give a 2 cm (¾ inch) depth. Add a pinch of salt and bring to the boil. Add the asparagus spears and cook for 4-5 minutes until almost tender. Drain, reserving 75 ml (5 tbsp) of the cooking water. Cut the asparagus into 5 cm (2 inch) lengths and set aside.
**2** Peel and finely chop the onion. Melt the butter in the frying pan. Add the onion and cook over a medium high heat for about 5 minutes until softened and beginning to colour. Stir in the asparagus and cook for 1 minute. Pour in the reserved cooking water and the wine. Cook over a high heat until almost all the liquid has evaporated.
**3** Meanwhile, cook the pasta in a large pan of boiling salted water until *al dente.*
**4** Add the cream to the sauce, stir well and heat until bubbling. Stir in half of the grated Parmesan, herbs if using and salt and pepper to taste.
**5** Drain the pasta thoroughly, add to the sauce and toss well. Serve at once, sprinkled with the remaining Parmesan and pepper to taste.

## MUSHROOM AND PASTA GRATIN

**SERVES 4**
PREPARATION
10 minutes
COOKING TIME
40-45 minutes
FREEZING
Not suitable
CALS/SERVING
700

225 g (8 oz) dried pasta shells
salt and pepper
450 g (1 lb) button mushrooms, wiped
25 g (1 oz) butter
90 ml (3 fl oz) brandy (optional)
15 ml (1 tbsp) chopped fresh tarragon
15 ml (1 tbsp) chopped fresh chives
300 ml (½ pint) double cream
50 g (2 oz) Parmesan cheese, freshly grated

**1** Cook the pasta in a large pan of boiling salted water until *al dente*. Drain and immediately refresh under cold water, then drain well and toss with a little oil to prevent sticking.
**2** Halve or quarter the mushrooms if large. Melt the butter in a large frying pan, add the mushrooms and stir-fry for 4-5 minutes until golden. Add the brandy if using and boil rapidly until only 30 ml (2 tbsp) liquid remains. Stir in the chopped herbs and remove from the heat.
**3** Toss the mushrooms with the pasta and transfer to a lightly oiled gratin dish. Mix the cream with half of the Parmesan and pour over the pasta. Sprinkle the remaining cheese over the top.
**4** Bake in the oven at 190°C (375°F) Mark 5 for 20-25 minutes until bubbling and golden. Serve hot.

## SPAGHETTI WITH WILD MUSHROOMS AND SAGE

**SERVES 4-6**
PREPARATION
25 minutes, plus soaking
COOKING TIME
About 20 minutes
FREEZING
Not suitable
CALS/SERVING
660-440
COLOUR INDEX
Page 37

15 g (½ oz) dried porcini mushrooms
125 ml (4 fl oz) boiling water
575 g (1¼ lb) mixed fresh mushrooms, such as field, chestnut, oyster, plus chanterelles or other wild types, if available, cleaned
3 shallots
2-3 garlic cloves
75 ml (5 tbsp) extra-virgin olive oil
300 ml (½ pint) dry white wine
30 ml (2 tbsp) chopped fresh sage
30 ml (2 tbsp) chopped fresh parsley
salt and pepper
400 g (14 oz) dried spaghettini
25-40 g (1-1½ oz) Parmesan cheese shavings, to serve (optional)

**1** Put the dried mushrooms in a small bowl, pour on the boiling water and leave to soak for 20 minutes. Drain, reserving the soaking liquor. Rinse and chop the porcini.
**2** Slice large field mushrooms; quarter chestnut mushrooms; leave oyster mushrooms and any others whole (unless very large).
**3** Peel and chop the shallots and garlic. Heat the olive oil in a large frying pan. Add the shallots and sauté over a medium heat for 5 minutes until softened. Stir in the garlic and cook for a further 1-2 minutes.
**4** Add the chopped dried mushrooms to the frying pan with the soaking liquor and the wine. Bring to the boil, then lower the heat a little and allow to bubble for 8-10 minutes until the liquid has reduced by about half.
**5** Add the fresh mushrooms, except oyster mushrooms, to the pan with the sage. Cook for about 6 minutes until they are tender. Stir in the oyster mushrooms, parsley and seasoning. Cook for a further 2 minutes.
**6** Meanwhile, cook the spaghettini in a large pan of boiling salted water until *al dente*. Drain thoroughly and return to the pan.
**7** Add the mushroom mixture to the pasta and toss lightly to mix. Adjust the seasoning and serve at once, sprinkled with shavings of Parmesan if wished.

# SPINACH AND RICOTTA RAVIOLI

**SERVES 4**
PREPARATION
20 minutes, plus pasta
COOKING TIME
3 minutes
FREEZING
Suitable: Stage 5
CALS/SERVING
525

1 quantity Pasta Dough (see page 122)
FILLING
300 g (10 oz) frozen spinach, thawed and squeezed dry
125 g (4 oz) ricotta or curd cheese
1.25 ml (¼ tsp) freshly grated nutmeg
2.5 ml (½ tsp) salt
pepper, to taste
TO FINISH
beaten egg, to seal
75 g (3 oz) butter, melted
25 g (1 oz) Parmesan cheese shavings

**1** To make the filling, place all the ingredients in a food processor or blender and process until smooth. Cover and refrigerate.

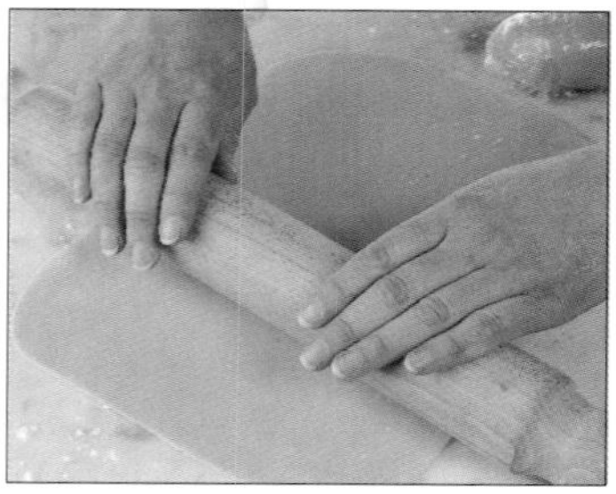

**2** If using a pasta machine, roll manageable portions of dough into strips. If rolling out by hand, cut the dough in half and re-wrap one piece in cling film. Roll the other piece out thinly on a lightly floured surface to a rectangle and cover with a clean damp tea-towel. Repeat with the remaining pasta dough.

**3** Spoon heaped teaspoonfuls of filling on one half of the dough, spacing them at 4 cm (1½ inch) intervals. Brush the dough in between with beaten egg.

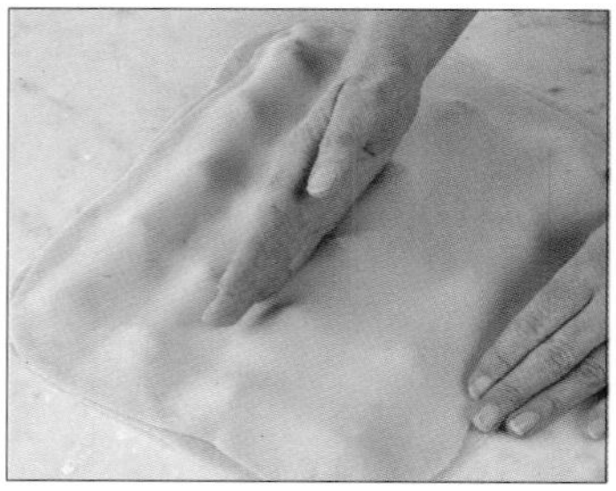

**4** Using a rolling pin, carefully lift the other sheet(s) of pasta over the top. Press down firmly between the pockets of filling, pushing out any trapped air.

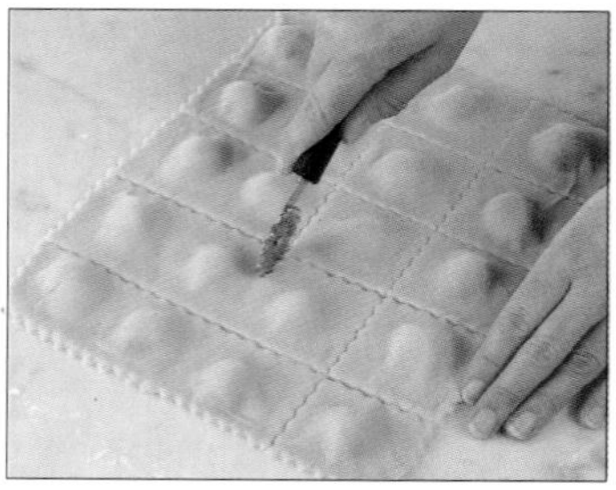

**5** Cut into squares, using a serrated ravioli cutter or sharp knife. Transfer to a floured tea-towel and leave to rest for 1 hour before cooking.

**6** Put a large pan of salted water on to boil. Add the ravioli and cook for about 3 minutes, until puffy. Drain well, toss with the butter and serve with Parmesan.

# HERBED MUSHROOM RAVIOLI

**SERVES 4 (or 6 as a starter)**
PREPARATION
25 minutes, plus pasta
COOKING TIME
5 minutes
FREEZING
Suitable: Stage 3
CALS/SERVING
550
COLOUR INDEX
Page 38

1 quantity Herb Pasta Dough (see page 122)
MUSHROOM FILLING
225 g (8 oz) mixed wild mushrooms, or 175 g (6 oz) dark flat mushrooms plus 40 g (1½ oz) dried porcini
2 shallots, peeled
25 g (1 oz) black olives, stoned
4 sun-dried tomatoes in oil, drained
50 g (2 oz) butter
15 ml (1 tbsp) dry sherry
salt and pepper
freshly grated nutmeg
beaten egg, for brushing
TO SERVE
50 g (2 oz) butter, melted
few sautéed wild mushrooms
Parmesan cheese

**1** To prepare the filling, wipe the fresh mushrooms clean, then chop finely. If using dried mushrooms, soak in hot water to cover for 10-15 minutes. Remove and chop finely. Strain the soaking liquid through a filter paper and reserve.
**2** Peel and finely chop the shallots. Finely chop the olives and sun-dried tomatoes. Melt the butter in a pan, add the shallots and cook for 5 minutes until soft and golden. Add all the mushrooms, olives and sun-dried tomatoes; cook,

tirring, over a high heat for 1-2 minutes. Add the sherry .nd reserved liquid; cook for 1 minute. Season well with alt, pepper and nutmeg. Transfer to a bowl; allow to cool.
Roll out the pasta, shape and fill the ravioli (as for pinach and Ricotta Ravioli – steps 2-5, see left).
Bring a large pan of salted water to the boil, with a dash f oil added. Add the ravioli, bring back to the boil, turn off he heat and cover with a tight-fitting lid. Leave for 5 mintes, then drain well. Serve immediately, topped with meltd butter, sautéed mushrooms and Parmesan shavings.

## .ASAGNE WITH GOAT'S CHEESE TOPPING

**ERVES 6**
EPARATION
oout 1 hour
OOKING TIME
) minutes
EEZING
itable: Stage 5
ALS/SERVING
35
OLOUR INDEX
ge 38

4 red, orange or yellow peppers
2 medium aubergines
2 onions
4 garlic cloves
75 ml (5 tbsp) extra-virgin olive oil
75 ml (5 tbsp) red wine or water
45 ml (3 tbsp) chopped fresh oregano
90 ml (6 tbsp) sun-dried tomato paste
salt and pepper
12 sheets dried lasagne

TOPPING
350 g (12 oz) soft goat cheese or ricotta
2 eggs
150 ml (¼ pint) single cream
45 ml (3 tbsp) day-old white breadcrumbs
30 ml (2 tbsp) freshly grated Parmesan cheese

Grill the whole peppers, turning from time to time, until ne skins are blackened and blistered all over. This will take oout 20 minutes. Allow to cool slightly, then skin, deseed nd roughly chop the flesh, reserving the juices.
Meanwhile, cut the aubergines into 1 cm (½ inch) cubes. eel and chop the onions. Peel and thinly slice the garlic.
Heat the oil in a large saucepan. Add the onions and ook, stirring frequently, for about 8 minutes until soft and olden. Add the garlic and cook for a further 2 minutes. dd the wine and let bubble for 1 minute, then stir in the ubergine, oregano and tomato paste. Cover and cook over medium heat for 15-20 minutes, stirring frequently. Take ff the heat and stir in the grilled peppers and seasoning.
If necessary, pre-cook the lasagne in a large pan of boilg salted water according to packet instructions.
Spread one third of the filling in the base of an oiled bakg dish, measuring about 25x18x8 cm (10x7x3½ inches). over with a layer of pasta, trimming to fit the dish as necssary. Add another third of the filling and cover with pasta before. Cover with the last of the filling and arrange the maining pasta sheets over the top.
To make the topping, place the goat's cheese in a bowl, dd the eggs and beat well. Stir in the cream and seasong. Pour over the lasagne and spread evenly. Sprinkle with e breadcrumbs and Parmesan, then bake for about 35-40 inutes, until heated through and lightly browned on top.

**ARIATION** Replace the goat's cheese topping with 350 g 2 oz) mozzarella, cut into slices.

## ARTICHOKE AND MUSHROOM LASAGNE

**SERVES 4**
PREPARATION
20 minutes
COOKING TIME
1 hour 40 minutes
FREEZING
Not suitable
CALS/SERVING
785

225 g (8 oz) onions
1.1 kg (2½ lb) mixed mushrooms, such as brown-cap and button
400 g can artichoke hearts in water
45 ml (3 tbsp) olive oil
3 garlic cloves, peeled and crushed
25 g (1 oz) walnuts
125 g (4 oz) cherry tomatoes
50 g (2 oz) butter
50 g (2 oz) plain flour
1.1 litres (2 pints) milk
2 bay leaves
30 ml (2 tbsp) lemon juice
salt and pepper
200 g (7 oz) chilled fresh lasagne
75 g (3 oz) Parmesan cheese, freshly grated
herb sprigs, to garnish

**1** Peel and roughly chop the onions; quarter the mushrooms. Drain and halve the artichokes.
**2** Heat the oil in a large pan, add the onions and fry gently for 10 minutes until soft. Add the garlic and walnuts and fry for 3-4 minutes. Stir in the mushrooms and cook for 10 minutes. Bubble briskly for a further 10 minutes or until the liquid is totally evaporated. Add the tomatoes and set aside.
**3** Melt the butter in a saucepan, add the flour and stir over a low heat for 1 minute. Slowly whisk in the milk to make a smooth sauce. Bring to the boil, add the bay leaves and stir over a gentle heat for 10 minutes. Add the lemon juice and seasoning to taste. Discard the bay leaves.
**4** Arrange a layer of lasagne over the base of a greased shallow ovenproof dish. Spoon on half of the mushroom mixture, followed by half the artichokes. Cover with another layer of lasagne, then half the sauce. Repeat the mushroom and artichoke layers, then top with the rest of the lasagne.
**5** Stir the Parmesan into the remaining sauce and spoon over the top. Bake at 200°C (400°F) Mark 6 for 40-50 minutes until golden and bubbling. Garnish with herbs to serve.

# TORTELLONI WITH ROASTED SQUASH AND SAGE BUTTER

**SERVES 4 (or 6 as a starter)**
PREPARATION 45-50 minutes, plus chilling
COOKING TIME 2-3 minutes
FREEZING Suitable: Stage 5
CALS/SERVING 655-435

1 quantity Pasta Dough (see page 122)
FILLING
300 g (10 oz) butternut squash
1 garlic clove, peeled and crushed
10 ml (2 tsp) chopped fresh thyme
30 ml (2 tbsp) olive oil
75 g (3 oz) ricotta cheese
25 g (1 oz) Parmesan cheese, freshly grated
pinch of freshly grated nutmeg
squeeze of lemon juice
salt and pepper
SAGE BUTTER
125 g (4 oz) unsalted butter, softened
30 ml (2 tbsp) chopped fresh sage leaves

**1** For the filling, peel and deseed the squash. Cut squash into cubes and place in a baking tin with the garlic, thyme and oil; toss well. Roast at 220°C (425°F) Mark 7 for 20 minutes until softened.

**2** Mash the roasted squash, then leave to cool completely. Beat in the ricotta, Parmesan, nutmeg, lemon juice and seasoning. Cover and chill in the refrigerator for 30 minutes.

**3** Divide the pasta dough into 8 pieces and roll out each one, using a pasta machine if possible, to a thin sheet (see page 123). Keep all except one of the pasta sheets covered with cling film. Using a 6 cm (2½ inch) pastry cutter, stamp out 6 rounds from the single pasta sheet.

**4** Place 5 ml (1 tsp) of the squash mixture in the middle of each round. Brush the edge of one half of each round with water, then fold the other half over to enclose the filling. Press the edges together to seal well.

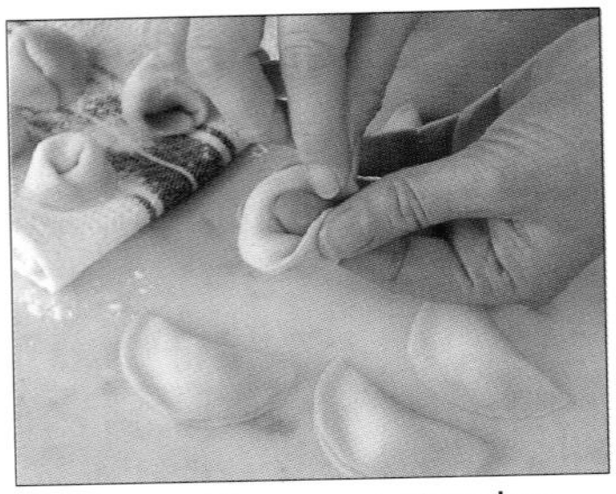

**5** Curve the semi-circular parcel around your finger and pinch the ends together, turning the sealed edge up to form a neat curved tortelloni as you do so. Place on a well floured tea-towel. Repeat with the remaining pasta and filling to make 48 tortelloni.

**6** Cook the tortelloni in a large pan of boiling salted water for 2-3 minutes until *al dente*. Drain well.

**7** At the same time, melt the butter with the sage in a large frying pan until foaming. Add the tortelloni and toss well. Serve at once, sprinkled with black pepper, and extra grated Parmesan if wished.

**NOTES**

❑ For the filling, you should have 225 g (8 oz) prepared weight of squash.

❑ If rolling the pasta dough by hand, divide into 4 pieces and roll out on a floured surface as thinly as possible (see page 123). Stamp out 12 rounds from each sheet of pasta.

## SIMPLE ORIENTAL NOODLES

**ERVES 4**
REPARATION
) minutes
OOKING TIME
2-15 minutes
REEZING
ot suitable
ALS/SERVING
50

- 250 g (9 oz) packet dried medium Chinese egg noodles
- 2 garlic cloves
- 2 small red chillies
- 60 ml (4 tbsp) light olive oil
- 10 ml (2 tsp) sesame oil
- 2.5 ml (½ tsp) grated fresh root ginger
- grated zest and juice of 1 lime
- 30-45 ml (2-3 tbsp) chopped fresh coriander
- 15-30 ml (1-2 tbsp) chopped fresh basil
- salt and pepper
- coriander sprigs, to garnish

. Bring a large saucepan of salted water to the boil, add he egg noodles and remove from the heat. Leave to stand or 4 minutes; the noodles will cook in the residual heat. )rain, reserving 90 ml (6 tbsp) of the cooking water. mmediately refresh under cold water, then drain the oodles thoroughly and toss with a little oil to prevent ticking; set aside.

: Peel and slice the garlic. Deseed and finely chop the hillies. Heat the two oils together in a large wok. Add the arlic, ginger, chillies and lime zest and fry gently for about 0 seconds until the garlic starts to release its aroma. Vhisk in the reserved 90 ml (6 tbsp) water and bring to the oil.

: Stir the pasta into the sauce with the herbs and lime uice and toss over the heat for a few seconds until heated hrough. Season with salt and pepper to taste and serve mmediately, garnished with coriander.

**OTE** Serve this simple, tasty dish on its own as a quick nack, or accompanied by stir-fried or grilled vegetables as light meal.

## PAD THAI

**SERVES 4**
PREPARATION
20 minutes
COOKING TIME
8-10 minutes
FREEZING
Not suitable
CALS/SERVING
410

- 225 g (8 oz) plain tofu
- oil, for deep-frying
- 125 g (4 oz) flat rice or egg noodles
- 30 ml (2 tbsp) sunflower oil
- 2 eggs, lightly beaten
- salt and pepper
- 2 red chillies
- 6 spring onions, trimmed
- 1 garlic clove, peeled and crushed
- 50 g (2 oz) bean sprouts
- 30 ml (2 tbsp) smooth peanut butter
- 30 ml (2 tbsp) dark soy sauce
- 30 ml (2 tbsp) lime juice
- 15 ml (1 tbsp) sugar
- 15 ml (1 tbsp) chopped fresh coriander
- 15 ml (1 tbsp) chopped fresh mint

**1** Cut the tofu into 2.5 cm (1 inch) cubes and drain well on kitchen paper. Heat the oil in a deep saucepan to 180°C (350°F) or until a cube of bread dropped in crisps in 40 seconds. Deep-fry the tofu in batches for 2-3 minutes until golden; drain on kitchen paper and set aside.

**2** Cook the noodles according to the packet instructions. Drain, refresh under cold water and dry well.

**3** Heat half of the sunflower oil in a large frying pan. Season the eggs and swirl into the pan. Cook over a gentle heat until the omelette is just set, then remove from the pan. Let cool slightly then cut into thin strips; set aside.

**4** Deseed and chop the chillies. Slice the spring onions. Heat remaining oil in a large wok, add the garlic, chillies, spring onions and bean sprouts and stir-fry for 1 minute.

**5** Heat the peanut butter, soy sauce, lime juice, sugar and 60 ml (4 tbsp) water in another pan, stirring until smooth.

**6** Add the noodles to the wok with the tofu and sauce. Toss over the heat until the noodles are coated with the sauce. Add the egg strips and herbs, and serve immediately.

# RICE AND GRAINS

# WILD MUSHROOM RISOTTO

**SERVES 4**
PREPARATION
25 minutes, plus soaking
COOKING TIME
30 minutes
FREEZING
Not suitable
CALS/SERVING
550

- 15 g (½ oz) dried porcini mushrooms
- 150 ml (¼ pint) boiling water
- 1 red onion
- 2 garlic cloves
- 90 ml (6 tbsp) extra-virgin olive oil
- 10 ml (2 tsp) chopped fresh thyme
- 5 ml (1 tsp) grated lemon zest
- 350 g (12 oz) Arborio rice
- 150 ml (¼ pint) dry white wine
- 900 ml (1½ pints) vegetable stock
- 450 g (1 lb) mixed fresh mushrooms, such as oyster, shiitake, blueits, ceps etc
- 25 g (1 oz) Parmesan cheese, freshly grated
- 30 ml (2 tbsp) chopped fresh parsley
- salt and pepper

**1** Place the dried porcini in a small bowl, pour over the boiling water and leave to soak for 20 minutes. Drain the porcini; strain and reserve the liquid. Dry the porcini and chop finely.

**2** Peel and finely chop the onion and garlic. Heat half the oil in a heavy-based saucepan. Add the porcini, onion, garlic, thyme and lemon zest; fry for 5 minutes until softened. Add the rice; stir-fry for 1 minute until the grains are glossy.

**3** Add the wine and boil rapidly until almost all of it is evaporated. At the same time, heat the stock and reserved mushroom liquid in a separate pan to a steady, low simmer.

**4** Gradually add the stock to the rice, a ladleful at a time allowing each addition to be absorbed before adding more, stirring constantly. Continue until the rice is tender. This will take about 25 minutes; it may not be necessary to add all of the stock.

**5** Meanwhile, wipe the fresh mushrooms and slice any large ones. About 5 minutes before the rice will be ready, heat the remaining oil in a large frying pan. Add the mushrooms and stir-fry over a high heat for 4-5 minutes until golden.

**6** Immediately stir the mushrooms into the rice with the Parmesan and parsley. Season with salt and pepper to taste and serve at once, with extra Parmesan if wished.

**NOTES**

❑ Arborio is the classic risotto rice which has the capacity to absorb plenty of liquid during cooking, without turning mushy. It is available from larger supermarkets and delicatessens. You can use long-grain rice as an alternative if necessary, but you will need to use less stock.

❑ The stock added to a risotto should always be just below boiling point; this will ensure a constant heat, necessary for the perfect texture of the dish.

## PUMPKIN AND BARLEY RISOTTO

**SERVES 4**
PREPARATION
20 minutes
COOKING TIME
35 minutes, plus resting
FREEZING
Not suitable
CALS/SERVING
560

450 g (1 lb) peeled and deseeded pumpkin
2 leeks, trimmed
2 garlic cloves
1 red chilli
60 ml (4 tbsp) extra-virgin olive oil
15 ml (1 tbsp) finely chopped fresh rosemary
15 ml (1 tbsp) chopped fresh sage
350 g (12 oz) pearl barley
1.2 litre (2 pints) vegetable stock
50 g (2 oz) Parmesan cheese, freshly grated
60 ml (4 tbsp) double cream
salt and pepper
extra Parmesan cheese, to serve

**1** Dice the pumpkin. Thinly slice the leeks; peel and finely chop the garlic; deseed and finely dice the chilli. Heat the oil in a large saucepan, add the leeks, garlic, chilli and herbs and fry for 5 minutes until softened.
**2** Add the barley and stir-fry for 1 minute until all the grains are glossy.
**3** Meanwhile bring the vegetable stock to a steady simmer in another saucepan.
**4** Add the pumpkin to the barley and stir well. Pour in 150 ml (¼ pint) of the hot stock and stir over a medium heat until absorbed.
**5** Gradually add the remaining simmering stock a ladleful at a time, stirring occasionally, and making sure each addition is absorbed before adding the next. Continue until the barley is tender and all the stock absorbed; this will take about 30 minutes.
**6** Remove from the heat and stir in the Parmesan and cream. Cover and allow to stand for 5 minutes. Season with salt and pepper to taste and serve at once, with extra Parmesan if wished.

**NOTE** Barley is used here as its cooked texture is quite similar to Arborio, the Italian risotto rice.

**VARIATION**
PUMPKIN AND BARLEY BAKE Follow the recipe to the end of step 2. Add the pumpkin and 900 ml (1½ pints) stock, bring to the boil and transfer to a deep baking dish. Cover with foil and bake in the oven at 180°C (350°F) Mark 4 for about 1 hour. Remove the foil, scatter some grated Parmesan over the top and grill until golden.

## SUMMER VEGETABLE RISOTTO

**SERVES 4**
PREPARATION
5 minutes
COOKING TIME
About 25 minutes
FREEZING
Not suitable
CALS/SERVING
350-375
COLOUR INDEX
Page 39

700 g (1½ lb) mixed green vegetables, such as French beans, broad beans, mangetout, peas and asparagus
12 pitted black olives
4 sun-dried tomatoes in oil, plus 15 ml (1tbsp) oil from jar
350 g (12 oz) tomatoes
225 g (8 oz) mixed wild and long-grain rice (see note)
350 ml (12 fl oz) vegetable stock
1 garlic clove, peeled and crushed
salt and pepper

**1** Trim the green vegetables and blanch separately in boiling water until barely tender. Drain and refresh under cold running water; drain well. Halve the olives. Dice the sun-dried and fresh tomatoes.
**2** Put the rice and stock in a saucepan. Bring to the boil, lower the heat and simmer, covered, for about 20 minutes or until all the liquid has been absorbed and the rice is tender.
**3** Heat the tomato oil in a large non-stick frying pan or wok. Add the garlic and cook, stirring, for 1-2 minutes.
**4** Add the tomatoes and rice. Cook, stirring, over a gentle heat for 3-4 minutes. Stir in the blanched vegetables and olives. Increase the heat and cook, stirring, for 1 minute until piping hot. Season with salt and pepper to taste and serve immediately.

**NOTE** Packets of mixed wild and long-grain rice are readily available from supermarkets. Refer to the packet instructions for the recommended cooking time. To test if rice is cooked, remove a few grains from the pan and press between finger and thumb. If it squashes easily and there is no hard core the rice is ready.

# MUSHROOM AND AUBERGINE RISOTTO

**SERVES 4**
PREPARATION
20 minutes, plus soaking
COOKING TIME
25-30 minutes
FREEZING
Not suitable
CALS/SERVING
680

25 g (1 oz) dried porcini mushrooms
1 aubergine
salt and pepper
175 g (6 oz) fresh mushrooms (preferably wild)
1 small onion
125 g (4 oz) butter
350 g (12 oz) Arborio rice
150 ml (¼ pint) dry white wine
1.2 litres (2 pints) hot vegetable stock
30 ml (2 tbsp) chopped fresh parsley
15 ml (1 tbsp) chopped fresh sage (optional)
60 ml (4 tbsp) freshly grated Parmesan cheese

**1** Put the dried mushrooms in a small bowl, add sufficient warm water to cover and leave to soak for 20 minutes. Drain, reserving the liquid. Rinse the porcini, drain then chop finely.
**2** Trim and dice the aubergine and put into a colander. Sprinkle liberally with salt and leave to degorge for 30 minutes. Rinse the aubergine thoroughly and drain well.
**3** Halve or quarter fresh mushrooms, or leave whole, according to size.
**4** Peel and finely chop the onion. Melt half of the butter in a heavy-based saucepan over a medium heat. Add the onion and cook for 5 minutes until softened. Stir in the rice and cook for 2-3 minutes until the grains are translucent. Add the aubergine and fresh mushrooms. Cook, stirring, for 2 minutes.
**5** Add the wine, the chopped porcini and the reserved soaking liquor. Cook for about 3 minutes, until all the liquid is absorbed.
**6** Add 600 ml (1 pint) of the stock to the pan, lower the heat, cover and simmer for 10 minutes until the stock is absorbed. Add a further 150 ml (¼ pint) and continue cooking as before until the liquid is absorbed. Continue to add the stock a ladleful at a time until the rice is tender. This will take 20-25 minutes. It may not be necessary to add all of the stock.
**7** Stir in the chopped herbs and remaining butter, together with half of the grated Parmesan. Serve sprinkled with the remaining Parmesan.

# SPINACH RISOTTO

**SERVES 4**
PREPARATION
5 minutes
COOKING TIME
30 minutes
FREEZING
Not suitable
CALS/SERVING
345
COLOUR INDEX
Page 39

400 g (14 oz) fresh spinach leaves, or 125 g (4 oz) frozen leaf spinach
1 onion
1 garlic clove
25 g (1 oz) butter
225 g (8 oz) Arborio rice
salt and pepper
750 ml (1¼ pints) vegetable stock
60 ml (4 tbsp) freshly grated Parmesan cheese
extra Parmesan cheese to serve

**1** Remove any tough stalks from fresh spinach and chop roughly. Peel and finely chop the onion. Peel and slice the garlic.
**2** Melt the butter in a heavy-based saucepan. Add the onion and garlic and cook for about 5 minutes or until the onion is beginning to soften.
**3** Add the rice, salt and pepper and cook, stirring, for about 2-3 minutes. Add just enough stock to cover the rice and continue cooking, stirring all the time until most of the stock has been absorbed. Continue adding the stock in this way until it is completely absorbed and the rice is tender.
**4** Squeeze the excess liquid from the frozen spinach, if using. Stir the fresh or frozen spinach into the rice. Heat through for 1-2 minutes or until the fresh spinach is just wilted.
**5** Remove from the heat and stir in the grated Parmesan. Adjust the seasoning and serve immediately, with a little extra grated Parmesan.

# RISOTTO GALETTE WITH TALEGGIO

**SERVES 6-8**
PREPARATION
15 minutes, plus cooling
COOKING TIME
1 hour
FREEZING
Not suitable
CALS/SERVING
540-405

- large pinch of saffron strands
- 900 ml (2 pints) hot vegetable stock
- 1 onion
- 50 g (2 oz) butter
- 3 garlic cloves, peeled and crushed
- 350 g (12 oz) Arborio rice
- 120 ml (4 fl oz) dry white wine
- 60 ml (4 tbsp) chopped mixed fresh herbs, such as basil, chives, parsley and tarragon
- 25 g (1 oz) Parmesan or Cheddar cheese, freshly grated
- 2 large eggs, beaten
- 225 g (8 oz) derinded taleggio cheese, diced
- salt and pepper
- oil, for shallow-frying

**1** Infuse the saffron strands in the hot stock for 10 minutes, then transfer to a saucepan. Peel and finely chop the onion.

**2** Melt the butter in a large heavy-based frying pan, add the onion and garlic and fry for 10 minutes until soft and golden.

**3** Add the rice to the onion and stir over the heat for 1 minute until all the grains are glossy. Add the wine and boil rapidly until almost all of the liquid is evaporated. Heat the saffron infused stock and keep at a very low simmer.

**4** Add a ladleful of the saffron stock to the rice. Simmer gently, stirring constantly, until the liquid is absorbed. Continue to add the stock and stir the rice for 20-25 minutes until all the liquid is used up and the rice is just cooked.

**5** Remove from the heat; stir in the herbs and Parmesan or Cheddar. Cover the surface with a piece of greaseproof paper and leave to cool.

**6** Stir the beaten eggs into the risotto, then divide the mixture in half. Pour a little oil into a 23 cm (9 inch) non-stick (grill-proof) frying pan and heat gently.

**7** Spoon half the risotto into the pan and spread evenly to the edges with a palette knife. Sprinkle over the taleggio and carefully spread the remaining risotto on top. Cook over a low heat for 20 minutes until golden underneath.

**8** Position the frying pan under the grill and cook for 10 minutes until the top is golden all over. Turn out onto a large plate and allow to cool slightly for 10-15 minutes. Serve warm, cut into wedges, accompanied by a green salad.

**NOTE** Taleggio is a rich, soft cheese from Italy with a wonderful melting texture. Use either mozzarella or fontina as an alternative if you are unable to find taleggio.

## BABY ONION AND FRESH PEA RISOTTO

**SERVES 4**
PREPARATION
30 minutes
COOKING TIME
35 minutes
FREEZING
Not suitable
CALS/SERVING
495
COLOUR INDEX
Page 40

225 g (8 oz) baby onions
50 g (2 oz) butter
30 ml (2 tbsp) olive oil
4 garlic cloves, peeled
30 ml (2 tbsp) chopped fresh sage
10 ml (2 tsp) soft brown sugar
5 ml (1 tsp) sea salt
225 g (8 oz) Arborio rice
150 ml (¼ pint) red wine
60 ml (2 fl oz) port (optional)
900 ml-1.2 litres (1½-2 pints) vegetable stock
125 g (4 oz) shelled peas (see note)
15-30 ml (1-2 tbsp) olive paste
25 g (1 oz) Parmesan cheese, freshly grated
TO GARNISH
sage sprigs

**1** Put the baby onions in a saucepan, add cold water to cover and bring to the boil. Simmer for 30 seconds, then drain and refresh under cold water. Peel away the skins and halve the onions if large.
**2** Melt half the butter with the oil in a frying pan. Add the onions and garlic cloves and fry over a medium heat for 15 minutes, stirring occasionally, until caramelised. Stir in the sage, sugar and salt and fry for a further 10 minutes.
**3** Meanwhile, melt the remaining butter in a heavy-based frying pan. Add the rice and stir-fry for 1-2 minutes until all the grains are glossy. Add the wine, and port if using, and boil rapidly until almost totally reduced.
**4** Heat the stock in a small pan and keep it at a very gentle simmer. Gradually add the simmering stock to the rice, a ladleful at a time, stirring the rice constantly and making sure each addition is absorbed before adding the next. Continue for about 20 minutes, until most of the stock has been added and the rice is almost cooked.
**5** Add the onion mixture to the rice with the remaining stock and the peas and continue to cook, stirring, until the liquid is absorbed and the rice is just tender. Remove the pan from the heat and stir in the olive paste and two thirds of the Parmesan. Season, cover with foil and allow the risotto to stand for 5 minutes.
**6** Serve topped with the remaining Parmesan and garnished with sage.

### NOTES
❑ For optimum results use fresh peas when they are in season: you will need about 300 g (10 oz) peas in the pod to give this shelled weight.
❑ Frozen peas can be used when fresh ones are not available; stir them into the risotto at the end, just to heat through.

## VEGETABLE AND RICE TIAN

**SERVES 4**
PREPARATION
20 minutes
COOKING TIME
1½ hours
FREEZING
Not suitable
CALS/SERVING
310

125 g (4 oz) long-grain rice
1 onion
1 red chilli
1 red pepper
1 yellow pepper
2 courgettes
30 ml (2 tbsp) olive oil
2 garlic cloves, peeled and crushed
5 ml (1 tsp) ground cumin
5 ml (1 tsp) ground cinnamon
5 ml (1 tsp) ground coriander
10 ml (2 tsp) chopped fresh thyme
30 ml (2 tbsp) sun-dried tomato paste
two 400 g (14 oz) cans chopped tomatoes
200 ml ( (7 fl oz) vegetable stock
5 ml (1 tsp) sugar
1 bay leaf
TOPPING
15 g (½ oz) ground almonds
15 g (½ oz) fresh breadcrumbs
15 g (½ oz) Parmesan cheese, freshly grated (optional)
30 ml (2 tbsp) chopped fresh parsley
salt and pepper
TO FINISH
olive oil, for drizzling

**1** Put the rice in a bowl, add plenty of cold water to cover and leave to soak for 30 minutes. Drain thoroughly in a sieve and shake dry.
**2** Peel and chop the onion; deseed and chop the chilli and peppers; dice the courgettes.
**3** Heat the oil in a saucepan, add the onion, garlic, spices and thyme and fry gently for 10 minutes, stirring often. Add the peppers, chilli and courgettes with a little more oil

if necessary. Stir-fry for 5 minutes until lightly golden.
**4** Stir in the sun-dried tomato paste, tomatoes, stock, sugar and bay leaf. Bring to the boil, cover and simmer gently for 30 minutes. Remove the bay leaf. Season with salt and pepper to taste.
**5** Spoon half of the vegetables into a lightly oiled baking dish. Sprinkle the rice evenly over the surface, then cover with the rest of the vegetables.
**6** Cover the dish with foil and bake in the oven at 190°C (375°F) Mark 5 for 40 minutes. Meanwhile, mix the topping ingredients together. Remove the foil from the baking dish, sprinkle the topping over the vegetables and drizzle liberally with oil. Bake for a further 15-20 minutes until the topping is golden.
**7** Allow to stand for a few minutes before serving, with jacket potatoes topped with butter and cheese if desired.

**VARIATION** Omit the Parmesan and scatter some grated Cheddar or gruyère over the crumb topping.

## CATALAN RED PEPPERS

**SERVES 4**
PREPARATION
20 minutes, plus chilling
COOKING TIME
15-20 minutes
FREEZING
Not suitable
CALS/SERVING
340
COLOUR INDEX
Page 40

4 red peppers
olive oil, for brushing
175 g (6 oz) mixed long-grain and wild rice
salt and pepper
8 tomatoes
8 spring onions, trimmed
few pitted olives, chopped
30 ml (2 tbsp) capers
90 ml (6 tbsp) olive oil
30 ml (2 tbsp) white wine vinegar
1 large garlic clove, peeled and crushed
Guacamole (see page 88), to serve (optional)

**1** Put the peppers on a baking sheet and brush lightly with oil. Bake in the oven at 220°C (425°F) Mark 7 for 15-20 minutes or until tender.
**2** Meanwhile, cook the rice in boiling salted water according to the packet instructions until tender. Drain, rinse under cold running water then drain well.
**3** Chop the tomatoes and spring onions. Add to the rice with the olives and capers. Fork through to mix.
**4** When the peppers are cool enough to handle, halve lengthwise and remove the core and seeds. Pat dry with kitchen paper.
**5** Whisk the olive oil, vinegar and garlic together in a bowl; season with salt and pepper. Add to the rice and toss to mix.
**6** Pile the rice into the pepper halves and arrange on serving plates. Cover and chill in the refrigerator for 30 minutes before serving. If preferred, serve topped with a spoonful of guacamole.

**NOTE** These stuffed peppers are equally good served hot. Rinse the rice with boiling, rather than cold water, pile into the hot peppers and serve immediately.

## VEGETABLE PILAU

**SERVES 4-6**
PREPARATION
10 minutes
COOKING TIME
20 minutes
FREEZING
Not suitable
CALS/SERVING
475-315
COLOUR INDEX
Page 40

125 g (4 oz) button mushrooms
175 g (6 oz) cauliflower florets
2-3 shallots
30 ml (2 tbsp) ghee or oil
1-2 garlic cloves, peeled and crushed
1 bay leaf
2.5 ml (½ tsp) turmeric
6 cloves
6 cardamoms
1 cinnamon stick, halved
1 dried red chilli
350 g (12 oz) white basmati rice
125 g (4 oz) peas
salt and pepper
25 g (1 oz) butter (optional)
handful of roughly chopped fresh coriander (optional)
finely grated zest of 1 lemon or lime
toasted flaked almonds or chopped fresh coconut, to garnish

**1** Thickly slice the mushrooms and cauliflower. Peel and halve the shallots.
**2** Heat the ghee or oil in a heavy-based saucepan. Add the shallots and cook, stirring, for a few minutes until beginning to soften. Add the garlic, mushrooms and cauliflower and cook briefly, stirring over a high heat, until softened and just tinged with brown.
**3** Add the bay leaf and spices. Cook for 1-2 minutes, stirring all the time.
**4** Add the rice, 600 ml (1 pint) water, the peas and plenty of salt. Bring quickly to the boil, then lower the heat, cover with a lid and simmer gently for about 10-15 minutes or until the rice is tender and the water absorbed. Add the butter and coriander if using, and lemon or lime zest. Season with pepper. Recover and leave to stand for 5 minutes before serving.
**5** Serve garnished with toasted flaked almonds or chopped fresh coconut.

**NOTE** Serve this pilau either as an accompaniment to a curry or as part of an Indian meal with a pulse dish, such as Chick Peas with Ginger and Tomatoes (see page 163).

**VARIATIONS** Almost any vegetables can be used instead of – or as well as – the peas, mushrooms and cauliflower. Try green beans, carrots, okra and courgettes.

## COURGETTE AND CHEESE PILAF

**SERVES 4**
PREPARATION
20 minutes
COOKING TIME
30 minutes
FREEZING
Not suitable
CALS/SERVING
490

- 1 onion
- 1 red chilli
- 1 courgette
- 60 ml (4 tbsp) olive oil
- 2 garlic cloves, peeled and crushed
- 225 g (8 oz) bulghar wheat
- 300 ml ($\frac{1}{2}$ pint) vegetable stock
- 50 g (2 oz) raisins or sultanas
- 25 g (1 oz) pine nuts, toasted
- salt and pepper
- 125 g (4 oz) mozzarella or fontina cheese, shredded
- 15 ml (1 tbsp) chopped fresh mint

**1** Peel and chop the onion; deseed and chop the chilli; dice the courgette. Heat the oil in a deep frying pan or saucepan. Add the onion, garlic and chilli and fry for 5 minutes, then add the courgette and fry for a further 5-10 minutes until golden. Remove with a slotted spoon and set aside.
**2** Add the bulghar wheat to the pan and stir over a low heat for 30 seconds until the grains are glossy. Add the stock and raisins or sultanas. Bring to the boil, cover and simmer for 5-10 minutes until the bulghar is softened and the water absorbed.
**3** Return the courgette and onion mixture to the pan and cook for a further 5 minutes until heated through. Add the pine nuts and season with salt and pepper to taste. Remove the pan from the heat and add the cheese. Cover and leave to stand for 5 minutes until the cheese is melted, then stir in the mint. Serve hot.

**NOTE** Serve this pilaf as part of a main meal with other vegetarian dishes, or as an accompaniment to a vegetable stew or curry.

## PUY LENTIL AND RICE PILAF

**SERVES 4-6**
PREPARATION
20 minutes
COOKING TIME
$1\frac{1}{4}$ hours
FREEZING
Not suitable
CALS/SERVING
390-260

- 125 g (4 oz) Puy lentils
- 125 g (4 oz) brown rice or red Camargue rice
- 4 ripe tomatoes
- 2 large onions
- 60 ml (4 tbsp) olive oil
- 2 garlic cloves, peeled and crushed
- 5 ml (1 tsp) each ground cinnamon, cumin and turmeric
- 10 ml (2 tsp) ground coriander
- 1.25-2.5 ml ($\frac{1}{4}$-$\frac{1}{2}$ tsp) cayenne pepper
- 30 ml (2 tbsp) lemon juice
- 60 ml (4 tbsp) chopped fresh parsley
- 25 g (1 oz) butter or margarine
- salt and pepper

**1** Rinse the lentils and place in a saucepan. Add plenty of cold water to cover. Bring to the boil, partially cover and simmer gently for 25-30 minutes until the lentils are cooked. Drain and refresh under cold water, drain thoroughly.
**2** Wash and dry the rice and cook as for the lentils, allowing 30 minutes for brown rice, or 20 minutes for red rice. Drain, refresh and dry well.
**3** Meanwhile, immerse the tomatoes in a bowl of boiling water for 30 seconds. Remove and peel away the skins, then chop the tomato flesh.
**4** Peel and slice the onions. Heat the oil in a heavy-based frying pan, add the onions and garlic and fry gently for 15 minutes. Add the spices and fry, stirring, for 3-4 minutes. Add the tomatoes, lemon juice and 60 ml (4 tbsp) water. Cover and simmer for a further 20 minutes.
**5** Stir in the cooked lentils and rice, add the butter and parsley and heat through for 2-3 minutes, stirring constantly. Season with salt and pepper to taste. Serve at once, with toasted pitta bread, and yogurt or crème fraîche if wished.

# VEGETABLE BIRYANI

**SERVES 4**
PREPARATION
25 minutes
COOKING TIME
40 minutes
FREEZING
Not suitable
CALS/SERVING
670

- 1 large onion
- 225 g (8 oz) waxy potatoes
- 125 g (4 oz) French beans
- 2 carrots
- 225 g (8 oz) cauliflower florets
- 350 g (12 oz) basmati rice
- about 60 ml (4 tbsp) ghee or oil
- 25 g (1 oz) unsalted pistachio nuts
- 25 g (1 oz) slivered blanched almonds
- 25 g (1 oz) raisins
- 2 large pinches of saffron strands
- 1 cinnamon stick
- 6 black peppercorns
- 6 cloves
- 4 cardamoms
- 5 ml (1 tsp) ground cumin
- 5 ml (1 tsp) cayenne pepper
- 3 garlic cloves, peeled and crushed
- 75 g (3 oz) shelled peas
- 150 ml (¼ pint) thick yogurt

TO SERVE
- hard-boiled eggs (optional)
- garam masala, to taste

**1** Peel and halve the onion, then cut into very thin semi-circular slices. Peel the potatoes and cut into chunks. Trim and halve the beans. Peel and slice the carrots. Break the cauliflower into small florets. Wash the rice in a sieve under cold running water; drain.
**2** Heat the ghee or oil in a heavy-based saucepan or flameproof casserole. Add the onion and cook over a high heat for about 5 minutes or until golden brown. Remove from the pan with a slotted spoon and drain on kitchen paper; set aside for the garnish.
**3** Add the nuts and raisins to the ghee or oil remaining in the pan and cook for 1 minute, or until the nuts are lightly browned. Remove from the pan with a slotted spoon and drain on kitchen paper; set aside.
**4** Add the spices and garlic to the pan, adding a little extra ghee or oil to the pan if necessary. Add the prepared vegetables and the peas and cook, stirring, for 2 minutes. Add the yogurt, a spoonful at a time, stirring thoroughly after each addition. Add 60 ml (4 tbsp) water, cover with a lid and simmer for 10 minutes or until the vegetables are just tender.
**5** Meanwhile, put the rice in another saucepan with 600 ml (1 pint) water and salt to taste. Bring quickly to the boil, then lower the heat, partially cover and simmer for 10 minutes or until barely tender and the liquid is absorbed.
**6** Add the rice to the vegetables, recover and simmer gently for 5-10 minutes or until the rice and vegetables are tender. Season with salt and pepper to taste.
**7** Pile onto a warmed serving platter and top with the nuts, raisins, fried onions, and hard-boiled eggs if using. Sprinkle with garam masala to taste and serve immediately, accompanied by Cauliflower and Lentil Dhal (see page 162) and a selection of chutneys.

# VEGETARIAN PAELLA

**SERVES 4**
PREPARATION
20 minutes
COOKING TIME
50 minutes, plus resting
FREEZING
Not suitable
CALS/SERVING
560
COLOUR INDEX
Page 41

- 2 red peppers
- 90 ml (6 tbsp) olive oil
- 2 onions
- 4 garlic cloves
- 10 ml (2 tsp) paprika
- 5 ml (1 tsp) turmeric
- 2.5 ml (½ tsp) cayenne pepper
- 350 g (12 oz) easy-cook Italian brown rice
- 1.2 litres (2 pints) vegetable stock
- 175 g (6 oz) French beans, halved
- 175 g (6 oz) frozen peas
- 30 ml (2 tbsp) chopped fresh parsley
- 50 g (2 oz) black olives
- salt and pepper

**1** Halve, core, deseed and slice the peppers. Heat 30 ml (2 tbsp) of the oil in a large, deep frying pan. Add the peppers and fry over a medium heat for 5-10 minutes until well browned and softened. Remove with a slotted spoon and set aside.
**2** Peel and chop the onion. Peel and finely chop the garlic. Add the remaining oil to the pan and fry the onions, garlic and spices for 10 minutes until golden. Add the rice, stir once and then pour in the stock. Bring to the boil and simmer gently for 15 minutes.
**3** Meanwhile, blanch the beans in boiling salted water for 1 minute. Drain and immediately refresh under cold water; set aside.
**4** Add the peppers, beans and peas to the rice and stir through. Cook for a further 15 minutes until the rice and vegetables are tender. Remove from the heat and stir in the parsley and olives. Season well, cover with a lid and allow to stand for 5 minutes before serving.

## SPANISH RICE WITH AIOLI

**SERVES 4-6**
PREPARATION
20 minutes
COOKING TIME
45 minutes
FREEZING
Not suitable
CALS/SERVING
750-500

2 onions
4 garlic cloves
60 ml (4 tbsp) olive oil
10 ml (2 tsp) hot paprika
5 ml (1 tsp) turmeric
pinch of cayenne pepper
350 g (12 oz) Spanish or Arborio rice
900 ml (1½ pint) hot vegetable stock
450 g (1 lb) ripe tomatoes
30 ml (2 tbsp) sun-dried tomato paste
30 ml (2 tbsp) chopped fresh parsley
AIOLI
2-4 garlic cloves, peeled
2.5 ml (½ tsp) coarse sea salt
2 egg yolks
15 ml (1 tbsp) lemon juice
300 ml (½ pint) light olive oil

**1** Peel and chop the onions and garlic. Heat the oil in a large, deep frying pan or saucepan, add the onions, garlic and spices and fry gently for 10 minutes until golden.
**2** Add the rice and stir-fry for 1 minute until the grains are glossy. Stir in the stock, bring to the boil and simmer for 10 minutes.
**3** Meanwhile immerse the tomatoes in a bowl of boiling water for 30 seconds, then remove and peel away the skins. Roughly chop the tomatoes and add to the pan with the sun-dried tomato paste. Simmer over a low heat for a further 20-25 minutes until the liquid is absorbed and the rice grains are tender. Add a little hot water during cooking if the rice becomes too dry.
**4** Meanwhile, make the aioli. Put the garlic cloves, salt, egg yolks and lemon juice in a food processor and blend for 30 seconds until pale and frothy. Then with the motor running, pour in the oil in a steady stream through the feeder tube, until the aioli is thickened and glossy. (If the sauce is too thick, add a little boiling water as you go.) Season with salt and pepper to taste.
**5** Add the chopped parsley to the rice and fork through. Season with salt and pepper to taste. Serve hot, with the aioli handed separately.

**NOTE** The quantity of aioli is more than is required as an accompaniment to this recipe but it isn't practical to make a smaller amount. Store the rest in the refrigerator for up to 1 week, and use as required.

## RICE CAKES WITH SAGE BUTTER

**SERVES 6-8**
PREPARATION
30 minutes, plus cooling
COOKING TIME
50 minutes
FREEZING
Not suitable
CALS/SERVING
525-395
COLOUR INDEX
Page 41

1.2 litres (2 pints) vegetable stock
large pinch of saffron strands
1 onion
3 garlic cloves
50 g (2 oz) butter
10 ml (2 tsp) chopped fresh thyme
350 g (12 oz) Arborio rice
150 ml (¼ pint) dry white wine
125 g (4 oz) ricotta cheese
50 g (2 oz) Parmesan cheese, freshly grated
salt and pepper
SAGE BUTTER
2 ripe tomatoes
125 g (4 oz) butter
15 ml (1 tbsp) chopped fresh sage
15 ml (1 tbsp) balsamic vinegar

**1** Put the stock and saffron in a pan; bring to a simmer.
**2** Peel and chop the onion and garlic. Melt half the butter in a medium pan and fry the onion gently for 5 minutes. Add the garlic and thyme and fry for a further 5 minutes. Add the rice, stir for 1 minute, then pour in the wine and bubble rapidly until totally evaporated.
**3** Add a ladleful of stock and cook over a medium heat, stirring constantly until the liquid is absorbed. Continue to add stock, a ladleful at a time, until the rice is cooked.
**4** Off the heat, stir in the ricotta, Parmesan and seasoning to taste. Spread out on a baking sheet and leave until cold.
**5** Heat remaining butter in a non-stick heavy-based frying pan. Add the rice mixture and press flat to the edges. Fry over a low heat for 10 minutes. Slide out onto a plate, invert frying pan over top, then flip back into pan. Fry for a further 10 minutes until the underside is crisp.
**6** Meanwhile, for the sage butter, skin, deseed and dice the tomatoes. Heat butter in a small pan and sauté the sage for 2-3 minutes until crisp; stir in tomatoes and vinegar.
**7** Turn the rice cake out onto a plate and cut into wedges. Serve drizzled with the sage butter. Accompany with a mixed leaf salad.

# MOZZARELLA-STUFFED RICE BALLS

**SERVES 4**
PREPARATION
45 minutes
COOKING TIME
10-15 minutes
FREEZING
Not suitable
CALS/SERVING
765

RISOTTO
1 red onion
75 g (3 oz) butter
150 ml (¼ pint) dry white wine
275 g (10 oz) Arborio rice
1 litre (1¾ pints) vegetable stock
salt and pepper
25 g (1 oz) freshly grated Parmesan cheese

TO FINISH
2 eggs, beaten
125 g (4 oz) mozzarella cheese
about 16 small basil leaves
125 g (4 oz) dried white breadcrumbs
oil, for deep-frying

**1** To make the risotto, peel and finely chop the onion. Melt the butter in a large saucepan, add the onion and fry gently for 5 minutes or until soft but not coloured. Pour in the wine and boil rapidly until almost totally reduced. Add the rice and stir to coat with the butter and wine.

**2** Add a ladleful of stock and simmer, stirring, until absorbed. Continue adding the stock ladle by ladle until the rice is tender and creamy but still has some bite to it; this should take about 20 minutes. Make sure each addition of stock is absorbed before adding the next. (You may not need to use all of the stock.)

**3** Season generously and stir in the Parmesan. Allow to cool completely. Beat the eggs into the cold risotto. Cut the mozzarella into small cubes.

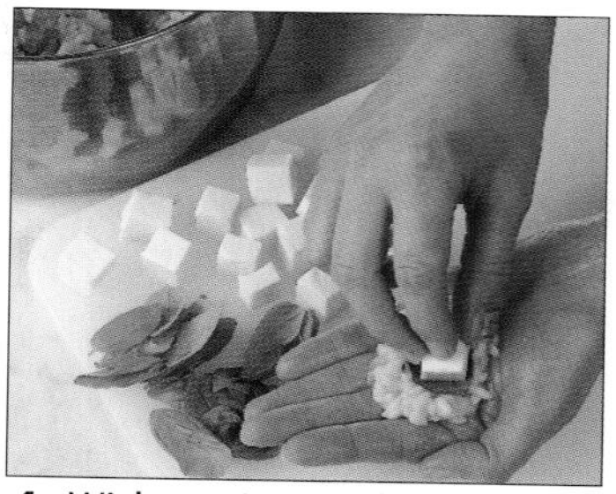

**4** With moistened hands, take 15 ml (1 tbsp) risotto and spread in the palm of one hand. Lay a small basil leaf and a cube of mozzarella in the middle.

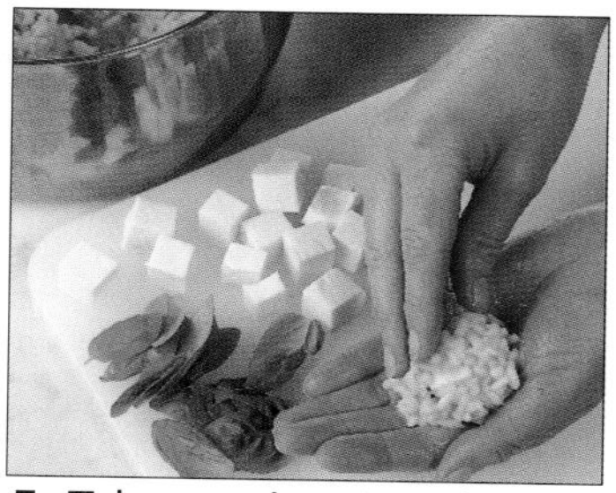

**5** Take another 15 ml (1 tbsp) of risotto and place over the mozzarella and basil to enclose. Shape into a smooth ball. Repeat to make about 16 in total.

**6** Spread the breadcrumbs in a shallow dish. Roll the rice balls in the breadcrumbs until evenly covered.

**7** Heat the oil in a deep-fryer to 180°C (350°F) or until a crumb dropped in sizzles immediately. Fry the rice balls, a few at a time, for 3-5 minutes until golden and crisp. Drain on kitchen paper, sprinkle with salt and keep hot while cooking the remainder. Serve immediately.

**NOTE** These rice balls are a good way to use up leftover risotto, but worth making from scratch too. Serve with a hearty salad, as a lunch or supper, or on their own as a substantial snack. Alternatively made as tiny bite-sized morsels, they are ideal finger food to serve with drinks.

## COUSCOUS-STUFFED PEPPERS

**SERVES 4-6**
PREPARATION
25 minutes
COOKING TIME
30 minutes
FREEZING
Not suitable
CALS/SERVING
435-290

6 red or yellow peppers
1 red onion
25 g (1 oz) butter or margarine
250 ml (8 fl oz) water
5 ml (1 tsp) oil
2.5 ml (½ tsp) salt
175 g (6 oz) quick-cook couscous
25 g (1 oz) raisins
25 g (1 oz) pine nuts
30 ml (2 tbsp) chopped fresh mint
15 ml (1 tbsp) balsamic vinegar
salt and pepper
1 egg yolk
DRESSING
60 ml (4 tbsp) olive oil
15 ml (1 tbsp) white wine vinegar
15 ml (1 tbsp) chopped fresh mint

**1** Make a slit in the side of each pepper and carefully remove the core and seeds.
**2** Peel and finely chop the onion. Melt the butter in a small pan, add the onion and cook until softened.
**3** Bring the water to the boil in a saucepan. Add the oil and salt. Remove from the heat, add the couscous, stir once, then leave to stand, covered, for 5 minutes. Stir in the onion, raisins, pine nuts, mint and balsamic vinegar. Season generously and stir in the egg yolk to bind the mixture.
**4** Using a teaspoon, three-quarters fill the peppers with the couscous mixture; do not over-fill as the couscous will swell during baking. Brush the peppers with oil and bake at 200°C (400°F) Mark 6 for 30-35 minutes until tender.
**5** Meanwhile put the ingredients for the dressing in a screw-topped jar and shake vigorously to combine.
**6** Serve the stuffed peppers warm or cold, with the dressing spooned over.

## VEGETABLE COUSCOUS WITH HARISSA

**SERVES 4-6**
PREPARATION
30 minutes
COOKING TIME
20 minutes
FREEZING
Not suitable
CALS/SERVING
445-300
COLOUR INDEX
Page 42

2 small onions
1 bunch of baby fennel, or 1 large fennel bulb
225 g (8 oz) pumpkin
225 g (8 oz) baby carrots
450 g (1 lb) quick-cook couscous
40 g (1½ oz) butter or margarine
2 garlic cloves, peeled and crushed
good pinch of saffron strands
2 cinnamon sticks
30 ml (2 tbsp) coriander seeds, crushed
5 ml (1 tsp) paprika
1 red chilli
225 g (8 oz) tomatoes
225 g (8 oz) courgettes
175 g (6 oz) shelled fresh or frozen broad beans (optional)
50 g (2 oz) raisins
450 ml (¾ pint) vegetable stock
salt and pepper
15 ml (1 tbsp) harissa paste (see note)
chopped coriander, to garnish

**1** Peel and quarter the onions. Trim baby fennel; quarter, core and chop large fennel, if using. Peel and chop the pumpkin. Trim and scrub the carrots.
**2** Put the couscous in a bowl and moisten with some water, according to the packet instructions. Drain well and place in a steamer or colander lined with muslin. Steam over boiling water for about 20 minutes, forking it through occasionally, until tender and fluffed up.
**3** Meanwhile, cook the vegetables. Melt the butter in a large saucepan and add the onions, garlic, fennel, pumpkin and carrots. Cook, stirring, for 3 minutes. Crumble in the saffron and stir in the cinnamon, coriander and paprika. Lower the heat, cover and cook for 5 minutes.
**4** In the meantime, finely slice the chilli, discarding the seeds if you prefer; skin and chop the tomatoes; thickly slice the courgettes; skin the broad beans if using. Add these vegetables to the saucepan with the raisins and stock. Season with salt and pepper to taste. Cook, uncovered, over a medium heat for 10-12 minutes, stirring frequently, until the vegetables are tender and the stock has reduced a little.
**5** Just before serving, pour about 200 ml (7 fl oz) of the cooking liquor into a small bowl and stir in the harissa paste.
**6** Pile the couscous onto a warmed platter or individual plates and top with the vegetables. Sprinkle with coriander and serve with the harissa sauce.

**NOTE** Harissa paste is a fiery hot red chilli paste, flavoured with garlic, coriander, cumin and mint. It is used widely in North African cookery and is available from ethnic shops in tubes or small cans. If you can't find it, make your own alternative. Flavour 30 ml (2 tbsp) tomato paste with a little crushed garlic and paprika and cayenne pepper to taste. Use as a substitute.

# COUSCOUS-FILLED AUBERGINES WITH A CORIANDER DRESSING

**SERVES 2 (or 4 as a starter)**
PREPARATION
30 minutes
COOKING TIME
20-30 minutes, plus reheating
FREEZING
Not suitable
CALS/SERVING
320 (or 160)

2 aubergines, each about 250 g (9 oz)
30 ml (2 tbsp) lemon juice
sea salt and pepper
50 g (2 oz) quick-cook couscous
6 sun-dried tomatoes in oil, drained
25 g (1 oz) dried apricots (no soak)
8 fresh mint sprigs
15 ml (1 tbsp) pine nuts
4 spring onions, trimmed

CORIANDER DRESSING
1 cm (½ inch) piece fresh root ginger
1 garlic clove, peeled
150 ml (¼ pint) yogurt
finely grated zest of 1 lime
30 ml (2 tbsp) chopped fresh coriander
squeeze of lime juice

TO GARNISH
coriander sprigs

**1** Cut the aubergines in half lengthways and score the cut sides deeply, without damaging the skins. Place, scored-side up, on a baking sheet.

**2** Rub in the lemon juice and sprinkle with a little sea salt. Bake in the oven at 200°C (400°F) Mark 6 for 20-30 minutes until the flesh is soft and tender.

**3** Meanwhile, put the couscous in a bowl, pour on 150 ml (¼ pint) boiling water and leave to soak and fluff up. Chop the sun-dried tomatoes, dried apricots, mint, pine nuts and spring onions; mix together in a bowl, seasoning with salt and pepper.

**4** Scoop the flesh out from the cooked aubergines and chop finely. Fork through the soaked couscous to separate the grains, then add the chopped aubergine and sun-dried tomato mixture. Stir gently, using a fork, until evenly combined.

**5** To make the dressing, peel and finely grate the ginger; crush the garlic. In a bowl, mix the yogurt with the ginger, garlic, lime zest, coriander and lime juice to taste. Chill until ready to serve.

**6** Spoon the filling into the aubergine shells, piling it up well. If serving hot, reheat in the oven for 15 minutes. Alternatively allow to cool, then chill in the refrigerator. Serve the aubergines either hot or cold, garnished with coriander and topped with the coriander dressing.

**NOTE** Serve a whole aubergine as a light meal, or one half as a starter. A tomato salad makes an ideal accompaniment.

**VARIATIONS** Other vegetables can be used instead of – or as well as – aubergines. Try baby peppers, baby courgettes and tomatoes.

## TAMALE PIE

**SERVES 4-6**
PREPARATION
15 minutes
COOKING TIME
55 minutes
FREEZING
Suitable: Stage 3
CALS/SERVING
450-300

- 1 onion
- 1 green pepper
- 1 green chilli
- 60 ml (4 tbsp) olive oil
- 2 garlic cloves, peeled and crushed
- 10 ml (2 tsp) sweet paprika
- 5 ml (1 tsp) ground coriander
- 5 ml (1 tsp) ground cumin
- 2.5 ml (½ tsp) chilli powder
- 125 g (4 oz) coarse cornmeal or polenta
- 225 g (8 oz) frozen sweetcorn kernels, thawed
- 600 ml (1 pint) vegetable stock
- 400 g (14 oz) can chopped tomatoes
- 75-125 g (3-4 oz) Cheddar cheese, grated
- salt and pepper

TO SERVE

- 90-120 ml (3-4 fl oz) soured cream
- 4 spring onions, trimmed

**1** Peel and chop the onion. Halve, core and deseed the green pepper and chilli, then chop finely.
**2** Heat the oil in a saucepan. Add the onion, garlic, green pepper and chilli, then add all of the spices and fry gently for 10 minutes until lightly golden.
**3** Stir in the cornmeal or polenta, sweetcorn, stock and tomatoes. Bring to the boil, cover and simmer over a low heat for about 30 minutes until the stew is thickened. You may need to add a little extra stock if it becomes too thick. Season with salt and pepper to taste.
**4** Spoon the stew into a lightly oiled 1.2 litre (2 pint) deep baking dish and cover with the grated cheese. Bake in the oven at 200°C (400°F) Mark 6 for 15-20 minutes until golden. Leave to stand for 5 minutes before serving with the soured cream and chopped spring onions.

**NOTE** If the cheese topping exudes any oil during baking, carefully pour off and discard on removing from the oven.

## BAKED CABBAGE WITH FRUITED BULGHAR WHEAT STUFFING

**SERVES 4**
PREPARATION
30 minutes
COOKING TIME
40-45 minutes
FREEZING
Not suitable
CALS/SERVING
355
COLOUR INDEX
Page 42

- 8 large green cabbage leaves
- 125 g (4 oz) bulghar wheat
- 2 large onions
- 175 g (6 oz) carrots
- 50 g (2 oz) no-soak dried apricots
- 30 ml (2 tbsp) olive oil
- 50 g (2 oz) hazelnuts, roughly chopped
- 1 garlic clove, peeled and crushed
- 10 ml (2 tsp) coriander seeds, lightly crushed
- 45 ml (3 tbsp) chopped fresh parsley
- 25 g (1 oz) raisins
- salt and pepper
- 10 ml (2 tsp) plain white flour
- 450 ml (¾ pint) vegetable stock
- chopped coriander or parsley, to garnish

**1** Remove the stalks from the cabbage leaves. Add to a large pan of boiling water and blanch for 1-2 minutes until softened. Drain.
**2** Put the bulghar wheat in a bowl and cover with plenty of boiling water. Leave to soften for 10 minutes, then drain.
**3** Peel and slice the onions; peel and dice the carrots; roughly chop the apricots.
**4** Heat the oil in a large frying pan. Add the onions and fry for 3-5 minutes. Add the chopped hazelnuts fry for a further 3-5 minutes until the onions are starting to brown. Remove three quarters of the mixture from the pan and set aside.
**5** Add the garlic, carrots, apricots, bulghar wheat, coriander, parsley and raisins to the pan. Stir well and season with salt and pepper to taste.
**6** Divide this stuffing between the cabbage leaves, spooning it into the centre. Fold in the sides of the leaves over the filling, then roll up to enclose the stuffing completely. If necessary, secure with cocktail sticks.
**7** Place the reserved onion mixture in a flameproof casserole over a medium heat. Stir in the flour, then gradually stir in the stock. Bring to the boil and season lightly. Place the cabbage parcels in the casserole in a single layer.
**8** Cover and bake in the oven at 200°C (400°F) Mark 6 for 30 minutes. Scatter with coriander or parsley to serve.

**VARIATIONS** Use prunes in place of the apricots. Brazil nuts, almonds or walnuts can be used instead of hazelnuts.

# BULGHAR WHEAT AND WALNUT PATTIES WITH TOMATO SAUCE

**SERVES 4**
PREPARATION
35 minutes, plus soaking
COOKING TIME
20 minutes
FREEZING
Suitable: See note
CALS/SERVING
450

PATTIES
175 g (6 oz) bulghar wheat
1 small onion
1 garlic clove
30 ml (2 tbsp) olive oil
finely grated zest of 1 lemon
5 ml (1 tsp) dried oregano
125 g (4 oz) mozzarella cheese
50 g (2 oz) walnuts, toasted and ground
30 ml (2 tbsp) chopped fresh mint
2.5 ml (½ tsp) each ground cumin and cinnamon
1 large egg
salt and pepper

SIMPLE TOMATO SAUCE
400 g (14 oz) can chopped tomatoes
15 ml (1 tbsp) olive oil
1 garlic clove, peeled and crushed
15 ml (1 tbsp) chopped fresh basil
pinch of sugar

TO GARNISH
basil sprigs

**1** Place the bulghar wheat in a large bowl, cover with plenty of boiling water and set aside to soak for 20 minutes. Drain well.

**2** Meanwhile, place all the ingredients for the sauce in a pan, season and bring to the boil. Cover and simmer for 15 minutes. Keep warm.

**3** Peel and finely chop the onion and garlic. Heat the oil in a frying pan, add the onion, garlic, lemon zest and oregano and fry gently for 5 minutes. Add the bulghar wheat and stir-fry for 1 minute.

**4** Transfer the bulghar mixture to a food processor. Roughly chop the mozzarella and add to the processor with the ground walnuts, mint, spices and egg. Season liberally and process until smooth.

**5** Divide the mixture into 8 equal portions and shape into patties, using floured hands. Dust each one lightly with flour. Reheat the tomato sauce.

**6** Heat a shallow layer of oil in a heavy-based frying pan. When hot, fry the patties, two at a time, for 2-3 minutes on each side until golden. Drain on kitchen paper; keep hot while cooking the rest. Serve garnished with basil and accompanied by the tomato sauce.

**NOTE** Open-freeze the cooled, cooked patties, then pack in a polythene bag, seal and freeze for up to 2 months. Freeze sauce separately. Thaw at room temperature, then reheat the patties in a moderate oven for 15-20 minutes.

# PULSES AND NUTS

# WHITE BEAN STEW WITH TAPENADE

**SERVES 4**
PREPARATION
25 minutes, plus overnight soaking
COOKING TIME
35 minutes
FREEZING
Suitable
CALS/SERVING
420

225 g (8 oz) dried cannellini beans, soaked overnight in cold water
pinch of saffron strands
450 g (1 lb) ripe tomatoes
1 onion
3 garlic cloves
60-90 ml (4-6 tbsp) olive oil
15 ml (1 tbsp) finely chopped fresh rosemary
5 ml (1 tsp) grated lemon zest
225 g (8 oz) broccoli florets
15 ml (1 tbsp) lemon juice
salt and pepper

TAPENADE
125 g (4 oz) pitted black olives
2 garlic cloves, peeled and chopped
30 ml (2 tbsp) capers in brine, drained and rinsed
30 ml (2 tbsp) chopped fresh parsley
5 ml (1 tsp) chopped fresh thyme
60 ml (4 tbsp) olive oil

**1** Drain the beans, place in a saucepan and cover with cold water by at least 10 cm (4 inches). Bring to the boil and boil steadily for 10 minutes. Skim the surface, lower heat, cover and simmer for 45 minutes or until tender.

**2** Drain the beans, reserving 300 ml (½ pint) liquid. Add the saffron to the liquid and set aside to infuse. Immerse the tomatoes in a bowl of boiling water for 30 seconds, then remove and peel away the skins; roughly chop the flesh.

**3** Peel and chop the onion and garlic. Heat the oil in a large saucepan, add the onion, garlic, rosemary and lemon zest and fry gently for 10 minutes. Add the chopped tomatoes, cover and simmer for a further 10 minutes.

**4** Cut the broccoli into small florets. Add the beans to the tomato mixture with the saffron stock, broccoli and lemon juice. Bring to the boil and simmer gently, uncovered, for 10-15 minutes until the cannellini beans are starting to fall apart and the broccoli is tender. Season with salt and pepper to taste.

**5** Meanwhile, make the tapenade. Place all the ingredients, except the oil, in a blender or food processor and process briefly to form a rough paste. Add the oil, blend again briefly and season to taste. Spoon the bean stew into warmed bowls, top each one with a spoonful of the tapenade and serve at once.

**VARIATIONS**

❑ Use canned instead of dried beans. You will need two 400 g (14 oz) cans cannellini beans. Drain and add to the stew at stage 4 after 5 minutes' cooking. At stage 2, use 300 ml (½ pint) vegetable stock.

❑ Omit the broccoli. Before serving, toast 4 slices ciabatta and spread with tapenade. Top each serving of bean stew with a tapenade toast.

## MIXED BEAN CHILLI

**SERVES 6**
PREPARATION
20 minutes, plus overnight soaking
COOKING TIME
$2\frac{1}{2}$-3 hours
FREEZING
Suitable
CALS/SERVING
275
COLOUR INDEX
Page 43

125 g (4 oz) dried red kidney beans, soaked overnight in cold water
125 g (4 oz) dried black-eye beans, soaked overnight in cold water
salt and pepper
1 red onion
2-3 dried hot red chillies
700 g ($1\frac{1}{2}$ lb) mixed vegetables, such as carrots, potatoes, peppers, aubergines
60 ml (4 tbsp) olive oil
3 garlic cloves, peeled and crushed
15 ml (1 tbsp) mild paprika
15 ml (1 tbsp) tomato paste
10 ml (2 tsp) cumin seeds
2 bay leaves
1 cinnamon stick
425 g (15 oz) can chopped tomatoes
15 ml (1 tbsp) lime or lemon juice
large handful of fresh coriander
TO SERVE
tortillas or rice
soured cream (optional)
grated Manchego or Cheddar cheese (optional)

**1** Drain the beans and put them in separate pans with enough fresh cold water to cover. Bring each to the boil and boil rapidly for 10 minutes, then lower the heat. Simmer until just tender: the red kidney beans will take 1-$1\frac{1}{2}$ hours; the black-eye beans $1\frac{1}{2}$ hours. Add salt towards the end of the cooking time. Drain and rinse with cold water.
**2** Peel and finely chop the onion. Crumble the chillies, removing the seeds if a milder flavour is preferred.
**3** Prepare the vegetables as necessary, cutting them into fairly large chunks.
**4** Heat half of the oil in a large saucepan or flameproof casserole. Add the onion, half of the garlic and half of the chillies. Cook, stirring, for about 5 minutes or until the onion is softened.
**5** Add the paprika, tomato paste and cumin seeds; cook, stirring, for 2 minutes. Add the bay leaves and cinnamon.
**6** Add the beans and prepared vegetables, stirring to coat in the onion mixture. Cook for 2 minutes, then add the tomatoes and about 150 ml ($\frac{1}{4}$ pint) water. Bring to the boil, lower the heat and simmer for about 45 minutes - 1 hour until the vegetables are tender. If the mixture begins to stick, add a little extra water. About halfway through cooking, taste and add more chilli if necessary.
**7** Meanwhile, whisk together the rest of the oil, lime or lemon juice and remaining garlic. Roughly chop the coriander and stir into the oil mixture. Leave to stand while the chilli is cooking.
**8** When the chilli is cooked, stir in the coriander mixture. Check the seasoning if necessary. Serve with tortillas or rice, and soured cream and grated cheese if desired.

**NOTE** Ready-made tortillas are available from larger supermarkets and delicatessens.

## CRUSTED BEAN AND PESTO BAKE

**SERVES 4**
PREPARATION
15 minutes
COOKING TIME
35 minutes
FREEZING
Suitable
CALS/SERVING
510

1 onion
2 garlic cloves
30 ml (2 tbsp) olive or sunflower oil
15 ml (1 tbsp) chopped fresh mixed herbs
400 g (14 oz) can chopped tomatoes
30 ml (2 tbsp) sun-dried tomato pesto (see page 292)
400 g (14 oz) can borlotti beans
400 g (14 oz) can cannellini beans, drained
salt and pepper
TOPPING
100 g ($3\frac{1}{2}$ oz) fresh breadcrumbs
75 g (3 oz) Cheddar cheese, finely grated
25 g (1 oz) ground almonds

**1** Peel and chop the onion and garlic. Heat the oil in a flameproof casserole, add the onion, garlic and herbs and fry for 5 minutes until softened. Add the tomatoes and pesto; stir well.
**2** Add the borlotti beans together with their liquid, and the drained cannellini beans. Bring to the boil, cover and simmer gently for 15 minutes. Remove from the heat and season with salt and pepper to taste.
**3** Mix all the topping ingredients together until evenly combined. Scatter evenly over the top of the stew and bake in the oven at 200°C (400°F) Mark 6 for 15 minutes until the topping is crisp and golden. Serve with a green vegetable and warm bread.

**VARIATION** For a different crust, arrange thin slices of baguette overlapping on top of the stew. Brush with garlic-flavoured olive oil, scatter over some chopped fresh herbs and grated Parmesan, then bake as above.

## QUICK VEGETABLE AND BEAN MOLE

**SERVES 4-6**
PREPARATION
20 minutes
COOKING TIME
35 minutes
FREEZING
Suitable
CALS/SERVING
400-270

- 2 red onions
- 2 garlic cloves
- 2 potatoes
- 60 ml (4 tbsp) sunflower oil
- 5 ml (1 tsp) ground cumin
- 5 ml (1 tsp) ground coriander
- 5 ml (1 tsp) paprika
- 1.25 ml (¼ tsp) chilli powder
- two 400 g (14 oz) cans red kidney beans
- 400 g (14 oz) can chopped tomatoes
- 150 ml (¼ pint) tomato juice
- 225 g (8 oz) button mushrooms
- 15 g (½ oz) dark chocolate, grated
- 15 ml (1 tbsp) lime juice
- 30-45 ml (2-3 tbsp) chopped fresh coriander
- salt and pepper
- coriander sprigs, to garnish

**1** Peel and finely chop the onions and garlic. Peel the potatoes and cut into bite-sized cubes.
**2** Heat 45 ml (3 tbsp) of the oil in a saucepan, add the onions, garlic, potatoes and spices and fry, stirring, for 5 minutes until lightly golden.
**3** Add the kidney beans together with their liquid, the tomatoes and tomato juice. Bring to the boil, cover and simmer gently for 25 minutes.
**4** Heat the remaining oil in a frying pan, add the mushrooms and stir-fry for 4-5 minutes until golden. Add to the stew with the chocolate, lime juice and coriander. Cook for a further 5 minutes. Season with salt and pepper to taste. Serve at once, garnished with coriander and accompanied by plain boiled rice.

**VARIATION** Make half the quantity of mole; meanwhile bake 4 large potatoes in a moderate oven until tender. Halve the potatoes and place in a gratin dish. Top with the mole and a dollop of soured cream. Scatter generously with grated cheese and grill until melted.

## BOSTON BAKED BEANS

**SERVES 4**
PREPARATION
10 minutes, plus overnight soaking
COOKING TIME
2-2½ hours
FREEZING
Suitable
CALS/SERVING
345
COLOUR INDEX
Page 43

- 225 g (8 oz) black-eyed beans, soaked overnight in cold water
- 1 large garlic clove
- 1 large onion
- 30 ml (2 tbsp) olive oil
- 600 ml (1 pint) dry cider
- 150 ml (¼ pint) passata
- 15 ml (1 tbsp) black treacle
- 30 ml (2 tbsp) tomato paste (preferably sun-dried)
- 15 ml (1 tbsp) demerara sugar
- 5 ml (1 tsp) French mustard
- coarse sea salt and pepper
- parsley sprigs, to garnish

**1** Drain the beans, rinse under cold water and place in a large saucepan. Cover with plenty of fresh cold water, bring to the boil and boil steadily for 10 minutes. Remove any scum from the surface with a slotted spoon. Lower the heat, cover and simmer for a further 20 minutes.
**2** Peel and finely chop the garlic. Peel and chop the onion. Heat the oil in a saucepan, add the onion and garlic and fry gently until tender. Add the cider, passata, black treacle, tomato paste, demerara sugar and mustard. Bring to the boil.
**3** Drain the black-eyed beans and transfer to a casserole. Stir in the tomato mixture. Cover and cook in the oven at 170°C (325°F) Mark 3 for 1½-2 hours or until the beans are tender. Check and stir the beans occasionally during cooking and add a little extra cider or water if necessary to prevent them drying out; the finished sauce should be thick and syrupy.
**4** Season with salt and pepper to taste. Serve garnished with parsley and accompanied by hot crusty garlic bread or jacket potatoes and a crisp, colourful salad.

**NOTE** The cooking time for pulses varies considerably. The longer the beans have been stored, the longer they will take to cook.

**VARIATION** Instead of black-eyed beans, use haricot beans or another pulse, adjusting the cooking time accordingly.

## CLAY POT STEW

**SERVES 6**
PREPARATION
20 minutes, plus overnight soaking
COOKING TIME
2½-2¾ hours
FREEZING
Suitable
CALS/SERVING
190

50 g (2 oz) dried chick peas, soaked overnight in cold water
50 g (2 oz) haricot beans, soaked overnight in cold water
900 ml (1½ pints) vegetable stock
1 onion
2 carrots
2 parsnips
2 tomatoes
50 g (2 oz) bulghar wheat
60 ml (4 tbsp) olive oil
4 red chillies
15 ml (1 tbsp) chopped fresh thyme
15 ml (1 tbsp) chopped fresh mint
10 ml (2 tsp) dried oregano
5-10 ml (1-2 tsp) ground cumin
5-10 ml (1-2 tsp) ground coriander
5 ml (1 tsp) ground cinnamon
30 ml (2 tbsp) tomato paste
salt and pepper
TO SERVE
30 ml (2 tbsp) chopped fresh parsley
extra-virgin olive oil, for drizzling

**1** Drain the chick peas and haricot beans and place in a saucepan. Pour on the stock and bring to the boil. Cover and boil steadily for 10 minutes.
**2** Peel and dice the onion, carrots, parsnips and tomatoes.
**3** Transfer the pulses and stock to a large clay pot or casserole dish. Add the bulghar wheat, diced vegetables, tomatoes, olive oil, whole chillies, herbs and spices. Cover with a tight-fitting lid and bake in the oven at 180°C (350°F) Mark 4 for 2 hours.
**4** Remove the lid and stir in the tomato paste. Cover and return to the oven for a further 30-45 minutes until the beans and vegetables are tender.
**5** Remove the stew from the oven and season generously with salt and pepper. Allow to stand for 10 minutes before serving, sprinkled with the chopped parsley and drizzled with extra-virgin olive oil.

**NOTE** If possible, make this stew a day ahead to allow the flavours time to develop.

## VEGETABLE AND BEAN STEW WITH ROUILLE

**SERVES 4**
PREPARATION
30 minutes
COOKING TIME
25-30 minutes
FREEZING
Not suitable
CALS/SERVING
600
COLOUR INDEX
Page 44

2 large leeks, trimmed
225 g (8 oz) courgettes or green beans, trimmed
450 g (1 lb) small potatoes, scrubbed
225 g (8 oz) brown mushrooms
1 red pepper
2.5 cm (1 inch) piece fresh root ginger
45 ml (3 tbsp) olive oil
strip of orange zest
2 bay leaves
900 ml (1½ pints) vegetable stock
400 g (14 oz) can red kidney beans, rinsed and drained
generous pinch of saffron strands (optional)
60 ml (4 tbsp) double cream (optional)
salt and pepper
ROUILLE
1 red pepper
1 red chilli
4 garlic cloves, peeled
75 ml (5 tbsp) olive oil
25 g (1 oz) fresh breadcrumbs

**1** First make the rouille. Halve, core and deseed the red pepper and chilli. Place in a food processor or blender with the garlic and oil. Work to a purée, then add the breadcrumbs and blend to a smooth paste. Transfer to a small serving dish.
**2** To prepare the stew, slice the leeks and courgettes or green beans. Halve the potatoes and mushrooms unless very small. Halve, core, deseed and slice the red pepper. Peel and grate the ginger.
**3** Heat the oil in a large saucepan. Add the leeks, ginger, orange zest and bay leaves and fry for 3 minutes. Add the stock and potatoes and bring to the boil. Reduce the heat and simmer gently for 10 minutes or until the potatoes are almost tender.
**4** Add the red pepper, courgettes, mushrooms, beans and saffron. Cover and simmer gently for 10-15 minutes until all the vegetables are tender but not pulpy. Add the cream if using, and season with salt and pepper to taste.
**5** Serve in warmed soup plates, with the rouille handed separately.

## ORIENTAL-STYLE BEAN STEW

**SERVES 4**
PREPARATION
20 minutes, plus overnight soaking
COOKING TIME
1¼ hours
FREEZING
Not suitable
CALS/SERVING
200

125 g (4 oz) dried soya beans, soaked overnight in cold water
50 g (2 oz) arame seaweed (optional)
450 g (1 lb) tomatoes
1 leek, trimmed
30 ml (2 tbsp) oil
2 garlic cloves, peeled and crushed
150 ml (¼ pint) vegetable stock
15 ml (1 tbsp) dark soy sauce
5-10 ml (1-2 tsp) chilli sauce
5 ml (1 tsp) sugar
30 ml (2 tbsp) chopped fresh coriander
salt and pepper

**1** Drain the beans and place in a saucepan with plenty of cold water to cover by at least 10 cm (4 inches). Bring to the boil and boil steadily for 10 minutes. Skim the surface, lower the heat, partially cover and simmer gently for 1 hour or until the beans are tender. Drain and set aside.
**2** If using seaweed, cook according to the packet instructions; drain, dry well and set aside.
**3** Meanwhile, immerse the tomatoes in a bowl of boiling water for 30 seconds, then remove and peel away the skins; dice the tomato flesh. Slice the leek.
**4** Heat the oil in a large frying pan. Add the garlic and leek and fry gently for 5 minutes. Stir in the tomatoes and fry for 1 minute, then add the stock, soy sauce, chilli sauce and sugar. Bring to the boil, cover and simmer gently for 10 minutes.
**5** Stir in the cooked beans, herbs and seaweed, if using. Heat through for 5 minutes, season with salt and pepper to taste and serve piping hot.

## ROOT VEGETABLE AND LENTIL CASSEROLE

**SERVES 6**
PREPARATION
20 minutes
COOKING TIME
About 1 hour
FREEZING
Not suitable
CALS/SERVING
260
COLOUR INDEX
Page 44

5 ml (1 tsp) cumin seeds
15 ml (1 tbsp) coriander seeds
5 ml (1 tsp) mustard seeds
25 g (1 oz) fresh root ginger
3 onions
450 g (1 lb) carrots
350 g (12 oz) leeks, trimmed
350 g (12 oz) mooli (white radish)
450 g (1 lb) button mushrooms
45 ml (3 tbsp) olive oil
2 garlic cloves, peeled and crushed
1.25 ml (¼ tsp) turmeric
175 g (6 oz) split red lentils
50 g (2 oz) brown or green lentils, rinsed and drained
750 ml (1¼ pints) boiling water
salt and pepper
30 ml (2 tbsp) chopped coriander leaves (optional)
parsley sprigs, to garnish

**1** Crush the cumin, coriander and mustard seeds together, using a pestle and mortar, (or in a strong bowl with the end of a rolling pin). Peel and grate or finely chop the ginger.
**2** Peel and slice the onions, carrots and leeks. Peel and roughly chop the mooli; halve the mushrooms if large.
**3** Heat the oil in a large flameproof casserole. Add the onions, carrots, leeks and mooli, and fry for 2-3 minutes, stirring constantly. Add the mushrooms, garlic, ginger, turmeric and crushed spices, and fry for a further 2-3 minutes, stirring.
**4** Add the lentils and boiling water. Season with salt and pepper and return to the boil. Cover and cook in the oven at 180°C (350°F) Mark 4 for about 45 minutes or until the vegetables and lentils are tender.
**5** Stir in the coriander if using, and adjust the seasoning. Serve garnished with parsley and accompanied by a green vegetable, such as broccoli or spinach, and plenty of warm crusty bread.

**VARIATION** Replace the mooli (white radish) with parsnips or young turnips.

## PASTA E FAGIOLI

**SERVES 6**
PREPARATION
25 minutes
COOKING TIME
45-50 minutes
FREEZING
Not suitable
CALS/SERVING
440

1 onion
1 leek, trimmed
1 carrot
1 large potato
2 celery sticks
60 ml (4 tbsp) extra-virgin olive oil
2 garlic cloves, peeled and crushed
10 ml (2 tsp) chopped fresh thyme
5 ml (1 tsp) finely chopped fresh rosemary
500 g (1 lb 2 oz) carton passata
600 ml (1 pint) vegetable stock
225 g (8 oz) small conchiglie or ditali pasta
two 400 g (14 oz) cans borlotti beans, drained
60 ml (4 tbsp) chopped fresh basil
salt and pepper
TO SERVE
75 g (3 oz) Parmesan cheese, freshly grated
a little extra-virgin olive oil

**1** Peel and chop the onion; slice the leek; peel and dice the carrot and potato; dice the celery.
**2** Heat the oil in a large saucepan, add the onion, leek, carrot, potato, celery, garlic and herbs and fry gently for 10 minutes until softened slightly, stirring occasionally to prevent them sticking.
**3** Add the passata and stock. Bring to the boil, cover and simmer for 20 minutes.
**4** Meanwhile add the pasta to a large pan of lightly salted boiling water and cook for 5-6 minutes until *al dente* (tender but firm to the bite). Drain and immediately refresh under cold water. Drain well and toss with a little olive oil.
**5** Add the beans to the stew. Cover and cook for a further 10 minutes until the vegetables are tender. Stir in the pasta and basil, heat through and season with salt and pepper to taste.
**6** Spoon into warmed bowls and sprinkle generously with Parmesan. Drizzle with olive oil to serve.

## NUT ROAST WITH ONION AND PORT GRAVY

**SERVES 8**
PREPARATION
45 minutes
COOKING TIME
1¼ hours
FREEZING
Suitable: Stage 3
CALS/SERVING
480
COLOUR INDEX
Page 45

1 onion, peeled
2 celery sticks
50 g (2 oz) butter
2 garlic cloves, peeled and crushed
grated zest and juice of 1 lemon
15 ml (1 tbsp) chopped fresh thyme
225 g (8 oz) mixed nuts
225 g (8 oz) cooked red or brown rice (see note)
125 g (4 oz) Cheddar cheese, grated
2 eggs, lightly beaten
30 ml (2 tbsp) chopped mixed fresh herbs
salt and pepper
ONION GRAVY
900 g (2 lb) onions
50 g (2 oz) butter
1 garlic clove, peeled and crushed
15 ml (1 tbsp) chopped fresh thyme
pinch of sugar
120 ml (4 fl oz) ruby port
600 ml (1 pint) vegetable stock

**1** Chop the onion and celery. Melt the butter in a pan, add the onion, celery, garlic, lemon zest and thyme and fry gently for about 10 minutes until softened.
**2** Meanwhile finely chop and toast the nuts. Place in a food processor with the sautéed mixture, rice, cheese, eggs and herbs. Pulse until evenly blended, seasoning liberally.
**3** Spoon into a greased and base-lined 900 g (2 lb) loaf tin. Smooth the surface and cover with a piece of greased non-stick baking parchment, then a layer of foil. Bake in the oven at 190°C (375°F) Mark 5 for 1¼ hours or until a skewer inserted into the middle comes out hot.
**4** Meanwhile make the gravy. Peel and chop the onions. Melt the butter in a saucepan. Add the onions, with the garlic, thyme, sugar and a pinch of salt, and fry gently for 20 minutes until golden and caramelised.
**5** Add the port and reduce by half, then stir in the stock and simmer covered for 15 minutes. Strain through a sieve into a clean pan, pressing through as much residue as possible; keep warm.
**6** Leave the nut roast to stand in the tin for 10 minutes, then unmould onto a warmed plate. Serve cut into slices, with the onion gravy and seasonal roast vegetables.

**NOTE** You will need about 125 g (4 oz) uncooked weight to give this quantity of cooked rice.

## CAULIFLOWER AND LENTIL DHAL

**SERVES 4**
PREPARATION
20 minutes
COOKING TIME
35 minutes
FREEZING
Not suitable
CALS/SERVING
420

1 onion
1 garlic clove
2.5 cm (1 inch) piece fresh root ginger
60 ml (4 tbsp) sunflower oil
5 ml (1 tsp) ground coriander
5 ml (1 tsp) ground cumin
2.5 cm (½ tsp) turmeric
2.5 cm (½ tsp) garam masala
75 g (3 oz) red lentils
300 ml (½ pint) vegetable stock
30 ml (2 tbsp) hot curry paste
575 g (1¼ lb) cauliflower florets
300 ml (½ pint) coconut milk
125 g (4 oz) frozen peas, thawed
30 ml (2 tbsp) chopped fresh coriander
15 ml (1 tbsp) lemon juice
salt and pepper

**1** Peel and finely chop the onion and garlic; peel and grate the ginger. Heat half the oil in a saucepan, add the onion, garlic, ginger and dry spices and fry gently for 5 minutes.
**2** Add the lentils, stir well and pour in the stock. Bring to the boil, cover and simmer gently for 10 minutes.
**3** Meanwhile, heat the remaining oil in a frying pan. Add the curry paste and fry gently for 3 minutes. Add the cauliflower and stir-fry over a medium heat for 3 minutes; remove from the heat.
**4** Add the coconut milk and spicy cauliflower to the lentils and return to the boil. Cover and simmer for a further 10 minutes.
**5** Stir in the peas, coriander and lemon juice and heat through gently for 2-3 minutes until the peas are tender. Check the seasoning. Serve the dhal as a meal with rice and naan bread, or as part of a selection of Indian dishes.

## EGYPTIAN-STYLE LENTILS

**SERVES 4**
PREPARATION
15 minutes
COOKING TIME
1¼ hours
FREEZING
Not suitable
CALS/SERVING
350

225 g (8 oz) Puy lentils
1-2 red chillies
1 red pepper
30 ml (2 tbsp) olive oil
2 garlic cloves, peeled and crushed
10 ml (2 tsp) ground coriander
5 ml (1 tsp) ground cumin
5 ml (1 tsp) turmeric
grated zest of ½ lemon
salt and pepper
TO GARNISH
1 large onion
25 g (1 oz) butter
4 hard-boiled eggs
a little chopped parsley
Greek-style yogurt (optional)

**1** Wash the lentils under cold running water. Drain, place in a large saucepan and cover with plenty of cold water. Bring to the boil, partially cover and simmer for 25-30 minutes until almost tender.
**2** Meanwhile, prepare the garnish. Peel and slice the onion. Melt the butter in a heavy-based frying pan and add the onion. Fry over a medium heat for 20 minutes until golden, stirring occasionally to prevent burning.
**3** Drain the lentils, reserving 150 ml (¼ pint) of the liquid and set aside. Deseed and chop the chillies; halve, core, deseed and thinly slice the red pepper.
**4** Heat the oil in a saucepan, add the garlic, chilli(es), spices and lemon zest and fry gently for 5 minutes. Add the red pepper and fry for a further 10 minutes.
**5** Stir in the lentils and reserved liquid. Bring to the boil, cover and simmer for 10 minutes.
**6** Transfer to a warmed serving bowl and garnish with fried onion, hard-boiled eggs and chopped parsley. Serve at once, with a dollop of yogurt if desired.

**NOTE** If preferred cook the eggs for 7 minutes only, and allow the just setting yolks to run into the lentil mixture.

# SPRING GREEN, LENTIL AND RED PEPPER STIR-FRY

**ERVES 4**
REPARATION
0 minutes
OOKING TIME
0 minutes
REEZING
Not suitable
ALS/SERVING
70

350 g (12 oz) spring greens or curly kale
1 large red pepper
1 red onion
2.5 cm (1 inch) piece fresh root ginger
30 ml (2 tbsp) sunflower oil
10 ml (2 tsp) sesame oil
1 garlic clove, peeled and crushed
400 g (14 oz) can green lentils, rinsed
30 ml (2 tbsp) sesame seeds, toasted

SAUCE
30 ml (2 tbsp) dark soy sauce
15 ml (1 tbsp) lime juice
15 ml (1 tbsp) chilli sauce
15 ml (1 tbsp) preserved stem ginger syrup or thin honey
45 ml (3 tbsp) water

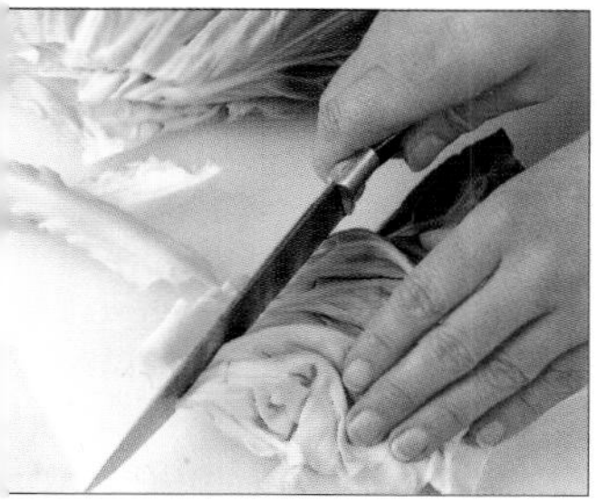

**1** Remove the tough stalks from the spring greens or kale, then shred the leaves. Halve, core deseed and thinly slice the pepper. Peel and thinly slice the onion. Peel and grate the ginger.

**2** To make the sauce, mix all the ingredients together in a small bowl.

**3** Blanch the spring greens or kale in a large pan of lightly salted boiling water for 1 minute, then drain, refresh under cold water and dry on kitchen paper.

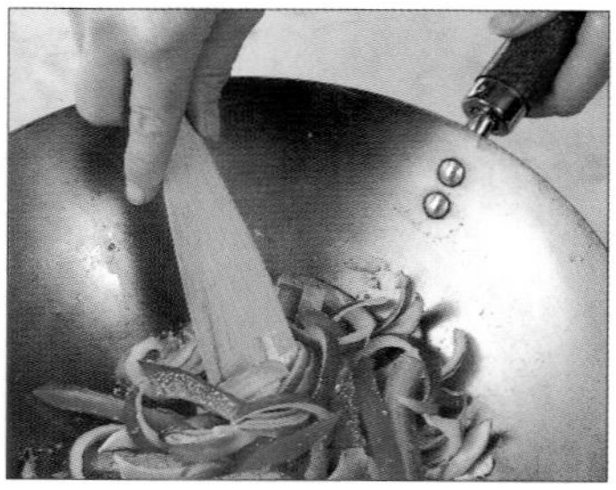

**4** Heat the sunflower and sesame oils in a wok or deep frying pan. When hot, stir-fry the red pepper, onion, ginger and garlic over a high heat for 3 minutes.

**5** Add the greens or kale, together with the well drained lentils and sauce. Stir well, cover and cook over a low heat for 3-4 minutes until the vegetables are tender. Scatter over the toasted sesame seeds and serve at once.

# CHICK PEAS WITH GINGER AND TOMATO

**SERVES 4**
PREPARATION
5 minutes, plus overnight soaking
COOKING TIME
$1\frac{3}{4}$-$2\frac{1}{4}$ hours
FREEZING
Not suitable
CALS/SERVING
260
COLOUR INDEX
Page 45

225 g (8 oz) dried chick peas, soaked overnight in cold water
5 cm (2 inch) piece fresh root ginger
1-2 garlic cloves
15 ml (1 tbsp) olive or sunflower oil
10 ml (2 tsp) garam masala
425 g (15 oz) can chopped tomatoes
salt and pepper
2 spring onions
150 ml ($\frac{1}{4}$ pint) thick yogurt or soured cream
5 ml (1 tsp) mild curry paste
30 ml (2 tbsp) chopped fresh mint
30 ml (2 tbsp) chopped fresh coriander (optional)

TO GARNISH
coriander sprigs
mint sprigs

**1** Drain the chick peas and put them in a large saucepan with plenty of fresh cold water to cover. Bring to the boil and boil steadily for 10 minutes, then lower the heat and simmer for $1\frac{1}{2}$-2 hours or until very tender. Drain thoroughly.
**2** Peel and finely chop the ginger and garlic. Heat the oil in a pan, add the ginger, garlic and garam masala and sauté for 2 minutes. Add the tomatoes, chick peas and seasoning. Bring to the boil, reduce heat and simmer for 15 minutes.
**3** Meanwhile, trim and finely chop the spring onions. Place in a bowl with the yogurt, curry paste, mint, and coriander if using. Mix thoroughly and season liberally.
**4** Turn the chick peas into a serving bowl and swirl in the yogurt. Serve garnished with coriander and mint.

# MASSAMAN CURRY

**SERVES 4-6**
PREPARATION
30 minutes
COOKING TIME
45 minutes
FREEZING
Suitable
CALS/SERVING
650-430

CURRY PASTE
½ small onion
1 red chilli
1 cm (½ inch) piece fresh root ginger
2 cloves
2.5 ml (½ tsp) cumin seeds
2.5 ml (½ tsp) coriander seeds
seeds from 1-2 cardamom pods
1 garlic clove, peeled and crushed
7.5 ml (1½ tsp) hot Indian curry paste
2.5 ml (½ tsp) turmeric
2.5 ml (½ tsp) sugar
FOR THE CURRY
225 g (8 oz) baby onions
30 ml (2 tbsp) sunflower oil
225 g (8 oz) small potatoes
225 g (8 oz) cauliflower florets
2 kaffir lime leaves, bruised
2 lemon grass stalks, bruised
400 g (14 oz) can coconut milk
400 g (14 oz) can chopped tomatoes
225 g (8 oz) frozen peas
90 g (3 oz) unsalted peanuts, toasted
30 ml (2 tbsp) chopped fresh coriander
salt and pepper
TO GARNISH
coriander sprigs

**1** To make the curry paste, peel and chop the onion; deseed and chop the chilli; peel and grate the ginger. Dry-fry the cloves, cumin, coriander and cardamom seeds in a small frying pan until browned and starting to give off their aroma.

**2** Place the dry-fried spices in a spice grinder or blender with the onion, chilli, ginger, garlic, curry paste, turmeric sugar and seasoning. Work to a smooth paste, adding about 15 ml (1 tbsp) water if necessary.

**3** For the curry, peel the onions and halve if large. Heat the oil in a saucepan, add the onions and curry paste and fry gently for 5 minutes. Meanwhile, peel the potatoes and cut into chunks. Add to the pan with the cauliflower florets and stir-fry for 5 minutes.

**4** Add the lime leaves, lemon grass, coconut milk and tomatoes. Bring to the boil, cover and simmer for 20 minutes. Add the peas and cook for a further 10 minutes until all the vegetables are tender.

**5** Stir in the peanuts and coriander and heat through for a few seconds. Check the seasoning. Serve the curry garnished with coriander sprigs and accompanied by plain boiled rice.

**NOTE** If you prefer a milder curry, only use half of the curry paste prepared at stage 1. The rest can be stored in a screw-topped jar in the refrigerator for up to 1 month.

## CHICK PEA, AUBERGINE AND MUSHROOM TAGINE

**SERVES 4**
PREPARATION
20 minutes
COOKING TIME
40 minutes
FREEZING
Suitable:
Stage 3
CALS/SERVING
540

1 large onion
2 garlic cloves
1 large aubergine, about 350 g (12 oz)
105 ml (7 tbsp) sunflower oil
10 ml (2 tsp) ground coriander
10 ml (2 tsp) paprika
5 ml (1 tsp) ground cumin
5 ml (1 tsp) ground cinnamon
5 ml (1 tsp) turmeric
1.25 ml (¼ tsp) cayenne pepper
400 g (14 oz) can chick peas
400 g (14 oz) can chopped tomatoes
300 ml (½ pint) vegetable stock
225 g (8 oz) button mushrooms
75 g (3 oz) dried apricots
salt and pepper
TO SERVE
225 g (8 oz) quick-cook couscous
25 g (1 oz) flaked almonds, toasted
15 ml (1 tbsp) chopped fresh parsley

**1** Peel and thinly slice the onion, peel and finely chop the garlic; trim and dice the aubergine. Heat 30 ml (2 tbsp) of the oil in a frying pan, add the onion, garlic and spices and fry over a medium heat for 5 minutes until golden. Using a slotted spoon, transfer to a saucepan. Add the chick peas with their liquid, tomatoes and stock.
**2** Heat another 45 ml (3 tbsp) oil in the frying pan, add the aubergine and fry, stirring, over a high heat for 5 minutes until evenly browned.
**3** Add the aubergine to the chick pea mixture. Bring to the boil, cover and simmer gently for 20 minutes.
**4** Meanwhile halve or quarter the mushrooms if large; roughly chop the apricots.
**5** Heat the remaining oil in the frying pan and stir-fry the mushrooms for 4-5 minutes until browned.
**6** Add the mushrooms to the stew with the apricots and cook for a further 10 minutes. Check the seasoning. In the meantime, steam the couscous in a muslin-lined steamer for 10 minutes, or according to the packet instructions.
**7** Fork through the couscous to separate the grains and pile onto a warmed serving dish. Scatter over the toasted almonds and chopped parsley and serve at once.

## CARIB STEW

**SERVES 4-6**
PREPARATION
15-20 minutes
COOKING TIME
55 minutes
FREEZING
Suitable:
Stage 4
CALS/SERVING
430-290
COLOUR INDEX
Page 46

1 onion
2 red chillies
2 large potatoes
2 red peppers
60 ml (4 tbsp) olive oil
4 garlic cloves, peeled and crushed
10 ml (2 tsp) jerk spices
600 ml (1 pint) tomato juice
600 ml (1 pint) vegetable stock
400 g (14 oz) can red kidney beans, drained
50 g (2 oz) creamed coconut
225 g (8 oz) spinach leaves, trimmed
30 ml (2 tbsp) chopped fresh coriander
salt and pepper
TO GARNISH
soured cream (optional)
chopped spring onion (optional)
diced avocado (optional)

**1** Peel and chop the onion; deseed and finely chop the chillies. Peel and dice the potatoes; halve, core, deseed and dice the peppers.
**2** Heat half the oil in a flameproof casserole, add the onion, garlic, chillies and spices and fry gently for 10 minutes.
**3** Add the remaining oil to the casserole and heat, then add the potatoes and peppers. Fry for a further 10 minutes until softened and golden, stirring occasionally to prevent them sticking.
**4** Add the tomato juice, stock and kidney beans. Bring to the boil, cover and simmer for 30 minutes. Transfer a few spoonfuls of the pan juices to a bowl and stir in the creamed coconut until melted. Stir this mixture into the casserole.
**5** Shred the spinach leaves and add to the stew with the chopped coriander. Season with salt and pepper to taste and heat gently for 5 minutes until the coconut is melted.
**6** Spoon into warmed bowls and top each serving with a little soured cream, chopped spring onion and some diced avocado if wished.

## STIR-FRIED CABBAGE WITH CASHEWS

**SERVES 4**
PREPARATION
20 minutes
COOKING TIME
10 minutes
FREEZING
Not suitable
CALS/SERVING
190

1-2 small red chillies
125 g (4 oz) French beans, trimmed
225 g (8 oz) Savoy cabbage
1 large carrot
30 ml (2 tbsp) sunflower oil
75-125 g (3-4 oz) cashew nuts
2 garlic cloves, peeled and crushed
5 ml (1 tsp) grated fresh root ginger

SAUCE
30 ml (2 tbsp) light soy sauce
15 ml (1 tbsp) lime juice
15 ml (1 tbsp) dry sherry
45 ml (3 tbsp) water
pepper

TO SERVE
egg-fried rice or noodles
a little sesame oil

**1** First mix the sauce ingredients together in a bowl.
**2** Deseed and chop the chilli(es); halve the beans; shred the cabbage. Peel the carrot and cut into matchsticks.
**3** Heat the oil in a wok or large, deep frying pan, add the cashews and stir-fry over a low heat until golden. Remove the nuts with a slotted spoon and drain on kitchen paper.
**4** Heat the oil remaining in the wok until it starts to smoke, then add the garlic, ginger and chilli. Stir-fry for 30 seconds, then add the French beans and stir-fry for 3 minutes. Add the cabbage and carrot and stir-fry for a further 2-3 minutes until the vegetables are wilted.
**5** Pour in the sauce, lower the heat and cook for 1 minute. Add the nuts and toss to mix. Serve immediately, on a bed of rice or noodles, drizzled with a little sesame oil.

## SPINACH AND CHICK PEA SAUTÉ

**SERVES 4**
PREPARATION
20 minutes
COOKING TIME
40 minutes
FREEZING
Not suitable
CALS/SERVING
450

1 onion
60 ml (4 tbsp) olive oil
3 garlic cloves, peeled and crushed
10 ml (2 tsp) ground cumin
5 ml (1 tsp) turmeric
2 ripe tomatoes
two 400 g (14 oz) cans chick peas, drained
200 ml (7 fl oz) vegetable stock
350 g (12 oz) spinach leaves, trimmed
50 g (2 oz) raisins
25 g (1 oz) pine nuts, toasted
salt and pepper
30 ml (2 tbsp) chopped fresh parsley, to garnish

**1** Peel and chop the onion. Heat the oil in a large frying pan, add the onion, garlic and spices and fry gently for 10 minutes until lightly golden.
**2** In the meantime, immerse the tomatoes in a bowl of boiling water for 30 seconds, then remove and peel away the skins; roughly chop the flesh. Add to the spice mixture and cook for a further 5 minutes.
**3** Stir in the chick peas and stock. Bring to the boil, cover and simmer for 20 minutes.
**4** Meanwhile, roughly shred the spinach leaves. Stir into the pilaf with the raisins and cook for a further 5 minutes until the spinach is wilted.
**5** Stir in the pine nuts and season with salt and pepper to taste. Serve at once, garnished with the chopped parsley and accompanied by plenty of warm crusty bread, such as olive bread or naan.

## SPICED CHICK PEA, RICE AND CARROT PILAF

**SERVES 4**
PREPARATION
15 minutes
COOKING TIME
20 minutes, plus standing
FREEZING
Not suitable
CALS/SERVING
490
COLOUR INDEX
Page 46

225 g (8 oz) basmati rice
seeds from 4-5 cardamom pods
1 cinnamon stick, bruised
10 ml (2 tsp) cumin seeds
2 bay leaves, bruised
1 onion
2 carrots
30 ml (2 tbsp) olive oil
2 garlic cloves, peeled and crushed
5 ml (1 tsp) grated fresh root ginger
5 ml (1 tsp) turmeric
5 ml (1 tsp) ground coriander
1.25 ml (¼ tsp) cayenne pepper
400 g (14 oz) can chick peas, drained
50 g (2 oz) raisins
750 ml (1¼ pints) vegetable stock
30 ml (2 tbsp) lemon juice
5 ml (1 tsp) salt
50 g (2 oz) cashew nuts, toasted
30 ml (2 tbsp) chopped fresh coriander
pepper
TO GARNISH
lemon wedges
coriander sprigs

**1** Wash the rice in a sieve under cold running water until it runs clear; set aside.
**2** Dry-fry the whole spices and bay leaves in a small frying pan for about 2 minutes until they start to pop and release their aroma.
**3** Peel and finely chop the onion; peel and dice the carrots. Heat the oil in a large saucepan, add the onion, garlic, ginger, carrots and ground spices and fry for 10 minutes until the vegetables are golden. Add the dry-fried spice mixture to the pan with the rice and stir-fry for 1 minute until all the rice grains are glossy.
**4** Add the chick peas, raisins, stock, lemon juice and salt to the pan. Bring to the boil, stir once and cover with a tight-fitting lid. Simmer over a low heat for 10 minutes, then take off the heat and leave undisturbed for 5 minutes.
**5** Fork through the cashew nuts and coriander. Check the seasoning and serve at once, garnished with lemon wedges and coriander sprigs.

**NOTE** If preferred, serve this dish with a mild vegetable curry.

## AFRICAN SWEET POTATO STEW

**SERVES 4-6**
PREPARATION
20 minutes
COOKING TIME
40-45 minutes
FREEZING
Suitable
CALS/SERVING
305-205

1 onion
60 ml (4 tbsp) groundnut oil
2 garlic cloves, peeled and crushed
10 ml (2 tsp) grated fresh root ginger
1.25 ml (½ tsp) cayenne pepper
350 g (12 oz) sweet potatoes
15 ml (1 tbsp) mild or medium curry paste
300 ml (½ pint) passata
300 ml (½ pint) vegetable stock
225 g (8 oz) spinach leaves, trimmed
225 g (8 oz) button mushrooms
60 ml (4 tbsp) peanut butter
30 ml (2 tbsp) chopped fresh coriander
salt and pepper
coriander sprigs, to garnish

**1** Peel and chop the onion. Heat 45 ml (3 tbsp) of the oil in a saucepan, add the onion, garlic, ginger and cayenne and fry gently for 10 minutes.
**2** Meanwhile, peel the sweet potatoes and cut into cubes. Add the curry paste to the onion mixture and cook, stirring, for 1 minute. Add the sweet potatoes, stir to coat with the onion mixture and fry for 3-4 minutes. Add the passata and stock. Bring to the boil, cover and simmer for 15-20 minutes until the potatoes are almost tender.
**3** Meanwhile, roughly shred the spinach leaves. Heat the remaining oil in a frying pan, add the mushrooms and stir-fry for 4-5 minutes until beginning to release their juices. Add to the potatoes with the spinach and cook for a further 5 minutes or until the vegetables are cooked through.
**4** Mix a few spoonfuls of the stew juices with the peanut butter to soften it slightly, then stir back into the pan. Add the coriander, season with salt and pepper to taste and heat through. Serve garnished with coriander sprigs.

# NUTTY BEAN BURGERS WITH A MANGO AND GINGER RELISH

**SERVES 6**
PREPARATION
20 minutes, plus standing
COOKING TIME
25 minutes
FREEZING
Suitable: Uncooked burgers only
CALS/SERVING
480 (including buns)

1 small onion
30 ml (2 tbsp) olive oil
1 garlic clove, peeled and crushed
10 ml (2 tsp) chopped fresh thyme
400 g (14 oz) can red kidney beans, rinsed and drained
400 g (14 oz) can butter beans, rinsed and drained
50 g (2 oz) chopped mixed nuts
40 g (1½ oz) fresh white breadcrumbs
15 ml (1 tbsp) dark soy sauce
15 ml (1 tbsp) lemon juice
salt and pepper
oil, for shallow-frying

RELISH
1 red onion
1 large red chilli
30 ml (2 tbsp) olive oil
5 ml (1 tsp) grated fresh root ginger
1 ripe mango
2 ripe tomatoes
15 ml (1 tbsp) brown sugar
15 ml (1 tbsp) distilled malt vinegar

TO SERVE
6 soft burger buns

**1** Peel and chop the onion. Heat the oil in a frying pan and fry the onion, garlic and thyme for 10 minutes until softened. Add the beans and fry gently for a further 5 minutes. Transfer to a food processor; pulse briefly to form a rough paste.

**2** Transfer the bean mixture to a bowl and stir in the nuts, breadcrumbs, soy sauce and lemon juice; season generously. Cover and set aside for several hours to allow the flavours to develop.

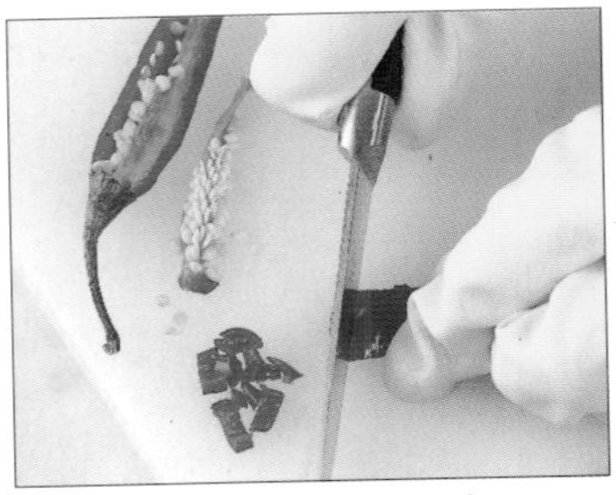

**3** Meanwhile, make the relish. Peel and dice the onion. Deseed and finely chop the chilli. Heat the oil in a small saucepan, add the onion, ginger and chilli and fry for 10 minutes until the onion is softened.

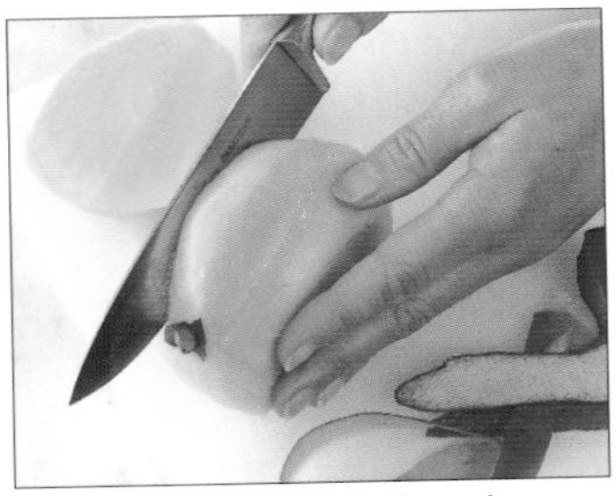

**4** Meanwhile, peel and roughly chop the mango and tomatoes. Add to the onion mixture, stir once, then add the sugar, vinegar and 15 ml (1 tbsp) water. Bring to the boil, cover and simmer for 5 minutes. Leave to cool.

**5** Divide the bean mixture into 6 equal portions and shape into burgers. Heat a little oil in a heavy-based frying pan and fry the burgers in two batches for 2-3 minutes on each side until golden and cooked through.

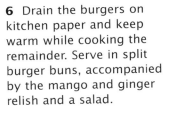

**6** Drain the burgers on kitchen paper and keep warm while cooking the remainder. Serve in split burger buns, accompanied by the mango and ginger relish and a salad.

## FESTIVE NUT AND CRANBERRY TERRINE

**SERVES 8-10**
PREPARATION
45 minutes, plus cooling
COOKING TIME
45-50 minutes
FREEZING
Not suitable
CALS/SERVING
490-395

FILLING
125 g (4 oz) long-grain rice
1 onion
1 leek, trimmed
4 celery sticks, trimmed
60 ml (4 tbsp) olive oil
60 ml (4 tbsp) chopped mixed fresh herbs, such as sage, parsley and thyme
40 g (1½ oz) fresh white breadcrumbs
40 g (1½ oz) walnuts, toasted and roughly ground
125 g (4 oz) dolcelatte cheese, crumbled
1 egg, lightly beaten
125 g (4 oz) fromage frais or crème fraîche
salt and pepper

PASTRY
225 g (8 oz) plain flour
pinch of salt
100 ml (3½ fl oz) water
45 g (1½ oz) white vegetable fat
15 g (1 oz) butter

TOPPING
125 g (4 oz) redcurrant jelly
5 ml (1 tsp) lemon juice
15 ml (1 tbsp) water
125 g (4 oz) cranberries or redcurrants, thawed if frozen
bay leaves, to garnish

**1** Cook the rice in boiling salted water according to the packet instructions until just tender; refresh under cold water, drain thoroughly and set aside. Peel and finely chop the onion; thinly slice the leek and celery.
**2** Heat the oil in a frying pan, add the onion, leek, celery and herbs and fry gently for 10 minutes until softened; transfer to a bowl. Add the rice and remaining filling ingredients, seasoning generously. Stir until evenly combined.
**3** For the pastry, sift the flour and salt into a bowl; make a well in the middle. Heat the water, fat and butter in a saucepan until the liquid comes to the boil. Pour into the flour and gradually work together, using a wooden spoon.
**4** When cool enough to handle, bring the dough together and knead lightly until smooth. Roll out on a lightly floured surface to a 25 x 20 cm (10 x 8 inch) rectangle and use to line a 1 kg (2 lb) loaf tin, pressing the dough into the corners; trim the overhanging pastry and reserve.
**5** Spoon the filling into the pastry case and smooth the surface. Divide the pastry trimmings in half, roll each piece into a long thin rope and plait the two lengths together.
**6** Dampen the edges of the pastry in the tin and top with the pastry plait, pressing down gently. Bake at 220°C (425°F) Mark 7 for 45-50 minutes until golden and a skewer inserted into the centre comes out hot. Leave to cool.
**7** For the topping, heat the redcurrant jelly in a small pan with the lemon juice and water until melted, then simmer for 3 minutes. Remove from the heat and stir in the fruit.
**8** To unmould the pie, upturn and tap gently, then set on a board. Spoon on the topping and leave to set. When cold, garnish with bay leaves and cut into slices to serve.

## VEGETABLE GRILL WITH WALNUT SAUCE

**SERVES 4**
PREPARATION
25 minutes
COOKING TIME
15-20 minutes
FREEZING
Not suitable
CALS/SERVING
540
COLOUR INDEX
Page 46

2 large carrots, trimmed
1 fennel bulb, trimmed
225 g (8 oz) sweet potatoes
225 g (8 oz) Jerusalem artichokes, scrubbed
225 g (8 oz) thick asparagus spears
8 baby leeks
60-90 ml (4-6 tbsp) olive oil
salt and pepper

WALNUT SAUCE
50 g (2 oz) day-old bread
75 g (3 oz) walnuts, toasted
2 garlic cloves, peeled and chopped
15 ml (1 tbsp) red wine vinegar
30 ml (2 tbsp) chopped fresh parsley
75 ml (3 fl oz) olive oil
50 ml (2 fl oz) walnut oil

**1** Start by preparing the walnut sauce. Crumble the bread into a bowl, add 30 ml (2 tbsp) water, then squeeze dry. Place the bread in a food processor with the toasted nuts, garlic, vinegar and parsley; blend until fairly smooth. Add the olive and walnut oils and process briefly to form a thick sauce. Season to taste and transfer to a serving dish.
**2** Prepare the vegetables. Cut the carrots into 5 mm (¼ inch) thick slices; thinly slice the fennel lengthwise; peel and thinly slice the sweet potatoes and artichokes. Trim the asparagus and leeks, but leave whole.
**3** Baste the vegetables with olive oil and grill in batches, turning once, for 2-6 minutes each side until charred and tender (see note); keep warm in a low oven while grilling the rest.
**4** Transfer all the vegetables to a warmed serving platter and season with a little salt and pepper. Serve accompanied by the walnut sauce and plenty of warm crusty bread.

**NOTE** The root vegetables will require the longest time under the grill whilst the asparagus and leeks will only take a short time to cook through.

# VEGETABLE DISHES

# FRITTO MISTO WITH ALMOND AIOLI

**SERVES 4-6**
PREPARATION
35 minutes
COOKING TIME
10-15 minutes
FREEZING
Not suitable
CALS/SERVING
745-500

900 g (2 lb) mixed vegetables, including asparagus tips, courgettes, peppers, fennel, onion
BATTER
2 eggs, separated
250 ml (8 fl oz) dry cider
150 g (5 oz) plain flour, sifted
2.5 ml (½ tsp) salt
30 ml (2 tbsp) chopped fresh chives
TO FINISH
oil, for deep-frying

ALMOND AIOLI
25 g (1 oz) day-old white bread, crusts removed
1-2 garlic cloves, peeled
25 g (1 oz) blanched almonds, toasted
1 egg yolk
juice of ½ lemon
150 ml (¼ pint) light olive oil
pinch of salt
pinch of cayenne pepper

**1** First make the aioli. Crumble the bread into a bowl, moisten with 15 ml (1 tbsp) water, then squeeze dry. Chop the garlic in a food processor, then add the toasted almonds and pulse briefly. Add the bread and work to a paste.

**2** Add the egg yolk and lemon juice, blend for a few seconds then, with the blade running, gradually pour in the oil through the feeder tube in a steady stream. Season, turn into a bowl, cover and set aside.

**3** Prepare the vegetables, trimming and peeling as necessary, then cut into slices, chunks or wedges.

**4** To make the batter, put the egg yolks, cider, flour, salt and chives into a bowl and beat together until smooth. In a separate bowl, whisk the egg whites until stiff, then fold into the batter until evenly incorporated.

**5** Heat a 10 cm (4 inch) depth of oil in a deep heavy based saucepan until it registers 180°C (350°F) on a sugar thermometer, or until a cube of bread dropped in browns in 30 seconds. Cook the vegetables in batches: dip a few pieces into the batter to coat, then deep-fry for 2-3 minutes until crisp and golden.

**6** Remove with a slotted spoon, drain on kitchen paper and keep warm in a low oven while frying the remaining vegetables. To serve, arrange the deep-fried vegetables on a large platter and serve the almond aioli as a dipping sauce.

**NOTE** The aioli can be made 2-3 days in advance; cover the surface with cling film and refrigerate until needed. If it becomes too thick, thin with a little hot water.

# POTATO GNOCCHI WITH RED PESTO

**SERVES 4**
PREPARATION
30 minutes
COOKING TIME
25-30 minutes
FREEZING
Not suitable
CALS/SERVING
980-655
COLOUR INDEX
Page 47

PESTO
1 large red pepper
50 g (2 oz) fresh basil leaves
1 garlic clove, peeled and crushed
30 ml (2 tbsp) pine nuts, toasted
6 sun-dried tomatoes in oil, drained
2 ripe tomatoes, peeled
45 ml (3 tbsp) tomato paste
2.5 ml (½ tsp) chilli powder
50 g (2 oz) Parmesan cheese, freshly grated
150 ml (¼ pint) olive oil
GNOCCHI
900 g (2 lb) floury potatoes
salt
50 g (2 oz) butter
1 egg, beaten
225-275 g (8-10 oz) plain white flour
TO GARNISH
basil leaves

**1** To make the pesto, place the pepper on the grill rack and grill, turning occasionally, under a high heat until blackened all over. Place in a covered bowl until cool enough to handle, then peel off the skin. Halve the pepper and remove the core and seeds. Place in a blender or food processor with the remaining pesto ingredients except the oil. Blend until smooth, then with the machine running, slowly add the oil.
**2** To make the gnocchi, cook the unpeeled potatoes in boiling water for 20-30 minutes until very tender; drain well. Halve and press through a potato ricer, or peel and press through a sieve into a bowl.
**3** While still warm, add 5 ml (1 tsp) salt, the butter, beaten egg and half of the flour. Lightly mix together, then turn out onto a floured board. Gradually knead in enough of the remaining flour to yield a smooth, soft, slightly sticky dough.
**4** Roll the dough into thick sausages, 2.5 cm (1 inch) in diameter. Cut into 2 cm (¾ inch) pieces and roll each piece over the back of a fork with your floured thumb, to form an indentation on one side and ridges on the other. Lay on a floured tea-towel.
**5** Bring a large pan of salted water to the boil. Cook the gnocchi in batches. Drop them into the boiling water and cook for 2-3 minutes, until they float to the surface. Remove with a slotted spoon and keep hot while cooking the remainder. Toss the gnocchi with the red pesto and serve immediately, garnished with basil.

**NOTES**
❑ It takes a little practice to make gnocchi really light – overworking makes them tough.
❑ The red pesto can be stored in a jar, covered with a layer of oil, for up to 2 weeks in the refrigerator.

**VARIATION** Serve the gnocchi with a classic pesto (see page 292).

# VEGETABLES À LA GRECQUE

**SERVES 4**
PREPARATION
20 minutes, plus cooling
COOKING TIME
40 minutes
FREEZING
Not suitable
CALS/SERVING
330

900 g (2 lb) mixed baby vegetables, such as carrots, turnips, fennel, cauliflower, broccoli, asparagus, courgettes and broad beans
75 ml (5 tbsp) olive oil
juice of ½ lemon
BOUILLON
2 shallots
75 ml (5 tbsp) olive oil
1 garlic clove, peeled and crushed
150 ml (¼ pint) dry white wine
15 ml (1 tbsp) white wine vinegar
2 fresh thyme sprigs, bruised
2 bay leaves
6 coriander seeds, bruised
large pinch of saffron strands
2 strips of orange zest
1.25 ml (¼ tsp) sea salt
6 white peppercorns, lightly crushed
300 ml (½ pint) water

**1** First prepare the bouillon. Peel and finely chop the shallots. Heat half the oil in a saucepan, add the shallots and garlic and fry over a low heat for 5 minutes until softened and translucent. Add the remaining ingredients, bring to the boil and simmer gently for 20 minutes.
**2** Meanwhile, prepare the vegetables, trimming and peeling as necessary; halve or quarter the larger ones. Heat the oil in a large sauté pan. Add the slower-cooking root vegetables (carrots, turnips and fennel) and cook for 5 minutes. Add the cauliflower and broccoli and cook for 3 minutes. Finally add the fast-cooking asparagus, courgettes and beans and cook for a final 2-3 minutes.
**3** Pour the bouillon into the pan, bring to the boil and poach the vegetables for 5 minutes; remove from the heat and allow to cool. Squeeze in the lemon juice and serve at room temperature, with soft wholemeal bread.

## BARBECUED AUBERGINE BAGUETTE

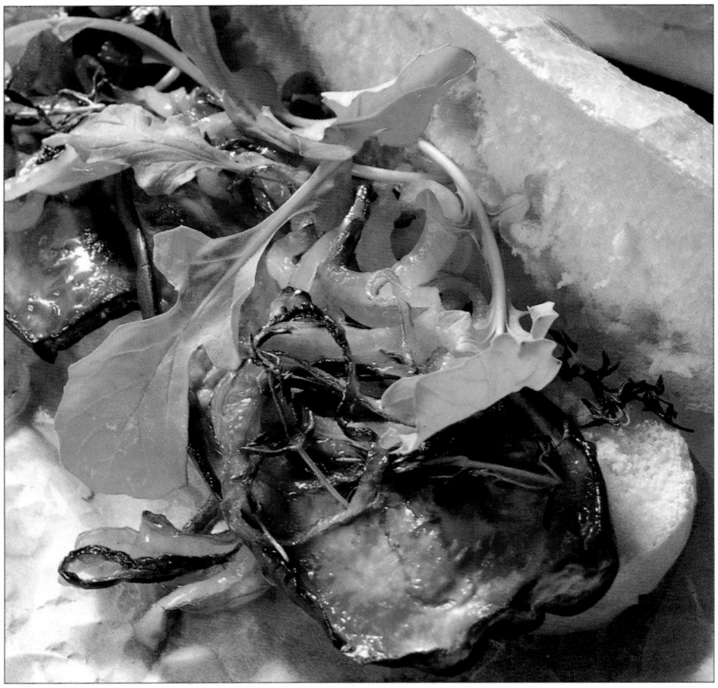

**SERVES 4**
PREPARATION
10 minutes
COOKING TIME
10-15 minutes
FREEZING
Not suitable
CALS/SERVING
300

2 long, thin aubergines, each about 225 g (8 oz)
2 onions
30 ml (2 tbsp) olive oil, plus extra for brushing
10 ml (2 tsp) chopped fresh thyme
4 medium petite baguettes
25 g (1 oz) rocket or other salad leaves

BARBECUE SAUCE
1 garlic clove, peeled and crushed
5 ml (1 tsp) English mustard
90 ml (3 fl oz) tomato ketchup
30 ml (2 tbsp) clear honey
15 ml (1 tbsp) Worcestershire sauce
5 ml (1 tsp) vinegar
few drops of Tabasco (optional)
salt and pepper

**1** Remove a thin slice from each side of the aubergines and discard, then cut each one lengthwise into four 5 mm (¼ inch) thick slices.
**2** To prepare the sauce, mix all the ingredients together in a small bowl until evenly combined; set aside.
**3** Peel and thinly slice the onions. Heat the oil in a frying pan, add the onions and chopped thyme and fry gently for 10-15 minutes until softened and lightly golden; keep warm.
**4** Meanwhile, lay the aubergine slices on a foil-lined grill rack. Brush with oil and grill for 2 minutes, then turn, oil and grill the other side for 2 minutes.
**5** Brush the aubergine slices with the barbecue sauce and grill for 3 minutes. Turn the aubergine slices again, brush the other side with sauce and grill for a further 3 minutes.
**6** Split the baguettes and fill each one with two aubergine slices, some onions and rocket leaves. Serve at once.

**NOTE** If you have time, sprinkle the sliced aubergines with sea salt and leave to drain for 30 minutes before grilling. Wash well to remove the salt and pat dry on kitchen paper. This will remove any slight bitterness that the aubergines may have and also reduce their high water content.

## HERB GNOCCHI WITH GRILLED TOMATO SAUCE

**SERVES 4**
PREPARATION
25 minutes
COOKING TIME
30-35 minutes
FREEZING
Not suitable
CALS/SERVING
490
COLOUR INDEX
Page 47

900 g (2 lb) floury potatoes
2 eggs, beaten
10 ml (2 tsp) salt
30 ml (2 tbsp) finely chopped fresh rosemary
150-175 g (5-6 oz) plain flour

SAUCE
900 g (2 lb) mixed red and yellow cherry tomatoes
3-4 garlic cloves, peeled and sliced
10 ml (2 tsp) grated lemon zest
30 ml (2 tbsp) chopped fresh thyme
30 ml (2 tbsp) chopped fresh basil
60 ml (4 tbsp) olive oil
salt and pepper
pinch of sugar

TO SERVE
extra-virgin olive oil
freshly grated Parmesan cheese
rosemary sprigs, to garnish

**1** Cook the potatoes in lightly salted boiling water for 15-20 minutes until tender; drain well and return to the pan. Set over a gentle heat to dry the potatoes out, then leave to cool slightly.
**2** Bring a large pan of water to a steady simmer. Mash the potatoes smoothly, then work in the eggs, salt, rosemary and enough flour to form a soft dough. Add a little more flour if the mixture is too sticky. Transfer to a piping bag fitted with a large plain nozzle.
**3** Meanwhile make the sauce. Halve the tomatoes and place in a gratin dish. Add the garlic, lemon zest, herbs, oil and seasoning and toss together. Sprinkle over the sugar and grill as close to the heat source as possible for 10 minutes until the tomatoes are charred and tender.
**4** In the meantime, cook the gnocchi in batches. Pipe about six 5 cm (2 inch) lengths directly into the boiling water, using a sharp knife to cut them off at the nozzle. Cook for 3-4 minutes until the gnocchi float to the surface.
**5** Remove with a slotted spoon, drain on kitchen paper and transfer to a large warmed bowl. Toss with a little olive oil and keep warm in a low oven while cooking the rest.
**6** Toss the gnocchi with the tomato sauce. Serve at once, dusted with Parmesan and garnished with rosemary.

**VARIATION** Spoon the cooked gnocchi into 4 individual gratin dishes, spoon on the tomato sauce and top with slices of mozzarella and grated Parmesan. Grill for 3-4 minutes.

# THAI GRILLED VEGETABLES

**SERVES 4**
PREPARATION
20 minutes, plus marinating
COOKING TIME
25 minutes
FREEZING
Not suitable
CALS/SERVING
350
COLOUR INDEX
Page 47

- 2 small red chillies
- 15 g (½ oz) fresh root ginger, peeled
- grated zest and juice of 1 large lime
- 2 garlic cloves, peeled and crushed
- 15 ml (1 tbsp) light soy sauce
- 5 ml (1 tsp) soft brown sugar
- 15 ml (1 tbsp) peanut butter
- 400 g (14 oz) can coconut milk
- 1 lemon grass stalk
- 450 g (1 lb) courgettes
- 1 bunch of spring onions, trimmed
- 450 g (1 lb) asparagus spears, trimmed
- 125 g (4 oz) rice noodles

**1** To prepare the marinade, halve and deseed the chillies, then place in a blender or food processor with the ginger, lime zest and juice, garlic, soy sauce, sugar and peanut butter. Work to a purée, then add the coconut milk and process briefly until evenly blended.
**2** Bruise the lemon grass with the end of a rolling pin and add to the marinade.
**3** Thickly slice the courgettes and spring onions. Place in a shallow dish with the asparagus. Pour on the marinade, cover and leave in a cool place for at least 1 hour.
**4** Remove the vegetables from the marinade with a slotted spoon, discarding the lemon grass; reserve the marinade. Grill the vegetables in batches, turning and basting occasionally with the reserved marinade, for 5-10 minutes until tender.
**5** Meanwhile, add the noodles to a pan of boiling water and cook for 2-3 minutes, stirring occasionally. Pour the reserved marinade into a saucepan, and reduce to a syrupy consistency.
**6** Drain the noodles and toss with the reduced marinade. Serve at once, topped with the grilled vegetables.

# ROASTED RED ONIONS WITH MUSHROOM AND THYME SAUCE

**SERVES 6**
PREPARATION
20 minutes
COOKING TIME
2-2¼ hours
FREEZING
Not suitable
CALS/SERVING
300
COLOUR INDEX
Page 48

- 12 red onions, each about 125 g (4 oz)
- 150 ml (¼ pint) port
- 30 ml (2 tbsp) balsamic vinegar
- 125 g (4 oz) butter or margarine
- salt and pepper
- 125 g (4 oz) large brown-cap or field mushrooms
- 225 g (8 oz) tomatoes
- 1 onion
- 900 ml (1½ pints) water
- 15 ml (1 tbsp) chopped fresh thyme or 5 ml (1 tsp) dried thyme

**1** Peel the red onions, leaving the root end intact; reserve the peelings. Trim the roots so that the onions will stand upright. Place in a single layer in a roasting tin just large enough to hold them. Drizzle over the port and balsamic vinegar.
**2** Dot the onions with half of the butter and season generously with salt and pepper. Roast in the oven at 200°C (400°F) Mark 6 for about 1½ hours until tender and slightly charred. Cover with foil and cook for a further 40 minutes or until very tender. Baste occasionally with the pan juices during roasting.
**3** Meanwhile, trim stalks and gills from the mushrooms, leaving only the thick, fleshy part; reserve the trimmings. Finely dice the flesh; set aside. Quarter the tomatoes, remove the pulp and seeds; reserve. Finely dice the tomato flesh and set aside with the diced mushrooms. Peel and finely dice the onion, reserving the skin.
**4** Place the reserved onion skins, mushroom trimmings and tomato pulp in a large pan. Pour on the water, bring to the boil and boil steadily, uncovered, for about 20 minutes or until reduced by about half. Strain through a fine sieve into a jug and season well.
**5** Melt 25 g (1 oz) butter in a small saucepan, add the diced onion, mushrooms and thyme and fry gently for 15-20 minutes or until soft and golden brown. Increase the heat and let bubble for a few minutes to evaporate excess liquid. Stir in the tomatoes and take off the heat.
**6** Pour the pan juices from the roasted onions into the mushroom mixture, then add the strained stock. Bring to the boil and let bubble for 10-12 minutes until the sauce becomes syrupy. Gradually whisk in the remaining butter, a piece at a time to make the sauce glossy. Check the seasoning.
**7** Serve the roasted onions with the mushroom and thyme sauce spooned over. Steamed spinach and a potato gratin are ideal accompaniments.

# ROASTED VEGETABLES WITH SALSA VERDE

**SERVES 4**
PREPARATION
35-40 minutes
COOKING TIME
40-50 minutes
FREEZING
Not suitable
CALS/SERVING
415

2 small aubergines
1 red pepper
1 yellow pepper
2 courgettes
8 garlic cloves, unpeeled
90 ml (6 tbsp) extra-virgin olive oil
15 ml (1 tbsp) chopped fresh herbs, such as rosemary, sage and thyme
6 ripe plum tomatoes, quartered
salt and pepper

SALSA VERDE
60 ml (4 tbsp) chopped fresh parsley
30 ml (2 tbsp) chopped fresh mint
2 garlic cloves, peeled
1 red chilli, seeded
5 ml (1 tsp) Dijon mustard
7.5 ml (1½ tsp) lemon juice
120 ml (4 fl oz) extra-virgin olive oil
TO GARNISH
mint leaves

**1** First prepare the salsa verde. Place all the ingredients, except the oil, in a food processor and work until fairly smooth. Add the oil, process briefly and season with salt and pepper to taste. Transfer to a bowl, cover and set aside.

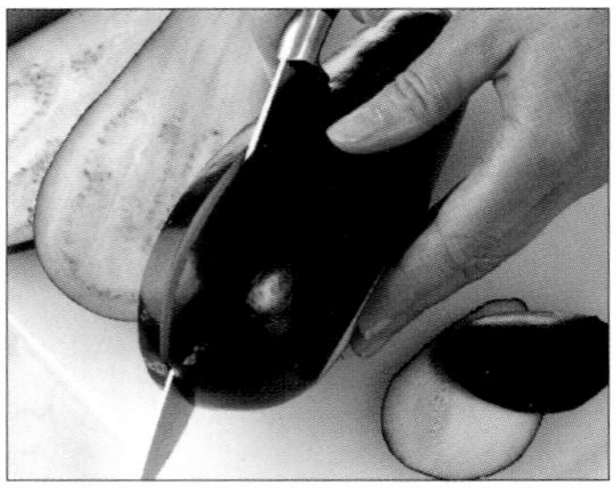

**2** Remove a thin slice from each side of the aubergines and discard, then cut each one lengthwise into 5 mm (¼ inch) thick slices. Place on a lightly oiled large baking sheet.

**3** Halve, core and deseed the peppers, then cut into thick strips. Cut the courgettes into 1 cm (½ inch) slices. Put the peppers, courgettes and garlic cloves in a roasting dish large enough to hold them in a single layer.

**4** Mix the oil and herbs together and drizzle half over the vegetables, turning to coat them evenly. Brush the aubergine slices with the herb-flavoured oil.

**5** Place the roasting tin on the top shelf of the oven at 230°C (450°F) Mark 8, with the aubergines on the next shelf. Roast for 30 minutes, stirring the vegetables in the roasting tin halfway through cooking.

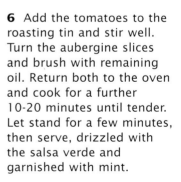

**6** Add the tomatoes to the roasting tin and stir well. Turn the aubergine slices and brush with remaining oil. Return both to the oven and cook for a further 10-20 minutes until tender. Let stand for a few minutes, then serve, drizzled with the salsa verde and garnished with mint.

## GOULASH WITH TARRAGON AND HORSERADISH DUMPLINGS

**SERVES 6**
PREPARATION
40 minutes
COOKING TIME
1-1¼ hours
FREEZING
Suitable:
Without dumplings
CALS/SERVING
320

2 large onions
2 large carrots
2 large potatoes
60 ml (4 tbsp) olive oil
2 garlic cloves, peeled and crushed
15 ml (1 tbsp) chopped fresh thyme
10 ml (2 tsp) paprika
600 ml (1 pint) tomato juice
450 ml (¾ pint) vegetable stock
30 ml (2 tbsp) tomato paste
10 ml (2 tsp) chilli sauce
2 bay leaves
2 red peppers

DUMPLINGS
75 g (3 oz) self-raising flour
2.5 ml (½ tsp) salt
50 g (2 oz) vegetarian suet
15 ml (1 tbsp) chopped fresh tarragon
30 ml (2 tbsp) grated fresh horseradish
60 ml (4 tbsp) water

TO SERVE
soured cream (optional)
shredded spring onions

**1** Peel and thinly slice the onions. Peel and chop the carrots and potatoes. Heat 45 ml (3 tbsp) of the oil in a flameproof casserole, add the onions, garlic, thyme and paprika and fry gently for 5 minutes.
**2** Add the carrots and potatoes and continue to fry for a further 10 minutes, stirring from time to time to prevent the vegetables sticking.
**3** Add the tomato juice, stock, tomato paste, chilli sauce and bay leaves. Bring to the boil, cover and simmer for 30 minutes. In the meantime, halve, deseed and slice the peppers. Heat the remaining oil in a frying pan, add the peppers and fry over a medium heat for 6-8 minutes, until charred and softened; set aside.
**4** Meanwhile, prepare the dumplings. Sift the flour and salt into a bowl and stir in the suet, tarragon and horseradish. Gradually work in enough water to form a soft dough. Knead lightly, then shape into 12 balls; set aside.
**5** Add the peppers and dumplings to the goulash. Cover and simmer gently for a further 25 minutes until the vegetables are cooked and the dumplings are puffed up and firm to the touch. Check the seasoning.
**6** Serve each portion topped with a spoonful of soured cream if wished, and a little shredded spring onion.

**VARIATION** Omit the dumplings. Stir 10 ml (2 tsp) creamed horseradish into 150 ml (¼ pint) soured cream. Serve each portion topped with a generous spoonful of horseradish cream, and accompanied by buttered noodles.

## SPRING VEGETABLE STEW

**SERVES 4**
PREPARATION
30 minutes
COOKING TIME
25-30 minutes
FREEZING
Not suitable
CALS/SERVING
255
COLOUR INDEX
Page 48

225 g (8 oz) new potatoes, scrubbed
salt and pepper
4 shallots
75 g (3 oz) unsalted butter
1 garlic clove, peeled and crushed
10 ml (2 tsp) chopped fresh thyme
5 ml (1 tsp) grated lime zest
6 baby leeks, sliced into 5 cm (2 inch) lengths
125 g (4 oz) baby carrots, scrubbed
125 g (4 oz) freshly podded new peas
125 g (4 oz) freshly podded broad beans
300 ml (½ pint) vegetable stock
1 Little Gem lettuce, shredded
60 ml (4 tbsp) chopped fresh herbs, such as chervil, chives, mint and parsley

**1** Put the potatoes into a saucepan with plenty of cold water to cover. Add a little salt, bring to the boil, cover and cook for 5 minutes. Drain and immediately refresh under cold water.
**2** Meanwhile, peel and thinly slice the shallots. Melt half of the butter in a large sauté pan, add the shallots, garlic, thyme and lime zest and fry gently for 5 minutes until softened and lightly golden. Add the leeks and carrots and sauté for a further 5 minutes.
**3** Stir in the potatoes, peas and broad beans, then pour in the stock. Bring to the boil, cover and simmer gently for 10 minutes. Remove the lid and cook, uncovered, for a further 5-8 minutes until all the vegetables are tender.
**4** Meanwhile shred the lettuce. Add to the vegetable stew with the herbs and remaining butter. Heat through until the butter is melted. Check the seasoning and serve at once.

## PROVENÇAL VEGETABLE PIE

**SERVES 4-6**
PREPARATION
20 minutes
COOKING TIME
1¼ hours
FREEZING
Suitable
CALS/SERVING
510-340

1 red onion
1 small fennel bulb
2 courgettes
30 ml (2 tbsp) olive oil
1 quantity hot Tomato Sauce (see page 291)
400 g (14 oz) can flageolet beans
125 g (4 oz) pitted black olives, chopped
15 ml (1 tbsp) capers in brine, drained
salt and pepper

TOPPING
1 French stick
90 ml (6 tbsp) extra-virgin olive oil
30 ml (2 tbsp) finely chopped fresh basil
15 ml (1 tbsp) finely chopped fresh parsley
1 clove garlic, peeled and crushed
25 g (1 oz) Parmesan or Cheddar cheese, freshly grated

**1** Peel and slice the onion; trim and dice the fennel and courgettes. Heat the oil in a frying pan and fry the onion and fennel for 10 minutes until softened and lightly golden, then add the courgettes and fry for a further 5 minutes. Stir into the hot tomato sauce, together with the beans and their liquid, the olives, capers and seasoning to taste.
**2** Transfer to a lightly oiled deep 1.5 litre (3 pint) baking dish and cover with foil. Bake in the oven at 200°C (400°F) Mark 6 for 40 minutes.
**3** Meanwhile, cut the French stick into thin slices. Mix the oil, herbs and garlic together in a shallow bowl. Remove the stew from the oven, dip the slices of bread into the oil mixture one at a time and arrange, overlapping, on top of the vegetables to form a crust.
**4** Scatter the cheese over the bread crust and bake for a further 15-20 minutes until crisp and golden. Serve with a green vegetable.

## VEGGIE CRUMBLE

**SERVES 4-6**
PREPARATION
45 minutes
COOKING TIME
35-40 minutes
FREEZING
Suitable
CALS/SERVING
895-595

225 g (8 oz) baby onions
225 g (8 oz) carrots
225 g (8 oz) peeled and seeded butternut squash
225 g (8 oz) broccoli
25 g (1 oz) butter
1 garlic clove, peeled and crushed
30 ml (2 tbsp) chopped fresh sage
400 g (14 oz) can chopped tomatoes
300 ml (½ pint) double cream
200 ml (7 fl oz) milk
salt and pepper

CRUMBLE TOPPING
175 g (6 oz) wholemeal flour
pinch of salt
75 g (3 oz) butter, diced
50 g (2 oz) walnuts, finely chopped
25 g (1 oz) Cheddar cheese, grated

**1** Halve the baby onions if large. Peel and chop the carrots; cut the squash into cubes. Cut the broccoli into florets.
**2** Melt the butter in a frying pan and fry the onions, garlic and sage for 10 minutes. Add the carrots and squash and fry for a further 10 minutes. Add the tomatoes, cover and simmer for 15 minutes until the vegetables start to soften. Let cool slightly.
**3** Meanwhile, prepare the crumble topping. Sift the flour and salt into a bowl, then rub in the butter until the mixture resembles breadcrumbs. Stir in the walnuts and cheese.
**4** Add the broccoli, cream and milk to the squash mixture and season well. Spoon into a 2 litre (3½ pint) pie dish and sprinkle with the crumble topping. Cover with foil and bake in the oven at 190°C (375°F) Mark 5 for 20 minutes.
**5** Uncover and bake for a further 15-20 minutes until bubbling and golden. Serve with a green vegetable.

# SUMMER VEGETABLE PIE WITH A HERBY CHEESE CRUST

**SERVES 4-6**
PREPARATION
40 minutes
COOKING TIME
About 1 hour
FREEZING
Not suitable
CALS/SERVING
660-440

- 2 leeks, trimmed
- 2 courgettes
- 30 ml (2 tbsp) olive oil
- 2 garlic cloves, peeled and crushed
- grated zest of 1 lemon
- 4 ripe tomatoes
- 150 ml (¼ pint) vegetable stock
- 30 ml (2 tbsp) sun-dried tomato paste
- 150 ml (¼ pint) double cream
- 30 ml (2 tbsp) chopped mixed fresh parsley and oregano
- salt and pepper

SCONE TOPPING

- 225 g (8 oz) self-raising flour
- 2.5 ml (½ tsp) salt
- 75 g (3 oz) butter, diced
- 15 ml (1 tbsp) chopped fresh basil
- 50 g (2 oz) red Leicester or Cheddar cheese, grated
- 45-60 ml (3-4 tbsp) milk

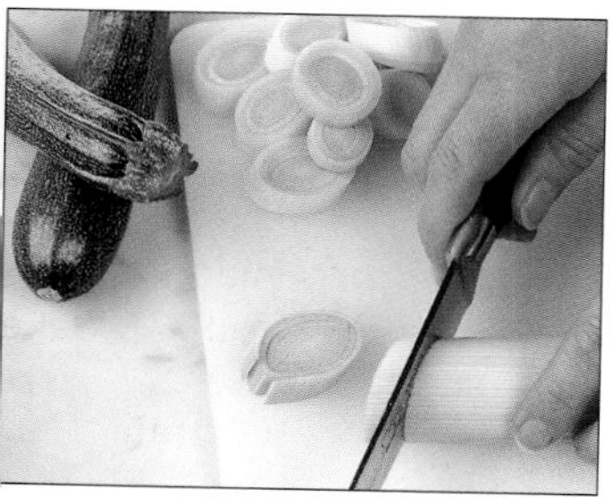

**1** Slice the leeks and the courgettes. Heat the oil in a large sauté pan, add the leeks, garlic and lemon zest and fry gently for 5 minutes. Add the courgettes and fry for a further 5 minutes, until softened.

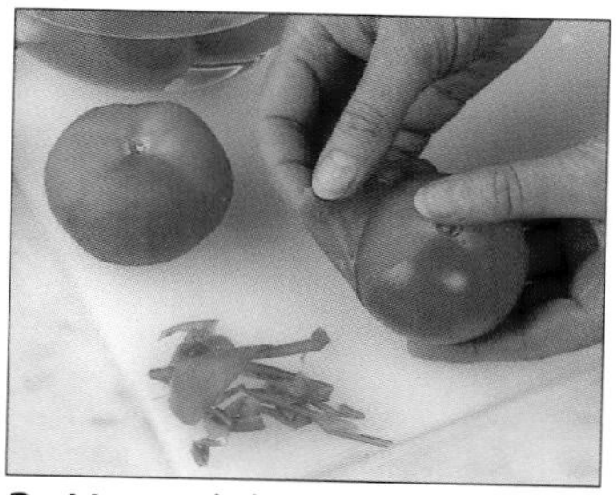

**2** Meanwhile immerse the tomatoes in a bowl of boiling water for 30 seconds. Remove and peel away the skins, then dice the flesh. Add to the sauté pan with the stock, tomato paste and cream. Stir, then bring to the boil, cover and simmer gently for 20 minutes. Add the herbs and season with salt and pepper to taste.

**3** Meanwhile, prepare the topping. Sift the flour and salt into a bowl, then rub in the butter until the mixture resembles fine breadcrumbs. Stir in the basil and half of the cheese, then gradually work in enough milk to form a soft dough.

**4** Lightly knead the dough on a floured surface and gently roll out to a circle, about 1 cm (½ inch) thick. Using a 5 cm (2 inch) pastry cutter, stamp out rounds. Re-roll the trimmings as necessary and repeat to make 12 scones in total.

**5** Transfer the vegetable stew to an ovenproof dish and carefully arrange the scones around the edge of the dish, overlapping them slightly.

**6** Brush the scones with a little extra milk and sprinkle with the remaining cheese. Bake in the oven at 220°C (425°F) Mark 7 for 20-25 minutes until puffed up and golden. Serve with a green vegetable, such as broccoli or French beans.

## AUBERGINE CANNELLONI

**SERVES 6**
PREPARATION
20-25 minutes
COOKING TIME
20-25 minutes
FREEZING
Suitable
CALS/SERVING
370

3 long, thin aubergines, each about 225 g (8 oz)
olive oil, for brushing
three 150 g (5 oz) packets mozzarella cheese
60 ml (4 tbsp) Pesto (see page 292)
50-75 g (2-3 oz) Cheddar cheese, grated
½ quantity Tomato Sauce (see page 291)
salt and pepper

**1** Remove a thin slice from the side of each aubergine and discard, then cut each one lengthwise into thin slices, to give 16-18 slices in total. Preheat a griddle or the grill. Brush each aubergine slice with a little oil and cook in batches for 3-4 minutes each side until charred and softened. Allow to cool.
**2** Lightly oil a shallow, rectangular 1.5-1.8 litre (2½-3 pint) ovenproof dish. Cut the mozzarella into thin slices. Lay two slices of mozzarella side by side on each aubergine slice. Spread with a little pesto, then sprinkle over a little grated cheese. Carefully roll the aubergines up into tight rolls and place, seam-side down, in the prepared dish.
**3** Spoon the tomato sauce over the aubergine rolls, then sprinkle the remaining cheese on top. Bake in the oven at 200°C (400°F) Mark 6 for 20-25 minutes until bubbling and golden. Check the seasoning and serve hot, accompanied by plenty of crusty bread and a leafy salad.

## ROASTED VEGETABLE RATATOUILLE

**SERVES 6**
PREPARATION
30 minutes
COOKING TIME
1½ hours
FREEZING
Not suitable
CALS/SERVING
335
COLOUR INDEX
Page 49

350 g (12 oz) sweet potatoes
salt and pepper
225 g (8 oz) plum tomatoes
225 g (8 oz) courgettes
225 g (8 oz) aubergines
225 g (8 oz) red peppers
225 g (8 oz) onions, peeled
2 garlic cloves, peeled
5 ml (1 tsp) chopped fresh thyme
50 ml (2 fl oz) olive oil
50 ml (2 fl oz) white wine
225 g (8 oz) passata or 400 g can chopped plum tomatoes
5 ml (1 tsp) caster sugar
175 g (6 oz) firm goat's cheese, thickly sliced
TO GARNISH
thyme sprigs
roasted garlic slivers (optional)

**1** Peel and roughly chop the sweet potatoes, then cook in a pan of boiling salted water for 10 minutes or until tender; drain. Roughly chop the tomatoes, courgettes, aubergines, red peppers and onions.
**2** Place all of the vegetables in a large roasting tin with the garlic, thyme and oil. Season generously with salt and pepper. Bake at 220°C (425°F) Mark 7 for 45 minutes to 1 hour; turning occasionally, until golden brown.
**3** Meanwhile, place the wine, passata and sugar in a pan. Bring to the boil and bubble for 10 minutes or until thick, then season well.
**4** Place the roasted vegetables in an ovenproof dish. Mash the roasted garlic and mix into the tomato sauce. Spoon over the vegetables.
**5** Arrange the goat's cheese on top and return to the oven for 20 minutes or until golden. Leave to stand for 5 minutes, then garnish with thyme and roasted garlic slivers if wished. Serve in small pots.

**NOTE** For convenience, prepare ahead to the end of stage 4. Cover and chill for up to 24 hours. To serve, continue from step 5, allowing an extra 5-10 minutes in the oven.

# RED CABBAGE TIMBALES WITH MUSHROOM STUFFING

**SERVES 6**
PREPARATION
1 hour, plus cooling
COOKING TIME
1 hour
FREEZING
Not suitable
CALS/SERVING
400
COLOUR INDEX
Page 49

STUFFING
450 g (1 lb) brown-cap mushrooms
75 g (3 oz) toasted, salted cashew nuts
200 g (7 oz) onions
50 g (2 oz) butter
90 ml (4 tbsp) chopped fresh parsley
125 g (4 oz) fresh breadcrumbs
2 large eggs, beaten
salt and pepper

TIMBALES
1 red cabbage, about 1.4 kg (3 lb)
350 g (12 oz) onions
40 g (1½ oz) butter
45 ml (3 tbsp) balsamic vinegar

SAUCE
60 ml (4 tbsp) caster sugar
60 ml (4 tbsp) red wine vinegar
150 ml (¼ pint) red wine
15 ml (1 tbsp) lemon juice

**1** For the stuffing, roughly chop the mushrooms and cashew nuts; peel and finely chop the onions.
**2** Melt the butter in a pan, add the onions and cook until soft and golden. Add the mushrooms and fry over a brisk heat until the moisture has evaporated. Mix in the parsley, cashew nuts and breadcrumbs. Leave to cool, then stir in the beaten eggs and seasoning, mixing well. Cover and set aside.
**3** To make the timbales, place the cabbage in a large pan of boiling water. Bring to the boil, lower the heat and simmer until the outside leaves have softened enough to be eased away. Lift the cabbage out of the pan and set aside, reserving the water. Remove the 3 outer leaves and boil these for a further 3-4 minutes; place in a bowl of cold water. Quarter and core the reserved whole cabbage. Weigh 700 g (1½ lb) and cut away any heavy central vein from the leaves. Shred the leaves very finely, cover and set aside.
**4** Line six 150 ml (¼ pint) individual pudding moulds with microwave cling film. Drain the whole cabbage leaves and cut in half either side of the central vein; discard the vein. Use these leaves to line the moulds. Fill with the stuffing mixture and cover with foil.
**5** Stand in a roasting tin and surround with enough warm water to come halfway up the sides. Cook at 190°C (375°F) Mark 5 for 30 minutes or until just set to the centre.
**6** Meanwhile, peel and finely chop the onions. Melt the butter in a pan, add the onions and cook until soft. Mix in the reserved shredded cabbage, vinegar, 45 ml (3 tbsp) water, salt and pepper. Cook, stirring from time to time, for 15-20 minutes or until beginning to soften.
**7** To make the sauce, put the sugar and vinegar in a small pan and dissolve over a gentle heat, then bring to the boil and cook to a rich caramel. Pour in the wine and reduce by half. Add lemon juice to taste and season.
**8** Turn out the timbales on to warmed serving plates. Spoon the shredded cabbage on top and drizzle over the red wine sauce. Serve at once.

# VEGETABLE AND CHICK PEA BALTI

**SERVES 6**
PREPARATION
30 minutes
COOKING TIME
1¼ hours
FREEZING
Suitable
CALS/SERVING
245

1 large onion
4 garlic cloves
4 red chillies
10 ml (2 tsp) grated fresh root ginger
60 ml (4 tbsp) sunflower oil
10 ml (2 tsp) ground coriander
5 ml (1 tsp) each ground cinnamon, fenugreek, paprika, turmeric and mustard powder
2.5 ml (½ tsp) ground cumin
3 whole cloves
3 cardamom pods, bruised
450 g (1 lb) tomatoes
350 g (12 oz) peeled potatoes
350 g (12 oz) peeled butternut squash
30 ml (2 tbsp) lemon juice
400 g (14 oz) can chick peas, drained
450 ml (¾ pint) water
225 g (8 oz) French beans, trimmed
salt and pepper
30 ml (2 tbsp) fresh coriander leaves

**1** Peel and chop the onion and garlic. Deseed and chop the chillies. Put the onion, garlic, chillies and ginger in a food processor and blend until fairly smooth.
**2** Heat the oil in a saucepan, add the onion mixture and fry gently for 10 minutes until lightly golden, then stir in the spices. Chop the tomatoes, add to the pan and fry for a further 5 minutes.
**3** Meanwhile, cut the potatoes and butternut squash into bite-sized pieces. Add to the pan with the lemon juice, chick peas and water. Bring to the boil, partially cover and simmer for 30-45 minutes until the potatoes are tender.
**4** Halve the beans, add to the pan and cook for a further 5-10 minutes. Season with salt and pepper to taste.
**5** Scatter over the coriander and serve accompanied by naan and poppadoms.

## MIXED VEGETABLE CURRY

**SERVES 4-6**
PREPARATION
20 minutes
COOKING TIME
About 1 hour
FREEZING
Suitable
CALS/SERVING
685-445
COLOUR INDEX
Page 49

1.4 kg (3 lb) mixed vegetables, including cauliflower, carrots, potato, parsnip and frozen peas
1 onion
2.5 cm (1 inch) piece fresh root ginger
2 green chillies
1-2 garlic cloves, peeled
30 ml (2 tbsp) ghee or vegetable oil
10 ml (2 tsp) turmeric
10 ml (2 tsp) ground coriander
10 ml (2 tsp) ground cumin
5 ml (1 tsp) ground fenugreek
8 whole cloves
8 green cardamom pods
1 cinnamon stick
600 ml (1 pint) canned coconut milk
300 ml (½ pint) water
salt and pepper
coriander sprigs, to garnish

**1** First prepare the vegetables. Divide the cauliflower into florets. Peel the carrots, potato and parsnip and cut into chunks.
**2** Peel and chop the onion and ginger. Halve and deseed the chillies. Put the onion, ginger, garlic and chillies in a blender or food processor and process until almost smooth.
**3** Heat the ghee or oil in a large heavy-based saucepan, add the onion mixture and fry for 5 minutes, stirring constantly. Add all the spices and cook over a high heat for 3-4 minutes, stirring all the time.
**4** Add the vegetables to the pan and stir to coat in the spice paste. Gradually stir in the coconut milk and water. Bring to the boil, then lower the heat, cover and simmer for 45-55 minutes or until the vegetables are just tender, depending on the type of vegetables used. Season with salt and pepper to taste.
**5** Leave the curry to stand for 5 minutes to let the flavours develop before serving, garnished with coriander sprigs. Accompany with naan bread, pickles and plain boiled rice.

**NOTE** If canned coconut milk is unavailable use one 225 g (8 oz) block creamed coconut or 100 g (3.5 oz) packet coconut milk powder with 600 ml (1 pint) boiling water.

## VEGETABLE PASANDA

**SERVES 6**
PREPARATION
30 minutes
COOKING TIME
50 minutes
FREEZING
Not suitable
CALS/SERVING
450
COLOUR INDEX
Page 50

75 g (3 oz) blanched almonds
10 ml (2 tsp) cumin seeds
5 ml (1 tsp) fennel seeds
10 ml (2 tsp) coriander seeds
2.5 cm (1 inch) piece fresh root ginger
2 onions
2 garlic cloves, peeled
6 cloves
8 black peppercorns
ghee or vegetable oil, for frying
300 ml (½ pint) double cream
175 ml (6 fl oz) water
350 g (12 oz) waxy potatoes
3 courgettes
1 medium aubergine
125 g (4 oz) green beans
225 g (8 oz) small cauliflower florets
450 g (1 lb) spinach leaves
salt
TO GARNISH
crisp-fried onions
toasted shredded almonds

**1** Put the almonds in a heavy-based frying pan and dry-fry over a gentle heat until just golden brown. Remove from the pan and leave to cool. Add the cumin, fennel and coriander seeds to the pan and dry-fry in the same way, shaking the pan all the time until the spices release their aroma. Leave to cool.
**2** Peel the ginger and chop roughly. Peel and thinly slice the onions.
**3** Tip the almonds into a food processor or blender and process until finely chopped. Add the ginger, garlic and 15 ml (1 tbsp) water. Work to a purée.
**4** Crush the dry-fried spices with the cloves and black peppercorns, using a pestle and mortar.
**5** Heat 30 ml (2 tbsp) ghee or oil in a large saucepan, add the onions and cook over a fairly high heat until tinged brown. Add the almond mixture and cook for 2 minutes.
**6** Add the crushed spices and cook for 2 minutes. Add the cream and water. Bring slowly to the boil, then lower the heat and simmer very gently for 10 minutes.
**7** Meanwhile, peel the potatoes and cut into chunks. Cut the courgettes and aubergine into chunks. Heat a little ghee or oil in a frying pan and fry these vegetables in batches over a high heat until thoroughly browned on all sides. Drain on crumpled kitchen paper.
**8** Add the fried vegetables to the sauce with the green beans and cauliflower. Simmer gently for 20 minutes or until the vegetables are tender; if the mixture becomes too dry, add a little extra water.
**9** Meanwhile, trim and roughly tear the spinach leaves. Add to the pan and simmer for 1-2 minutes until just wilted. Add salt to taste. Serve garnished with crisp-fried onions and toasted almonds.

**NOTE** It isn't essential to fry the potatoes, courgettes and aubergines. You can add them to the sauce at stage 8, but they will take longer to cook.

## SPICED VEGETABLES WITH COCONUT

**SERVES 4**
PREPARATION
30 minutes
COOKING TIME
30 minutes
FREEZING
Not suitable
CALS/SERVING
395
COLOUR INDEX
Page 50

1 small or medium coconut
150 ml (¼ pint) water
2 onions
2 garlic cloves
2.5 cm (1 inch) piece fresh root ginger
1 hot green chilli (optional)
5 ml (1 tsp) turmeric
10 ml (2 tsp) ground coriander
10 ml (2 tsp) coriander seeds
30 ml (2 tbsp) ghee or oil
2 large green peppers
2 carrots
8 spring onions
125 g (4 oz) green beans
salt and pepper

**1** Wrap the coconut in a tea-towel, grip it firmly and crack with a hammer. Remove the coconut flesh and peel off the hard brown skin, using a potato peeler or sharp knife. You will need about 225 g (8 oz) coconut flesh (use the rest for another dish). Roughly chop the flesh then place in a blender or food processor and work until very finely chopped. Add the water and process again. Transfer the mixture from the blender to a bowl and set aside.
**2** Peel and quarter the onions. Peel and halve the garlic cloves. Peel and roughly chop the ginger. Chop the chilli, if using, discarding the seeds if a milder flavour is preferred. Add the onions, garlic, ginger, chilli if using, turmeric, ground coriander and coriander seeds to the blender and process until finely chopped. Add a spoonful of water and process again to make a smooth purée.
**3** Heat the ghee or oil in a large saucepan, add the onion and spice mixture and cook over a moderate heat, stirring for about 10 minutes until soft and golden brown.
**4** Meanwhile, halve, core, deseed and roughly chop the peppers. Peel and slice the carrots; trim and halve the spring onions; trim the green beans.
**5** Add the prepared vegetables to the pan and stir to coat n the onion and spice mixture. Add the coconut and eason with salt and pepper to taste. Bring to the boil, then ower the heat. Cover and simmer very gently for about 0 minutes or until the vegetables are just tender. Check he pan from time to time to make sure that the vegetables re still moist; if they look dry, add a little extra water.
Serve with rice or naan.

**IOTE** The technique suggested for cracking a coconut is ie quick way – be prepared for the milk to spill out! If you refer to catch it, pierce the 'eyes' with a screwdriver and rain the milk before you crack open the coconut.

**ARIATION** If fresh coconut is unobtainable, use 150 ml ¼ pint) coconut milk instead, omitting stage 1.

## SPICED POTATOES AND CAULIFLOWER

**SERVES 4**
PREPARATION
15 minutes
COOKING TIME
15 minutes
FREEZING
Not suitable
CALS/SERVING
270

450 g (1 lb) waxy potatoes
450 g (1 lb) cauliflower
1 onion
5 cm (2 inch) piece fresh root ginger
1 hot green chilli
60 ml (4 tbsp) ghee or vegetable oil
5 ml (1 tsp) black mustard seeds
5 ml (1 tsp) cumin seeds
5 ml (1 tsp) ground cumin
2.5 ml (½ tsp) turmeric
salt and pepper

**1** Peel the potatoes and cut into large chunks. Place in a saucepan with enough salted water to cover, bring to the boil and boil for 5 minutes. Drain.
**2** Meanwhile, cut the cauliflower into small florets. Peel and finely chop the onion and ginger. Finely slice the chilli, discarding the seeds if a milder flavour is preferred.
**3** Heat the ghee or oil in a large frying pan. Add the onion and ginger and cook over a medium heat until the onion is golden brown but not burnt. Add the chilli and spices and cook for 2 minutes, stirring all the time.
**4** Add the potatoes and cauliflower, stirring to coat them in the spice mixture. Season with salt and pepper and stir in 45 ml (3 tbsp) water. Cover with a lid and cook gently over a medium heat for about 10 minutes or until the potatoes and cauliflower are tender. Check the pan occasionally during cooking, adding a little extra water if necessary to prevent sticking. Don't overcook the vegetables; they should retain their shape.
**5** Serve with rice or naan as a supper dish, or as part of an Indian meal with a selection of other dishes.

## MATTAR PANEER

**SERVES 4**
PREPARATION
20-30 minutes, plus pressing
COOKING TIME
20 minutes
FREEZING
Suitable
CALS/SERVING
375
COLOUR INDEX
Page 50

- 2.3 litres (4 pints) full-fat milk
- 75 ml (5 tbsp) lemon juice (approximately)
- 1 onion
- 5 cm (2 inch) piece fresh root ginger
- 450 g (1 lb) fresh ripe tomatoes
- 45 ml (3 tbsp) ghee or vegetable oil
- 5 ml (1 tsp) turmeric
- 5 ml (1 tsp) ground coriander
- 5 ml (1 tsp) cumin seeds
- 2.5-5 ml (½-1 tsp) cayenne pepper
- 350 g (12 oz) shelled fresh or frozen peas (see note)
- 5 ml (1 tsp) sugar
- salt and pepper
- 30 ml (2 tbsp) chopped fresh coriander
- 15 ml (1 tbsp) chopped fresh mint (optional)
- garam masala, to taste
- coriander and mint sprigs, to garnish

**1** To make the paneer, bring the milk to the boil in a deep saucepan. As soon as it boils, remove from the heat and add the lemon juice, all at once. Stir thoroughly, then return to the heat for about 1 minute; the curds and whey should separate very quickly. Immediately remove the pan from the heat. If they don't separate, add another 15 ml (1 tbsp) lemon juice and repeat.
**2** Line a large sieve or colander with a double thickness of muslin or cheesecloth and place over a large bowl. Pour the curds and whey into the lined sieve or colander and leave to drain and cool slightly.
**3** When the muslin is cool enough to handle, gather it up around the curds and squeeze to remove excess whey. Reserve 120 ml (4 fl oz) of the whey and keep, covered, in the refrigerator; discard the rest.
**4** Wrap the cheesecloth tightly around the curds, then place on a chopping board. Put a second board on top and weigh it down with a few large cans or heavy weights. Leave undisturbed for about 4 hours, or until the cheese feels firm to the touch.
**5** When ready, cut the paneer cheese into small cubes. Peel and chop the onion and ginger. Skin the tomatoes if preferred, then chop the flesh.
**6** Heat the ghee or oil in a large frying pan. Add the paneer and cook until golden brown on all sides; remove from the pan with a slotted spoon and set aside.
**7** Add the onion and ginger to the pan and cook over a medium heat until the onion is golden brown. Add the spices and cook for 2 minutes, stirring all the time.
**8** Add the tomatoes and the reserved whey and bring to the boil. Simmer for 2-3 minutes, then add the peas, with the cheese, sugar and salt and pepper to taste. Cover and simmer gently until the peas are tender.
**9** Stir in the coriander and mint if using. Sprinkle with garam masala before serving, garnished with herbs.

**NOTE** If using fresh peas, you will need to buy about 900 g (2 lb) in the pod.

## AFRICAN VEGETABLE AND FRUIT CURRY

**SERVES 4**
PREPARATION
25 minutes
COOKING TIME
1 hour
FREEZING
Suitable
CALS/SERVING
260

- 1 onion
- 2 red chillies
- 225 g (8 oz) potatoes
- 225 g (8 oz) carrots
- 60 ml (4 tbsp) groundnut or sunflower oil
- 2 garlic cloves, peeled and crushed
- 5 ml (1 tsp) grated fresh root ginger
- 5 ml (1 tsp) fennel seeds, lightly crushed
- 5 ml (1 tsp) ground cumin
- 5 ml (1 tsp) ground coriander
- 5 ml (1 tsp) turmeric
- 2.5 ml (½ tsp) ground cinnamon
- 1.25 ml (¼ tsp) each ground cloves and cardamom
- 25 g (1 oz) dried pears, diced
- 25 g (1 oz) dried apricots, diced
- 600 ml (1 pint) vegetable stock
- 225 g (8 oz) green beans, trimmed
- 30 ml (2 tbsp) mango chutney
- 15 ml (1 tbsp) lemon juice
- salt and pepper
- 25 g (1 oz) cashew nuts, toasted and chopped

**1** Peel and chop the onion. Deseed and chop the chillies. Peel and dice the potatoes and carrots.
**2** Heat the oil in a large deep frying pan, add the onion, garlic, ginger and chillies and fry for 5 minutes, then add the spices and fry for a further 2-3 minutes.
**3** Add the potatoes, carrots and dried fruit and stir to coat with the spice mixture. Fry over a low heat for 10 minutes, stirring from time to time to prevent sticking.
**4** Add the stock, bring to the boil, cover and simmer for 30 minutes. Halve the beans and add to the pan with the mango chutney and lemon juice. Cook for a further 10-15 minutes until the beans are tender. Check the seasoning.
**5** Serve hot, sprinkled with the cashew nuts and accompanied by bread.

# STIR-FRIED VEGETABLES WITH HOISIN AND TOFU

**SERVES 4**
PREPARATION
20 minutes
COOKING TIME
30 minutes
FREEZING
Not suitable
CALS/SERVING
410

- 275 g (10 oz) packet tofu, drained
- 30 ml (2 tbsp) hoisin sauce
- 30 ml (2 tbsp) dark soy sauce
- 30 ml (2 tbsp) sherry vinegar
- 15 ml (1 tbsp) chilli sauce
- 15 ml (1 tbsp) thin honey
- 10 ml (2 tsp) sesame oil
- 2 carrots
- 175 g (6 oz) broccoli
- 125 g (4 oz) shiitake mushrooms
- 1 leek, trimmed
- 4 spring onions, trimmed
- 125 g (4 oz) mangetout, trimmed
- 45 ml (3 tbsp) sunflower oil
- toasted sesame seeds, to garnish

**1** Cut the tofu into 2.5 cm (1 inch) cubes and place in a shallow roasting dish.

**2** For the glaze, combine the hoisin sauce, soy sauce, vinegar, chilli sauce, honey and sesame oil in a bowl.

**3** Pour two thirds of the glaze over the tofu and toss to coat. Bake on the top shelf of the oven at 230°C (450°F) Mark 8 for 20 minutes, stirring halfway through cooking.

**4** Meanwhile, prepare the vegetables. Peel and thinly slice the carrots; cut the broccoli into small florets; halve the mushrooms; slice the leek and spring onions; halve the mangetout.

**5** Heat the sunflower oil in a wok or large frying pan. When hot, add the carrots, broccoli and mushrooms and stir-fry for 3 minutes. Add the leek, spring onions and mangetout and stir-fry for a further 2 minutes.

**6** Stir 45 ml (3 tbsp) water into the remaining glaze; add to the wok. Cook for 3-4 minutes until all the vegetables are tender. Stir in the roasted tofu and serve at once, sprinkled with the sesame seeds.

**NOTE** If serving with noodles, add an extra 15 ml (1 tbsp) water to the sauce.

**VARIATION** Omit the tofu and simply serve the stir-fried vegetables with plain-boiled rice or noodles.

## GRILLED POLENTA WITH MUSHROOMS

**SERVES 6-8**
PREPARATION
15 minutes, plus cooling
COOKING TIME
15-20 minutes
FREEZING
Not suitable
CALS/SERVING
220-165

- 450 g (1 lb) field or flat mushrooms, wiped
- 4 shallots
- 50 g (2 oz) butter
- 2 garlic cloves, peeled and crushed
- salt and pepper
- 175 g (6 oz) quick-cook polenta
- 50 g (2 oz) Parmesan cheese, freshly grated
- 30 ml (2 tbsp) chopped fresh chives
- 30 ml (2 tbsp) chopped fresh parsley

TO SERVE
- rocket leaves
- extra-virgin olive oil

**1** Slice the mushrooms and dry-fry in a heavy-based frying pan, stirring to prevent sticking, until cooked through and most of the liquid has evaporated. Drain and leave to cool.
**2** Peel and finely chop the shallots. Melt the butter in a pan, add the shallots and garlic and cook until softened.
**3** Bring 750 ml (1¼ pints) water to the boil in a large pan. Add 2.5 ml (½ tsp) salt, then pour in the polenta in a thin steady stream, stirring constantly as you do so. Stir and cook for about 5 minutes (or according to the packet instructions) until it leaves the side of the pan.
**4** Remove the polenta from the heat and stir in the mushrooms, sautéed shallots, cheese, herbs and plenty of seasoning. Spoon the mixture into an oiled 900 g (2 lb) loaf tin, tapping it firmly to get rid of any air bubbles. Level the surface and leave to cool completely.
**5** Turn out the terrine onto a board and cut into thick slices. Brush with olive oil and grill for about 5 minutes each side until crisp and golden brown. Serve piping hot on a bed of rocket leaves, drizzled with olive oil.

## SMOKED TOFU, AUBERGINE AND SHIITAKE MUSHROOM KEBABS

**SERVES 4**
PREPARATION
15 minutes, plus marinating
COOKING TIME
10-15 minutes
FREEZING
Not suitable
CALS/SERVING
370

- 225 g (8 oz) smoked tofu
- 30 ml (2 tbsp) sesame oil
- 60 ml (4 tbsp) light soy sauce
- 30 ml (2 tbsp) thin honey
- 10 ml (2 tsp) chilli oil
- 1 medium aubergine
- 1 red pepper
- 16 even-sized shiitake mushrooms
- 15 ml (1 tbsp) toasted sesame seeds
- lime wedges, to garnish

**1** Cut the smoked tofu into 2.5 cm (1 inch) cubes. In a small bowl, mix together the sesame oil, soy sauce, honey and chilli oil. Add the tofu and toss to coat. Leave to marinate for 30 minutes. Remove the tofu with a slotted spoon, reserving the marinade.
**2** Cut the aubergine into 2.5 cm (1 inch) cubes. Halve, core and deseed the pepper, then cut into 2.5 cm (1 inch) squares.
**3** Thread the aubergine, tofu, mushrooms and pepper alternately onto kebab skewers. Lay on a rack set over the grill pan and grill for 10-15 minutes until tender, turning frequently and basting with the reserved marinade.
**4** Serve on a bed of rice, with the basting juices spooned over and sprinkled with the toasted sesame seeds. Garnish with lime wedges.

**NOTE** To toast sesame seeds, simply dry-fry them in a small frying pan, stirring constantly, until golden.

# SPICY VEGETABLE AND TOFU KEBABS

**SERVES 6**
PREPARATION 30 minutes, plus marinating
COOKING TIME 8-10 minutes
FREEZING Not suitable
CALS/SERVING 395

12 button onions
12 new potatoes
12 button mushrooms
2 courgettes
295 g (9½ oz) packet smoked tofu
2 garlic cloves, peeled and crushed
5 ml (1 tsp) ground coriander
5 ml (1 tsp) turmeric
2.5 ml (½ tsp) ground cumin
2.5 ml (½ tsp) sea salt
5 ml (1 tsp) chilli sauce
15 ml (1 tbsp) tomato paste
juice of ½ lemon
60 ml (4 tbsp) olive oil

YOGURT SAUCE
225 g (8 oz) Greek-style yogurt
1 garlic clove, peeled and crushed
30 ml (2 tbsp) chopped fresh coriander
salt and pepper

TO SERVE
lemon wedges

**1** Bring a large saucepan of lightly salted boiling water to the boil, add the onions and blanch for 3 minutes; drain, refresh under cold water and peel.

**2** Put the potatoes in a saucepan. Cover with cold water, bring to the boil and simmer for 8 minutes; then drain and refresh under cold water.

**3** Blanch the mushrooms in boiling water for 1 minute; drain and refresh under cold water. Cut each courgette into 6 thick slices and blanch for 1 minute; drain and refresh.

**4** Dry all the vegetables on kitchen paper and place in a large shallow dish. Cut the tofu into 2.5 cm (1 inch) cubes and add to the dish.

**5** Mix the garlic, spices, salt, chilli sauce, tomato paste, lemon juice and olive oil together in a small bowl. Add to the vegetables and tofu and toss until well coated. Cover and set aside in a cool place to marinate for several hours.

**6** Thread the tofu and vegetables onto 6 kebab skewers alternating them, so that on each skewer you have at least 2 cubes of tofu, 2 potatoes, 2 onions, 2 courgette slices and 2 mushrooms.

**7** Lay the kebabs on a rack set over the grill pan and grill for about 8-10 minutes until the vegetables are evenly charred and cooked through, turning frequently and basting with the marinade juices.

**8** Meanwhile in a small bowl, mix together the ingredients for the yogurt sauce and season with salt and pepper to taste. Serve the kebabs accompanied by the yogurt dip and lemon wedges.

**NOTE** If available use metal kebab skewers; alternatively if using wooden skewers pre-soak them in cold water for at least 30 minutes to prevent scorching under the grill.

# OKRA TAGINE

**SERVES 4-6**
PREPARATION
15 minutes
COOKING TIME
40 minutes
FREEZING
Not suitable
CALS/SERVING
160-110

- 2.5 ml (½ tsp) saffron strands
- 2 onions
- 30 ml (2 tbsp) olive oil
- 3 garlic cloves, peeled and crushed
- 5 ml (1 tsp) ground ginger
- 5 ml (1 tsp) turmeric
- 5 ml (1 tsp) caraway seeds
- 2.5 ml (½ tsp) ground cloves
- 10 ml (2 tsp) paprika
- finely grated zest and juice of 1 lemon
- 300 ml (½ pint) vegetable stock
- 1 large fennel bulb
- handful of fresh coriander or parsley
- 3 fresh oregano sprigs
- salt and pepper
- 425 g (15 oz) can plum tomatoes
- 350 g (12 oz) okra
- 8 baby courgettes, about 225 g (8 oz)
- handful of black olives

TO SERVE
- harissa sauce (see note)

**1** Put the saffron in a small bowl, pour on 150 ml (¼ pint) warm water and leave to soak.
**2** Peel and roughly chop the onions. Heat the oil in a large casserole dish, add the onions and garlic and sauté until softened. Add the spices and cook, stirring constantly, for 2 minutes. Stir in the lemon zest and juice, the saffron with its soaking liquid, and the stock. Slowly bring to the boil.
**3** Meanwhile, trim the fennel and cut into 6 wedges. Roughly chop half of the herbs. Add the fennel and chopped herbs to the casserole and season liberally with salt and pepper. Lower the heat, cover and simmer gently for about 15 minutes or until the fennel is softened.
**4** Meanwhile drain the tomatoes, being careful not to break them up. Trim the stalk ends of the okra if necessary, being careful not to cut right through into the pod itself. Halve the baby courgettes lengthwise.
**5** Add the tomatoes, okra and baby courgettes to the casserole. Simmer gently for 10-15 minutes until the okra and courgettes are cooked. Check the seasoning.
**6** Add the remaining fresh herbs and the olives. Serve immediately, with harissa sauce and plenty of bread, rice or couscous to mop up the juices.

**NOTE** Harissa sauce is a hot pepper sauce available from delicatessens and specialist food stores. It is a traditional accompaniment to many North African dishes.

**VARIATIONS**
❑ Add 175 g (6 oz) cooked or rinsed canned pulses, such as chick peas, with the fennel.
❑ Add 150 ml (¼ pint) thick yogurt with the tomatoes and okra, for a milder flavour.

# BAKED JACKET POTATOES

**SERVES 8**
PREPARATION
15 minutes
COOKING TIME
About 1½ hours
FREEZING
Not suitable
CALS/SERVING
240
COLOUR INDEX
Page 51

- 8 large baking potatoes, each about 175 g (6 oz)

CHEESY CARROT FILLING
- 350 g (12 oz) carrots
- 30 ml (2 tbsp) oil
- 10 ml (2 tsp) mustard seeds
- salt and pepper
- 45 ml (3 tbsp) mayonaise
- 50 g (2 oz) mature Cheddar cheese, grated
- squeeze of lemon juice

**1** Wash and scrub the potatoes and prick all over with a fork. Place on a baking sheet and bake in the oven at 200°C (400°F) Mark 6 for about 1½ hours or until the potatoes feel soft when gently squeezed, turning them over once during cooking.
**2** For the filling, peel and coarsely grate the carrots. Heat the oil in a wide-based saucepan, add the mustard seeds and fry over a high heat for a few seconds, taking care as they will 'spit'. Add the carrots and stir-fry for 1 minute. Take off the heat, season with salt and pepper and toss with the mayonnaise, cheese and lemon juice to taste.
**3** When the potatoes are cooked, score a deep cross on each one and mash the flesh lightly with a fork. Top with the filling and serve at once.

**VARIATIONS**
❑ Serve the potatoes with a chilli bean filling. Use either the Quick Vegetable and Bean Mole (see page 158), or Mixed Bean Chilli (see page 157).
❑ For an easy supper, simply top jacket potatoes with grated cheese, or crème fraîche and chopped chives. Serve with a salad.

## ROAST PEPPERS STUFFED WITH MUSHROOMS

SERVES 4
PREPARATION
20 minutes
COOKING TIME
30-35 minutes
FREEZING
Not suitable
CALS/SERVING
315
COLOUR INDEX
Page 51

2 large orange or red peppers
2 large yellow peppers
FILLING
450 g (1 lb) tomatoes, or a 400 g (14 oz) can chopped tomatoes
1 large onion
2-3 garlic cloves
45 ml (3 tbsp) extra-virgin olive oil
30 ml (2 tbsp) tomato paste
5 ml (1 tsp) sugar
salt and pepper
50 g (2 oz) mushrooms
50 g (2 oz) pine nuts or flaked almonds
15 ml (1 tbsp) fresh marjoram leaves, roughly torn
50 g (2 oz) black olives
25-50 g (1-2 oz) Parmesan cheese, freshly grated (optional)
marjoram sprigs, to garnish

**1** Halve the peppers lengthwise, remove the core and seeds, then place cut-side down on a baking sheet. Roast in the oven at 200°C (400°F) Mark 6 for 15 minutes, turning from time to time.
**2** Meanwhile make the filling. If using fresh tomatoes, place in a bowl, add boiling water to cover and leave for 30 seconds. Remove and peel away the skins, then roughly chop the tomato flesh.
**3** Peel and finely chop the onion and garlic. Heat 30 ml (2 tbsp) of the oil in a saucepan, add the onion and garlic and fry gently until softened and lightly coloured. Add the tomatoes, tomato paste, sugar, salt and pepper. Cook, uncovered, for 15-20 minutes until reduced to a thick sauce. Check the seasoning.
**4** Meanwhile, thickly slice the mushrooms. Heat the remaining 15 ml (1 tbsp) oil in a pan and sauté the mushroom slices until softened.
**5** Place the peppers, cut-side up, in an ovenproof dish. Transfer two thirds of the tomato mixture to a bowl and stir in the mushrooms, nuts, marjoram and olives. Fill the peppers with the mixture and top with the grated Parmesan if using. Bake in the oven for 15-20 minutes until thoroughly heated through.
**6** Garnish with marjoram sprigs and serve with a green salad and plenty of crusty bread or baked tomato and sesame bread (see note).

**NOTE** Use the remaining tomato mixture to make a tasty accompaniment. Spread on thick slices of crusty bread and sprinkle with sesame seeds. Warm through in the oven.

## OVEN-ROASTED SPAGHETTI SQUASH WITH HERB BUTTER

SERVES 4
PREPARATION
10 minutes
COOKING TIME
40-45 minutes
FREEZING
Not suitable
CALS/SERVING
325

2 large spaghetti squash, each about 700 g (1½ lb)
HERB BUTTER
125 g (4 oz) unsalted butter, softened
30 ml (2 tbsp) chopped fresh thyme
15 ml (1 tbsp) chopped fresh chives
grated zest and juice of ½ lemon
pinch of cayenne pepper
salt and pepper

**1** First prepare the herb butter. Place all the ingredients in a food processor and process briefly until evenly combined; transfer to a bowl.
**2** Cut each squash in half lengthwise, then carefully scoop out and discard the seeds. Place the halves, cut-side up, in a shallow baking tin.
**3** Divide the herb butter between the squash halves, spreading it on the cut flesh as well as in the hollow. Cover loosely with foil. Bake at 220°C (425°F) Mark 7 for 30 minutes, then remove the foil and bake for a further 10-15 minutes until the squash is golden and tender.
**4** Either serve the squash halves just as they are, or scoop out the flesh into its spaghetti-like strands and pile onto warmed serving plates.

**VARIATION** If you can't find spaghetti squash, use butternut instead – the result will be just as good. Cut in half lengthwise, then scoop out and discard the seeds. Continue as above.

## BAKED BEEF TOMATOES STUFFED WITH PESTO RICE

**SERVES 4**
PREPARATION
20 minutes
COOKING TIME
30 minutes
FREEZING
Not suitable
CALS/SERVING
185

50 g (2 oz) long-grain rice
4 large beef tomatoes, each about 225 g (8 oz)
50 g (2 oz) mozzarella cheese, shredded
30 ml (2 tbsp) pesto
25 g (1 oz) Parmesan cheese, freshly grated
salt and pepper
basil leaves, to garnish

**1** Cook the rice according to the packet instructions; drain and set aside.
**2** Meanwhile, cut a sliver from the base of each tomato so that it will sit flat. Cut a slightly thicker slice from the top of each one, then scoop out the seeds and pulp, taking care to avoid cutting through the skins; discard the seeds.
**3** Finely chop the tomato pulp and stir into the rice with the mozzarella, pesto and half of the Parmesan. Season with salt and pepper to taste.
**4** Spoon the rice mixture into the hollowed-out tomato skins and scatter over the remaining Parmesan. Place in a small roasting dish and bake at 220°C (425°F) Mark 7 for 20 minutes until bubbling and golden. Serve hot or warm, garnished with basil and accompanied by a green salad.

**VARIATION** Hollow out 6 medium tomatoes, stuff and bake as above. Serve as a side dish to a stew or vegetable roast.

## MUSHROOM, SPINACH AND ROASTED POTATO BAKE

**SERVES 6**
PREPARATION
45 minutes
COOKING TIME
35 minutes
FREEZING
Suitable: Stage 6
CALS/SERVING
775
COLOUR INDEX
Page 52

900 g (2 lb) small potatoes, scrubbed
90 ml (6 tbsp) olive oil
25 g (1 oz) dried porcini mushrooms (optional)
2 onions, peeled
450 g (1 lb) mixed mushrooms, such as shiitake and brown cap
400 g (14 oz) large spinach leaves, trimmed
2 garlic cloves, peeled and crushed
30 ml (2 tbsp) tomato paste
60 ml (4 tbsp) sun-dried tomato paste
10 ml (2 tsp) chopped fresh thyme
300 ml (½ pint) white wine
300 ml (½ pint) vegetable stock
300 ml (½ pint) double cream
175 g (6 oz) gruyère cheese, grated
75 g (3 oz) Parmesan cheese, freshly grated
salt and pepper
2 eggs, beaten
300 ml (½ pint) Greek-style yogurt
TO GARNISH
flat-leaf parsley
thyme sprigs

**1** Quarter the potatoes and place in a large roasting tin. Drizzle with 60 ml (4 tbsp) oil and turn to coat. Roast in the oven at 200°C (400°F) Mark 6 for 40 minutes or until tender and golden.
**2** Meanwhile, soak the dried porcini in warm water to cover if using. Drain and chop roughly. Roughly chop the onions, mushrooms and spinach.
**3** Heat the remaining 30 ml (2 tbsp) oil in a large, heavy-based saucepan. Add the onions and cook gently for 10 minutes or until soft. Add the fresh mushrooms and garlic and cook over a high heat for 5 minutes.
**4** Stir in the tomato pastes, porcini mushrooms if using, and the thyme and wine. Bring to the boil and simmer for 2 minutes. Add the stock and cream, bring back to the boil and let bubble for 20 minutes or until well reduced and syrupy.
**5** Transfer the mushroom mixture to a 2.3 litre (4 pint) ovenproof dish. Stir in the potatoes, spinach, gruyère and half of the Parmesan. Season well.
**6** In a bowl, beat the eggs with the yogurt and seasoning until evenly blended. Spoon over the vegetable mixture and sprinkle with the remaining Parmesan.
**7** Bake at 200°C (400°F) Mark 6 for 30-35 minutes, or until golden and bubbling. Garnish with parsley and thyme and serve with a crisp green salad and plenty of crusty bread.

**NOTE** If frozen, thaw overnight at cool room temperature, then cook as above for 40-45 minutes.

## BAKED STUFFED PUMPKIN

**SERVES 4-6**
PREPARATION
45 minutes
COOKING TIME
1¼-1½ hours
FREEZING
Not suitable
CALS/SERVING
430-285

1 pumpkin, about 1.4-1.8 kg (3-4 lb)
2 leeks, trimmed
30 ml (2 tbsp) olive oil
2 garlic cloves, peeled and crushed
30 ml (2 tbsp) chopped fresh thyme
10 ml (2 tsp) paprika
5 ml (1 tsp) turmeric
125 g (4 oz) long-grain rice
2 tomatoes
125 g (4 oz) gruyère or Cheddar cheese, grated
50 g (2 oz) cashew nuts, toasted
salt and pepper

**1** Cut a 5 cm (2 inch) slice from the top of the pumpkin and set aside for the lid. Scoop out and discard the seeds. Using a knife and a spoon, cut out most of the pumpkin flesh, leaving a thin shell. Cut the pumpkin flesh into small pieces and set aside.

**2** Chop the leeks. Heat the oil in a large pan, add the leeks with the garlic, thyme and spices, and fry for 10 minutes. Add the chopped pumpkin flesh and fry for a further 10 minutes, until golden, stirring frequently to prevent sticking. Transfer to a bowl.

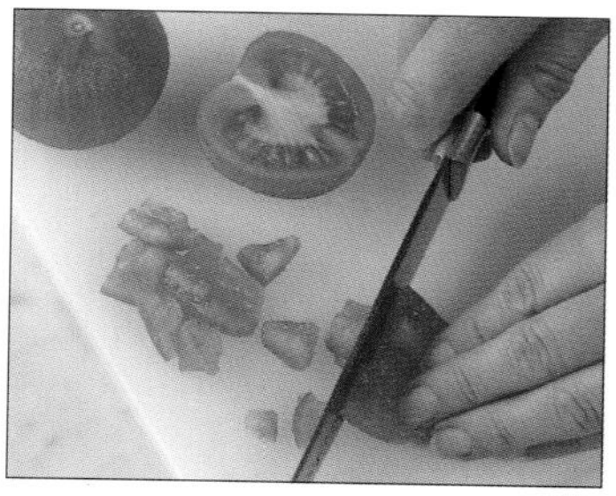

**3** In the meantime, cook the rice according to the packet directions. Skin, deseed and dice the tomatoes. Roughly chop the cashew nuts.

**4** Drain the rice and add to the pumpkin mixture with the tomatoes, cheese and cashews. Fork through to mix and season with salt and pepper to taste.

**5** Spoon the mixture into the pumpkin shell, top with the lid and bake at 180°C (350°F) Mark 4 for 1¼-1½ hours until softened and the skin is browned. Remove from the oven and let stand for 10 minutes. Cut into wedges to serve.

## TURKISH AUBERGINES

**SERVES 6**
PREPARATION
15 minutes, plus chilling
COOKING TIME
1½ hours
FREEZING
Not suitable
CALS/SERVING
365
COLOUR INDEX
Page 52

6 small aubergines
450 g (1 lb) onions
200 ml (7 fl oz) olive oil
3 garlic cloves, peeled and crushed
450 g (1 lb) tomatoes
60 ml (4 tbsp) chopped fresh parsley
3.75 ml (¾ tsp) ground allspice
salt and pepper
5 ml (1 tsp) sugar
30 ml (2 tbsp) lemon juice
chopped parsley, to garnish

**1** Halve the aubergines lengthwise, then scoop out the flesh, leaving a substantial shell so that they do not disintegrate. Chop the aubergine flesh and set aside.
**2** Peel and finely slice the onions. Heat 45 ml (3 tbsp) of the olive oil in a saucepan, add the onions and garlic and fry gently for about 15 minutes or until soft but not coloured. In the meantime, peel and chop the tomatoes.
**3** Add the tomatoes to the onions with the reserved aubergine flesh, parsley, allspice and seasoning. Simmer gently for 20 minutes or until the mixture is reduced.
**4** Spoon the tomato mixture into the aubergine halves and place in a shallow ovenproof dish in which they fit snugly.
**5** Mix the remaining oil with 150 ml (¼ pint) water, the sugar, lemon juice and seasoning. Pour this around the aubergines and cover the dish. Cook in the oven at 150°C (300°F) Mark 2 for about 1 hour or until tender.
**6** Leave to cool, then chill for at least 2 hours before serving. Sprinkle with parsley to serve.

# PIES, FLANS AND PIZZAS

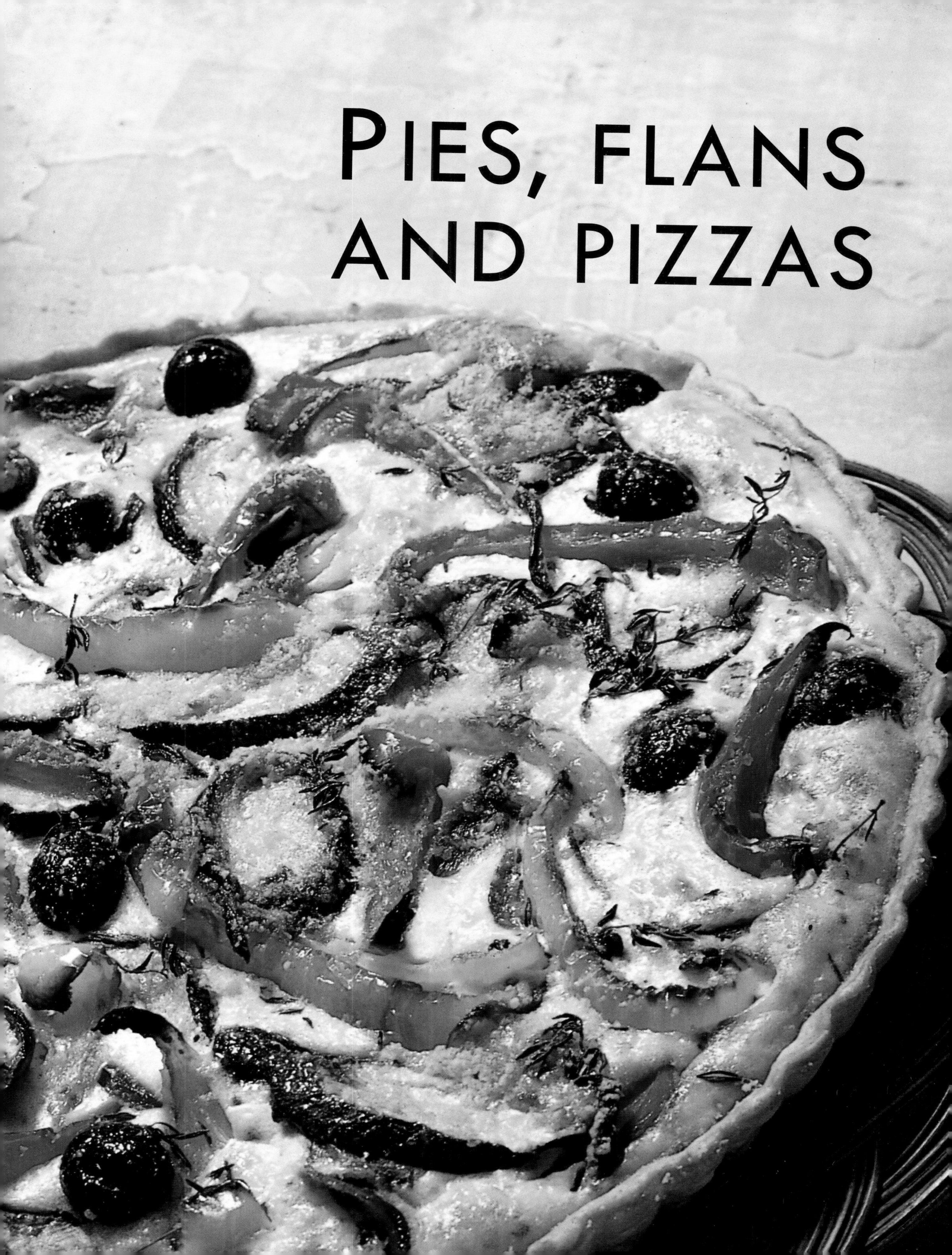

## LINING A FLAN CASE

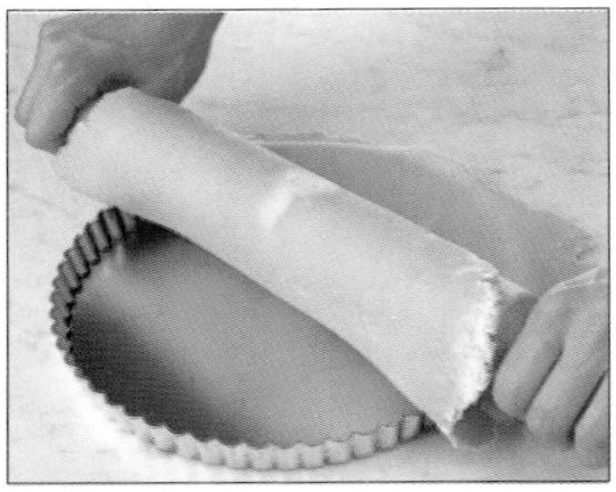

**1** Roll out the pastry on a lightly floured surface until 5-7.5 cm (2-3 inches) larger all round than the flan tin, depending on depth of tin. Using the rolling pin, lift the pastry over the tin.

**2** Lift the edges of the pastry so that it falls down into the tin, then gently press the pastry against the edges of the flan tin so that there are no gaps between the pastry and the tin.

**3** Turn any surplus pastry outwards over the rim, then trim away using a sharp knife to leave a neat edge. Chill in the refrigerator for 20-30 minutes to rest the pastry; this helps to minimise shrinkage during baking.

## BAKING BLIND

If a recipe instructs you to 'bake blind' you need to bake, or part-bake the pastry case without its filling.

**1** Prick the pastry base all over with a fork, then line with a large piece of grease-proof paper.

**2** Fill with a layer of ceramic baking beans or dried pulses.

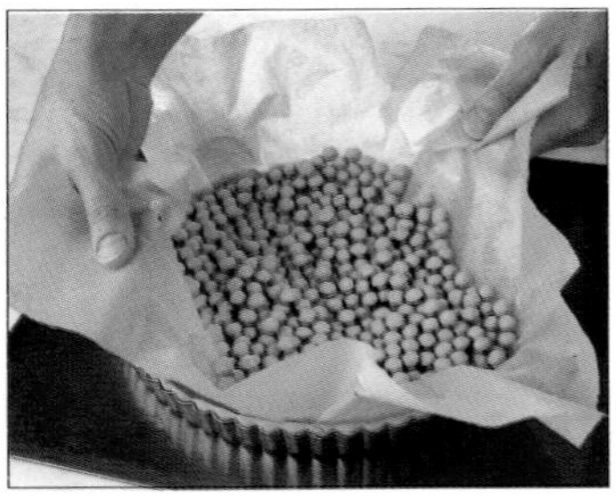

**3** Bake as directed in the recipe until the case looks set, then carefully remove the paper and beans bake for a further 5 minutes until the base is firm to the touch and lightly coloured, or longer if the flan case requires complete baking.

## COVERING A PIE DISH

**1** Using the inverted pie dish as a guide, roll out the pastry on a lightly floured surface until it is at least 5 cm (2 inches) larger all round than the dish.

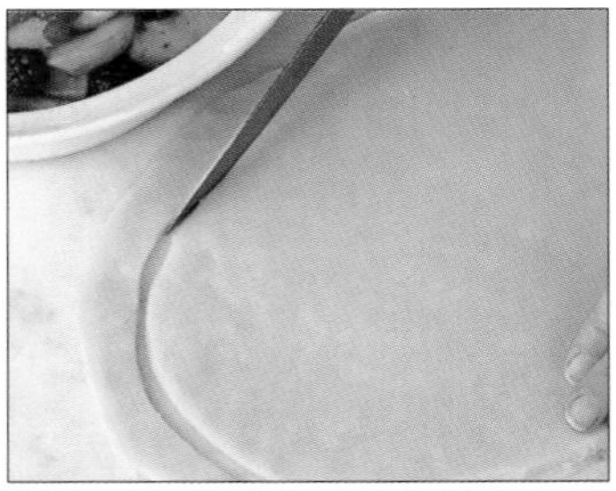

**2** Cut off a 2.5 cm (1 inch) strip from around the edge. Moisten the rim of the pie dish and position the strip on the rim; brush with water.

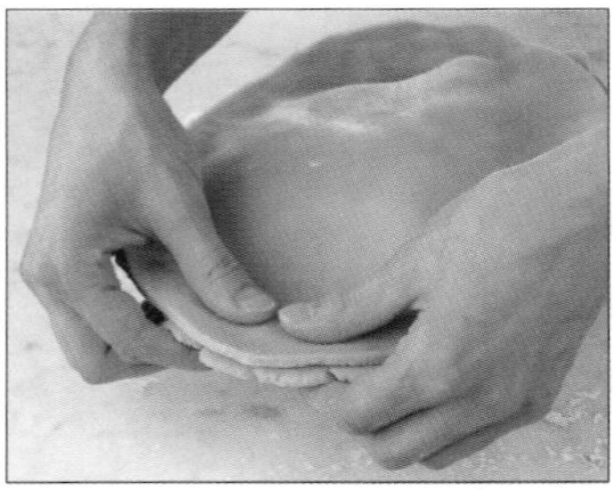

**3** Fill the dish generously so the surface of the filling is slightly rounded; use a pie funnel if there isn't enough filling to do this. Using the rolling pin, lift the pastry lid into position. Press the pastry edges together to seal.

**4** Using a sharp knife, held at an angle away from the dish, trim off excess pastry.

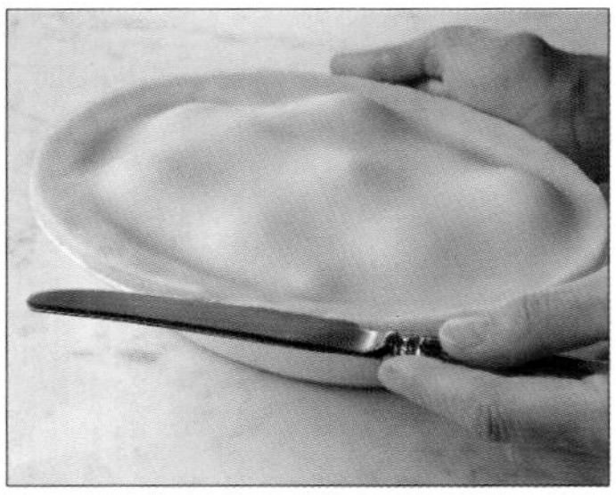

**5** Knock up the edge of the pastry by holding the blunt edge of a knife horizontally against the pastry rim and tapping sharply; this seals the edge and prevents the filling leaking out.

**6** To flute the edge, press your thumb on the rim of the pastry and at the same time gently draw back the floured blade of a round-bladed knife about 1 cm (½ inch) towards the centre. Repeat at 2.5 cm (1 inch) intervals around the edge. Make a hole in the top of the pie.

# VEGETABLE CHEESE PIE WITH POTATO CRUST

**SERVES 4**
PREPARATION
1 hour, plus chilling
COOKING TIME
30-35 minutes
FREEZING
Suitable
CALS/SERVING
645
COLOUR INDEX
Page 53

POTATO PASTRY
225 g (8 oz) plain white flour
pinch of salt
100 g (3½ oz) butter, diced
175 g (6 oz) cooled mashed potato
20-25 ml (4-5 tsp) cold water
FILLING
2 large onions
2 large carrots
350 g (12 oz) celeriac
175 g (6 oz) broccoli
125 g (4 oz) French beans
25 g (1 oz) butter
4 garlic cloves, peeled and crushed
50 g (2 oz) plain white flour
300 ml (½ pint) vegetable stock
300 ml (½ pint) milk
freshly grated nutmeg
salt and pepper
400 g (14 oz) can pinto or red kidney beans, drained
225 g (8 oz) Cheddar cheese, grated
beaten egg, to glaze

**1** To make the pastry, sift the flour and salt into a bowl. Add the butter and rub in with the fingertips until the mixture resembles fine breadcrumbs. Add the mashed potato and sufficient water to mix to a firm dough; knead lightly. Wrap in cling film and chill in the refrigerator while making the filling.
**2** To make the filling, peel and slice the onions; peel the carrots and celeriac and cut into chunks. Divide the broccoli into small florets; cut the French beans into short lengths.
**3** Melt the butter in a large saucepan. Add the onions and garlic and fry gently for 5 minutes. Add the carrots and celeriac; fry for a further 10 minutes. Stir in the flour and cook for 1 minute. Gradually stir in the stock and milk and bring just to the boil, stirring.
**4** Add the broccoli and French beans. Season with nutmeg, salt and pepper to taste. Cover and cook gently for 15 minutes. Cool slightly, then stir in the canned beans and cheese. Turn the filling into a 1.4 litre (2½ pint) pie dish.
**5** Roll out the pastry on a lightly floured surface until 5 cm (2 inches) larger than the diameter of the dish. Cut off a 2.5 cm (1 inch) strip of pastry from around the edge.
**6** Moisten the rim of the pie dish with water and position the strip on the rim. Dampen the pastry strip and position the pastry lid, pressing the edges firmly together to seal. Trim and flute the edge, and make a hole in the top of the pie to allow the steam to escape. If wished, decorate with leaves cut from the pastry trimmings.
**7** Brush the pie with beaten egg to glaze and sprinkle with a little grated nutmeg. Bake at 200°C (400°F) Mark 6 for 30-35 minutes until the pastry is golden.

# CREAMY CAULIFLOWER PIE

**SERVES 4**
PREPARATION
25 minutes
COOKING TIME
25 minutes
FREEZING
Not suitable
CALS/SERVING
720

375 g (13 oz) packet ready-made puff pastry
FILLING
800 g (1¾ lb) cauliflower
1 onion
50 g (2 oz) butter
25 g (1 oz) plain white flour
350 ml (12 fl oz) milk
2.5 ml (½ tsp) ground mace
5 ml (1 tsp) Dijon mustard
15 ml (1 tbsp) mustard seeds (optional)
50 g (2 oz) Parmesan or gruyère cheese, freshly grated
30 ml (2 tbsp) chopped fresh parsley
salt and pepper
60 ml (4 tbsp) single cream
TO FINISH
beaten egg, to glaze
15 g (½ oz) Parmesan cheese, freshly grated

**1** To prepare the filling, cut the cauliflower into large florets and blanch in boiling water for 2 minutes; drain.
**2** Peel and chop the onion. Melt the butter in a saucepan and fry the onion for 3 minutes. Add the flour and cook, stirring, for 1 minute. Remove from the heat and gradually blend in the milk. Stir in the mace, mustard, mustard seeds if using, cheese, parsley and seasoning. Cook, stirring, until thickened.
**3** Add the cream and cauliflower to the sauce and toss until coated. Turn into a 1.4 litre (2½ pint) pie dish.
**4** Roll out the pastry on a lightly floured surface and use to cover the dish (see opposite). Flute the edge and make a hole in the top of the pie to allow the steam to escape. If wished, decorate with leaves cut from the pastry trimmings.
**5** Brush with beaten egg and sprinkle the grated cheese over the pastry. Bake at 220°C (425°F) Mark 7 for about 25 minutes until the pastry is risen and golden.

# CHESTNUT AND VEGETABLE PIE

**SERVES 6-8**
PREPARATION
1 hour, plus chilling
COOKING TIME
50 minutes
FREEZING
Suitable
CALS/SERVING
1060-795

SHORTCRUST PASTRY
- 350 g (12 oz) plain white flour
- large pinch of salt
- 75 g (3 oz) lightly salted butter, diced
- 75 g (3 oz) white vegetable fat, diced
- 60-75 ml (4-5 tbsp) chilled water

STUFFING BALLS
- 75 g (3 oz) walnut pieces
- 2 large onions, peeled
- 4 celery sticks
- 60 ml (4 tbsp) oil
- 4 garlic cloves, peeled and crushed
- 30 ml (2 tbsp) chopped fresh rosemary
- 30 ml (2 tbsp) chopped fresh parsley
- 175 g (6 oz) soft white breadcrumbs
- 1 egg, beaten
- salt and pepper

FILLING
- 225 g (8 oz) baby onions or shallots
- 450 g (1 lb) carrots
- 350 g (12 oz) parsnips
- 225 g (8 oz) turnips
- 50 g (2 oz) butter
- 30 ml (2 tbsp) mustard seeds
- 25 g (1 oz) plain white flour
- 450 ml (¾ pint) strong beer
- 450 ml (¾ pint) vegetable stock
- 3 bay leaves
- 30 ml (2 tbsp) chopped fresh oregano
- two 240 g (8½ oz) cans whole chestnuts, or 450 g (1lb) cooked fresh ones, peeled
- 225 g (8 oz) button mushrooms

TO FINISH
- beaten egg, to glaze

**1** To make the pastry, sift the flour and salt into a bowl and rub in the fats until the mixture resembles breadcrumbs. Add enough cold water to mix to a firm dough. Knead lightly, then wrap in cling film and chill in the refrigerator while preparing the filling.

**2** To make the stuffing balls, finely chop the nuts, onions and celery. Heat 30 ml (2 tbsp) of the oil in a frying pan and fry the nuts, onions and garlic for 3 minutes. Add the celery and fry for 1 minute. Let cool slightly, then stir in the remaining ingredients.

**3** Shape the stuffing into small balls, 2.5 cm (1 inch) in diameter. Heat remaining oil in a clean frying pan and fry the stuffing balls for 2 minutes or until golden. Drain and leave to cool.

**4** For the filling, peel the onions or shallots, but leave whole. Peel and slice the carrots and parsnips. Peel the turnips and cut into chunks.

**5** Melt the butter in a large pan and fry the mustard seeds until starting to pop. Add the onions and carrots; fry for 2 minutes. Stir in the flour, then gradually stir in the beer and stock. Add the parsnips, turnips, herbs and seasoning. Cover and simmer for 15 minutes. Discard bay leaves; let cool.

**6** Add the chestnuts, mushrooms and stuffing balls to the filling, stir carefully, then turn into a 2.3 litre (4 pint) pie dish. Roll out the pastry on a lightly floured surface and use to cover the pie dish (see page 194). Flute the edge.

**7** Brush with egg and decorate with pastry leaves and a rose shaped from the trimmings. Bake at 200°C (400°F) Mark 6 for 25 minutes, then at 160°C (325°F) Mark 3 for a further 25 minutes. Serve with a green vegetable.

**IOTE** To make this pie suitable for vegans, use margarine nstead of butter.

## MEDITERRANEAN VEGETABLE FLAN

**ERVES 4-6**
REPARATION
5 minutes,
lus chilling
OOKING TIME
5 minutes
REEZING
uitable
ALS/SERVING
45-565
OLOUR INDEX
age 53

SHORTCRUST PASTRY
225 g (8 oz) plain white flour
pinch of salt
125 g (4 oz) butter, diced
45-60 ml (3-4 tbsp) chilled water

FILLING
1 red onion
1 small red pepper
1 small yellow pepper
1 small courgette
45 ml (3 tbsp) extra-virgin olive oil
1 garlic clove, crushed
15 ml (1 tbsp) chopped fresh thyme
10 ml (2 tsp) dried oregano
225 g (8 oz) ricotta cheese
25 g (1 oz) Parmesan cheese, freshly grated
2 eggs
150 ml (¼ pint) double cream
salt and pepper
25 g (1 oz) pitted black olives

To make the pastry, sift the flour and salt into a bowl, hen rub in the butter until the mixture resembles fine readcrumbs. Add sufficient water to mix to a firm dough. nead lightly, then wrap in cling film and chill in the refrigrator for 30 minutes. Preheat a baking sheet in the oven.

Roll out the pastry on a lightly floured surface and use to ne a 25 cm (10 inch) flan tin. Chill for 20 minutes.

Prick the base with a fork, then line with greaseproof aper and baking beans. Place on the preheated baking heet and bake blind in the oven at 200°C (400°F) Mark 6 or 10 minutes. Remove the foil and beans and bake for a urther 10 minutes until the pastry is golden. Lower the ven setting to 190°C (375°F) Mark 5.

Meanwhile, peel and thinly slice the onion; deseed and hinly slice the peppers; trim and slice the courgette. Heat he oil in a large frying pan, add the vegetables, garlic and erbs and stir-fry over a high heat for 5-6 minutes until ghtly golden. Drain on kitchen paper.

In a bowl, beat the ricotta, Parmesan and eggs together ntil evenly blended, then stir in the cream and season enerously with salt and pepper.

Spoon the vegetables into the pastry case and scatter he olives on top. Pour on the ricotta mixture and bake for 5 minutes, or until risen and firm to the touch. Serve varm or cold, with a tomato and basil salad.

## ROASTED VEGETABLE TATIN

**SERVES 4**
PREPARATION
10 minutes
COOKING
40 minutes
FREEZING
Not suitable
CALS/SERVING
495
COLOUR INDEX
Page 53

175 g (6 oz) celeriac
175 g (6 oz) carrots
175 g (6 oz) swede
175 g (6 oz) shallots
3 garlic cloves
125 g (4 oz) trimmed leeks
5 ml (1 tsp) coriander seeds
5 ml (1 tsp) fennel seeds
45 ml (3 tbsp) olive oil
salt and pepper
225 g (8 oz) ready-made puff pastry
50 g (2 oz) butter
10 ml (2 tsp) sugar
50 ml (2 fl oz) water
15 ml (1 tbsp) lemon juice
75 g (3 oz) no-soak dried apricots

**1** Peel the celeriac, carrots and swede, then cut into chunks. Peel the shallots; cut in half, if large. Peel the garlic cloves; leave whole. Cut the leeks into chunks.
**2** Finely grind the coriander and fennel seeds, using a pestle and mortar, or in a bowl with the end of a rolling pin.
**3** Place the celeriac, carrot, swede and shallots in a roasting tin and scatter over the ground spices. Drizzle with the olive oil and season generously with salt and pepper. Roast in the oven at 220°C (425°F) Mark 7 for 20 minutes.
**4** Add the garlic cloves and roast for another 10-15 minutes, then stir in the leeks and return to the oven for a further 10 minutes.
**5** Roll out the pastry on a lightly floured surface to a 25 cm (10 inch) round and prick all over with a fork. Chill in the refrigerator for 10 minutes.
**6** Meanwhile, melt the butter in a heavy-based ovenproof frying pan, about 20 cm (8 inches) in diameter. Add the sugar, water and lemon juice and dissolve over a low heat. Increase the heat and cook until the mixture is a golden caramel colour.
**7** Roughly chop the apricots and mix with the vegetables. Spoon on top of the caramel mixture and cook over a moderate heat for 10 minutes.
**8** Place the chilled pastry round on top of the vegetables and immediately transfer to the oven. Bake for 20 minutes or until the pastry is golden.
**9** Leave to stand for 5 minutes, then carefully invert onto a warmed plate and serve immediately.

# ONION AND POTATO TART

**SERVES 4**
PREPARATION
30 minutes, plus chilling
COOKING TIME
30-35 minutes
FREEZING
Not suitable
CALS/SERVING
605

SHORTCRUST PASTRY
- 175 g (6 oz) plain white flour
- pinch of salt
- 75 g (3 oz) butter, diced
- 30-45 ml (2-3 tbsp) chilled water

FILLING
- 3 small potatoes, about 225 g (8 oz)
- 2 onions
- 60 ml (4 tbsp) olive oil
- 2 garlic cloves, peeled and crushed
- 10 ml (2 tsp) each chopped fresh thyme and sage
- 30 ml (2 tbsp) Olive Pesto (see page 292)
- 30 ml (2 tbsp) capers in brine, drained
- 125 g (4 oz) gruyère or Cheddar cheese, grated
- salt and pepper

**1** To make the pastry, sift the flour and salt into a bowl, then rub in the butter until the mixture resembles fine breadcrumbs. Add sufficient water to mix to a firm dough. Knead lightly, wrap in cling film and chill for 30 minutes. Preheat a baking sheet in the oven.

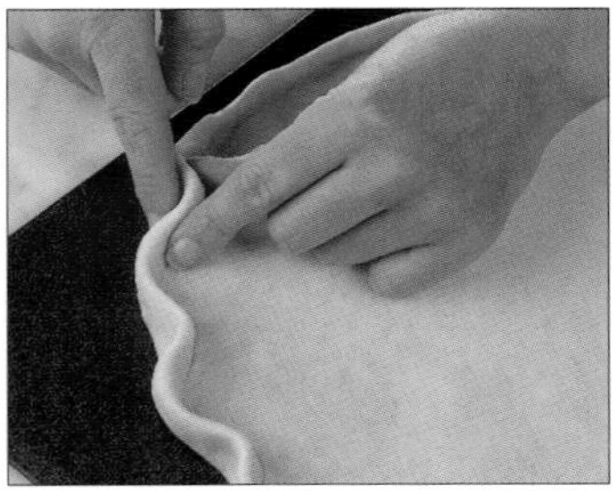

**2** Roll out the pastry on a lightly floured surface to a 30 cm (12 inch) round, then lift onto another baking sheet. Using fingers and thumbs, form a slight rim around the edge. Prick the base with a fork and line with greaseproof paper and baking beans.

**3** Slide the baking sheet onto the heated baking sheet and bake blind at 220°C (425°F) Mark 7 for 10 minutes. Remove the paper and beans and bake for a further 5-8 minutes or until the pastry is crisp.

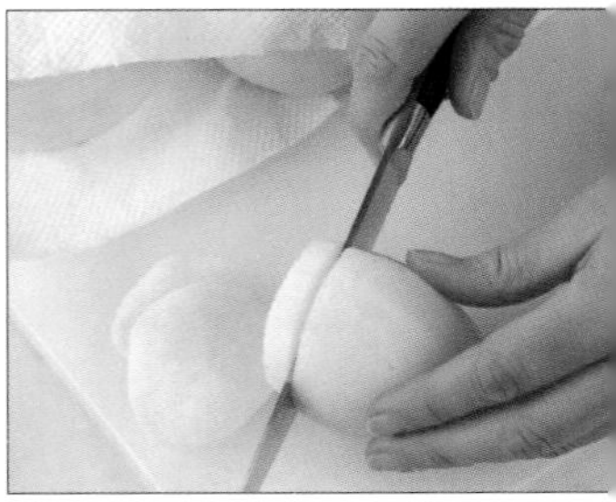

**4** Meanwhile, cook the potatoes in lightly salted boiling water for 10-15 minutes until just tender. Drain and immediately refresh under cold water. Pat dry and cut into thin slices.

**5** Peel and slice the onions. Heat the oil in a frying pan add the onions, garlic and herbs and fry gently for 10 minutes until softened and lightly golden.

**6** Spread the olive pesto over the pre-baked pastry base, then top with the sliced potatoes, onion mixture and capers.

**7** Scatter over the grated cheese and season generously with salt and pepper. Bake the tart in the oven for 20-25 minutes until the cheese is melted and golden. Serve at once, with a tomato salad.

**NOTE** For convenience, you can buy a 225 g (8 oz) packet ready-made shortcrust pastry, rather than make your own.

## SAFFRON TART WITH WILD MUSHROOMS

**SERVES 4-6**
PREPARATION
25 minutes, plus chilling
COOKING TIME
45-50 minutes
FREEZING
Suitable
CALS/SERVING
820-550

SAFFRON PASTRY
large pinch of saffron strands
10 ml (2 tsp) boiling water
225 g (8 oz) plain white flour
salt and pepper
125 g (4 oz) lightly salted butter, diced
15-30 ml (1-2 tbsp) chilled water
FILLING
450 g (1 lb) mixed wild mushrooms (see note)
1 large onion
50 g (2 oz) lightly salted butter
2-3 garlic cloves, peeled and crushed
2 eggs
200 ml (7 fl oz) double cream
TO GARNISH
Parmesan cheese shavings (optional)
chervil or parsley sprigs

**1** Put the saffron in a small bowl with the boiling water and set aside to infuse until cool. Sift the flour and a pinch of salt into a bowl and add a little pepper. Rub in the butter until the mixture resembles fine breadcrumbs. Stir in the saffron liquid and sufficient water to mix to a firm dough. Knead lightly, wrap in cling film and chill for 30 minutes.
**2** Roll out the pastry on a lightly floured surface and use to line a 24 cm (9½ inch) loose-based flan tin, about 2.5 cm (1 inch) deep. Bake blind at 200°C (400°F) Mark 6 for 15 minutes until beginning to colour around the edges. Remove the beans and paper and bake for a further 5 minutes.
**3** Meanwhile, prepare the filling. Wipe the mushrooms; peel and finely chop the onion. Melt the butter in a frying pan, add the onion and garlic and fry for 3 minutes. Add the mushrooms and fry for a further 2 minutes. Turn into the pastry case.
**4** In a bowl, beat together the eggs, cream and seasoning, then pour over the mushrooms. Bake in the oven for about 25-30 minutes until just set in the centre. Serve topped with Parmesan if preferred and garnished with herbs.

**NOTE** If wild mushrooms are unavailable, use a mixture of chestnut, button and oyster mushrooms instead. For extra flavour, include 25 g (1 oz) dried porcini; soak in hot water for 15 minutes, then drain and chop before using.

## COURGETTE, FETA AND THYME TART

**SERVES 6**
PREPARATION
45 minutes, plus chilling
COOKING TIME
About 1 hour
FREEZING
Suitable
CALS/SERVING
620
COLOUR INDEX
Page 54

PASTRY
125 g (4 oz) chilled butter, diced
125 g (4 oz) plain white flour
pinch of salt
FILLING
350 g (12 oz) courgettes, trimmed
1 bunch of spring onions, trimmed
125 g (4 oz) feta cheese
30 ml (2 tbsp) olive oil
15 ml (1 tbsp) fresh thyme leaves
salt and pepper
300 g (11 oz) medium-fat soft goat's cheese
2 eggs
200 ml (7 fl oz) double cream
TO FINISH
beaten egg, to glaze

**1** To make the pastry, put the butter into a food processor with the flour and salt. Process for 2-3 seconds, then add 60 ml (4 tbsp) cold water and process for 3-4 seconds or until the mixture just comes together in a ball. Turn out on to a floured surface and knead lightly until the dough is smooth but the butter is still in small pieces. Wrap in cling film and chill in the refrigerator for at least 2 hours.
**2** For the filling, roughly chop the courgettes; slice the spring onions; crumble the feta cheese into large pieces.
**3** Heat the olive oil in a large frying pan. Add the spring onions and cook for 1-2 minutes. Add the courgettes and cook for a further 2-3 minutes. Add the thyme, pepper and a little salt if required. Turn into a bowl and allow to cool.
**4** In a large bowl, beat the goat's cheese with the eggs and cream until evenly blended. Stir in the feta cheese and cooled courgettes. Set aside in a cool place.
**5** Roll out the pastry thinly on a lightly floured surface and use to line a 23 cm (9 inch) loose-bottomed flan tin; chill in the refrigerator for 20 minutes.
**6** Line the pastry case with greaseproof paper and baking beans. Bake blind in the oven at 200°C (400°F) Mark 6 for 15 minutes. Remove the paper and beans and bake for a further 10 minutes or until the pastry is deep golden brown. Allow to cool for 5 minutes, then brush the inside of the pastry case with beaten egg and return to the oven for 4-5 minutes until the egg has formed a seal. Pour in the courgette and cheese mixture and bake for 30-35 minutes or until the filling is just set.
**7** Leave to stand for 5 minutes, then carefully unmould. Serve warm or cold, accompanied by salad leaves.

## CREAMY LEEK TART

**SERVES 6**
PREPARATION
30 minutes, plus chilling
COOKING TIME
35-40 minutes
FREEZING
Not suitable
CALS/SERVING
640

PATE BRISÉE
250 g (9 oz) plain white flour
5 ml (1 tsp) salt
125 g (4½ oz) butter, softened
1 egg yolk
FILLING
1.4 kg (3 lb) leeks, trimmed
50 g (2 oz) butter
30 ml (2 tbsp) water
salt and pepper
3 egg yolks
300 ml (½ pint) crème fraîche or double cream
freshly grated nutmeg

**1** To make the pastry, sift the flour and salt onto a sheet of greaseproof paper. Put the butter and egg yolk in a food processor and blend until smooth. Shoot in the flour and work until just combined. Turn out onto a lightly floured work surface and knead gently until smooth. Form into a ball, flatten and wrap in cling film. Chill in the refrigerator for at least 30 minutes. Allow to come to room temperature before rolling out.
**2** Meanwhile, prepare the filling. Slice or chop the leeks. Melt the butter in a large saucepan, add the leeks and stir to coat in the butter. Add the water, cover and cook gently, stirring occasionally, for about 20 minutes until very soft, but not coloured. Season well. Set aside to cool.
**3** Roll out the pastry thinly on a lightly floured surface and use to line a 25 cm (10 inch) loose-bottomed flan tin. Chill for 20 minutes, then lightly prick the base with a fork.
**4** Beat the egg yolks and cream together, adding a little freshly grated nutmeg. Spread the leeks in the pastry case and pour over the egg and cream mixture.
**5** Bake in the oven at 200°C (400°F) Mark 6 for 15 minutes, then lower the oven setting to 190°C (375°F) Mark 5 and bake for a further 20-25 minutes until set and browned on top. Serve warm or cold.

**VARIATION** Sprinkle 125 g (4 oz) grated gruyère over the top of the flan before cooking.

## TARTE AU ROQUEFORT

**SERVES 6-8**
PREPARATION
30 minutes, plus chilling
COOKING TIME
45-50 minutes
FREEZING
Not suitable
CALS/SERVING
905-680
COLOUR INDEX
Page 54

PATE BRISÉE
250 g (9 oz) plain white flour
5 ml (1 tsp) salt
125 g (4½ oz) butter, softened
1 egg yolk
FILLING
225 g (8 oz) cream cheese, at room temperature
150 ml (¼ pint) crème fraîche or double cream
3 eggs, beaten
175 g (6 oz) Roquefort cheese
pepper
freshly grated nutmeg
45 ml (3 tbsp) chopped fresh chives
TOPPING
3 garlic cloves
30 ml (2 tbsp) olive oil
125 g (4 oz) walnut halves
15 ml (1 tbsp) walnut oil
45 ml (3 tbsp) chopped fresh parsley

**1** To make the pastry, sift the flour and salt onto a sheet of greaseproof paper. Put the butter and egg yolk in a food processor and blend until smooth. Shoot in the flour and work until just combined. Turn out onto a lightly floured work surface and knead gently until smooth. Form into a ball, flatten and wrap in cling film. Chill in the refrigerator for at least 30 minutes. Allow to come to room temperature before rolling out.
**2** To prepare the filling, beat the cream cheese in a bowl until softened, then beat in the cream and eggs. Crumble in the Roquefort and mix gently. Season liberally with pepper and a little nutmeg. As the cheese is salty, you probably won't need to add salt. Stir in the chives; set aside.
**3** Roll out the pastry on a lightly floured surface and use to line a 25 cm (10 inch) loose-bottomed flan tin. Chill for 20 minutes, then lightly prick the base with a fork. Line the base with greaseproof paper and baking beans and bake blind in the oven at 200°C (400°F) Mark 6 for 10 minutes. Remove the paper and beans and bake for a further 5 minutes. Let cool slightly. Lower the oven setting to 190°C (375°F) Mark 5.
**4** Pour the filling into the pastry case and bake for 30-35 minutes or until puffed and lightly browned.
**5** Meanwhile, peel and slice the garlic. Heat the olive oil in a frying pan and add the garlic and walnuts. Stir-fry until the garlic is golden and the walnuts are browned. Stir in the walnut oil and parsley. Serve the tart warm or cold, topped with the warm garlic and walnut topping. A chicory, pear and watercress salad is the ideal complement.

## OATMEAL AND COURGETTE QUICHE

**SERVES 6**
PREPARATION
25 minutes, plus chilling
COOKING TIME
About 1 hour
FREEZING
Suitable
CALS/SERVING
515

OATMEAL PASTRY
50 g (2 oz) plain white flour
50 g (2 oz) plain wholemeal flour
pinch of salt
50 g (2 oz) medium oatmeal
40 g (1½ oz) lightly salted butter, diced
40 g (1½ oz) white vegetable fat, diced
30-45 ml (2-3 tbsp) chilled water
FILLING
350 g (12 oz) onions
450 g (1 lb) small courgettes
60 ml (4 tbsp) olive oil
2 eggs
1 egg yolk
200 g (7 oz) crème fraîche
30 ml (2 tbsp) grainy mustard (optional)
salt and pepper
30 ml (2 tbsp) pine nuts
30 ml (2 tbsp) freshly grated Parmesan cheese

**1** To make the pastry, place the flours, salt and oatmeal in a bowl, then rub in the fats until the mixture resembles breadcrumbs. Add enough cold water to mix to a firm dough. Knead lightly, then wrap in cling film and chill in the refrigerator for 30 minutes.
**2** Roll out the pastry on a lightly floured surface and use to line a 28 x 20 cm (11 x 8 inch) rectangular loose-based flan tin, about 2.5 cm (1 inch) deep (see note). Bake blind in the oven at 200°C (400°F) Mark 6 for 15 minutes until beginning to colour around the edges. Remove the beans and paper and bake for a further 5 minutes.
**3** Meanwhile, prepare the filling. Peel and thinly slice the onions. Trim the courgettes, halve lengthwise, then cut across into slices. Heat the oil in a frying pan. Add the onions and fry for 2 minutes. Add the courgettes and fry for a further 3-5 minutes until golden. Spread in the pastry case.
**4** In a bowl, beat the eggs, egg yolk and crème fraîche with the mustard if using, and seasoning. Pour over the courgettes. Sprinkle with the pine nuts and cheese and bake for 35-40 minutes until golden. Serve warm.

**NOTE** Use a 25 cm (10 inch) round flan tin if you don't have a rectangular one.

## SPRING VEGETABLE STRUDEL

**SERVES 6**
PREPARATION
30 minutes, plus standing
COOKING TIME
35-40 minutes
FREEZING
Suitable: Stage 6
CALS/SERVING
515
COLOUR INDEX
Page 54

4 large sheets filo pastry
50 g (2 oz) butter, melted
FILLING
450 g (1 lb) waxy potatoes, such as Maris Bard or Wilja
450 g (1 lb) carrots
225 g (8 oz) leeks
4-5 spring onions
125 ml (4 fl oz) water
75 g (3 oz) butter
30 ml (2 tbsp) olive oil
450 g (1 lb) spring greens
1 garlic clove, peeled and crushed
15 ml (1 tbsp) lemon juice
300 ml (½ pint) fromage frais
pinch of ground mixed spice
salt and pepper
pinch of paprika
TO ASSEMBLE
75 g (3 oz) ground almonds
poppy seeds, for sprinkling

**1** To prepare the filling, peel and dice the potatoes and carrots. Trim and slice the leeks and spring onions. Melt 50 g (2 oz) of the butter with 15 ml (1 tbsp) olive oil in a large saucepan. Add the potatoes, carrots, leeks and spring onions and fry for 4-5 minutes, stirring all the time. Add the water, reduce the heat, cover and cook gently for 10-15 minutes. Leave to cool.
**2** Meanwhile, remove the thick stalks from the spring greens and shred the leaves. Heat the remaining butter and olive oil in a large frying pan. Add the spring greens and garlic and stir-fry for 2-3 minutes or until just softened; do not overcook. Stir in the lemon juice and leave to cool.
**3** Stir the fromage frais into the potato and leek mixture and season with mixed spice, salt, pepper and paprika.
**4** Lay one sheet of filo pastry on a clean surface and brush lightly with melted butter. Take a second sheet of pastry and place it slightly overlapping the first sheet to make a 45 cm (18 inch) square. Brush lightly with butter. Repeat with the remaining filo to make a double thickness. Sprinkle the ground almonds evenly over the pastry.
**5** Spoon half of the potato mixture over the bottom quarter of the pastry, leaving a border around the edge. Cover with the spring green mixture, then top with the remaining potato mixture.
**6** Fold in the sides of the pastry, then roll up like a Swiss roll. Carefully transfer to a baking sheet, seam-side down.
**7** Brush with melted butter, sprinkle with poppy seeds and bake at 200°C (400°F) Mark 6 for 20-25 minutes until golden brown. Leave to stand for 5 minutes before serving.

# SPANAKOPITTA STRUDEL

**SERVES 4-6**
PREPARATION
25 minutes
COOKING TIME
25-30 minutes
FREEZING
Suitable:
Stage 7
CALS/SERVING
490-330

- 5 large sheets filo pastry
- 1 red onion
- 30 ml (2 tbsp) oil
- 2 garlic cloves, peeled and crushed
- 10 ml (2 tsp) ground coriander
- 2.5 ml (½ tsp) each ground cumin and cinnamon
- 10 ml (2 tsp) dried oregano
- 450 g (1 lb) frozen leaf spinach, thawed
- 175 g (6 oz) feta cheese, crumbled
- 15 ml (1 tbsp) chopped fresh mint
- salt and pepper
- 100 g (3½ oz) unsalted butter
- 25 g (1 oz) ground almonds
- 25 g (1 oz) fresh breadcrumbs

TO SERVE
- mint leaves, to garnish
- Tomato Sauce (see page 291)

**1** Peel and finely chop the onion. Heat the oil in a frying pan, add the onion, garlic, spices and oregano and fry gently for 5 minutes to soften. Transfer to a bowl.

**2** Drain the spinach and squeeze out all excess liquid, then add to the onion mixture. Stir in the feta, mint and seasoning to taste; set aside.

**3** Melt 25 g (1 oz) of the butter in a clean frying pan add the ground almonds and breadcrumbs and stir-fry over a medium heat for 3-4 minutes until golden.

**4** Melt the remaining butter in a small pan. Lay one sheet of filo pastry on a clean surface, brush with a little butter, then sprinkle over a quarter of the crumb mixture.

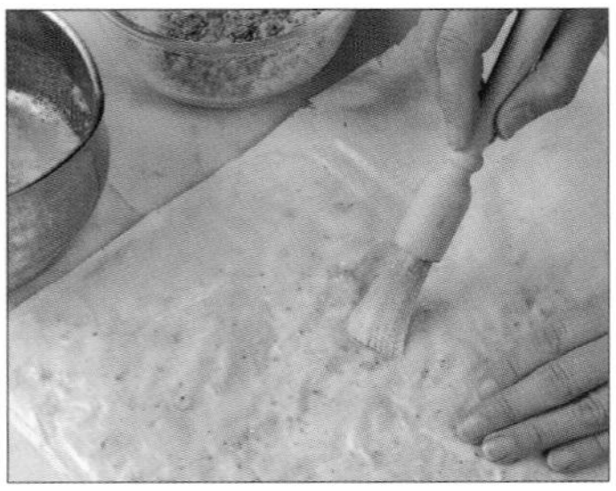

**5** Repeat these layers, brushing each pastry layer with butter and finishing with the final sheet of filo pastry. Brush the top sheet with butter.

**6** Carefully spread the spinach mixture over the filo pastry, leaving a clear 2.5 cm (1 inch) border around the edge.

**7** Roll up from a short end, like a Swiss roll. Carefully transfer to a baking sheet, making sure the seam is underneath.

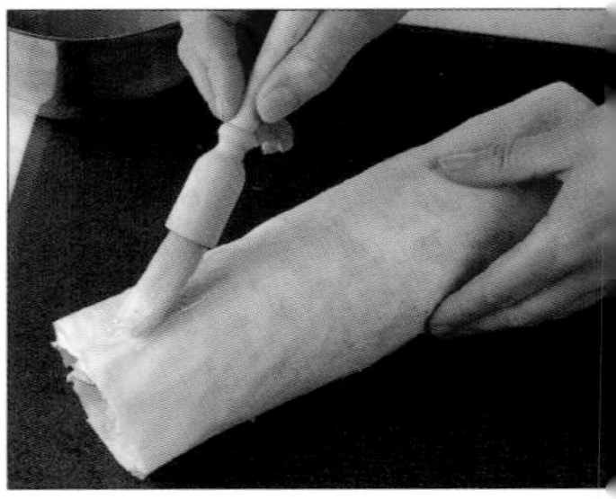

**8** Brush with the remaining butter and bake at 200°C (400°F) Mark 6 for 25-30 minutes until the pastry is golden and crisp. Leave to stand for a few minutes, then cut into slices. Serve garnished with mint and accompanied by the tomato sauce.

**NOTE** Always keep filo pastry covered with a damp tea-towel until ready to use or it will dry out and crumble.

## ONION, FETA CHEESE AND PINE NUT TARTS

**SERVES 4**
PREPARATION 15 minutes, plus chilling
COOKING TIME 35 minutes
FREEZING Suitable
CALS/SERVING 710
COLOUR INDEX Page 55

450 g (1 lb) ready-made puff pastry
700 g (1½ lb) onions
60 ml (4 tbsp) olive oil, plus extra for brushing
25 g (1 oz) pitted black olives
25 g (1 oz) sun-dried tomatoes
25 g (1 oz) pine nuts
25 g (1 oz) raisins (optional)
50 g (2 oz) feta cheese, crumbled
25 g (1 oz) capers
salt and pepper
oregano sprigs, to garnish

**1** Roll out the puff pastry on a lightly floured surface, then cut out 4 circles, each 15 cm (6 inches) in diameter. Chill the pastry circles for 30 minutes.
**2** Preheat 2 baking sheets in the oven at 220°C (425°F) Mark 7. Meanwhile, peel and slice the onions. Heat the oil in a large heavy-based frying pan. Add the onions and cook over a low heat for 10-15 minutes, stirring occasionally, until golden and caramelised. Set aside to cool.
**3** Roughly chop the black olives and sun-dried tomatoes. Add to the onions with the pine nuts, raisins if using, feta cheese and capers. Toss to mix.
**4** Prick the pastry circles with a fork and brush with a little oil. Divide the onion mixture between the pastry circles, leaving a 1 cm (½ inch) margin around the edges. Season well with salt and pepper.
**5** Place the tarts on the hot baking sheets and bake in the oven for approximately 15 minutes or until the pastry is crisp, golden and risen around the edges. Garnish with oregano sprigs to serve.

**NOTE** If frozen, reheat from frozen at 220°C (425°F) Mark 7 for 10 minutes.

## FILO MUSHROOM TARTLETS

**SERVES 6**
PREPARATION 30 minutes, plus cooling
COOKING TIME 25-30 minutes
FREEZING Not suitable
CALS/SERVING 375

8-10 sheets filo pastry
15 ml (1 tbsp) sunflower oil
FILLING
2 small red onions
125 g (4 oz) chestnut mushrooms
125 g (4 oz) flat mushrooms
15 ml (1 tbsp) sunflower oil
2 garlic cloves, peeled and crushed
5 sun-dried tomatoes in oil, drained
10 ml (2 tsp) lemon juice
15 ml (1 tbsp) chopped fresh parsley
salt and pepper
6 medium eggs
15 g (½ oz) Parmesan cheese, freshly grated
TO SERVE
mixed salad leaves
a little balsamic vinegar

**1** Lightly grease six 9 cm (3½ inch), 2.5 cm (1 inch) deep flan tins. Cut eighteen 11 cm (4½ inch) squares from the filo pastry. Brush each square with a little sunflower oil. Layer 3 sheets in each tin, arranging them at an angle to each other so the points form a star. Press the pastry into the sides of the tins. Bake in the oven at 190°C (375°F) Mark 5 for 10-15 minutes until just golden; don't overcook.
**2** Meanwhile, prepare the filling. Peel and finely chop the onions. Trim the mushrooms, then chop finely. Heat the oil in a pan, add the onions and fry until softened and transparent. Add the garlic and mushrooms to the pan and cook until the juices start to run.
**3** Finely chop the sun-dried tomatoes and add to the mushrooms with the lemon juice, parsley and seasoning.
**4** Divide the filling between the filo pastry cases. Make a well in the centre of one with the back of a spoon, pushing the filling to the side. Break an egg into a small saucer or cup, then slide into the well. Repeat with the remainder.
**5** Sprinkle with the Parmesan and bake for 14-16 minutes until the eggs are softly set and creamy. Serve with a mixed leaf salad drizzled with balsamic vinegar.

# MOROCCAN FILO PIE

**SERVES 6-8**
PREPARATION
20 minutes, plus cooling
COOKING TIME
40-45 minutes
FREEZING
Suitable: Stage 5
CALS/SERVING
540-410

12 sheets filo pastry (see note)
75 g (3 oz) unsalted butter, melted
FILLING
1 onion
60 ml (4 tbsp) olive oil
2-3 garlic cloves, peeled and crushed
5 ml (1 tsp) ground mixed spice
10 ml (2 tsp) ground cumin
450 g (1 lb) spinach leaves, trimmed
two 400 g (14 oz) cans green lentils, drained
2 eggs, beaten
175 g (6 oz) feta cheese, crumbled
25 g (1 oz) Parmesan cheese, freshly grated
60 ml (4 tbsp) chopped mixed fresh herbs such as coriander, dill and parsley
salt and pepper

**1** To prepare the filling, peel and finely chop the onion. Heat the oil in a saucepan, add the onion, garlic and spices and fry over a low heat for about 10 minutes.

**2** Meanwhile, shred the spinach. Add to the pan and cook until wilted. Stir in the lentils, cover and heat through for 5 minutes. Mash the lentils slightly with a fork, then transfer to a bowl and let cool slightly.

**3** Stir the eggs into the cooled filling, then add the feta cheese, Parmesan, herbs and seasoning. Toss to mix, then set aside.

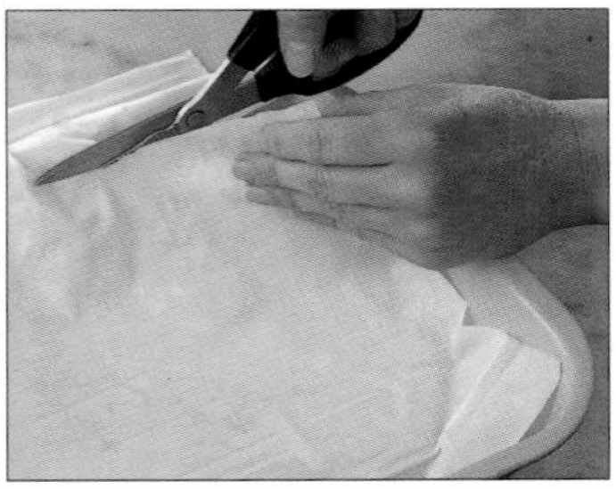

**4** Lay one sheet of filo pastry in the base of a lightly oiled 25 x 20 cm (10 x 8 inch) baking tin, trimming to fit as necessary and brush with melted butter. Layer five more filo sheets in the tin, brushing each one with butter.

**5** Spoon in the filling and level the surface. Layer the remaining sheets of filo pastry on top, again brushing each with butter.

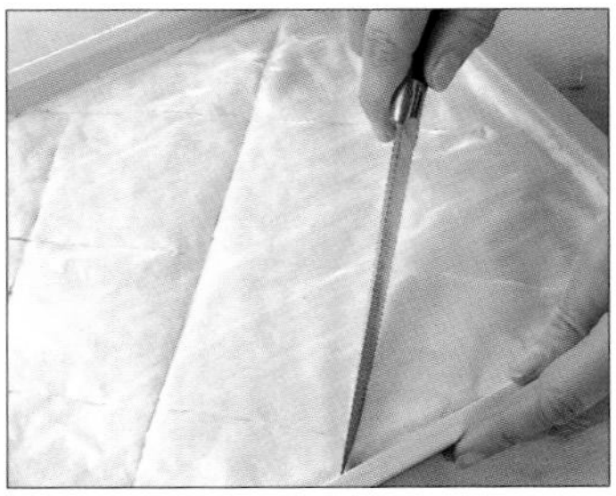

**6** Score the top of the pie into a diamond pattern, using a sharp knife. Bake in the oven at 180°C (350°F) Mark 4 for 40-45 minutes until golden brown. Leave to stand for 5 minutes, then cut into portions and serve with a salad.

**NOTE** Filo pastry sheets vary in size. If the sheets are large, you will only need six as they can be cut in half. In any case, you may need to trim the pastry to fit the dimensions of the tin.

# CRUSTY VEGETABLE PARCELS

**SERVES 8**
PREPARATION
30 minutes
COOKING TIME
1¼ hours
FREEZING
Suitable: Stage 6
CALS/SERVING
480
COLOUR INDEX
Page 55

450 g (1 lb) ready-made puff pastry
FILLING
700 g (1½ lb) mixed vegetables, such as carrots, leeks, courgettes, red or yellow peppers, aubergines, sweet potatoes
30 ml (2 tbsp) olive oil
salt and pepper
225 g (8 oz) onions
2 garlic cloves, peeled and crushed
400 g (14 oz) can chopped tomatoes
15 ml (1 tbsp) sun-dried tomato paste
125 g (4 oz) gruyère cheese, grated
200 g (7 oz) mascarpone cheese
50 ml (2 fl oz) single cream
30 ml (2 tbsp) finely chopped fresh chives
50 g (2 oz) pine nuts, toasted
TO FINISH
1 egg, beaten
chopped chives, to garnish

**1** Prepare the vegetables (except the onions) as necessary and cut into 2.5 cm (1 inch) chunks. Place in a small roasting tin and drizzle with 15 ml (1 tbsp) olive oil. Season generously with salt and pepper. Bake in the oven at 200°C (400°F) Mark 6 for 40-45 minutes or until just tender, stirring occasionally. Remove from the oven and leave to cool.
**2** Peel and roughly chop the onions. Heat the remaining olive oil in a frying pan. Add the onions and garlic and fry for 5 minutes or until lightly coloured. Add the tomatoes and tomato paste and simmer, uncovered, for 15-20 minutes until thick and pulpy. Set aside.
**3** Mix 75 g (3 oz) of the gruyère with the mascarpone, cream and chives.
**4** Add the roasted vegetables to the tomato sauce with 25 g (1 oz) pine nuts. Stir to mix and check the seasoning.
**5** Roll out the pastry quite thinly to two oblongs, each measuring about 35 x 30 cm (14 x 12 inches). Place on a baking sheet. Spoon half of the vegetable filling along the centre of each oblong, in a 10 cm (4 inches) wide band. Top with the cheese mixture. Brush the pastry around the filling with beaten egg.
**6** Using a sharp knife, make diagonal cuts about 2.5 cm (1 inch) apart, down each side of the pastry to within 2.5 cm (1 inch) of the filling. Plait the strips by overlapping them alternately from either side across the filling; tuck any loose pastry under the base.
**7** Brush liberally with beaten egg to glaze and sprinkle with the remaining grated cheese, pine nuts and seasoning. Bake in the oven at 220°C (425°F) Mark 7 for 25 minutes or until golden brown, covering loosely with foil if the pastry appears to be browning too quickly.
**8** Serve cut into slices, sprinkled with chopped chives.

**NOTE** As you plait the pastry strips over the filling; make sure that they cross over or the parcel might burst open during cooking.

# MEDITERRANEAN CHEESE PUFFS

**MAKES 8**
PREPARATION
25 minutes
COOKING TIME
15 minutes
FREEZING
Not suitable
CALS/SERVING
345

450 g (1 lb) ready-made puff pastry
FILLING
150 g (5 oz) halloumi cheese
200 g (7 oz) ricotta cheese
25 g (1 oz) pine nuts, toasted
30 ml (2 tbsp) extra-virgin olive oil
12 black olives, pitted
30 ml (2 tbsp) chopped fresh coriander, basil or thyme
2.5 ml (½ tsp) black mustard seeds
pepper
TO FINISH
beaten egg, to glaze
extra black mustard seeds, for sprinkling

**1** To make the filling, cut the halloumi into small cubes and place in a bowl with the ricotta, pine nuts, oil, olives, herbs and mustard seeds. Toss to mix and season with pepper to taste.
**2** Roll out half of the pastry on a lightly floured surface to a 25 cm (10 inch) square, then cut into four 12 cm (5 inch) squares. Repeat with the rest of the pastry to make 8 squares.
**3** Brush the edges of the squares with beaten egg. Spoon the filling onto one side of the squares. Fold the pastry over the filling to enclose and press the edges together to seal; flute the edges. Transfer the pastries to a lightly greased large baking sheet.
**4** Lightly brush the pastries with beaten egg, then score the top of each one with a sharp knife. Scatter with extra mustard seeds. Bake in the oven at 220°C (425°F) Mark 7 for about 15 minutes until well risen and golden. Serve warm, with a selection of roasted vegetables, such as tomatoes, peppers and aubergine.

# PEPPER, PARMESAN AND ALMOND FILOS

**SERVES 6**
PREPARATION
30 minutes, plus cooling
COOKING TIME
25 minutes
FREEZING
Suitable: Stage 6
CALS/SERVING
400

270 g (9½ oz) packet filo pastry

FILLING
350 g (12 oz) onions
2 red peppers
1 yellow pepper
50 g (2 oz) sun-dried tomatoes in oil, drained
60 ml (4 tbsp) extra-virgin olive oil
4 garlic cloves, peeled and crushed
50 g (2 oz) chopped mixed nuts
400 g (14 oz) can chopped tomatoes
large handful of basil leaves
large pinch of sugar
salt and pepper

TO ASSEMBLE
30 ml (2 tbsp) olive oil
40 g (1½ oz) Parmesan cheese, grated

TO GARNISH
salad leaves

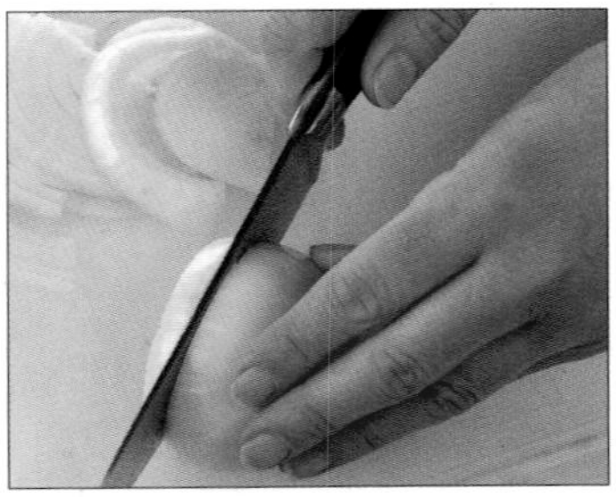

**1** To make the filling, peel and slice the onions. Halve, core, deseed and slice the peppers. Roughly chop the sun-dried tomatoes.

**2** Heat the oil in a large pan. Add the onions, garlic and nuts and fry for 3 minutes. Add the peppers and fry for 2 minutes. Stir in the sun-dried and canned tomatoes. Bring to the boil and cook for 10 minutes until pulpy. Stir in the basil, sugar and seasoning to taste; let cool.

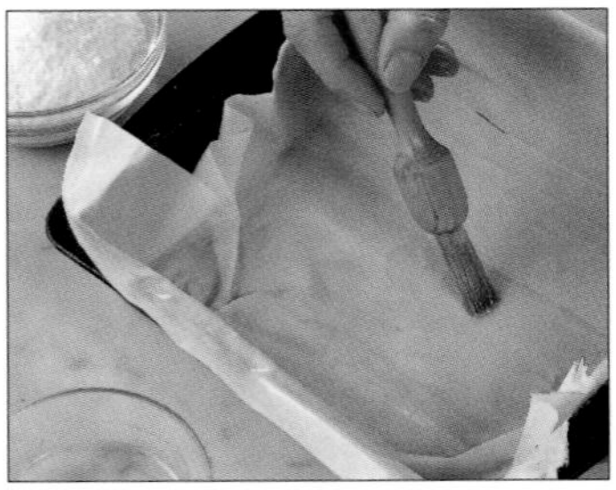

**3** Lay one filo pastry sheet in a 23 cm (9 inch) square baking tin, which is about 3 cm (1¼ inches) deep, allowing the excess pastry to overhang the edges. Brush with a little oil and sprinkle with a little Parmesan.

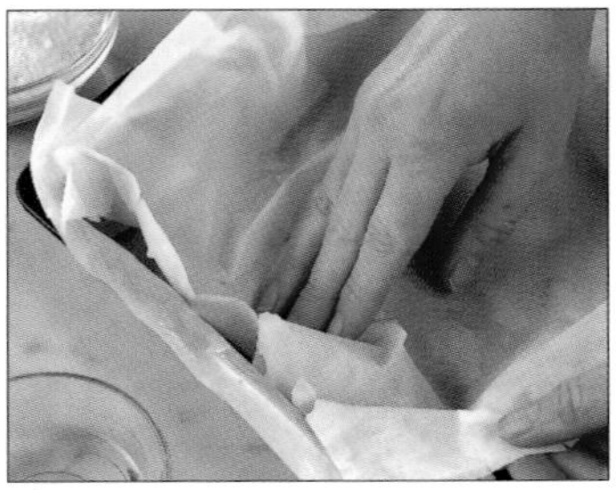

**4** Lay another sheet of pastry on top, crumpling it up slightly over the base and letting the excess fall over the sides. Brush with more oil and sprinkle with Parmesan.

**5** Repeat the layers until you have used half of the filo pastry sheets. Spread the filling in the tin, then fold the overhanging pastry over the top.

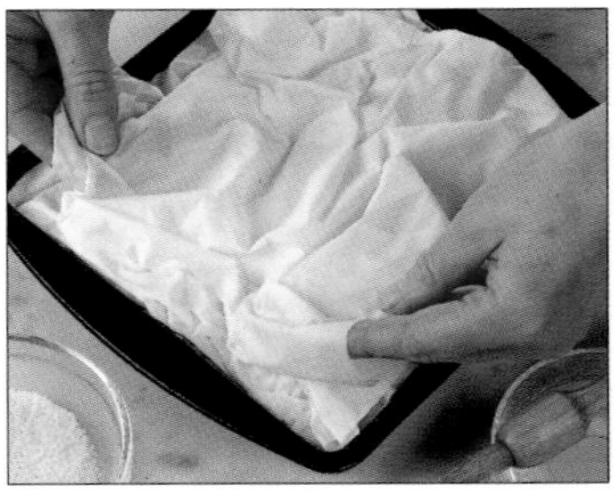

**6** Crumple the remaining filo sheets and layer on top of the filling, brushing with more oil and sprinkling with Parmesan. Sprinkle the top sheets with the remaining Parmesan.

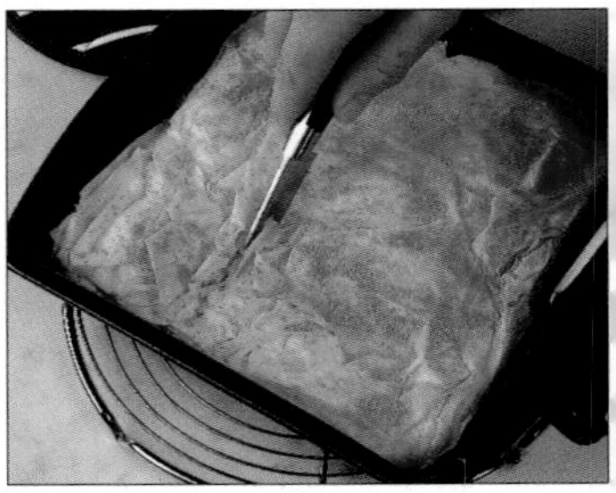

**7** Bake in the oven at 190°C (375°F) Mark 5 for 25 minutes until the pastry is deep golden and crisp. Cut into squares and serve with a crisp green salad.

## PIZZA BASE DOUGH

This basic pizza dough can be rolled out to any shape but, as a rough guide, it will make one 30 cm (12 inch) round pizza or two thin 20 cm (8 inch) pizzas.

PREPARATION
5 minutes, plus rising

225 g (8 oz) strong plain flour
2.5 ml (½ tsp) sea salt
2.5 ml (½ tsp) fast-action dried yeast
120 ml (4 fl oz) warm water
15 ml (1 tbsp) extra-virgin olive oil

**1** Sift the flour and salt into a bowl and stir in the yeast. Make a well in the centre and gradually work in the water and oil to form a soft dough.

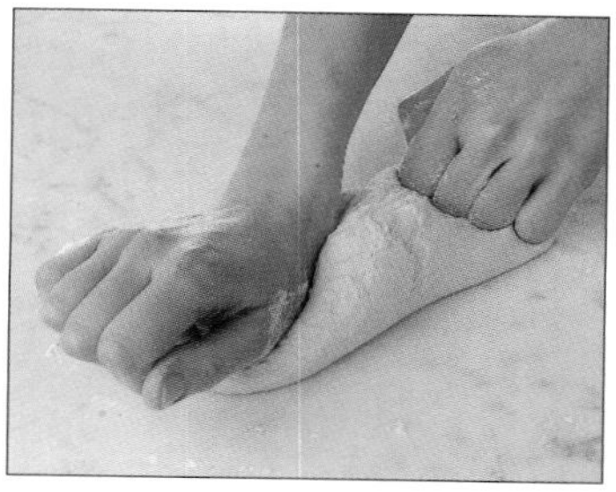

**2** Knead the dough on a lightly floured surface for 8-10 minutes (or using a large food mixer with a dough hook) until smooth and elastic.

**3** Place in an oiled bowl, turn the dough once to coat the surface with oil and cover the bowl with cling film. Leave to rise in a warm place for up to 45 minutes until doubled in size. Once risen, turn out and knock back the dough.

**NOTE** If you haven't time to make your own pizza dough buy ready-made pizza base mix. A 155 g (5¼ oz) packet is equivalent to this quantity.

### ROLLING OUT PIZZA DOUGH

Roll out or stretch the dough with your fingers to a large round. Using your fingertips and thumbs, form a shallow rim around the edge of the pizza base if required.

## ARTICHOKE AND DOLCELATTE PIZZA

**SERVES 2-4**
PREPARATION
15 minutes
COOKING TIME
15-20 minutes
FREEZING
Not suitable
CALS/SERVING
995-495

1 quantity Pizza Base Dough (see left) or 155 g (5¼ oz) packet pizza-base mix
TOPPING
400 g (14 oz) can artichoke hearts
45 ml (3 tbsp) sun-dried tomato pesto (see page 292), or sun-dried tomato paste
175 g (6 oz) dolcelatte cheese, diced
25 g (1 oz) pitted black olives
10 ml (2 tsp) dried oregano
25 g (1 oz) Parmesan cheese, freshly grated
pepper
extra-virgin olive oil, for drizzling

**1** Make up the pizza base dough and preheat a baking sheet on the top shelf of the oven.
**2** Drain and rinse the artichokes, then halve and pat dry.
**3** Roll out the dough on a lightly floured surface to a 30 cm (12 inch) round and transfer to a lightly greased baking sheet. Using fingertips and thumbs, form a shallow rim around the edge of the dough. Prick with a fork.
**4** Spread the tomato pesto over the pizza base to within 1 cm (½ inch) of the edge and scatter over the artichokes, dolcelatte, olives, oregano, Parmesan and pepper.
**5** Slide the pizza onto the preheated baking sheet in the oven and bake at 220°C (425°F) Mark 7 for 15-20 minutes until the base is crisp and the topping is golden. Drizzle with olive oil and serve with a tomato salad.

## TOMATO AND GARLIC PIZZA

**SERVES 2**
PREPARATION
15 minutes
COOKING TIME
20 minutes
FREEZING
Not suitable
CALS/SERVING
485

1 quantity Pizza Base Dough (see page 207), or 155 g (5¼ oz) packet pizza base mix
15 ml (1 tbsp) chopped fresh rosemary
TOPPING
1 garlic bulb
olive oil, for basting
4 flavourful tomatoes, about 400 g (14 oz)
salt and pepper
75 g (3 oz) feta cheese
handful of black olives
handful of fresh basil leaves

**1** Make up the pizza dough and knead in the rosemary.
**2** Divide the garlic into cloves, discarding the outer, papery layers, but leaving the inner skins intact. Toss in a little oil.
**3** Meanwhile, roughly chop the tomatoes and place in a bowl with 5 ml (1 tsp) salt. Mix well.
**4** Preheat a lightly oiled baking sheet on the top shelf of the oven. Roll out the dough thinly to a 30 cm (12 inch) round on a lightly floured surface. Prick with a fork. Transfer to a lightly greased and floured baking sheet.
**5** Spoon the tomatoes over the pizza base to within 1 cm (½ inch) of the edge and crumble the feta cheese on top. Scatter the olives, garlic cloves and basil over the top. Season with pepper only.
**6** Slide the pizza onto the preheated sheet in the oven and bake at 220°C (425°F) Mark 7 for 20 minutes or until the base is crisp and the topping is golden. Serve immediately, mashing down the garlic cloves as you eat.

**NOTE** On baking the garlic loses its pungency and becomes deliciously soft with a mild nutty flavour.

**VARIATION** Replace the garlic, olives and feta cheese with a 340 g (12 oz) jar of pimientos, drained; 20 ml (4 tsp) capers; and 75 g (3 oz) smoked cheese.

## FOUR-CHEESE PIZZA

**SERVES 4**
PREPARATION
30 minutes, plus cooling
COOKING TIME
40-50 minutes
FREEZING
Not suitable
CALS/SERVING
450
COLOUR INDEX
Page 56

1 quantity Pizza Base Dough (see page 207), or 155 g (5¼ oz) packet pizza base mix
TOPPING
400 g (14 oz) can chopped tomatoes
5 ml (1 tsp) dried oregano
15 ml (1 tbsp) sun-dried tomato paste
pepper
125 g (4 oz) mozzarella cheese, thinly sliced
50 g (2 oz) dolcelatte cheese, chopped
125 g (4 oz) ricotta cheese, crumbled
30 ml (2 tbsp) freshly grated Parmesan cheese
few olives
TO GARNISH
basil leaves

**1** To make the topping, put the tomatoes, oregano and tomato paste in a saucepan, seasoning with pepper. Bring to the boil, reduce the heat and simmer, uncovered, for 15-20 minutes or until thick and pulpy. Remove from the heat and leave to cool.
**2** Make up the pizza base dough and preheat a baking sheet on the top shelf of the oven.
**3** Roll out the pizza dough to a 30 cm (12 inch) round and place on a lightly greased baking sheet. Fold up the edges of the dough slightly to form a rim. Prick lightly with a fork.
**4** Spread the sauce over the dough to within 1 cm (½ inch) of the edge. Scatter the mozzarella, dolcelatte and ricotta cheeses evenly over the sauce. Top with the Parmesan and olives.
**5** Slide the pizza onto the preheated sheet in the oven and bake at 200°C (400°F) Mark 6 for 25-30 minutes or until the base is crisp and the cheese is melted and golden. Serve piping hot, garnished with basil.

**VARIATIONS**
❑ Omit the dolcelatte cheese. Grill 2 large red peppers until blackened. Skin, deseed and slice the peppers. Scatter over the pizza before baking.
❑ Sauté 125 g (4 oz) sliced mushrooms in olive oil with a little crushed garlic. Scatter over the pizza before baking.

# ROASTED ONION AND OLIVE CALZONE

**SERVES 4**
PREPARATION
40 minutes
COOKING TIME
35-40 minutes
FREEZING
Suitable
CALS/SERVING
475

1 quantity Pizza Base Dough (see page 207)
FILLING
4 red onions
1 garlic clove, peeled and crushed
5 ml (1 tsp) chopped fresh rosemary
5 ml (1 tsp) grated lemon zest
60 ml (4 tbsp) olive oil
125 g (4 oz) fontina or mozzarella cheese
125 g (4 oz) ricotta cheese
30 ml (2 tbsp) olive paste
salt and pepper
TO GARNISH
salad leaves

**1** Make up the pizza base dough and set aside to rise. Meanwhile, make the filling. Peel the onions and cut into wedges.

**2** Place the onions in a roasting tin with the garlic, rosemary and lemon zest. Add the oil and toss until well coated. Roast at 230°C (450°F) Mark 8 for 30 minutes, stirring occasionally until softened and browned. Turn into a bowl; let cool.

**3** Dice the fontina or mozzarella cheese. Add to the cooled onion mixture with the ricotta, olive paste and seasoning to taste. Place a baking sheet on the top shelf of the oven to preheat.

**4** Knock back the risen dough and divide into 4 equal pieces. Keeping the other 3 pieces covered with cling film, roll out one piece on a well-floured surface to a 20 cm (8 inch) round. Transfer to a well-floured board.

**5** Spoon a quarter of the onion mixture onto one half of the dough and dampen the edges with a little water.

**6** Fold over the other half of the dough and press the edges together well to seal. Repeat to make 4 calzone in total.

**7** Transfer the calzone to the hot baking sheet on the top shelf of the oven and bake for 15 minutes until slightly puffed and golden. Leave to stand for 5 minutes. Serve garnished with salad leaves, accompanied by a tomato salad.

# EGGS AND CHEESE

## CLASSIC FRENCH OMELETTE

**SERVES 1**
PREPARATION
5 minutes
COOKING TIME
About 1 minute
FREEZING
Not suitable
CALS/SERVING
390
COLOUR INDEX
Page 57

2-3 eggs
salt and pepper
15 ml (1 tbsp) milk or water
25 g (1 oz) unsalted butter, for frying

**1** Whisk the eggs just enough to break them down; do not over-beat. Season with salt and pepper and add the milk or water.

**2** Heat the butter in an omelette pan or 18 cm (7 inch) non-stick frying pan over a gentle heat until it is foaming, but not brown.

**3** Add the beaten eggs. Stir gently with a fork or wooden spatula, drawing the mixture from the sides to the centre as it sets and letting the liquid egg run to the sides. When set, stop stirring and cook for a further 30 seconds or until the omelette is golden brown underneath and still creamy on top.

**4** Add any filling at this point. Tilt the pan away from you slightly and use a palette knife to fold over a third of the omelette to the centre, then fold over the opposite third. Slide the omelette on to a warmed plate, flipping it over so the folded sides are underneath. Serve at once, with a salad and warm bread.

### OMELETTE FLAVOURINGS AND FILLINGS

FINES HERBES: Add 5 ml (1 tsp) each finely chopped chervil, chives and tarragon or a large pinch of dried mixed herbs to the beaten egg mixture before cooking.

TOMATO Fry 2 skinned and chopped tomatoes in a little butter for 5 minutes or until soft and pulpy. Put in the centre of the omelette before folding.

CHEESE Sprinkle 25 g (1 oz) grated cheese over the omelette before folding.

MUSHROOM Thickly slice about 50 g (2 oz) mushrooms and cook in butter until soft. Put in the centre of the omelette before folding. (When available, use wild mushrooms.)

CURRIED VEGETABLE Roughly chop leftover vegetables, such as potato, green beans, broad beans or parsnips. Fry in oil with about 2.5 ml (½ tsp) curry powder and a little crushed garlic. Put in the centre of the omelette before folding.

GOAT'S CHEESE Soften about 25 g (1 oz) mild goat's cheese and blend with a little fromage frais. Season with salt and pepper and put in the centre of the omelette before folding.

## THAI-STYLE STUFFED OMELETTE

**SERVES 2**
PREPARATION
20 minutes
COOKING TIME
10-12 minutes
FREEZING
Not suitable
CALS/SERVING
650
COLOUR INDEX
Page 57

50 g (2 oz) aubergine
50 g (2 oz) shiitake or button mushrooms
½ small red pepper, deseeded
50 g (2 oz) French beans
2 spring onions
25 g (1 oz) shelled peas, thawed if frozen
45 ml (3 tbsp) sunflower oil
6 eggs
CORIANDER PESTO
1 shallot, peeled
1 garlic clove, peeled
½ small red chilli, deseeded
1 coriander root, scrubbed
15 g (½ oz) coriander leaves
pinch of caster sugar
10 ml (2 tsp) light soy sauce
15 ml (1 tbsp) sunflower oil
salt and pepper
TO SERVE
light soy sauce

**1** First make the coriander pesto. Roughly chop the shallot, garlic, chilli and coriander root, then grind to a paste with all the remaining ingredients, using a spice grinder or pestle and mortar. Season to taste and set aside.
**2** Prepare the vegetables. Dice the aubergine; thinly slice the mushrooms and red pepper; trim and slice the beans; trim and slice the spring onions; pat frozen peas dry.
**3** Heat 15 ml (1 tbsp) oil in a wok or frying pan, add the aubergine and fry, stirring, over a high heat for 3-4 minutes until golden. Add the remaining vegetables (except frozen peas) and stir-fry for 3-4 minutes until tender. (Add frozen peas for the last 30 seconds.) Remove from the heat and stir in the coriander pesto to taste.
**4** Beat the eggs together in a bowl and season with salt and pepper to taste. Heat the remaining 30 ml (2 tbsp) oil in a large non-stick frying pan, tip in the egg mixture and swirl to the edges of the pan. Cook the omelette until it is set and browned underneath, but still slightly runny on top.
**5** Spoon the vegetable mixture onto one half of the omelette, carefully flip the other half over and cook over a low heat for a few minutes until set and the vegetables are heated through. Serve at once, with soy sauce.

# OMELETTE CANNELLONI WITH MUSHROOM STUFFING

**SERVES 4**
PREPARATION
45 minutes
COOKING TIME
35-40 minutes
FREEZING
Not suitable
CALS/SERVING
505

MUSHROOM STUFFING
15 g (½ oz) dried ceps
100 ml (3½ fl oz) boiling water
3 shallots
350 g (12 oz) mixed fresh mushrooms, such as brown cap, oyster, shiitake and ceps, trimmed
25 g (1 oz) butter
1 garlic clove, peeled and crushed
225 g (8 oz) frozen leaf spinach, thawed
25 g (1 oz) walnuts, toasted
25 g (1 oz) fresh breadcrumbs
75 g (3 oz) ricotta cheese
salt and pepper
OMELETTES
4 large eggs
unsalted butter, for frying
SAUCE
25 g (1 oz) butter
25 g (1 oz) plain flour
5 ml (1 tsp) mustard powder
450 ml (¾ pint) milk
15 ml (1 tbsp) chopped fresh chervil
15 ml (1 tbsp) chopped fresh parsley
50 g (2 oz) Cheddar cheese, grated
TO GARNISH
parsley and/or chervil sprigs

**1** Put the dried ceps in a bowl, pour over the boiling water and leave to soak for 20 minutes. Drain, pat dry, then finely chop the ceps.
**2** Peel and finely chop the shallots. Finely chop the fresh mushrooms. Melt the butter in a frying pan, add shallots and garlic and sauté for 5 minutes. Increase the heat, add all of the mushrooms and fry for 5 minutes until starting to release their juices. Squeeze the spinach dry and add to the pan. Continue to cook until all the juices are evaporated.
**3** Transfer the mushroom mixture to a bowl and leave to cool slightly. Finely chop the walnuts and stir into the mushroom mixture with the breadcrumbs, ricotta and seasoning to taste.
**4** Next make the omelettes. Beat the eggs together in a bowl and season with plenty of salt and pepper. Melt a little unsalted butter in a non-stick frying pan. Swirl in a quarter of the beaten egg and cook gently until set; remove from the pan and set aside. Repeat to make 4 omelettes in total.
**5** To make the sauce, melt the butter in a saucepan, add the flour and mustard and cook for 30 seconds. Remove from the heat and gradually stir in the milk, then bring to the boil, stirring constantly, until thickened and smooth. Simmer for 2 minutes, then take off the heat and stir in the herbs and cheese. Season with salt and pepper to taste.
**6** Divide the mushroom mixture between the omelettes and roll each one up like a Swiss roll to enclose the filling.
**7** Place in an oiled shallow rectangular dish, measuring about 25 x 20 cm (10 x 8 inches) and pour over the cheese sauce. Bake in the oven at 190°C (375°F) Mark 5 for 20-25 minutes until bubbling and golden.
**8** Carefully transfer to warmed serving plates and garnish with herb sprigs to serve.

# EGG AND ROASTED PEPPER STEW

**SERVES 2-3**
PREPARATION
10 minutes
COOKING TIME
55 minutes
FREEZING
Not suitable
CALS/SERVING
540-360
COLOUR INDEX
Page 57

3 red peppers
4 tomatoes (preferably large plum)
225 g (8 oz) onions (preferably red)
1 red chilli
6 garlic cloves (unpeeled)
5 ml (1 tsp) sugar
few fresh thyme sprigs (optional)
salt and pepper
60 ml (4 tbsp) olive oil
30 ml (2 tbsp) sun-dried tomato paste
6 small eggs
chopped parsley, to garnish

**1** Halve and deseed the red peppers and tomatoes. Roughly chop the peppers and 2 tomato halves; place in a small roasting tin. Peel and roughly slice the onions and add to the tin, with the whole chilli and garlic cloves. Sprinkle with the sugar and thyme sprigs if using. Season well.
**2** Drizzle with the oil and roast in the oven at 230°C (450°F) Mark 8 for 25 minutes, stirring occasionally.
**3** Stir in the tomato paste. Sit the reserved tomato halves on top and bake for a further 20 minutes or until the peppers are charred.
**4** Reduce the oven setting to 180°C (350°F) Mark 4. Crack an egg into each tomato half and season well. Spoon the pan juices over the eggs and bake for 7 minutes or until the eggs are just set. Garnish with parsley and serve at once, with crusty bread, as a light lunch or supper.

## BROCCOLI, OLIVE AND GOAT'S CHEESE FRITTATA

**SERVES 4**
PREPARATION
10 minutes
COOKING TIME
20 minutes
FREEZING
Not suitable
CALS/SERVING
335

8 eggs
30 ml (2 tbsp) chopped fresh parsley
15 ml (1 tbsp) chopped fresh tarragon
salt and pepper (see note)
1 small green or red chilli
350 g (12 oz) broccoli
30 ml (2 tbsp) extra-virgin olive oil
1 garlic clove, peeled and crushed
150 g (5 oz) soft rindless goat's cheese
25 g (1 oz) pitted black olives

**1** Beat the eggs, herbs, salt and pepper together in a small bowl and set aside. Deseed and finely chop the chilli. Peel and thinly slice the broccoli stalk; cut the florets into small pieces.

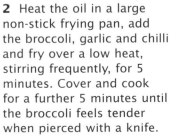

**2** Heat the oil in a large non-stick frying pan, add the broccoli, garlic and chilli and fry over a low heat, stirring frequently, for 5 minutes. Cover and cook for a further 5 minutes until the broccoli feels tender when pierced with a knife.

**3** Crumble over the goat's cheese and stir in the olives, then pour in the beaten egg mixture, making sure it reaches the edge of the pan.

**4** Cook the frittata over a medium heat for 6-8 minutes, then carefully slide out onto a plate.

**5** Flip the frittata back into the pan and cook the other side for 2-4 minutes. Slide onto a warmed plate and cut into wedges. Serve hot or warm, with a tossed mixed salad and plenty of crusty bread.

**NOTES**

❑ Use Herb Salt (see page 295) if possible.

❑ If you don't want to try flipping the frittata, after 6 minutes' cooking, transfer to a preheated grill and cook for about 2-3 minutes until the top is set.

## ASPARAGUS, BROAD BEAN AND PARMESAN FRITTATA

**SERVES 2-4**
PREPARATION
35 minutes
COOKING TIME
15-20 minutes
FREEZING
Not suitable
CALS/SERVING
720-360
COLOUR INDEX
Page 57

175 g (6 oz) small new potatoes
225 g (8 oz) asparagus spears
225 g (8 oz) frozen broad beans, thawed
6 eggs
salt and pepper
50 g (2 oz) Parmesan cheese, freshly grated
45 ml (3 tbsp) chopped mixed fresh herbs, such as parsley, oregano and thyme
50 g (2 oz) unsalted butter

**1** Cook the potatoes in boiling salted water for 15-20 minutes until tender. Allow to cool, then slice thickly.
**2** Meanwhile, trim the asparagus, removing any woody parts of the stems. Place in a steamer over boiling water and cook for 12 minutes until tender. Immediately plunge into cold water to set the colour and cool completely.
**3** Slip the broad beans out of their waxy skins. Drain the asparagus, pat dry, then cut into short lengths. Mix with the broad beans.
**4** Put the eggs in a bowl with a good pinch of salt, plenty

of pepper and half of the Parmesan cheese. Beat well, then stir in the asparagus, broad beans and chopped herbs.
**5** Melt 40 g (1½ oz) butter in a 25 cm (10 inch) heavy-based non-stick frying pan (see note, below right). When foaming, pour in the egg mixture. Turn down the heat to as low as possible. Cook for about 15 minutes, until the frittata is set but the top is still a little runny.
**6** Scatter the cooked sliced potato over the frittata and sprinkle with the remaining Parmesan cheese. Dot with the rest of the butter.
**7** Place under a hot grill until the cheese is golden and bubbling and the top is just set. Slide the frittata onto a warmed plate and cut into wedges to serve.

## SPANISH TORTILLA

**SERVES 6-8**
PREPARATION
15 minutes, plus standing
COOKING TIME
35-40 minutes
FREEZING
Not suitable
CALS/SERVING
300-225
COLOUR INDEX
Page 58

800 g (1¾ lb) potatoes
1 onion
90 ml (6 tbsp) olive oil
2 garlic cloves, peeled and crushed
10 ml (2 tsp) turmeric
30 ml (2 tbsp) water
6 eggs, lightly beaten
salt and pepper

**1** Peel the potatoes and cut into small chunks. Peel and chop the onion.
**2** Heat all but 15 ml (1 tbsp) of the oil in a non-stick frying pan, add the potatoes, onion, garlic and turmeric and fry over a gentle heat for 10 minutes, stirring occasionally to prevent sticking. Add the water and cook gently for a further 10 minutes until very soft.
**3** Turn the potato mixture into a bowl, let cool slightly, then stir in the eggs and season generously with salt and pepper. Leave to stand for 20 minutes.
**4** Heat the remaining 15 ml (1 tbsp) oil in the cleaned frying pan, tip in the omelette mixture and cook over a very low heat for 10-15 minutes until golden underneath and almost set through.
**5** Carefully slide the omelette out onto a large plate, hold the frying pan over the top, then flip the omelette back into the pan and cook the other side for 5 minutes or so until browned. Remove from the pan and leave to cool.
**6** Serve still slightly warm or cold cut into wedges.

## SWEET POTATO AND LEEK TORTILLA

**SERVES 4**
PREPARATION
10 minutes
COOKING TIME
About 20 minutes
FREEZING
Not suitable
CALS/SERVING
525

450 g (1 lb) sweet potato
salt and pepper
3 leeks, trimmed
60 ml (4 tbsp) olive oil
4 eggs
125 ml (4 fl oz) single cream or milk
125 g (4 oz) gruyère or mature Cheddar cheese, grated
30 ml (2 tbsp) chopped fresh parsley

**1** Peel the sweet potato and cut into 2.5 cm (1 inch) chunks. Cook in boiling salted water for 5-8 minutes, until just tender. Drain thoroughly.
**2** Thinly slice the leeks. Heat the oil in a large frying pan, add the leeks and cook until softened. Add the sweet potato and cook, stirring occasionally, until the potato is just beginning to colour.
**3** Meanwhile, beat the eggs and cream together in a bowl. Season with salt and pepper, then pour into the frying pan. Add the grated cheese, and stir a little until the cheese is evenly distributed. Cook gently until the tortilla is set on the bottom.
**4** Place the frying pan under the grill and cook until the tortilla is puffed up and golden. Serve straight from the pan, sprinkled with the parsley.

**NOTE** Make sure you use a frying pan which is suitable for placing under the grill.

**VARIATION** Use carrots instead of sweet potato.

# CRUNCHY CHICK PEA EGGS WITH AIOLI

**SERVES 6**
PREPARATION
30 minutes, plus chilling
COOKING TIME
15 minutes
FREEZING
Not suitable
CALS/SERVING
415
COLOUR INDEX
Page 58

1-2 red chillies
2 tomatoes (preferably plum)
4 spring onions
125 g (4 oz) pitted black olives
two 420 g (15 oz) cans chick peas, drained
2 garlic cloves, peeled and crushed
60 ml (4 tbsp) chopped fresh parsley
salt and pepper
6 hard-boiled eggs, shelled
1 egg, beaten
75 g (3 oz) fresh white breadcrumbs
oil, for deep-frying
AIOLI
300 ml (½ pint) bought mayonnaise
4 garlic cloves, peeled and crushed
30 ml (2 tbsp) lemon juice

**1** Deseed and finely chop the chillies and tomatoes. Roughly chop the spring onions and black olives.
**2** Place the chick peas in a food processor with the garlic and process for 1 minute or until roughly chopped. Turn into a bowl and add the chillies, spring onions, tomatoes, olives and parsley. Season well and mix thoroughly.
**3** Divide the mixture into 6 equal portions. Shape each into a flat cake and mould around a hard-boiled egg, as evenly as possible. Brush with beaten egg and roll in the breadcrumbs to coat thoroughly. Chill in the refrigerator, uncovered for 3-4 hours, or overnight.
**4** To prepare the aioli, in a bowl mix the mayonnaise with the garlic and lemon juice. Season generously with salt and pepper.
**5** Heat the oil in a deep-fat fryer or large deep, heavy saucepan to 160°C (325°F), or until a cube of bread dropped in begins to sizzle. Gently lower each egg into the oil and deep-fry for 7-8 minutes or until golden brown. Remove and drain on kitchen paper.
**6** Serve the chick pea eggs hot, accompanied by the aioli.

**NOTES**
❑ Buy a good quality, thick mayonnaise for the aioli.
❑ Make sure the shelled eggs are dry, to ensure the coating will adhere.

# SAVOURY PANCAKES

**MAKES 8**
PREPARATION
10 minutes, plus standing
COOKING TIME
15-20 minutes
FREEZING
Suitable
CALS/PANCAKE
105

125 g (4 oz) plain white flour
pinch of salt
1 egg
about 300 ml (½ pint) milk
15 ml (1 tbsp) oil
a little oil, for frying

**1** Sift the flour and salt into a bowl and make a well in the centre. Break the egg into the well and add a little of the milk. Mix the liquid ingredients together, then gradually beat in the flour until smooth.

**2** Beat in the oil and the remaining milk; the batter should be the consistency of thin cream. (Or mix in a blender.) Cover the batter and leave to stand in the refrigerator for about 20 minutes.

**3** Heat a pancake pan, then brush with the minimum of oil. Add a little extra milk to the batter if it is thick. Pour a small amount of batter into the pan and swirl around until it is evenly and thinly spread over the bottom of the pan.

**4** Cook over a moderate to high heat for about 1 minute or until the edges are curling away from the pan and the underside is golden. Flip the pancake over using a palette knife and cook the second side for 30 seconds - 1 minute, until browned.

**5** Turn the pancake out on to a sheet of greaseproof paper (or non-stick baking parchment). Loosely fold a clean tea-towel over the top; keep warm. Repeat until all the batter is used, lightly oiling the pan in between; stack the cooked pancakes.

**NOTE** Freeze pancakes interleaved with non-stick baking parchment. Defrost at room temperature, then reheat wrapped in foil at 190°C (375°F) mark 5 for 15 minutes.

**VARIATIONS**

WHOLEWHEAT PANCAKES Use a mixture of half white, half wholemeal flour.

BUCKWHEAT PANCAKES Use a mixture of half white, half buckwheat flour. Don't sift the buckwheat flour.

SPICED CHICK PEA PANCAKES Use chick pea (gram) flour. Toast 10 ml (2 tsp) cumin seeds under the grill, then grind to a powder. Add to the flour with 1.25 ml (¼ tsp) turmeric. Replace 150 ml (¼ pint) of the milk with water. Make slightly thicker pancakes. Use more oil if necessary.

**FILLINGS**

Almost any mixture of cooked vegetables, herbs and nuts – moistened with a little white sauce, soured cream or cream cheese – can be used.Try the following combinations:

❑ Sautéed spinach with pine nuts and feta cheese.
❑ Spiced cooked aubergine, peppers and tomatoes flavoured with chopped fresh coriander.
❑ Steamed broccoli in a cheese sauce.

MUSHROOM AND SPINACH PANCAKE LAYER Soak 25 g (1 oz) dried mushrooms in 300 ml (½ pint) stock. Sauté 450 g (1 lb) chopped brown cap mushrooms with 6-8 chopped spring onions until softened. Add soaked mushrooms and stock; simmer for 15-20 minutes until syrupy; season. Purée half the mixture; mix with remaining mushrooms. Stir 450 g (1 lb) cooked, well drained, chopped spinach with 225 g (8 oz) soft cheese; season. Spoon half this mixture into an oiled 1.1 litre (2 pint) shallow ovenproof dish. Layer 6-8 pancakes on top with the mushrooms and remaining spinach, finishing with a mushroom layer. Cook at 200°C (400°F) Mark 6 for 30 minutes. (Illustrated above, left)

# OVEN-BAKED MUSHROOM PANCAKE

**SERVES 6-8**
PREPARATION
15 minutes
COOKING TIME
40-45 minutes
FREEZING
Not suitable
CALS/SERVING
270-210

450 g (1 lb) mixed mushrooms, such as chestnut, oyster, shiitake and ceps, trimmed
30 ml (2 tbsp) olive oil
1 onion
2 garlic cloves, peeled and crushed
5 ml (1 tsp) chopped fresh thyme
5 ml (1 tsp) grated lemon zest
25 g (1 oz) unsalted butter

PANCAKE BATTER
125 g (4 oz) plain white flour
2.5 ml (½ tsp) salt
4 eggs, lightly beaten
450 ml (¾ pint) milk
60 ml (4 tbsp) chopped fresh herbs, such as chervil, chives and parsley
pepper
TO SERVE
Tomato Sauce (see page 291)

**1** Quarter the mushrooms. Heat the oil in a large frying pan. Add the onion and fry gently for 3-4 minutes until beginning to soften. Add the garlic, thyme and lemon zest and fry gently for 30 seconds.
**2** Increase the heat, add the mushrooms and stir-fry for 5-10 minutes until golden, then simmer to evaporate all the juices.
**3** To make the pancake batter, sift the flour and salt into a bowl and gradually beat in the eggs, milk, herbs and pepper until the batter is smooth.
**4** Put the unsalted butter into a 20 x 25 cm (8 x 10 inch) baking tin and place in the oven at 200°C (400°F) Mark 6 until it is foaming. Immediately add the mushrooms, then pour over the batter. Bake for about 25 minutes until puffed up, golden and firm in the centre. Serve at once, with the tomato sauce.

## BRUSCHETTA OF FIELD MUSHROOMS WITH POACHED EGGS

**SERVES 4**
PREPARATION
10 minutes
COOKING TIME
10 minutes
FREEZING
Not suitable
CALS/SERVING
300

450 g (1 lb) field mushrooms, wiped
4 thick slices country bread, such as pugliese or pain de campagne
2 garlic cloves, peeled
50 g (2 oz) butter
10 ml (2 tsp) chopped fresh thyme
4 eggs
salt and pepper
TO GARNISH
rocket or other salad leaves

**1** Thinly slice the mushrooms and set aside. Grill the bread on both sides until golden, then immediately rub all over with the garlic; keep warm in a low oven.
**2** Melt the butter in a large frying pan and stir-fry the mushrooms with the thyme over a high heat for 4-5 minutes until golden and starting to release their juices. Cover and keep warm.
**3** Poach the eggs either in an egg poacher or in a pan of gently simmering water – allowing 3 minutes for a soft yolk and up to 5 minutes for a firm yolk.
**4** Place a slice of garlic bread on each warmed serving plate. Spoon on the mushrooms and pan juices, then top each serving with a poached egg. Serve at once, garnished with rocket or other salad leaves.

## CURRIED EGGS ON TOAST

**SERVES 2**
PREPARATION
15 minutes
COOKING TIME
10 minutes
FREEZING
Not suitable
CALS/SERVING
575

1 small red onion
2.5 cm (1 inch) piece fresh root ginger
25 g (1 oz) butter
pinch of chilli powder
15 ml (1 tbsp) medium curry paste
6 large eggs
15 ml (1 tbsp) chopped fresh coriander
5 ml (1 tsp) lemon juice
salt and pepper
TO SERVE
1 naan bread, halved, or 2 pittas
soured cream or yogurt (optional)
coriander leaves, to garnish

**1** Peel and thinly slice the onion; peel and grate the ginger. Melt the butter in a non-stick frying pan, add the onion, ginger, chilli powder and curry paste and fry over a low heat for 5 minutes until softened.
**2** Meanwhile lightly beat the eggs in a bowl with the coriander, lemon juice and salt and pepper.
**3** Toast the naan bread or pittas under the grill and keep warm.
**4** Pour the eggs into the frying pan and stir over a low heat for 2-3 minutes until scrambled; take care to avoid overcooking the eggs or they will be tough.
**5** Spoon the curried eggs on top of the grilled bread and serve at once, topped with a spoonful of soured cream or yogurt if wished, and garnished with coriander.

**NOTE** Use a non-stick pan as scrambled egg pans are notoriously difficult to clean!

## MACARONI CHEESE

**SERVES 4**
PREPARATION
10 minutes
COOKING TIME
15 minutes
FREEZING
Not suitable
CALS/SERVING
755
COLOUR INDEX
Page 59

225 g (8 oz) short-cut macaroni or small pasta shapes
salt and pepper
50 g (2 oz) butter or margarine
50 g (2 oz) plain flour
900 ml (1½ pints) milk
pinch of freshly grated nutmeg or 2.5 ml (½ tsp) mustard
225 g (8 oz) mature Cheddar cheese, grated
45 ml (3 tbsp) fresh wholemeal breadcrumbs

**1** Cook the macaroni in a large pan of boiling salted water until *al dente*.
**2** Meanwhile, melt the butter in a saucepan, stir in the flour and cook, stirring, for 1 minute. Remove from the heat and gradually stir in the milk. Bring to the boil and cook, stirring, until the sauce thickens. Remove from the heat. Season with salt and pepper and add the nutmeg or mustard.
**3** Drain the macaroni and add to the sauce, together with three quarters of the cheese. Mix well, then turn into an ovenproof dish.
**4** Preheat the grill to high. Sprinkle the remaining cheese and the breadcrumbs over the macaroni cheese. Place under the grill until golden brown on top and bubbling. Serve immediately.

**NOTE** To prepare ahead, make up to the end of stage 3. When required, bake in a preheated oven at 200°C (400°F) Mark 6 for 25-30 minutes.

**VARIATIONS**
CAULIFLOWER CHEESE Divide ½ cauliflower into florets and cook in boiling salted water for about 10 minutes or until just tender; drain thoroughly. Mix with the cheese sauce and macaroni at stage 3. Finish as above.

LUXURY THREE-CHEESE MACARONI Flavour the sauce with a pinch of nutmeg and 10 ml (2 tsp) Dijon mustard. Replace the Cheddar with Italian fontina cheese. At stage 3, fold all of the fontina into the sauce, together with 125 g (4 oz) diced mozzarella cheese. At stage 4, sprinkle with white (rather than wholemeal) breadcrumbs, and plenty of freshly grated Parmesan cheese.

## PASTICCIO WITH SPINACH AND FETA

**SERVES 4-6**
PREPARATION
30 minutes
COOKING TIME
30-40 minutes
FREEZING
Suitable
CALS/SERVING
760-415

225 g (8 oz) dried penne, shells or other pasta shapes
salt and pepper
1 onion
30 ml (2 tbsp) olive oil
2 garlic cloves, peeled and crushed
15 ml (1 tbsp) chopped fresh thyme
450 g (1 lb) frozen leaf spinach, thawed
1 quantity Rich Tomato Sauce (see page 291)
225 g (8 oz) feta cheese, crumbled
4 egg yolks
225 g (8 oz) fromage frais
200 g (7 oz) crème fraîche

**1** Cook the pasta in a large pan of boiling salted water until *al dente*. Drain, refresh under cold water and drain thoroughly. Place the pasta in a large bowl, toss with a little oil to prevent sticking and set aside.
**2** Meanwhile, peel and finely chop the onion. Heat the oil in a frying pan, add the onion, garlic and thyme, and fry for 10 minutes until softened. Squeeze the spinach dry, add to the pan and stir until heated through.
**3** Reheat the tomato sauce if necessary, remove from the heat and stir in half of the feta. Add to the pasta, with the spinach mixture and toss to mix. Spoon into a lightly oiled deep baking dish.
**4** Put the egg yolks, fromage frais, crème fraîche and remaining feta in a food processor and process briefly until smooth; season generously with pepper.
**5** Pour the cream mixture over the pasta mixture and bake in the oven at 190°C (375°F) Mark 5 for 30-40 minutes until golden and firm to the touch. Leave to stand for a few minutes before serving, accompanied by a crisp salad.

# SPINACH AND POTATO MASCARPONE GRATIN

**SERVES 4**
PREPARATION
20 minutes
COOKING TIME
30-35 minutes
FREEZING
Not suitable
CALS/SERVING
505

4 medium potatoes
salt and pepper
450 g (1 lb) fresh spinach, trimmed
knob of butter
250 g (9 oz) mascarpone cheese
150 ml (¼ pint) single cream
large pinch of freshly grated nutmeg
50 g (2 oz) Cheddar cheese, grated

**1** Peel the potatoes, cut into quarters and cook in a large pan of lightly salted water until just tender, about 12-15 minutes. Drain thoroughly and cut into bite-sized pieces.
**2** Meanwhile, put the spinach in a saucepan with just the water clinging to the leaves after washing and cook gently, stirring, for 1-2 minutes until just wilted. Drain thoroughly, squeezing out any excess liquid. Roughly chop the spinach and toss with a knob of butter and seasoning to taste.
**3** Toss the spinach with the potatoes and spoon into a lightly oiled gratin dish.
**4** Stir the mascarpone and cream together in a bowl and season with nutmeg, a little salt and pepper. Spoon over the potatoes and scatter the cheese over the top.
**5** Bake in the oven at 200°C (400°F) Mark 6 for 30-35 minutes until bubbling. Leave to stand for 5 minutes before serving, with a crisp green salad and some French bread.

# MARINATED BAKED GOAT'S CHEESE WITH CHILLI DRESSING

**SERVES 4**
PREPARATION
15 minutes, plus marinating
COOKING TIME
20 minutes, plus warming
FREEZING
Not suitable
CALS/SERVING
425
COLOUR INDEX
Page 60

250 g (9 oz) ricotta cheese
225 g (8 oz) creamy fresh goat's cheese
75 g (3 oz) pecorino or Parmesan cheese, freshly grated
2 egg whites
salt and pepper
30 ml (2 tbsp) extra-virgin olive oil

CHILLI DRESSING
1 green chilli
120 ml (4 fl oz) olive oil
pinch of caster sugar
5 ml (1 tsp) Dijon mustard
10 ml (2 tsp) balsamic vinegar
15 ml (1 tbsp) capers
about 12 pitted olives

**1** Put all of the cheeses into a food processor or blender with the egg whites and process until evenly blended. Season liberally with pepper, but sparingly with salt as the pecorino is salty.
**2** Base-line a shallow ovenproof dish, measuring about 23 x 18 cm (9 x 7 inches), with non-stick baking parchment. Spoon the cheese mixture into the dish and spread evenly. Drizzle over the olive oil. Bake at 200°C (400°F) Mark 6 for about 20 minutes or until just firm. Allow to cool.
**3** Meanwhile, prepare the dressing. Deseed and finely slice the chilli. Whisk the olive oil, sugar, mustard and vinegar together in a bowl. Stir in the chilli, capers and olives.
**4** Turn the cooked cheese onto a board and cut into 2.5 cm (1 inch) squares. Place in a shallow, non-metallic ovenproof dish and spoon over the dressing. Cover and leave to marinate in a cool place overnight.
**5** When ready to serve, warm through in the oven at 180°C (350°F) Mark 4 for 5-10 minutes. Serve with plenty of warm focaccia bread and a tomato salad.

**VARIATION** Omit the goat's cheese and use 450 g (1 lb) ricotta instead.

# HERBY CHEESE AND VEGETABLES WITH SPICY CARROT SALSA

**SERVES 4**
PREPARATION
40 minutes
COOKING TIME
45 minutes
FREEZING
Not suitable
CALS/SERVING
485
COLOUR INDEX
Page 59

2 globe artichokes
salt and pepper
1 small red pepper
1 small yellow pepper
2 small red onions
1 bulb fennel, trimmed
2 large courgettes
1 small aubergine
4 large flat mushrooms
4 plum tomatoes
4 large asparagus spears, trimmed
2 garlic cloves
125 g (4 oz) halloumi or feta cheese
75 ml (5 tbsp) olive oil (approximately)
30 ml (2 tbsp) lemon juice
60 ml (4 tbsp) chopped fresh basil

SPICY CARROT SALSA
450 g (1 lb) carrots
2.5 ml (½ tsp) ground cinnamon
1 garlic clove, peeled and crushed
1.25 ml (¼ tsp) ground ginger
1.25 ml (¼ tsp) cayenne pepper
90 ml (6 tbsp) olive oil
30 ml (2 tbsp) wine vinegar

TO SERVE
4 slices sun-dried tomato or onion bread, toasted

**1** Cook the artichokes in boiling salted water for 35 minutes or until a leaf can be pulled away easily. Halve each artichoke and remove the hairy 'choke' at the base.
**2** Quarter, core and deseed the peppers. Peel and quarter the red onions. Thickly slice the fennel, courgettes and aubergine. Leave the mushrooms, tomatoes and asparagus spears whole. Peel and finely chop the garlic. Slice the halloumi or feta cheese.
**3** For the dressing, mix 60 ml (4 tbsp) of the olive oil with the lemon juice, basil and seasoning; set aside.
**4** Place the vegetables in a single layer in a roasting tin. Brush with olive oil, sprinkle with the garlic and season well. Roast at 200°C (400°F) Mark 6 for about 45 minutes until tender and well browned, turn once during cooking.
**5** Meanwhile, make the salsa. Peel and roughly chop the carrots. Cook in boiling salted water for 15-20 minutes until just tender; drain. Let cool slightly, then transfer to a food processor, add the remaining ingredients and process until finely chopped. Turn into a serving dish.
**6** To serve, grill the halloumi or feta cheese slices on each side for about 1-2 minutes. Place a slice of hot toast on each serving plate and top with the vegetables and cheese. Drizzle with the basil dressing and serve at once, with the warm carrot salsa.

**NOTE** Halloumi must be served while it is still warm; once cooled it will become rubbery.

# CAPONATA WITH CHEESY POTATO CRUST

**SERVES 4-6**
PREPARATION
30 minutes
COOKING TIME
30-35 minutes
FREEZING
Suitable
CALS/SERVING
540-360

675 g (1½ lb) floury potatoes
25 g (1 oz) butter
60 ml (4 tbsp) milk
125 g (4 oz) Cheddar cheese, grated
salt and pepper
1 aubergine, trimmed
1 onion
2 celery sticks
1 garlic clove, peeled and crushed
60 ml (4 tbsp) extra-virgin olive oil
400 g (14 oz) can chopped tomatoes
30 ml (2 tbsp) chopped fresh basil
30 ml (2 tbsp) sun-dried tomato pesto (see page 292)
30 ml (2 tbsp) capers, rinsed and drained (preferably French capers)
25 g (1 oz) pitted black olives
50 g (2 oz) fresh white breadcrumbs
basil and chervil sprigs, to garnish

**1** Peel the potatoes, cut into cubes and cook in boiling salted water for 15 minutes until tender; drain well. Mash with the butter, milk, half of the cheese and seasoning. Cover the surface with damp greaseproof paper; set aside.
**2** Meanwhile, dice the aubergine; peel and thinly slice the onion; slice the celery. Heat the oil in a flameproof casserole, add the aubergine, onion, celery and garlic and stir-fry for 10 minutes until softened and golden.
**3** Add the tomatoes, basil and tomato pesto. Bring to the boil and simmer gently for 15 minutes. Add the capers to the stew with the olives and seasoning to taste.
**4** Carefully spoon the mashed potatoes on top of the stew and smooth with a palette knife. Mix the remaining cheese with the breadcrumbs and scatter over the potato. Bake at 220°C (425°F) Mark 7 for 20-25 minutes until the cheese is melted and golden. Serve garnished with herbs.

# SUMMER VEGETABLE SOUFFLÉ

**SERVES 6**
PREPARATION
50 minutes, plus standing
COOKING TIME
About 1 hour
FREEZING
Not suitable
CALS/SERVING
420
COLOUR INDEX
Page 60

- 25 g (1 oz) Parmesan cheese, finely grated
- 300 ml (½ pint) milk
- 2 bay leaves
- 4 peppercorns
- 1 red pepper
- 1 onion
- 125 g (4 oz) courgettes
- 125 g (4 oz) aubergine
- 175 g (6 oz) tomatoes
- salt and pepper
- 350 g (12 oz) trimmed spinach leaves
- 60 ml (4 tbsp) olive oil
- 5 ml (1 tsp) chopped fresh thyme
- 2 garlic cloves, peeled and crushed
- 30 ml (2 tbsp) sun-dried tomato paste
- 120 ml (4 fl oz) dry white wine
- 50 g (2 oz) butter
- 50 g (2 oz) plain white flour
- 6 eggs, separated
- 50 g (2 oz) Gruyère cheese, finely grated

**1** Tie a double greaseproof paper collar around a 1.7 litre (3 pint) soufflé dish. Brush inside of dish and collar with melted butter; sprinkle with 30 ml (2 tbsp) Parmesan. Put the milk, bay leaves and peppercorns in a pan. Slowly bring to the boil; set aside for 30 minutes.

**2** Meanwhile, halve, core, deseed and finely dice the red pepper. Peel and chop the onion; dice the courgettes and aubergine. Immerse the tomatoes in boiling water for 1 minute, then drain and refresh in cold water. Peel, deseed and finely dice the flesh.

**3** Bring a pan of salted water to the boil, add the spinach and cook for 1 minute. Drain and refresh immediately in cold water; drain well, squeezing to remove excess water, then finely chop the spinach.

**4** Heat the oil in a frying pan; stir-fry the onion, thyme and garlic for 10 minutes. Add the pepper, courgettes and aubergine; cook, stirring, over a high heat for 5 minutes. Stir in tomato paste, tomatoes and wine. Simmer for 15 minutes, until the liquid has reduced; season. Let cool.

**5** Melt the butter in a saucepan, stir in the flour and cook for 1 minute, stirring. Off the heat, gradually whisk in the strained milk. Return to the heat and bring to the boil, stirring, until thickened.

**6** Add the spinach to the sauce and mix until evenly blended; allow to cool. Add the egg yolks and all but 30 ml (2 tbsp) of the grated Parmesan and Gruyère. Season well.

**7** In a mixing bowl, whisk the egg whites with a pinch of salt until they form soft peaks. Using a large metal spoon, stir a spoonful of the whisked egg whites into the cooled spinach and cheese mixture to lighten it, then fold in the rest.

**8** Spoon the courgette and aubergine mixture into the prepared soufflé dish and cover with the spinach mixture. Sprinkle the reserved cheese on top and chill in the refrigerator for up to 2 hours until ready to cook.

**9** Run a knife around the inside edge of the dish to ensure that the soufflé rises evenly. Bake in the oven at 190°C (375°F) Mark 5 for 55 minutes - 1 hour, or until the soufflé is well risen and golden on top. Serve immediately.

**NOTE** If fresh spinach is unobtainable, use a 300 g (10 oz) packet frozen leaf spinach, thawed, and well drained.

**VARIATION** To serve as a starter, make individual soufflés. Divide the mixture between 8-10 individual soufflé dishes and bake as above for 15-20 minutes.

# CHEESE SOUFFLÉ

**SERVES 4**
PREPARATION
20 minutes, plus standing
COOKING TIME
30 minutes
FREEZING
Not suitable
CALS/SERVING
295

15 ml (1 tbsp) freshly grated Parmesan cheese
200 ml (7 fl oz) milk
few onion and carrot slices
1 bay leaf
6 black peppercorns
25 g (1 oz) butter
30 ml (2 tbsp) plain white flour
10 ml (2 tsp) Dijon mustard
salt and pepper
large pinch of cayenne pepper
4 eggs, separated, plus 1 egg white
75 g (3 oz) Gruyère or mature Cheddar cheese, finely grated

**1** Grease a 1.3 litre ($2\frac{1}{4}$ pint) soufflé dish with butter. Sprinkle the Parmesan into the dish and tilt the dish, tapping the sides gently until they are evenly coated with cheese. Put the milk in a saucepan with the onion and carrot slices, bay leaf and peppercorns. Bring slowly to the boil, remove from the heat, cover and leave to infuse for 30 minutes; strain.
**2** Melt the butter in a saucepan and stir in the flour and mustard. Season with salt, pepper and cayenne, and cook for 1 minute, stirring. Remove from the heat and gradually stir in the milk. Bring to the boil slowly and cook, stirring, until the sauce thickens. Let cool slightly, then beat in the egg yolks, one at a time. Sprinkle the cheese over the sauce, reserving 15 ml (1 tbsp) for the topping.
**3** Stir the cheese into the sauce until evenly blended. Using a hand-held or electric mixer, whisk the egg whites in a bowl until they stand in soft peaks.
**4** Mix one large spoonful of egg white into the sauce to lighten it. Gently pour the sauce over the remaining egg whites and carefully fold the ingredients together, using a metal spoon; do not over-mix.
**5** Pour the soufflé mixture gently into the prepared dish; it should come about three-quarters of the way up the side of the dish. Sprinkle with the reserved cheese and run a knife around the edge. Stand the dish on a baking sheet and bake in the oven at 180°C (350°F) Mark 4 for about 30 minutes, until golden brown, well risen and just firm to the touch. Serve immediately. There should be a hint of softness in the centre of the soufflé.

**NOTES**
❑ Use a proper straight-sided soufflé dish to obtain the best possible rise.
❑ Running a knife around the edge of the mixture before baking helps to achieve the classic 'hat' effect.
❑ If necessary, the soufflé can be prepared ahead to the end of stage 2 and left to stand for 1-2 hours before finishing.

**VARIATIONS**
BLUE CHEESE Use a semi-hard blue cheese, such as Stilton or Wensleydale, instead of Gruyère or Cheddar.

MUSHROOM Replace cheese with 125 g (4 oz) mushrooms (preferably field or wild), chopped and sautéed in butter.

# AUBERGINE AND PEPPER PARMIGIANA

**SERVES 6**
PREPARATION
15 minutes
COOKING TIME
$1\frac{1}{4}$ hours
FREEZING
Suitable: Stage 5
CALS/SERVING
360
COLOUR INDEX
Page 60

4 large red peppers
3 aubergines
1 quantity Tomato Sauce (see page 291)
225 g (8 oz) Cheddar cheese, grated
50 g (2 oz) Parmesan cheese, freshly grated
pepper

**1** Quarter, core and deseed the peppers. Place, skin-side up, on the grill rack, brush with a little oil and grill for 5-6 minutes each side until charred and tender. Place in a bowl, cover tightly and leave until cool enough to handle.
**2** Cut the aubergines lengthwise into thick slices, place on the grill rack and brush with oil. Grill for 6-8 minutes each side, then leave to cool. Peel away the skin from the cooled peppers.
**3** Spoon a little tomato sauce over the base of a large greased baking dish and cover with a layer of aubergines and peppers. Sprinkle with Cheddar cheese. Repeat these layers of sauce, vegetables and cheese until all of these ingredients are used, finishing with a layer of cheese. Sprinkle with the Parmesan and pepper to taste.
**4** Bake in the oven at 200°C (400°F) Mark 6 for 30-40 minutes until bubbling and golden. Serve at once.

# SPINACH AND RICOTTA GNOCCHI

**SERVES 4**
PREPARATION
20 minutes
COOKING TIME
10 minutes
FREEZING
Not suitable
CALS/SERVING
490

15 g (½ oz) butter
1 large garlic clove, peeled and crushed
450 g (1 lb) frozen leaf spinach, thawed
100 g (3½ oz) ricotta cheese
45 ml (3 tbsp) plain white flour
75 g (3 oz) Parmesan cheese, freshly grated
3 medium egg yolks
large pinch of freshly grated nutmeg
salt and pepper

SAGE BUTTER
125 g (4 oz) unsalted butter
30 ml (2 tbsp) chopped fresh sage

TO GARNISH
sage leaves

**1** Melt the butter in a small pan and gently fry the garlic for 3 minutes until softened but not coloured; set aside.

**2** Squeeze out all excess liquid from the spinach, then chop finely. Place in a bowl with the garlic, ricotta, flour, Parmesan, egg yolks, nutmeg, salt and pepper; beat thoroughly.

**3** Using two tablespoons, shape the ricotta mixture into gnocchi by passing a little of the mixture from one spoon to the other. Place on a plate, liberally dusted with flour. Repeat to make 20 gnocchi.

**4** Bring a large pan of lightly salted water to the boil, then lower the heat until the water is at a steady simmer (see note). In the meantime, prepare the sage butter. Melt the butter in a small pan, add the sage leaves and heat until foaming; keep warm.

**5** Cook the gnocchi in batches. Lower into the gently simmering water, return to a simmer and cook for 3 minutes or until the gnocchi float to the surface.

**6** Remove with a slotted spoon and drain on kitchen paper; keep warm. Repeat with the remaining gnocchi. Transfer to warmed bowls, drizzle with the sage butter and garnish with sage. Serve at once.

**NOTE** You will need a very large pan and at least 2.5 litres (4 pints) water to cook the gnocchi.

**VARIATION** Make 1 quantity of Tomato Sauce (see page 291) and purée in a blender. Cook the gnocchi and divide between 4 individual gratin dishes. Pour over the hot tomato sauce, top each serving with 25 g (1 oz) shredded mozzarella cheese and grill until bubbling and golden.

# CHEESE SAUSAGES ON APPLE AND WATERCRESS SALAD

**SERVES 4**
PREPARATION
15 minutes
COOKING TIME
10 minutes
FREEZING
Suitable: Stage 4
CALS/SERVING
705
COLOUR INDEX
Page 60

125 g (4 oz) Caerphilly cheese, grated
200 g (7 oz) soft white breadcrumbs (see note)
2.5 ml (½ tsp) dried thyme
30 ml (2 tbsp) finely chopped fresh parsley
2 spring onions, trimmed
salt and pepper
freshly grated nutmeg
2 eggs
a little milk, if necessary
45 ml (3 tbsp) plain white flour
10 ml (2 tsp) mustard powder
oil for shallow-frying
SALAD
20 g (¾ oz) walnut halves
10 ml (2 tsp) sherry vinegar
45 ml (3 tbsp) olive oil
15 ml (1 tbsp) walnut oil
1 small red onion
50 g (2 oz) watercress
2 green eating apples

**1** Put the cheese in a bowl with the breadcrumbs, thyme and parsley. Finely chop the spring onions and add to the mixture. Season with a little salt, and plenty of pepper and nutmeg. Mix thoroughly.
**2** Separate one egg, dropping the white into a shallow dish. In another bowl, beat the whole egg and egg yolk lightly together, then add to the crumb mixture and mix thoroughly. If necessary, moisten with a little milk; the mixture must be soft enough to gather into balls.
**3** Prepare the salad dressing. Chop half the walnuts very finely by hand or in a food processor. Beat in the vinegar, olive and walnut oils, and seasoning.
**4** Scoop the cheese mixture into 8 balls and shape each one with your hands into a cylindrical sausage.
**5** Beat the reserved egg white lightly until frothy. Mix the flour and mustard powder on a plate.
**6** Heat the oil for shallow-frying in a frying pan. Brush the sausages lightly all over with egg white then, using two forks, roll them in the flour and mustard. Fry the sausages slowly enough to allow them to cook right through, turning frequently to ensure they brown evenly. Drain on kitchen paper.
**7** Meanwhile, peel and thinly slice the onion. Trim the watercress. Quarter, core and slice the apples. Toss these ingredients together and arrange on serving plates. Drizzle with the walnut vinaigrette and sprinkle with the remaining walnuts. Top with the cheese sausages and serve at once.

**NOTE** Soft white breadcrumbs are best made in a food processor from day-old bread.

**VARIATIONS**
- Use another sharp white cheese or a strong Cheddar in place of Caerphilly.
- Omit the apples from the salad. Toss the watercress with 50 g (2 oz) rocket leaves.

# PARSNIP, POTATO AND CHEESE RÖSTI

**SERVES 4**
PREPARATION
10 minutes
COOKING TIME
20 minutes
FREEZING
Not suitable
CALS/SERVING
370

1 onion
350 g (12 oz) waxy potatoes
225 g (8 oz) parsnip
1 garlic clove, peeled and crushed
15 ml (1 tbsp) chopped fresh sage
salt and pepper
1 egg, lightly beaten
30 ml (2 tbsp) sunflower oil
175 g (6 oz) fontina or Cheddar cheese, grated

**1** Peel and slice the onion. Peel and grate the potatoes and parsnip, using the medium grater attachment of a food processor; squeeze out excess liquid.
**2** Place the grated vegetables, onion, garlic and sage in a large bowl. Season generously with salt and pepper. Stir in the egg until evenly combined.
**3** Heat the oil in a large, non-stick frying pan. When hot, spread half of the vegetable mixture over the base of the pan. Scatter over the cheese, then top with the remaining vegetable mixture, spreading it flat.
**4** Cook over a low heat for approximately 10 minutes until golden underneath. Slide the rösti out onto a large plate and flip back into the pan. Cook for a further 10 minutes until the underside is browned and the vegetables are cooked through.
**5** Serve immediately, cut into wedges, as a lunch or light supper with a mixed leaf salad. Alternatively, serve as an accompaniment to a vegetable stew or grill.

**VARIATIONS**
- To make individual rösti, divide the potato mixture into 4 portions, shape into cakes and fry as above.
- For a more substantial lunch or supper dish, top with poached eggs, mushrooms and grilled tomatoes.

# Salads

# ROASTED VEGETABLE SALAD

**SERVES 8**
PREPARATION
20 minutes, plus standing
COOKING TIME
45-50 minutes
FREEZING
Not suitable
CALS/SERVING
250

2 aubergines
2 courgettes
salt and pepper
2 small onions, preferably red
1 head of fennel, trimmed
2 red peppers
15 ml (1 tbsp) chopped fresh thyme
15 ml (1 tbsp) chopped fresh sage
60 ml (4 tbsp) olive oil
1 small head of garlic
125 g (4 oz) fontina cheese, diced
30 ml (2 tbsp) chopped fresh basil
25 g (1 oz) pitted black olives
25 g (1 oz) pine nuts, toasted
DRESSING
10 ml (2 tsp) balsamic or sherry vinegar
60 ml (4 tbsp) extra-virgin olive oil
TO GARNISH
basil leaves

**1** Cut the aubergines and courgettes into 2.5 cm (1 inch) cubes. Layer in a large colander, sprinkling with 10 ml (2 tsp) salt. Set aside for 30 minutes, then rinse thoroughly to remove salt and dry well with kitchen paper.

**2** Peel the onions and cut into small wedges. Remove the tough outer layer and core from the fennel, then dice. Halve, core and deseed the peppers, then cut into 2.5 cm (1 inch) squares.

**3** Combine all of the vegetables in a large bowl. Add the thyme, sage and oil. Toss well, then transfer to a large roasting tin, arranging the vegetables in a single layer. (If necessary, use 2 roasting tins.)

**4** Slice the top from the head of garlic and stand on a small sheet of foil. Drizzle over a little oil, season with salt and pepper and seal the foil to form a parcel. Sit the parcel amongst the vegetables.

**5** Roast in the oven at 230°C (450°F) Mark 8 for 45-50 minutes, stirring from time to time to ensure even browning. Transfer the vegetables to a large bowl and stir in the diced cheese.

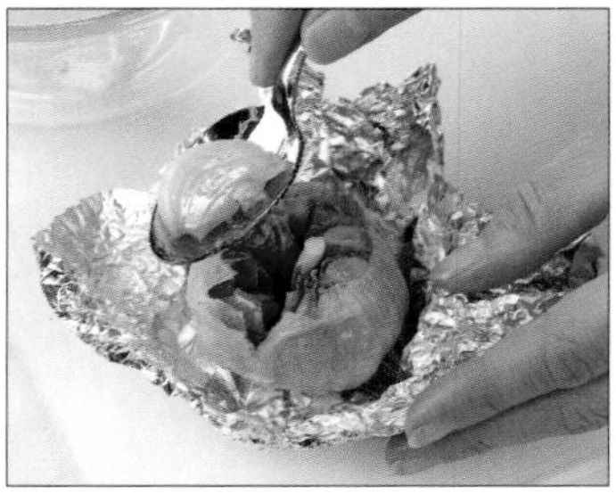

**6** Unwrap the garlic and scoop out the flesh into a bowl. Add the dressing ingredients, season with salt and pepper and whisk to combine.

**7** Pour the garlic dressing over the vegetables. Add the chopped basil, olives and pine nuts and toss lightly. Serve immediately, garnished with basil leaves.

**NOTES**

❑ If Italian fontina is unobtainable, use mozzarella cheese instead.

❑ This rich salad is best served with plenty of warm crusty bread – as a lunch or supper dish.

## INDONESIAN VEGETABLE SALAD

**SERVES 4-6**
PREPARATION
30 minutes, plus marinating
COOKING TIME
20 minutes
FREEZING
Not suitable
CALS/SERVING
350-235

1 medium sweet potato, or small butternut squash
2 large raw beetroot
1 fennel bulb, trimmed
2 large carrots
60 ml (4 tbsp) oil
20 ml (4 tsp) sesame oil
1 medium courgette
125 g (4 oz) cucumber
125 g (4 oz) radishes
125 g (4 oz) bean sprouts
salt and pepper

DRESSING
2.5 cm (1 inch) piece fresh root ginger
1 red chilli
1 garlic clove, peeled and crushed
5 ml (1 tsp) thin honey
grated zest and juice of 1 lime
15 ml (1 tbsp) chopped fresh coriander

TO SERVE
50 g (2 oz) raw peanuts, toasted
coriander sprigs, to garnish

**1** Peel the sweet potato or squash and slice thinly; peel and thinly slice the beetroot. Discard the tough outer layer from the fennel and thinly slice lengthwise. Peel the carrots, halve crosswise, then slice lengthwise.
**2** Mix the two oils together. Brush the sweet potato or squash slices with some of the oil and place on the grill rack. Grill as close to the heat as possible for 6-8 minutes on each side until charred and cooked through. Repeat with the beetroot and fennel, grilling for 5-6 minutes on each side, then the carrot, grilling for 4-5 minutes each side. Transfer to a large bowl and set aside to cool.
**3** Trim and very finely slice the courgette, cucumber and radishes, then place in a bowl with the bean sprouts.
**4** To make the dressing, peel and grate the ginger; halve, deseed and finely chop the chilli. Place in a screw-topped jar with the remaining oil, garlic, honey, lime zest and juice, and chopped coriander. Season with salt and pepper to taste and shake until evenly blended.
**5** Combine the raw vegetables with the cooked ones, pour over the dressing, toss well and leave to marinate for 1 hour.
**6** Just before serving, scatter the peanuts over the salad and garnish with coriander sprigs.

## THAI VEGETABLE SALAD WITH CRISPY NOODLES

**SERVES 4-6**
PREPARATION
30 minutes
COOKING TIME
5-8 minutes
FREEZING
Not suitable
CALS/SERVING
500-335
COLOUR INDEX
Page 61

2 carrots
1 red onion
½ small cucumber
2 tomatoes
2 Little Gem lettuce, trimmed
125 g (4 oz) bean sprouts, trimmed
125 g (4 oz) canned water chestnuts, drained

DRESSING
2 red chillies
3 garlic cloves
30 ml (2 tbsp) sesame seeds
45 ml (3 tbsp) sunflower oil
7.5 ml (1½ tsp) grated fresh root ginger
7.5 ml (1½ tsp) caster sugar
22 ml (1½ tbsp) sherry vinegar
45 ml (3 tbsp) light soy sauce
60 ml (4 tbsp) water

CRISPY NOODLES
1 sheet dried Chinese egg thread noodles
oil, for deep-frying

**1** First, prepare the dressing. Deseed and finely chop the chillies; peel and slice the garlic. Dry-fry the sesame seeds in a wok or frying pan until golden, remove from the pan and set aside. Heat the oil in the same pan and fry the chillies, garlic and ginger for 30 seconds. Add the sugar, vinegar, soy sauce and water, and simmer for 1 minute. Remove from the heat and allow to cool.
**2** Peel the carrots and thinly pare into ribbons, using a swivel vegetable peeler. Peel and thinly slice the onion. Halve the cucumber lengthwise, scoop out the seeds and cut the flesh into slices. Skin, deseed and chop the tomatoes. Halve the water chestnuts.
**3** Soak the noodles according to the packet instructions; drain and dry thoroughly. Heat a 10 cm (4 inch) depth of oil in a deep, heavy-based saucepan until it registers 180°C (350°F) on a sugar thermometer or until a cube of bread browns in 30 seconds. Deep-fry the noodles in batches for 1-2 minutes until crisp and golden. Drain on kitchen paper and set aside.
**4** Put all of the salad ingredients, except the noodles, in a large bowl. Add the dressing and toss well until all the vegetables are coated. Transfer to a serving platter and top with the sesame seeds and crispy noodles. Serve at once.

## TOMATO AND ROASTED BREAD SALAD

**SERVES 4**
PREPARATION
20 minutes
COOKING TIME
25 minutes
FREEZING
Not suitable
CALS/SERVING
530

- 2 red or green peppers
- 1 red onion
- ½ cucumber
- 1 small fennel bulb
- 6 ripe plum tomatoes
- handful of pitted black olives, halved
- handful of fresh basil leaves, shredded
- 15 ml (1 tbsp) chopped fresh oregano
- salt and pepper
- 225 g (8 oz) rustic bread (uncut)
- 25 g (1 oz) butter, melted

DRESSING

- 75 ml (5 tbsp) olive oil
- 30 ml (2 tbsp) balsamic vinegar
- 1 garlic clove, peeled and crushed

**1** Halve and deseed the peppers; place skin-side up on the grill rack and grill until the skin is blistered and blackened. Allow to cool slightly, then remove the skins. Cut the pepper flesh into thin strips and set aside.
**2** Peel and thinly slice the onion. Peel and dice the cucumber. Quarter, core and chop the fennel. Cut the tomatoes into wedges. Place these ingredients in a bowl with the reserved pepper strips, olives and herbs. Season with salt and pepper to taste and toss lightly.
**3** Cut the bread into 2.5 cm (1 inch) slices, discarding the crusts. Brush both sides of each slice with melted butter, then cut into 2.5 cm (1 inch) cubes. Place in a buttered shallow baking tin in a single layer. Bake at 200°C (400°F) Mark 6 for 8-12 minutes until crisp and golden brown.
**4** Meanwhile, mix the dressing ingredients together In a small bowl. Drizzle over the salad, add the piping hot croûtons and toss again. Serve at once.

## MEDITERRANEAN SALAD WITH A SPICY DRESSING

**SERVES 4-6**
PREPARATION
20 minutes
COOKING TIME
10 minutes
FREEZING
Not suitable
CALS/SERVING
520-345
COLOUR INDEX
Page 61

- 125 g (4 oz) French beans
- 225 g (8 oz) broad beans in their pods, or 125 g (4 oz) frozen broad beans
- 1 crisp Cos lettuce
- 225 g (8 oz) feta cheese
- 6 artichoke hearts in oil (optional)
- few sun-dried tomatoes (optional)
- handful of fresh herb sprigs, such as basil, oregano, parsley or chervil (optional)
- salt and pepper

HOT DRESSING

- 1-2 dried red chillies
- 1 garlic clove, peeled and crushed
- 10 ml (2 tsp) balsamic or red wine vinegar
- 60 ml (4 tbsp) olive oil

CROUTONS

- 3 thick slices of firm-textured bread
- olive oil for shallow-frying
- knob of butter

**1** First make the dressing. Toast the chillies in a dry heavy-based frying pan over a moderate heat for 2 minutes, shaking the pan so that they do not burn. Leave to cool, then crush. In a bowl, mix together the chilli(es), garlic and vinegar. Gradually whisk in the oil, with a fork, to make a thick dressing. Season with salt and pepper to taste.
**2** Trim the French beans and blanch in a pan of boiling salted water for 2 minutes. Drain, refresh under cold water, then drain thoroughly. Turn into a salad bowl and moisten with a little of the dressing.
**3** If using fresh broad beans, remove from their pods. Cook in boiling salted water for 1 minute only, then refresh with cold water. Drain, skin if preferred, and mix with the French beans. If using frozen broad beans, place in a heat-proof bowl, pour over sufficient boiling water to cover and leave until cool enough to handle. Drain, remove the skins, then add to the salad.
**4** Trim the lettuce, separate the leaves and tear into pieces. Toss with the beans.
**5** To make the croûtons, cut the bread into large cubes. Heat the oil and butter in a frying pan. Add the bread cubes and fry until golden brown on all sides. Remove from the pan with a slotted spoon and drain on crumpled kitchen paper.
**6** Break the feta cheese into large pieces. Halve the artichokes, if using. Chop the sun-dried tomatoes and herbs if using. Scatter the feta, artichokes, tomatoes, herbs and croûtons on top of the salad. Drizzle over the remaining dressing and season with salt and pepper. Toss lightly and serve immediately.

**VARIATION** Omit the feta cheese. Replace with a generous handful of assorted nuts – tossed in a little ground cumin and paprika and fried in the oil and butter used for cooking the croûtons.

## MEDITERRANEAN PASTA SALAD

**SERVES 4**
PREPARATION
15 minutes, plus standing
COOKING TIME
10 minutes
FREEZING
Not suitable
CALS/SERVING
415

175 g (6 oz) dried pasta shapes, such as penne
15 ml (1 tbsp) extra-virgin olive oil
4 sun-dried tomatoes in oil, drained
225 g (8 oz) cherry tomatoes
4-6 spring onions, trimmed
8-12 black olives
8-12 fresh basil leaves, torn

DRESSING
2 sun-dried tomatoes in oil, drained
30 ml (2 tbsp) oil (from the sun-dried tomato jar)
30 ml (2 tbsp) red wine vinegar
1 garlic clove, peeled
15 ml (1 tbsp) tomato paste
pinch of sugar (optional)
coarse sea salt and pepper
30 ml (2 tbsp) extra-virgin olive oil

TO GARNISH
small basil leaves

**1** Cook the pasta in a large pan of boiling salted water until *al dente*. Drain in a colander, refresh under cold running water, then drain thoroughly. Turn into large bowl and toss with the olive oil to prevent sticking.
**2** Slice the sun-dried tomatoes; half the cherry tomatoes; shred the spring onions. Add these ingredients to the pasta with the olives and basil, and toss to mix.
**3** To make the dressing, put the sun-dried tomatoes and oil, vinegar, garlic and tomato paste in a blender or food processor. Add the sugar if using, and salt and pepper. With the motor running, pour the olive oil through the feeder tube and process briefly to make a fairly thick dressing.
**4** Pour the dressing over the pasta and toss well. Cover and leave to stand for 1-2 hours if possible, to allow the flavours to develop. Garnish with basil to serve.

**VARIATION** Toss cubes of Cheddar cheese into the salad and serve with wholemeal bread and salad leaves for a more substantial dish.

## SALAD OF HARICOT BEANS AND SUMMER VEGETABLES

**SERVES 6-8**
PREPARATION
30 minutes, plus overnight soaking
COOKING TIME
1 hour
FREEZING
Not suitable
CALS/SERVING
320-235
COLOUR INDEX
Page 62

175 g (6 oz) dried haricot beans, soaked overnight in cold water (see note)
225 g (8 oz) baby carrots
225 g (8 oz) asparagus spears
125 g (4 oz) French beans
125 g (4 oz) shelled broad beans
125 g (4 oz) shelled peas
6 spring onions, trimmed
90 ml (6 tbsp) extra-virgin olive oil
15 ml (1 tbsp) brown mustard seeds
1 garlic clove, peeled and crushed
finely grated zest of 2 limes
30 ml (2 tbsp) lime juice
45 ml (3 tbsp) chopped fresh parsley
45-60 ml (3-4 tbsp) double cream (optional)
salt and pepper

**1** Drain and rinse the beans, then place in a saucepan and cover with plenty of cold water. Bring to the boil, boil steadily for 10 minutes, then reduce the heat, cover and simmer gently for 45 minutes or until tender.
**2** Meanwhile, scrub the carrots; remove the tough ends of the asparagus spears, then cut into 7.5 cm (3 inch) lengths; trim and halve the French beans.
**3** Bring a large pan of lightly salted water to the boil. Blanch the carrots for 4 minutes; drain and refresh immediately under cold water; pat dry. Repeat with the asparagus, French beans, broad beans and peas, but blanch for 2 minutes only.
**4** Drain the haricot beans; set aside. Slice the spring onions on the diagonal and set aside.
**5** Heat 15 ml (1 tbsp) of the oil in a large frying pan, add the mustard seeds and fry gently for 1 minute until they start to pop. Add the garlic to the pan with the grated lime zest. Fry for a further 2 minutes.
**6** Add the haricot beans and blanched vegetables. Stir-fry over a gentle heat for 3-4 minutes until warmed through.
**7** Stir in the lime juice, spring onions, remaining oil and parsley. Remove from the heat, stir in the cream if using, and season with salt and pepper to taste. Serve at once.

**NOTE** If you don't have time to pre-soak dried beans, use two 400 g (14 oz) cans of haricot beans instead. Rinse and drain the beans and add directly to the frying pan at stage 6.

# YELLOW PEPPER CAESAR SALAD

**SERVES 4-6**
PREPARATION
20 minutes
COOKING TIME
20-30 minutes
FREEZING
Not suitable
CALS/SERVING
505-340

3 large yellow peppers
1 Cos lettuce
25 g (1 oz) Parmesan cheese shavings
DRESSING
75 ml (5 tbsp) mayonnaise
45-60 ml (3-4 tbsp) water
1-2 garlic cloves
coarse sea salt and pepper
CROUTONS
1 small rustic white loaf (uncut)
75 g (3 oz) butter, melted
TO SERVE
Parmesan cheese shavings

**1** First make the dressing: Thin the mayonnaise to a pouring consistency with the water. Peel the garlic cloves and crush to a paste with a little coarse sea salt. Add to the mayonnaise with the grated Parmesan and stir well. Season with pepper and set aside.

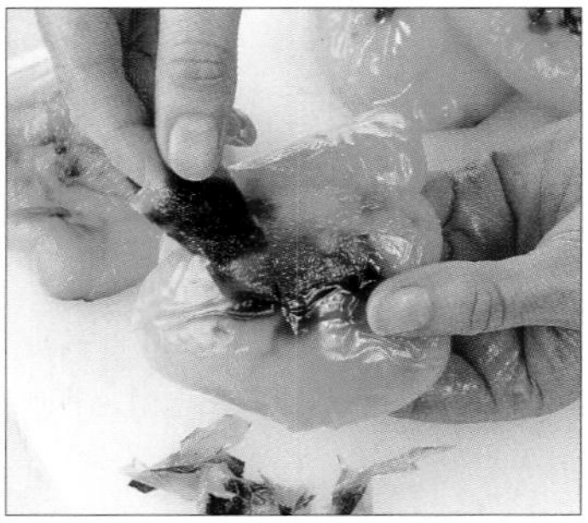

**2** Halve the peppers lengthwise and remove the seeds. Grill the pepper halves, skin-side up, for 10-15 minutes until blistered and blackened. Cover and leave to cool slightly, then peel off and discard the charred skin. Cut the peppers into long, thin strips.

**3** Separate the lettuce leaves, tear into pieces and place in a salad bowl. Add the pepper strips and set aside.

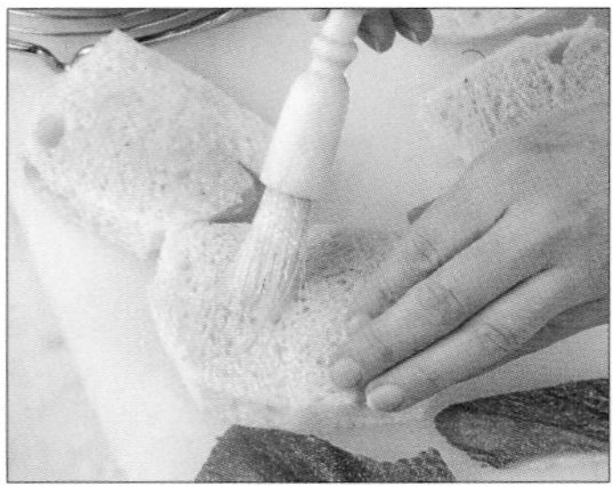

**4** To make the croûtons, cut the bread into 3 cm (1¼ inch) thick slices. Cut off the crusts and discard. Brush generously with melted butter, then cut into 3 cm (1¼ inch) cubes.

**5** Arrange the bread cubes in a buttered large shallow baking tin, in a single layer, brushing the cut sides with any remaining butter. Bake at 200°C (400°F) Mark 6 for 9-12 minutes until crisp and deep golden brown.

**6** Tip the piping hot croûtons into the salad, drizzle over the dressing and sprinkle the Parmesan shavings on top. Serve immediately.

# SPINACH AND FETA CHEESE SALAD

**SERVES 4**
PREPARATION
10 minutes
COOKING TIME
3-4 minutes
FREEZING
Not suitable
CALS/SERVING
350
COLOUR INDEX
Page 62

350 g (12 oz) young spinach leaves
2-3 spring onions
1 red or yellow pepper
salt and pepper
200 g (7 oz) feta cheese
DRESSING
2 garlic cloves
30 ml (2 tbsp) pine nuts
60 ml (4 tbsp) olive oil
30 ml (2 tbsp) wine vinegar

**1** Divide the spinach leaves between individual serving plates. Trim and finely shred the spring onions. Quarter, core, deseed and finely slice the red pepper. Scatter the red pepper and spring onions over the spinach and season with salt and pepper.
**2** Cut the cheese into 1 cm (½ inch) cubes and scatter over the salads.
**3** Immediately before serving, prepare the dressing. Peel and finely chop the garlic. Put the pine nuts in a small

heavy-based frying pan and shake over a moderate heat until they begin to colour and develop a toasted aroma.
**4** Immediately add the oil and garlic to the pan and shake the pan over the heat until the garlic sizzles and turns golden. Add the wine vinegar, then pour the dressing over the salads. Serve at once, with plenty of warm bread.

**NOTE** Packets of ready-washed spinach are widely available from supermarkets.

**VARIATION** Use batavia lettuce or a combinaton of frisée and radicchio instead of spinach leaves.

## ROCKET AND GOAT'S CHEESE SALAD WITH ROASTED PEPPER SALSA

**SERVES 4**
PREPARATION
20 minutes
COOKING TIME
25 minutes
FREEZING
Not suitable
CALS/SERVING
390
COLOUR INDEX
Page 62

1 small red pepper
1 small orange pepper
90 ml (6 tbsp) extra-virgin olive oil
1 small red onion
1 garlic clove
2 ripe plum tomatoes
22 ml (1½ tbsp) balsamic vinegar
pinch of sugar
30 ml (2 tbsp) chopped fresh chervil
salt and pepper
125 g (4 oz) goat's cheese (see note)
125 g (4 oz) rocket leaves
30 ml (2 tbsp) pine nuts, toasted (optional)

**1** Brush the peppers with a little olive oil and place in a roasting tin. Roast in the oven at 230°C (450°F) Mark 8 for 20 minutes, turning once, until charred. Transfer to a bowl, cover and set aside until cool enough to handle.
**2** Carefully peel the peppers over the bowl, to catch the juices, then discard the seeds. Dice the pepper flesh and add to the juices.
**3** Peel and finely chop the onion and garlic. Immerse the tomatoes in boiling water for 30 seconds, then remove and peel away the skins. Halve, deseed and dice the tomato flesh.
**4** Heat 15 ml (1 tbsp) of the oil in a small pan, add the onion and garlic and fry for about 3 minutes until softened. Add the diced tomatoes and fry gently for a further 2 minutes. Add to the peppers, toss to mix and set aside to cool.
**5** Combine the remaining oil with the vinegar, sugar, chervil and seasoning. Pour over the pepper mixture and toss to mix.
**6** Thinly slice the goat's cheese. Divide the rocket between individual serving plates and arrange the cheese in the centre. Spoon some of the salsa over the cheese and drizzle the rest liberally over the rocket. Scatter over the pine nuts and serve at once, with plenty of olive bread.

**NOTE** Buy a rindless soft goat's cheese for this recipe, such as Sainte-Maure or a Chabi. For a more pronounced flavour, opt for the cendré version of either cheese which are ripened in wood-ash and have a distinctive grey coating.

## GREEN PEA, POTATO AND WALNUT SALAD

**SERVES 4**
PREPARATION
10 minutes
COOKING TIME
15 minutes
FREEZING
Not suitable
CALS/SERVING
425

350 g (12 oz) baby new potatoes, scrubbed
4 fresh mint sprigs, bruised
salt and pepper
225 g (8 oz) sugar snap peas, trimmed
225 g (8 oz) shelled fresh peas
50 g (2 oz) sprouted seeds
50 g (2 oz) walnuts, toasted

DRESSING
90 ml (3 fl oz) walnut oil
60 ml (2 fl oz) light olive oil
15-30 ml (1-2 tbsp) white wine vinegar
5 ml (1 tsp) Dijon mustard

**1** Halve the potatoes if large, place in a saucepan and cover with cold water. Add the mint and a little salt, bring to the boil and cook for 8-10 minutes until tender. Drain off the water into a clean pan; transfer the potatoes to a bowl.
**2** Meanwhile, prepare the dressing. Put all the ingredients into a small bowl and season with salt and pepper.
**3** Pour half of the dressing over the hot potatoes, toss well and leave to cool.
**4** Cook the sugar snap peas and the fresh peas in the reserved water for 3-4 minutes until tender. Drain, refresh under cold water and toss with the remaining dressing.
**5** When the potatoes are cool, add the peas and sprouts; toss to mix. Roughly chop the walnuts and scatter over the salad. Check the seasoning and serve at once.

# LENTIL SALAD WITH GREEN VEGETABLES AND GOAT'S CHEESE

**SERVES 4-6**
PREPARATION
25 minutes, plus standing
COOKING TIME
35 minutes
FREEZING
Not suitable
CALS/SERVING
370-250

1 small onion, peeled
1 small carrot, peeled
1 small leek, trimmed
1 small celery stick, trimmed
30 ml (2 tbsp) olive oil
225 g (8 oz) Puy lentils
2 bay leaves
600 ml (1 pint) vegetable stock
125 g (4 oz) mangetout
125 g (4 oz) French beans, trimmed
125 g (4 oz) asparagus tips
125 g (4 oz) goat's cheese, crumbled

DRESSING
90 ml (6 tbsp) extra-virgin olive oil
30 ml (2 tbsp) lemon juice
1 garlic clove, peeled and crushed
1.25 ml (¼ tsp) paprika
pinch of cayenne pepper
salt and pepper
TO SERVE
croûtons (optional – see page 230)

**1** Finely chop the onion, carrot, leek and celery. Heat the oil in a large pan and sauté the chopped vegetables for 10 minutes. Stir in the lentils, bay leaves and stock. Bring to the boil, cover and simmer for 20-30 minutes until tender.

**2** In the meantime, place the ingredients for the dressing in a small bowl and whisk to emulsify.

**3** Drain the lentil mixture and place in a large bowl. Add the dressing, toss to mix and set aside to cool to room temperature.

**4** Bring a large pan of lightly salted water to the boil. Cook the mangetout, French beans and asparagus separately in the boiling water for 2-3 minutes until just tender. Drain, refresh under cold water and pat dry.

**5** When the lentils are cool, stir in the green vegetables, add the goat's cheese and toss well. Divide the salad between individual plates and serve topped with croûtons if wished.

# BULGHAR WHEAT SALAD WITH DRIED FRUIT AND PINE NUTS

**SERVES 4**
PREPARATION
15 minutes, plus standing
FREEZING
Not suitable
CALS/SERVING
635
COLOUR INDEX
Page 63

225 g (8 oz) bulghar wheat
1 lemon
1 large onion
4 ripe tomatoes
75 g (3 oz) mixed dried fruit, such as apricots, peaches and figs
60 ml (4 tbsp) chopped fresh coriander
30 ml (2 tbsp) chopped fresh mint
125 ml (4 fl oz) extra-virgin olive oil
5 ml (1 tsp) thin honey
50 g (2 oz) pine nuts, toasted
50 g (2 oz) pitted black olives
salt and pepper

**1** Place the bulghar wheat in a large bowl, pour over 300 ml (½ pint) boiling water and leave to soak for 30 minutes until softened; drain off any remaining liquid.
**2** Peel the lemon, removing all of the white pith, then cut into segments, discarding the membrane and pips. Finely dice the lemon and add to the bulghar wheat.
**3** Peel and finely chop the onion; skin the tomatoes if

preferred, then dice; chop the dried fruit. Add these ingredients to the bulghar wheat, with the herbs, oil and honey. Toss to mix, cover and chill for 1 hour to allow the flavours to develop.
**4** Add the toasted pine nuts and olives to the salad, season generously with salt and pepper and serve at once.

**NOTE** To toast the pine nuts, spread on a baking sheet and place in the oven at 200°C (400°F) Mark 6 for 6-8 minutes until golden, watching carefully as they quickly burn.

## CIABATTA, PLUM TOMATO AND MOZZARELLA SALAD

**SERVES 4-6**
PREPARATION
25 minutes
FREEZING
Not suitable
CALS/SERVING
440-295
COLOUR INDEX
Page 63

175 g (6 oz) ciabatta or pugliese bread
700 g (1½ lb) plum tomatoes
175 g (6 oz) mozzarella cheese
450 g (1 lb) cucumber
50 g (2 oz) sun-dried tomatoes in oil, drained
2 oz (50 g ) pitted black olives, such as Kalamata
125 g (4 oz) baby spinach or lamb's lettuce
DRESSING
30 ml (2 tbsp) red wine vinegar
60 ml (4 tbsp) olive oil
30 ml (2 tbsp) chopped basil
salt and pepper
TO GARNISH
basil leaves

**1** Cut the ciabatta or pugliese bread into 2.5 cm (1 inch) cubes. Place in a bowl and add about 150 ml (¼ pint) water. Leave to soak for 5 minutes, then drain and gently squeeze the bread to remove excess water.
**2** Cut the plum tomatoes, cheese and cucumber into rough chunks. Finely slice the sun-dried tomatoes.
**3** For the dressing, whisk together the wine vinegar, olive oil and chopped basil in a bowl. Season with salt and pepper.
**4** Put the bread, tomatoes, cheese, cucumber, sun-dried tomatoes, olives and spinach or lamb's lettuce into a bowl.
**5** Add the dressing and toss to mix. Turn into a serving bowl and garnish with basil leaves.

**VARIATION** Replace the mozzarella with brie, dolcelatte or gorgonzola cheese.

## MILLET SALAD WITH GRILLED PEPPERS

**SERVES 4**
PREPARATION
15 minutes
COOKING TIME
25-30 minutes
FREEZING
Not suitable
CALS/SERVING
400

225 g (8 oz) millet
600 ml (1 pint) vegetable stock
1 red pepper
1 yellow pepper
1 orange pepper
1 onion
2 garlic cloves
1 small red chilli
2 ripe tomatoes
90 ml (6 tbsp) extra-virgin olive oil
5 ml (1 tsp) ground mixed spice
30 ml (2 tbsp) balsamic vinegar
30 ml (2 tbsp) chopped fresh basil
salt and pepper
basil, to garnish

**1** Dry-fry the millet in a large frying pan for 3-4 minutes until golden and releasing a smoky aroma, then transfer to a saucepan. Add the stock, bring to the boil, cover and simmer gently for about 20-25 minutes until the grains are swollen and the stock is absorbed. Transfer to a large bowl.
**2** Meanwhile, grill the peppers under a high heat for 15-20 minutes, turning frequently until charred on all sides. Transfer to a bowl, cover and leave until cool enough to handle. Peel away the skin and remove the core and seeds over a bowl to catch the juices. Slice the pepper flesh.
**3** Peel and finely chop the onion and garlic. Deseed and finely chop the chilli. Skin the tomatoes if preferred; dice the flesh. Heat 15 ml (1 tbsp) of the oil in a frying pan, add the onion, garlic, chilli and mixed spice and fry gently for 5 minutes until softened and lightly golden. Add the tomatoes and remove from the heat.
**4** In a bowl, whisk the remaining oil with the vinegar and reserved pepper juices. Add to the cooked millet with the spiced mixture and chopped basil. Toss to mix and season with salt and pepper to taste. Serve while still warm.

## MESCLUN WITH TOASTED SEEDS

**SERVES 4**
PREPARATION
5 minutes
COOKING TIME
2-3 minutes
FREEZING
Not suitable
CALS/SERVING
215

175 g (6 oz) assorted salad leaves, such as rocket, lamb's lettuce, watercress, oak leaf, lollo rosso, chicory
25 g (1 oz) assorted fresh herb leaves, such as parsley, chives, basil, chervil and tarragon
25 g (1 oz) sunflower seeds
25 g (1 oz) pumpkin seeds
30 ml (2 tbsp) poppy seeds

DRESSING
60 ml (4 tbsp) extra-virgin olive oil
10 ml (2 tsp) wine or sherry vinegar
pinch of sugar
salt and pepper

TO GARNISH
edible flowers (optional)

**1** Place the salad leaves and herbs in a large salad bowl.
**2** Place a heavy-based frying pan over a medium heat. Add the sunflower, pumpkin and poppy seeds and stir-fry for 2-3 minutes until they are golden and begin to release their aroma. Immediately transfer to a plate and allow to cool.
**3** Shake all the dressing ingredients together in a screw-topped jar until evenly combined.
**4** Pour the dressing over the leaves and herbs, and toss gently until coated. Scatter over the toasted seeds and edible flowers if using. Serve at once.

**NOTE** For convenience, use one of the ready-prepared packets of mixed salad leaves which are readily available from most supermarkets.

**VARIATION** For a more substantial salad suitable to serve as a light lunch, add 125 g (4 oz) crumbled feta or diced gruyère cheese to the salad along with some croûtons and seedless grapes.

## MIXED LEAF SALAD WITH CROÛTONS

**SERVES 6-8**
PREPARATION
10 minutes
COOKING TIME
3-4 minutes
FREEZING
Not suitable
CALS/SERVING
140
COLOUR INDEX
Page 63

1 head of radicchio
1 bunch of watercress
½ head of frisée
5 thin slices of bread
50 g (2 oz) baby spinach leaves
50 g (2 oz) rocket leaves
250 g (9 oz) radishes, trimmed

DRESSING
30 ml (2 tbsp) olive oil
30 ml (2 tbsp) sunflower oil
22 ml (1½ tsp) white wine vinegar
pinch of sugar
1 small garlic clove, peeled and crushed
salt and pepper

**1** Tear the radicchio into bite-sized pieces; remove the stalks from the watercress; discard any tough outer leaves from the frisée.
**2** Using a heart-shaped or other cutter, stamp out shapes from the bread. Grill until golden on both sides.
**3** For the dressing, put all the ingredients in a screw-topped jar and shake vigorously to combine.
**4** To serve, transfer the salad leaves and radishes to a serving bowl. Pour on the dressing and toss lightly. Scatter the warm croûtons over the salad and serve at once.

## COURGETTE AND LEMON SALAD

**SERVES 6**
PREPARATION
10 minutes
FREEZING
Not suitable
CALS/SERVING
115
COLOUR INDEX
Page 64

900 g (2 lb) courgettes (preferably mixed green and yellow)
grated zest and juice of 1 lemon
small handful of fresh oregano leaves
1 large garlic clove, peeled and crushed
60 ml (4 tbsp) extra-virgin olive oil
salt and pepper
oregano sprigs, to garnish

**1** Trim and thinly slice the courgettes. Place in a large bowl.
**2** Add the lemon zest and juice, oregano, garlic and olive oil. Season generously with salt and pepper. Cover and leave to marinate in the refrigerator for about 3 hours.
**3** Toss lightly before serving, and check the seasoning. Garnish with oregano sprigs.

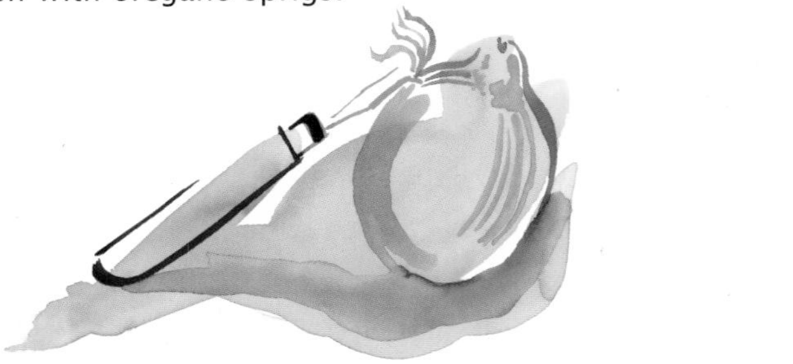

## THREE TOMATO SALAD WITH CAPERS AND OLIVES

**SERVES 4-6**
PREPARATION
10 minutes, plus standing
FREEZING
Not suitable
CALS/SERVING
215-110

30 ml (2 tbsp) small French capers, washed (see note)
2 large ripe beef tomatoes
3 ripe plum tomatoes
125 g (4 oz) red or yellow cherry tomatoes
40 g (1½ oz) small Nicoise olives
DRESSING
60 ml (4 tbsp) extra-virgin olive oil
30 ml (2 tbsp) lemon juice
5 ml (1 tsp) Dijon mustard
1.25 ml (¼ tsp) thin honey
salt and pepper
TO FINISH
15 g (½ oz) basil leaves
40 g (1½ oz) pecorino or Parmesan cheese (optional)

**1** Soak the capers in cold water for 30 minutes, then drain and pat dry.
**2** Thinly slice the beef tomatoes and arrange them in overlapping slices on a large plate. Slice the plum tomatoes lengthwise and arrange on top. Halve the cherry tomatoes and place in the centre of the plate.
**3** Stone the olives, if preferred, and scatter them over the tomatoes along with the capers.
**4** Place all the ingredients for the dressing in a screw-topped jar and shake well until amalgamated.
**5** Drizzle the dressing generously over the tomatoes. Cover and leave to stand for 30 minutes to infuse.
**6** Scatter the basil leaves over the salad, then top with slivers of pecorino or Parmesan cheese if desired. Serve immediately.

**NOTE** Small French capers come either packed in salt or in balsamic vinegar and are available from delicatessens. They have a firm, slightly crunchy texture, whereas the larger capers in brine can be soggy and taste strongly of brine. Ordinary capers will suffice for this recipe, but be sure to wash and dry them well before using.

## THREE BEAN SALAD

**SERVES 6**
PREPARATION
10 minutes, plus standing
COOKING TIME
10-15 minutes
FREEZING
Not suitable
CALS/SERVING
330
COLOUR INDEX
Page 64

1 red pepper
1 yellow pepper
425 g (15 oz) can black-eye beans
215 g (7 oz) can red kidney or aduki beans
425 g (15 oz) can chick peas
60 ml (4 tbsp) chopped fresh coriander
salt and pepper
DRESSING
5 ml (1 tsp) curry paste
2.5 ml (½ tsp) thin honey
1 garlic clove, peeled and crushed
25 ml (1½ tbsp) white wine vinegar
90 ml (6 tbsp) sunflower oil

**1** Halve the peppers lengthwise, then grill cut-side down until the skins are black and blistered. Cover with a damp tea-towel and let cool slightly.
**2** Peel away the skins, then discard the seeds and core. Cut the pepper flesh into strips.
**3** Drain the beans and chick peas and rinse under cold running water. Drain well and place in a bowl.
**4** To make the dressing, put the curry paste, honey and garlic in a small bowl and whisk together with a fork. Add the vinegar, then gradually blend in the oil, whisking vigorously with the fork. Season with salt and pepper.
**5** Add the peppers and coriander to the beans, then pour on the dressing. Toss well and leave at cool room temperature for 2-3 hours before serving, to allow the flavours to mingle.

## RED CABBAGE SLAW

**SERVES 4-6**
PREPARATION
20 minutes, plus standing
FREEZING
Not suitable
CALS/SERVING
495-335

225 g (8 oz) red cabbage, cored
2 medium carrots, peeled
50 g (2 oz) raw beetroot, peeled
1 red onion, peeled
2 green apples
50 g (2 oz) pecan nuts, toasted
1 garlic clove, peeled and crushed

DRESSING
½ quantity Mayonnaise (see page 292)
60 ml (4 tbsp) Greek-style yogurt
15 ml (1 tbsp) orange juice
15 ml (1 tbsp) red wine vinegar
salt and pepper
30 ml (2 tbsp) chopped fresh chives

**1** Coarsely grate or shred the cabbage, carrots and beetroot, using a food processor fitted with a medium grating disc. Finely slice the onion. Quarter, core and grate the apples.

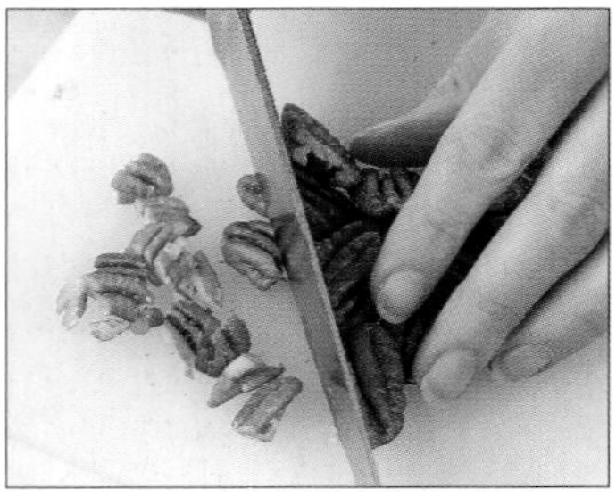

**2** Roughly chop the pecan nuts and place in a large bowl with all the prepared vegetables, apples and garlic.

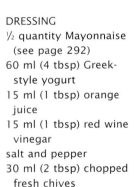

**3** To make the dressing, beat the mayonnaise, yogurt, orange juice, vinegar and seasoning together in a bowl. Stir in the chives.

**4** Spoon the dressing over the vegetables and nuts and toss well until coated. Cover and set aside for 30 minutes to allow the flavours to develop. Toss the salad before serving.

**NOTE** Use bought mayonnaise if you haven't time to make your own or if you are unhappy about using raw egg yolks; you will need 150 ml (¼ pint).

## FENNEL AND ORANGE SALAD

**SERVES 4**
PREPARATION
15 minutes
FREEZING
Not suitable
CALS/SERVING
280
COLOUR INDEX
Page 64

2 large oranges
1 fennel bulb, trimmed
1 small red onion
50 g (2 oz) rocket leaves

DRESSING
15 g (½ oz) pitted black olives
1 sun-dried tomato in oil, drained
1 small garlic clove, peeled and crushed
7.5 ml (½ tbsp) chopped fresh parsley
90 ml (6 tbsp) extra-virgin olive oil
10 ml (2 tsp) balsamic vinegar
salt and pepper

**1** First make the dressing. Roughly chop the olives and sun-dried tomato. Place in a blender or food processor with the garlic, parsley and 15 ml (1 tbsp) oil. Blend to a fairly smooth paste. Transfer to a bowl and whisk in the remaining oil, vinegar and seasoning to taste.
**2** Peel the oranges, removing all the white pith, then cut into segments between the membranes (do this over a bowl to catch the juice and add it to the dressing); place the orange segments in a large bowl.
**3** Discard the tough outer layer from the fennel, then slice very thinly. Finely slice the onion.
**4** Add the fennel, onion and rocket leaves to the oranges. Pour over the dressing and toss well until evenly coated. Serve at once.

**NOTE** Blood oranges are the ideal choice for this salad when in season, as they have a delicious sweet flavour and pretty ruby-coloured flesh.

## POTATO SALAD WITH BASIL DRESSING

**SERVES 4**
PREPARATION
10 minutes, plus standing
COOKING TIME
10-12 minutes
FREEZING
Not suitable
CALS/SERVING
345

700 g (1½ lb) pink fir apple potatoes (or other firm, waxy variety)
salt and pepper
4 spring onions, trimmed
25 g (1 oz) pine nuts, toasted
DRESSING
1 small red chilli
90 ml (3 fl oz) extra-virgin olive oil
1 garlic clove, peeled and crushed
grated zest of 1 lemon
30-45 ml (2-3 tbsp) chopped fresh basil
15 ml (1 tbsp) sherry vinegar
TO GARNISH
basil sprigs

**1** Scrub the potatoes, then place in a saucepan with cold salted water to cover. Bring to the boil and simmer gently for about 10 minutes until just tender.
**2** Meanwhile, make the dressing. Halve, deseed and finely chop the chilli. Heat 30 ml (2 tbsp) of the oil in a large frying pan, add the chilli, garlic and lemon zest and fry gently for 5 minutes until soft but not golden.
**3** Blend the remaining oil with the basil, vinegar and seasoning.
**4** Drain the potatoes and shake off excess water. Add to the frying pan and stir-fry for 1 minute. Stir in the vinegar, basil and oil mixture, and remove from the heat. Set aside to cool to room temperature.
**5** Just before serving, finely chop the spring onions and stir into the potato salad with the pine nuts. Check the seasoning and serve garnished with basil sprigs.

**NOTE** If you prefer the basil to retain its vibrant colour, add it with the spring onions, just prior to serving.

## NEW POTATO AND DILL SALAD

**SERVES 6**
PREPARATION
5 minutes
COOKING TIME
10 minutes
FREEZING
Not suitable
CALS/SERVING
215
COLOUR INDEX
Page 65

900 g (2 lb) baby new potatoes
salt and pepper
60 ml (4 tbsp) chopped fresh dill
DRESSING
60 ml (4 tbsp) Greek-style yogurt
60 ml (4 tbsp) mayonnaise
20 ml (4 tsp) wholegrain mustard
5 ml (1 tsp) lemon juice

**1** Scrub the new potatoes and place in a saucepan with cold salted water to cover. Bring to the boil and simmer gently for about 10 minutes until just tender.
**2** Meanwhile, mix the ingredients for the dressing together in a bowl and season with salt and pepper to taste.
**3** Drain the potatoes and let cool slightly, then toss with the dressing and dill while still warm. Serve warm or cool.

**VARIATION** Replace dill with 4-6 chopped spring onions and 30-45 ml (2-3 tbsp) chopped parsley or chervil.

## WILD RICE AND THYME SALAD

**SERVES 6-8**
PREPARATION
15 minutes, plus standing
COOKING TIME
35 minutes
FREEZING
Not suitable
CALS/SERVING
275-210
COLOUR INDEX
Page 65

150 g (5 oz) French beans
salt and pepper
150 g (5 oz) shelled broad beans
50 g (2 oz) wild rice
175 g (6 oz) long-grain white rice
50 g (2 oz) wild or button mushrooms
50 ml (2 fl oz) sunflower oil
30 ml (2 tbsp) chopped fresh thyme
25 ml (1 fl oz) walnut oil
30 ml (2 tbsp) white wine vinegar
15 ml (1 tbsp) Dijon mustard

**1** Halve the French beans and cook in boiling salted water for 10-12 minutes or until just tender. Drain, refresh under cold running water and set aside to cool completely.
**2** Cook the broad beans in boiling water for 5-7 minutes. Drain and refresh under cold running water, slipping off the skins if wished. Set aside to cool completely.
**3** Cook the wild rice in a large pan of boiling salted water for 20 minutes, then add the white rice. Boil together for a further 15 minutes or until both are just tender. Drain and refresh under cold running water. Stir together the French beans, broad beans and rice in a large mixing bowl.
**4** Roughly slice the mushrooms. Heat the sunflower oil in a small frying pan and fry the mushrooms with the thyme for 2-3 minutes, stirring. Remove from the heat and stir in the walnut oil, vinegar, mustard and seasoning. Add the rice mixture; toss to mix. Check the seasoning. Cover and leave to stand for at least 30 minutes before serving.

**NOTE** If fresh broad beans are out of season, use frozen ones instead, or replace with other cooked beans.

## ORZO SALAD WITH PESTO SAUCE

**SERVES 4**
PREPARATION
10 minutes
COOKING TIME
5-8 minutes
FREEZING
Not suitable
CALS/SERVING
385

225 g (8 oz) orzo (see note)
salt and pepper
60 ml (4 tbsp) Pesto or Olive Pesto (see page 292)
30 ml (2 tbsp) extra-virgin olive oil
15 ml (1 tbsp) balsamic vinegar
4 large spring onions, trimmed
25 g (1 oz) sun-dried tomatoes in oil, drained
25 g (1 oz) pitted black olives
25 g (1 oz) pine nuts, toasted

**1** Bring a large saucepan of water to the boil with 5 ml (1 tsp) salt added. Add the pasta, return to the boil and boil steadily for 5-8 minutes until the orzo is *al dente* (cooked but still firm to the bite).
**2** Meanwhile, prepare the dressing. Stir the pesto, olive oil and balsamic vinegar together in a small bowl until evenly blended.
**3** Drain the pasta, transfer to a bowl and stir in the dressing. Set aside to cool.
**4** Chop the spring onions, sun-dried tomatoes and olives. Add to the orzo with the pine nuts and toss to mix. Season with salt and pepper to taste. Serve warm or cold.

**NOTE** Orzo is a tiny rice-shaped pasta, which is available from Italian delicatessens and larger supermarkets. If unobtainable, use pasta shells or twists instead.

## GINGERED RICE SALAD

**SERVES 6**
PREPARATION
15 minutes
COOKING TIME
45 minutes
FREEZING
Not suitable
CALS/SERVING
240

175 g (6 oz) brown rice
30 ml (2 tbsp) sesame oil
60 ml (4 tbsp) sunflower oil
30 ml (2 tbsp) dark soy sauce
juice of ½ orange
3 ripe tomatoes
2 spring onions, trimmed
1 red pepper
½ cucumber
2 cm (¾ inch) piece fresh root ginger
15 ml (1 tbsp) sesame seeds
salt and pepper
45 ml (3 tbsp) chopped fresh coriander
15 ml (1 tbsp) chopped fresh mint

**1** Cook the rice in twice its volume of boiling salted water for about 45 minutes until all the water is absorbed.
**2** Turn the rice into a sieve and rinse under cold running water. Drain thoroughly and turn into a large bowl. Add the oils, soy sauce and orange juice; toss well. Leave to cool.
**3** Dice the tomatoes, discarding the seeds. Chop the spring onions finely. Halve, core and deseed the pepper, then slice thinly. Halve the cucumber lengthwise, deseed, then dice the flesh. Peel and finely chop the ginger. Add the ginger, tomatoes and vegetables to the rice; mix well.
**4** Preheat a small frying pan and dry-fry the sesame seeds, stirring, until golden. Add to the salad with the coriander, mint and seasoning to taste. Toss before serving.

**NOTE** This salad is best made the day before. Keep it refrigerated, but bring to room temperature before serving. Moisten with a little more oil, if necessary.

# CLASSIC TABBOULEH

**SERVES 4**
PREPARATION
30 minutes, plus standing
FREEZING
Not suitable
CALS/SERVING
270

125 g (4 oz) bulghar wheat
90 ml (6 tbsp) extra-virgin olive oil
juice of 1 small lemon
1 garlic clove, peeled and crushed
½ cucumber
2 ripe tomatoes
6 spring onions
60 ml (4 tbsp) chopped fresh parsley
30 ml (2 tbsp) chopped fresh mint
salt and pepper
mint sprigs, to garnish

**1** Put the bulghar wheat in a bowl, add plenty of cold water to cover and leave to soak for 30 minutes.

**2** Meanwhile, put the olive oil, lemon juice and garlic in a small bowl; stir to mix and set aside until required.

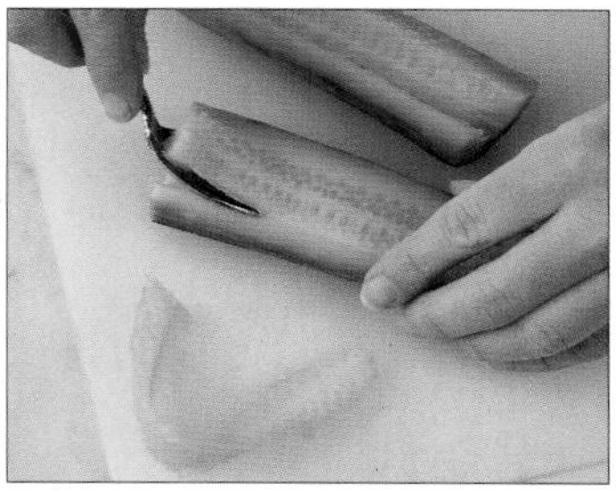

**3** Peel and halve the cucumber. Scoop out and discard the seeds, then dice the flesh.

**4** Skin the tomatoes if preferred, then dice the flesh. Trim and finely chop the spring onions.

**5** Drain the bulghar wheat thoroughly, shaking off as much excess liquid as possible.

**6** Place the bulghar wheat in a bowl with the cucumber, tomatoes, onions and herbs.

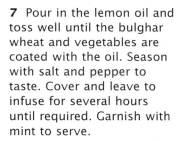

**7** Pour in the lemon oil and toss well until the bulghar wheat and vegetables are coated with the oil. Season with salt and pepper to taste. Cover and leave to infuse for several hours until required. Garnish with mint to serve.

**NOTE** This salad can be made a day ahead. Cover and leave to infuse in the refrigerator overnight.

# ACCOMPANIMENTS

## CRUNCHY-TOPPED ASPARAGUS AND COURGETTES

**SERVES 4-6**
PREPARATION
15 minutes
COOKING TIME
5-6 minutes
FREEZING
Not suitable
CALS/SERVING
445-300

225 g (8 oz) thin asparagus spears
225 g (8 oz) baby courgettes
salt and pepper
125 g (4 oz) butter
175 g (6 oz) fresh white breadcrumbs
50 g (2 oz) Parmesan cheese, freshly grated

**1** Trim the asparagus and cut into 5 cm (2 inch) lengths. Quarter the courgettes lengthwise. Add the asparagus and courgettes to a pan of boiling salted water, return to the boil and cook for 3 minutes. Drain and immediately refresh in cold water. Drain and pat dry on kitchen paper.
**2** Heat the butter in a frying pan and fry the breadcrumbs until light golden and crisp. Stir in the Parmesan cheese.
**3** Place the asparagus and courgettes in a warmed shallow flameproof dish. Cover thickly with the crumbs and place under the grill for 2-3 minutes until the topping is golden and the vegetables are heated through. Serve immediately.

**VARIATION** Replace the asparagus and/or courgettes with any other green vegetable – try broccoli florets, cauliflower, French beans, or even carrots, but be sure to half-cook them before adding the topping.

## GRILLED CHICORY AND RADICCHIO WITH ORANGE

**SERVES 4**
PREPARATION
15 minutes
COOKING TIME
10 minutes
FREEZING
Not suitable
CALS/SERVING
230
COLOUR INDEX
Page 66

2 plump heads of chicory
1 large firm head of radicchio
1 orange
olive oil, for basting
125 g (4 oz) fresh goat's cheese
a little chopped fresh thyme (optional)
pepper
30 ml (2 tbsp) pine nuts, toasted

**1** Cut the chicory in half lengthwise. Cut the radicchio into quarters. Over a bowl to catch the juice, peel the orange of all pith and cut into segments, discarding the membrane.
**2** Place the chicory and radicchio in a grill pan, cut-side up, and brush liberally with olive oil. Cook under a high grill, as close to the heat as possible, for about 3-4 minutes until just beginning to char and soften. Turn, baste with more olive oil and cook for a further 2-3 minutes.
**3** Transfer to a gratin dish, carefully turning the chicory and radicchio again. Arrange the orange segments on top and sprinkle with the reserved orange juice. Crumble the goat's cheese over the top. Brush with oil, sprinkle with thyme if using, and season with pepper. Place under the grill until the cheese is bubbling and begins to brown.
**4** Sprinkle with the toasted pine nuts to serve.

## BAKED FENNEL WITH LEMON AND OLIVES

**SERVES 4**
PREPARATION
10 minutes
COOKING TIME
45 minutes
FREEZING
Not suitable
CALS/SERVING
225
COLOUR INDEX
Page 66

3 large, or 4 medium fennel bulbs, trimmed
grated zest and juice of 1 lemon
90 ml (6 tbsp) olive oil
salt and pepper
12 black or green olives
30 ml (2 tbsp) chopped fresh parsley

**1** Halve the fennel lengthwise and remove the core; cut larger bulbs into quarters. Place cut-side up in a baking dish.
**2** Mix the lemon zest and juice with the olive oil, salt and pepper. Pour over the fennel and scatter the olives on top.
**3** Bake in the oven at 200°C (400°F) Mark 6 for 15 minutes. Turn the fennel and bake for a further 15 minutes. Turn once more and bake for a final 15 minutes until tender. Sprinkle with the parsley to serve.

**NOTE** For a softer texture, blanch the fennel in boiling water for 2 minutes and drain well before baking.

# FENNEL GRATIN

**SERVES 6**
PREPARATION
10 minutes
COOKING TIME
20-25 minutes
FREEZING
Not suitable
CALS/SERVING
305

3 fennel bulbs, trimmed
300 ml (½ pint) vegetable stock
25 g (1 oz) butter
1 bunch of spring onions, trimmed
1 garlic clove, peeled and crushed
30 ml (2 tbsp) chopped fresh fennel fronds or dill
300 ml (½ pint) double cream
50 g (2 oz) Cheddar cheese, grated
pepper

**1** Cut the fennel bulbs lengthwise into 5 mm (¼ inch) thick slices and place in a large shallow pan. Pour over the stock, add half of the butter and bring to the boil. Cover and simmer for 10-15 minutes until the fennel is just tender.
**2** Meanwhile, finely chop the spring onions. Melt the remaining butter in a saucepan, add the garlic and spring onions and fry gently for 5 minutes until softened. Stir in the fennel fronds or dill.
**3** Remove the poached fennel with a slotted spoon and drain on kitchen paper. Add 150 ml (¼ pint) of the cooking liquid to the spring onions. Pour in the cream, bring to the boil and simmer very gently for 1 minute. Remove from the heat and stir in the cheese and pepper.
**4** Arrange the fennel in a gratin dish in a double layer. Pour over the cream mixture and grill for 1-2 minutes until bubbling and golden.

**NOTE** If you are fortunate enough to buy fennel with the feathery leaves still attached to the bulb, use these – otherwise dill makes a good substitute.

# STIR-FRIED SUMMER VEGETABLES

**SERVES 4-6**
PREPARATION
15 minutes
COOKING TIME
7-8 minutes
FREEZING
Not suitable
CALS/SERVING
160-110
COLOUR INDEX
Page 66

1 large yellow pepper
125 g (4 oz) baby courgettes
125 g (4 oz) patty pan squashes (optional)
125 g (4 oz) baby carrots
125 g (4 oz) thin asparagus spears
125 g (4 oz) cherry tomatoes
2 garlic cloves
15 ml (1 tbsp) sunflower oil
15 ml (1 tbsp) olive oil
90 ml (3 fl oz) vegetable stock
salt and pepper
30 ml (2 tbsp) balsamic or sherry vinegar
5 ml (1 tsp) sesame oil
15 ml (1 tbsp) sesame seeds, toasted

**1** Halve, core and deseed the pepper, then cut into long triangular shapes. Halve the courgettes lengthwise. If using patty pans, cut them in half. Trim the carrots and peel if necessary, leaving on a tuft of stalk. Trim the asparagus spears. Halve the cherry tomatoes. Peel and roughly chop the garlic.
**2** Add the yellow pepper and carrots to a pan of boiling salted water and blanch for 2 minutes, then remove with a slotted spoon and refresh in cold water. Drain well and pat dry on kitchen paper.
**3** Heat a wok or deep frying pan until smoking, swirl in the sunflower and olive oils, then add the garlic and stir-fry for 20 seconds. Add all of the vegetables and stir-fry over a high heat for 1 minute. Add the tomatoes, stock and seasoning to taste. Stir-fry for 3-4 minutes until the vegetables are just tender.
**4** Add the balsamic vinegar and sesame oil, toss well and sprinkle with the sesame seeds. Serve immediately.

**NOTE** These are just a selection of the vegetables available throughout the summer: try other combinations, but always blanch or par-cook harder ones first.

**VARIATION** For a winter vegetable stir-fry, use 125 g (4 oz) each of cauliflower florets, broccoli florets and carrot sticks, plus 2-3 spring onions, sliced, and a little chopped fresh root ginger.

## ROAST SWEET PEPPERS WITH SAGE

**SERVES 4**
PREPARATION
20 minutes
COOKING TIME
20-25 minutes
FREEZING
Not suitable
CALS/SERVING
170

2 large red peppers
2 large orange or yellow peppers
1 small onion
1 garlic clove
30 ml (2 tbsp) olive oil
about 8 fresh sage leaves
300 ml (½ pint) vegetable stock
25 g (1 oz) pine nuts, toasted
coarse sea salt and pepper

**1** Place the peppers on a grill rack and grill, turning frequently, for 15-20 minutes until the skin is blistered and blackened. Cover with a damp cloth and leave to cool slightly.
**2** In the meantime, peel and chop the onion; peel and finely slice the garlic. Heat the oil in a small saucepan, add the onion and garlic and cook gently until softened. Add the sage leaves and cook over a moderate heat for 2-3 minutes until frazzled. Remove the sage with a slotted spoon and set aside. Add the stock to the pan and boil rapidly until reduced to a quarter of the original volume.
**3** When the peppers are ready, peel away the skins. Cut off the stalk, then halve the peppers and scrape out the core and seeds. Cut the peppers into broad strips, add to the garlic and onion mixture and toss lightly to mix.
**4** Arrange the peppers on a warmed serving dish and sprinkle with the toasted pine nuts and frazzled sage leaves. Serve immediately.

## BROAD BEANS IN A CREAM HERB SAUCE

**SERVES 4-6**
PREPARATION
20 minutes
COOKING TIME
20 minutes
FREEZING
Not suitable
CALS/SERVING
385-260
COLOUR INDEX
Page 67

2 garlic cloves
4 shallots
50 g (2 oz) butter
450 g (1 lb) shelled fresh or frozen broad beans (see note)
150 ml (¼ pint) vegetable stock
200 ml (7 fl oz) double cream
30 ml (2 tbsp) chopped fresh chervil or chives
30 ml (2 tbsp) chopped fresh parsley
grated zest of 1 lemon
salt and pepper

**1** Peel and finely chop the garlic and shallots. Melt the butter in a saucepan, add the garlic and shallots and cook gently for 3 minutes. Stir in the broad beans and stock. Bring to the boil, cover and simmer gently for 12-15 minutes, until the beans are tender. Drain, reserving the liquid.
**2** Pour the reserved cooking liquid into a blender or food processor, add 60 ml (4 tbsp) of the beans and blend to a purée, gradually adding the cream through the feeder tube to make a smooth sauce. Return to the pan.
**3** Add the rest of the broad beans, herbs, lemon zest and salt and pepper to taste. Reheat gently to serve.

**NOTE** Tender, fresh baby broad beans are best for this dish, or use frozen baby beans and skin before cooking.

## ROAST TOMATOES WITH A GARLIC CRUST

**SERVES 6**
PREPARATION
15 minutes
COOKING TIME
15-20 minutes
FREEZING
Not suitable
CALS/SERVING
185
COLOUR INDEX
Page 67

6 slices day-old bread
6 garlic cloves
45 ml (3 tbsp) chopped fresh parsley
salt and pepper
700 g (1½ lb) cherry or manhattan tomatoes
olive oil, for basting
chopped parsley, to garnish (optional)

**1** Break up the bread, place in a food processor or blender and process until you have fine breadcrumbs: there should be approximately 125 g (4 oz). Place in a heavy-based frying pan and dry-fry over a moderate heat until golden.
**2** Peel and finely chop the garlic. Add to the breadcrumbs with the parsley and salt and pepper to taste; stir to mix.
**3** Place the tomatoes in a shallow roasting tin or baking dish, positioning them close together and in a single layer. Sprinkle the breadcrumbs evenly over the tomatoes and drizzle liberally with olive oil.
**4** Bake in the oven at 220°C (425°F) Mark 7 for 15-20 minutes until the crust is golden and the tomatoes are soft; the tomatoes will have disintegrated slightly under the crust. Scatter with more parsley to serve if you like.

**VARIATION** Instead of cherry tomatoes, use halved plum tomatoes. Place cut-side up in the dish.

## MINTED PEAS WITH CUCUMBER AND SPRING ONIONS

**SERVES 4-6**
PREPARATION
5 minutes
COOKING TIME
About 10 minutes
FREEZING
Not suitable
CALS/SERVING
350-230

- 1 bunch of spring onions
- 175 g (6 oz) cucumber
- 450 g (1 lb) shelled fresh peas (see note)
- salt and pepper
- 50 g (2 oz) butter
- 150 ml (¼ pint) crème fraîche
- 45 ml (3 tbsp) dry vermouth, such as Noilly Prat
- 30 ml (2 tbsp) chopped fresh mint
- pinch of sugar
- mint sprigs, to garnish

**1** Trim and slice the spring onions. Halve the cucumber lengthwise, scrape out the seeds and slice thickly.
**2** Add the peas to a pan of boiling salted water and cook for 5-10 minutes until tender; drain.
**3** Meanwhile, heat the butter in a frying pan, add the spring onions and cucumber and sauté for 3 minutes. Add the crème fraîche and vermouth and bring to the boil. Let bubble for 2-3 minutes.
**4** Add the peas, mint and sugar. Season generously with salt and pepper and toss to mix. Serve at once, garnished with mint.

**NOTE** Frozen peas can be used when fresh ones are out of season. Adjust the cooking time accordingly.

## RUNNER BEANS WITH HAZELNUT BUTTER

**SERVES 4-6**
PREPARATION
15 minutes
COOKING TIME
20 minutes
FREEZING
Not suitable
CALS/SERVING
210-140

- 700 g (1½ lb) tender runner beans
- 50 g (2 oz) hazelnuts
- salt and pepper
- 50 g (2 oz) butter
- lemon juice, to taste

**1** Trim the beans, then slice thinly on the diagonal. Chop the hazelnuts roughly.
**2** Add the runner beans to a pan of boiling salted water. Bring back to the boil and cook for 3-4 minutes, until just tender.
**3** Meanwhile, melt the butter in a frying pan, add the hazelnuts and cook until golden.
**4** Drain the runner beans and immediately splash with a little cold water (see note). Toss the beans with the hazelnuts and lemon juice to taste. Serve at once, seasoned with coarsely ground black pepper.

**NOTE** Splashing the beans with half a cupful of cold water after cooking helps to preserve their bright green colour.

## SPICY GRILLED AUBERGINES

**SERVES 4**
PREPARATION
25 minutes, plus standing
COOKING TIME
15-20 minutes
FREEZING
Not suitable
CALS/SERVING
125

2 medium aubergines, or 4 baby ones
salt and pepper
2 garlic cloves
1 green chilli
15 ml (1 tbsp) chopped fresh rosemary
finely grated zest and juice of 1 lemon
45 ml (3 tbsp) chopped fresh parsley
olive oil, for basting

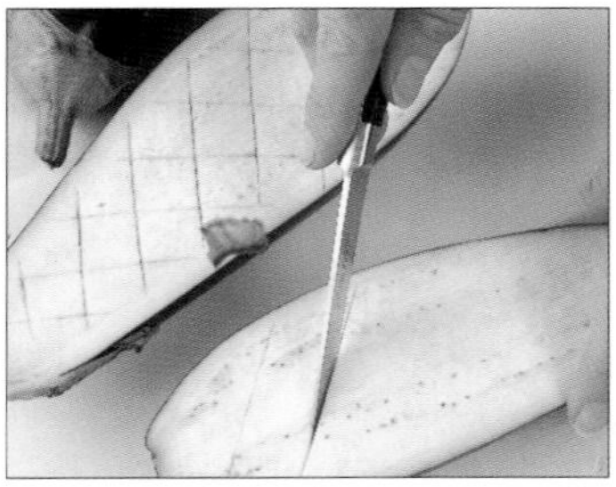

**1** Trim the aubergines and cut in half lengthwise. Deeply score the flesh in a criss-cross pattern, cutting almost, but not quite through to the skin. Sprinkle generously with salt and leave to degorge for 20 minutes.

**2** Meanwhile, peel and finely chop the garlic. Chop the chilli, discarding the seeds if a milder flavour is preferred. Mix the chilli, garlic, rosemary, lemon zest and parsley together in a small bowl.

**3** Rinse the aubergines thoroughly and pat dry with kitchen paper. Brush the scored sides with olive oil and place, cut-side uppermost, on the grill rack. Grill – not too close to the heat – for 10 minutes (see note).

**4** Spread with the herb mixture and drizzle with a little more olive oil. Position closer to the heat and grill for a further 5-10 minutes or until the aubergines are tender, brushing with oil occasionally. Sprinkle with a little lemon juice and olive oil to serve.

**NOTES**

❑ If you're short of time you could omit the degorging, but it does draw out any bitter juices and reduces the amount of oil the aubergines absorb during cooking.

❑ If the aubergines are quite plump, increase the initial cooking time to 15-20 minutes.

**VARIATION** Replace the chilli and herb topping with Coriander Pesto (see page 292). Spread on the aubergines and grill as above.

## HONEY-GLAZED SHALLOTS

**SERVES 4**
PREPARATION
15 minutes, plus standing
COOKING TIME
25 minutes
FREEZING
Not suitable
CALS/SERVING
95
COLOUR INDEX
Page 67

450 g (1 lb) shallots
25 g (1 oz) butter
15 ml (1 tbsp) thin honey
juice of ½ lemon
15 ml (1 tbsp) Worcestershire sauce
15 ml (1 tbsp) balsamic vinegar
salt and pepper

**1** Put the shallots in a bowl, pour on cold water to cover and leave to soak for 20 minutes; this makes it easier to peel them. Drain and peel away the skins.
**2** Put the shallots in a pan and add just enough cold water to cover. Bring to the boil, lower the heat and simmer for 5 minutes. Drain well and return to the pan.
**3** Add all of the remaining ingredients and stir until the shallots are well coated with the glaze. Cover and cook over a low heat, stirring occasionally until the shallots are tender.
**4** Remove the lid and let bubble for 2-3 minutes until the liquid is reduced and syrupy.

# OKRA WITH ONION AND TOMATO

**SERVES 4**
PREPARATION
20 minutes
COOKING TIME
25 minutes
FREEZING
Not suitable
CALS/SERVING
175

2 medium onions
45 ml (3 tbsp) ghee or oil
2 garlic cloves
2.5 cm (1 inch) piece fresh root ginger
1 chilli (optional)
3 tomatoes
450 g (1 lb) okra
10 ml (2 tsp) ground coriander
2.5 ml (½ tsp) turmeric
2.5 ml (½ tsp) ground cinnamon
salt and pepper
30 ml (2 tbsp) thick yogurt
30 ml (2 tbsp) chopped fresh coriander

MASALA SPICE MIX
15 ml (1 tbsp) coriander seeds
15 ml (1 tbsp) cumin seeds
10 ml (2 tsp) black peppercorns
3 dried red chillies

**1** First make the masala spice mix. Dry-fry the spices in a small frying pan for about 3 minutes until they begin to pop and release their aroma; stir frequently to ensure that they don't burn. Let cool slightly, then grind using a pestle and mortar or spice grinder. Store in an airtight jar until required (see note).
**2** Peel the onions. Halve and thinly slice one onion; quarter the other. Heat the ghee or oil in a frying pan, add the sliced onion and cook over a medium heat for about 10 minutes until dark golden brown and crisp. Drain on kitchen paper and set aside. Reserve the oil in the pan.
**3** Peel and roughly chop the garlic and ginger. Slice the chilli if using, discarding the seeds if a milder flavour is preferred. Skin the tomatoes if preferred; chop the flesh.
**4** Trim the okra, removing a small piece from each end; do not cut into the flesh, or the dish will acquire an unpleasant glutinous texture during cooking.
**5** Put the quartered onion, garlic and ginger in a blender with 15 ml (1 tbsp) water and process until smooth. Add the spices and process again.
**6** Reheat the ghee or oil remaining in the frying pan, add the onion paste and cook over a high heat for 2 minutes, stirring all the time. Lower the heat and cook for 5 minutes or until the onion paste is golden brown and softened.
**7** Add the chopped tomatoes, with the chilli if using. Season with salt and pepper to taste. Cook for 5 minutes until the tomato has reduced down, then add the okra and stir to coat in the mixture. Cover and simmer gently for about 5 minutes until the okra is just tender.
**8** Stir in the yogurt, a spoonful at a time, then add the coriander and heat through gently. Transfer to a serving dish and sprinkle with the crisp onions and a little of the masala spice mix to serve.

**NOTE** The quantity of masala spice mix is more than you need for this recipe, but it can be stored in an airtight jar and used as required. If you're short of time you could omit the spice mix and simply serve the okra sprinkled with the crisp-fried onions.

# RED CABBAGE WITH PINE NUTS

**SERVES 8**
PREPARATION
10 minutes
COOKING TIME
25 minutes
FREEZING
Not suitable
CALS/SERVING
135
COLOUR INDEX
Page 68

900 g (2 lb) red cabbage
2.5 cm (1 inch) piece fresh root ginger (optional)
30 ml (2 tbsp) olive oil
150 ml (¼ pint) light vegetable stock
salt and pepper
40 g (1½ oz) butter (optional)
30 ml (2 tbsp) balsamic vinegar
50 g (2 oz) pine nuts, toasted

**1** Halve the cabbage, remove the core, then shred finely. Peel and grate the ginger, if using. Heat the oil in a large saucepan and sauté the cabbage with the ginger, if using, over a high heat for 3-4 minutes until reduced in bulk, stirring occasionally.
**2** Add the stock and seasoning and bring to the boil. Cover and cook over a low heat for about 20 minutes, until just tender, stirring occasionally.
**3** Uncover and let bubble to reduce any excess liquid. Off the heat, stir in the butter if using, balsamic vinegar and pine nuts. Check the seasoning before serving.

# SWEET POTATO AND CHESTNUT CAKES WITH SPRING ONIONS

**SERVES 4-6**
PREPARATION
30 minutes, plus chilling
COOKING TIME
30 minutes
FREEZING
Suitable: Stage 4
CALS/SERVING
570-380

450 g (1 lb) sweet potatoes (see note)
225 g (8 oz) vacuum-packed chestnuts
6 spring onions
75 g (3 oz) butter
30 ml (2 tbsp) chopped fresh parsley
2.5 ml (½ tsp) ground mace
salt and pepper
flour, for coating
1 large egg, beaten
125 g (4 oz) fresh white breadcrumbs
sunflower oil, for shallow-frying
parsley sprigs, to garnish

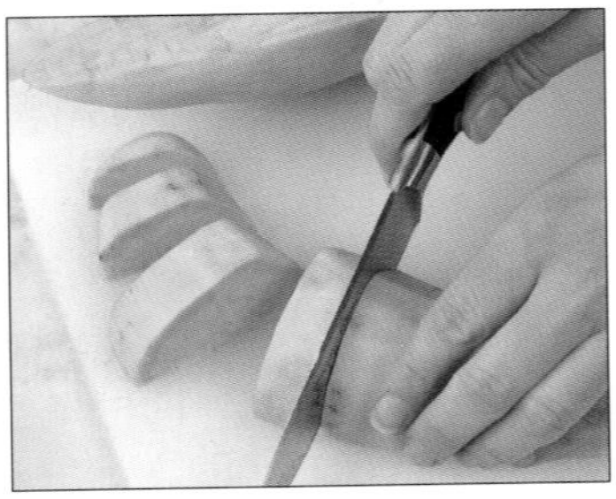

**1** Peel the sweet potatoes and cut into large chunks. Place in a steamer and steam for 15-20 minutes until tender. Remove the basket from the steamer and let rest for 2-3 minutes to allow excess moisture to evaporate.

**2** Place the potatoes and chestnuts in a bowl and mash until smooth. Trim and slice the spring onions.

**3** Heat the butter in a frying pan and add the spring onions. Fry for 1 minute until beginning to soften, then add to the potato with the parsley and mix well. Season with the mace, and salt and pepper to taste. Work the ingredients until the mixture comes together.

**4** Divide the mixture into eight and roll each portion into a ball. Flatten each one to make a thick cake. Transfer to a baking sheet and chill in the refrigerator for at least 30 minutes.

**5** Season a little flour and use to lightly coat the cakes. Dip each one into beaten egg, then coat with the breadcrumbs. Chill in the refrigerator for 30 minutes to set.

**6** Heat a 1 cm (½ inch) depth of oil in a frying pan until a breadcrumb dropped into the pan sizzles in 30 seconds. Fry the cakes in batches on both sides until golden. Drain on kitchen paper. Serve immediately, garnished with parsley.

## NOTES

❑ There are two kinds of sweet potato – one has a purply skin and orange flesh, the other has a brown skin and white flesh. Both taste good but the orange-fleshed variety has the edge.
❑ Avoid using canned chestnuts in brine – they will be too watery.

## VARIATIONS

❑ For a less rich version, use plain mashed potato rather than sweet potato.
❑ Serve with a Tomato Sauce (see page 291) and a crisp salad – as a light meal rather than an accompaniment.

## BABY CARROTS WITH BASIL

**SERVES 6**
PREPARATION
5 minutes
COOKING TIME
5-10 minutes
FREEZING
Not suitable
CALS/SERVING
90
COLOUR INDEX
Page 68

700 g (1½ lb) baby carrots
salt and pepper
75 ml (5 tbsp) double cream
60 ml (4 tbsp) roughly torn fresh basil

**1** Trim the carrots and peel if necessary, leaving on a tuft of stalk. Cook in boiling salted water for about 5 minutes, until almost tender. Drain thoroughly.
**2** Return the carrots to the pan and add the cream and basil. Lower the heat and cook for about 2 minutes, stirring occasionally. Season generously with salt and pepper and serve at once.

## PARSNIPS IN A LIME GLAZE

**SERVES 4**
PREPARATION
5 minutes
COOKING TIME
15 minutes
FREEZING
Not suitable
CALS/SERVING
225
COLOUR INDEX
Page 68

700 g (1½ lb) parsnips
1 lime
50 g (2 oz) butter
25 g (1 oz) light muscovado sugar
coarse sea salt and pepper
thyme sprigs, to garnish

**1** Peel the parsnips and cut in half lengthwise. (If using older, tougher parsnips cut into quarters and remove the woody core.) Add to a pan of boiling salted water and cook for 5 minutes.
**2** Meanwhile, using a zester or a vegetable peeler, carefully pare thin slivers of rind from the lime; set aside for the garnish. Halve the lime and squeeze the juice.
**3** Melt the butter in a large saucepan together with the sugar. Add the lime juice and heat gently, stirring, to dissolve the sugar.
**4** Drain the parsnips thoroughly in a colander, then add to the lime mixture in the saucepan. Toss in the buttery lime mixture and cook over a moderate heat, shaking the pan frequently, for approximately 10 minutes until golden brown. Season with salt and pepper to taste.
**5** Transfer to a warmed serving dish and garnish with the slivers of lime zest and thyme sprigs.

**VARIATIONS**
❑ Replace 1 parsnip with 3 eddoes. Peel and halve the eddoes and cook with the parsnips.
❑ Use carrots or turnips instead of parsnips.
❑ For added crunch, toss a handful of walnuts in towards the end of the cooking time.

## ROASTED WINTER VEGETABLES WITH CARDAMOM

**SERVES 6-8**
PREPARATION
20 minutes
COOKING TIME
About 1 hour
FREEZING
Not suitable
CALS/SERVING
355-265

350 g (12 oz) carrots
350 g (12 oz) parsnips
350 g (12 oz) celeriac
350 g (12 oz) sweet potato
150 ml (¼ pint) olive oil
4 cardamom pods, lightly crushed
15 ml (1 tbsp) soft brown sugar
coarse sea salt and pepper

**1** Peel all of the vegetables. Quarter the carrots and parsnips lengthwise. Cut the celeriac and sweet potato into chunks.
**2** Heat the olive oil in a roasting tin and add the vegetables, turning them to coat well. Roast in the oven at 200°C (400°F) Mark 6 for 30 minutes, turning the vegetables twice during cooking.
**3** Add the crushed cardamom pods and sugar to the vegetables, turning them to coat evenly. Return to the oven and bake for a further 30 minutes, until well browned and completely soft, but not disintegrating.
**4** Season liberally with coarse sea salt and pepper and transfer to a warmed serving dish to serve.

**VARIATION** For a more distinctive flavour, replace the brown sugar with maple syrup or honey.

## POTATO PARSNIP GALETTE

**SERVES 6**
PREPARATION
25 minutes
COOKING TIME
45-50 minutes
FREEZING
Not suitable
CALS/SERVING
340

900 g (2 lb) firm potatoes, such as Desirée, Romano, Estima or Wilja
225 g (8 oz) young parsnips
75 g (3 oz) unsalted butter
45 ml (3 tbsp) thin honey
30 ml (2 tbsp) lemon juice
freshly grated nutmeg
salt and pepper

**1** Peel the potatoes and parsnips. Slice them very thinly either by hand, with a mandolin, or in a food processor; do not rinse the potatoes. Divide the potatoes into three equal portions; don't worry if they discolour a little.
**2** To clarify the butter, slowly melt it in a small pan, then skim off any white residue or foam; keep warm. Heat the honey and lemon juice together in a small pan; keep warm.
**3** Pour 30 ml (2 tbsp) butter into a heavy 20 cm (8 inch) non-stick frying pan, suitable for oven use (see note). Layer one third of the potatoes over the bottom of the pan in neat overlapping circles, seasoning well.
**4** Lay half the sliced parsnips over the potato layer. Brush with the honey and lemon juice, and season with nutmeg, salt and pepper.
**5** Cover with another third of the potato slices, brushing with butter and seasoning well. Layer the remaining parsnips on top. Brush with the remaining honey and lemon juice, and season with nutmeg, salt and pepper. Cover with the rest of the potato slices, melted butter and seasoning.
**6** Place the pan over a medium heat and cook carefully for about 5 minutes or until the underside begins to turn golden. Test by carefully lifting up the edge with a palette knife.
**7** Press the potatoes down firmly and cover with a lid or buttered kitchen foil. Bake in the oven at 200°C (400°F) Mark 6 for 40-45 minutes or until the potatoes and parsnips are tender when pierced with a sharp knife and the underside is a deep golden brown.
**8** Loosen the galette with a palette knife. Place a warmed serving plate over the pan and quickly invert the galette onto the dish. Serve immediately.

**NOTE** Ideally you need a non-stick frying pan with an integral metal handle which can therefore be placed in the oven, such as Le Creuset. Alternatively, use a moule à manque pan instead, buttering it well.

## ROSTI WITH GARLIC AND THYME

**SERVES 6**
PREPARATION
20 minutes
COOKING TIME
35-40 minutes
FREEZING
Not suitable
CALS/SERVING
240
COLOUR INDEX
Page 69

700 g (1½ lb) potatoes
6 garlic cloves, peeled and crushed
30 ml (2 tbsp) chopped fresh thyme
salt and pepper
125 g (4 oz) unsalted butter

**1** Peel the potatoes and immerse in a bowl of cold water. Drain the potatoes, slice thinly, then cut into thin sticks, a little thicker than matchsticks. Place in a bowl; it won't matter if they discolour a little.
**2** Add the garlic and thyme to the potato matchsticks and toss well. Season liberally with salt and pepper.
**3** To clarify the butter, slowly melt the butter in a small pan, then skim off any impurities. Keep warm.
**4** Pour 30 ml (2 tbsp) of the butter into a heavy-based 25 cm (10 inch) non-stick frying pan, suitable for use in the oven (see above note). Transfer the potato sticks to the pan, spread evenly and press down firmly to form a 'cake'. Pour over the remaining butter. Cook over a moderate heat for 5 minutes or until the underside is golden; to check, carefully lift up the edge with a palette knife.
**5** Press the potatoes down firmly once more and cover with a lid or a buttered sheet of foil. Bake in the oven at 200°C (400°F) Mark 6 for 25-30 minutes, or until the potatoes are tender when pierced with a sharp knife and the underside is a deep golden brown.
**6** Place a lid or plate on top of the potato cake, invert onto the lid and slide back into the pan. Cook over a medium heat for 5 minutes, or until golden and crisp. Loosen the cake with a palette knife so that it moves freely.
**7** Place a warmed serving plate over the pan and invert the potato cake onto the plate. Serve immediately.

## POTATO GRATIN

**SERVES 4-6**
PREPARATION
15-20 minutes
COOKING TIME
1¼ hours
FREEZING
Suitable
CALS/SERVING
460-305

450 ml (¾ pint) milk
150 ml (¼ pint) double cream
2 bay leaves, bruised
2 fresh rosemary sprigs, bruised
2 strips lemon zest, bruised
pinch of saffron strands
900 g (2 lb) even-sized, small waxy potatoes
1 small onion
2 garlic cloves
25 g (1 oz) butter, diced
salt and pepper

**1** Put the milk, cream, bay leaves, rosemary and lemon zest into a saucepan. Bring slowly to the boil, remove from the heat, stir in the saffron and set aside to infuse for 10 minutes.
**2** Meanwhile, peel the potatoes, then cut into wafer-thin slices, using a mandolin or a food processor fitted with a fine slicing blade.
**3** Peel and grate the onion. Peel and finely chop the garlic.
**4** Arrange a layer of potatoes over the base of a 1.5 litre (2½ pint) gratin dish. Scatter over some of the onion, garlic and butter and season well. Repeat the layers, finishing with a layer of potatoes and a few pieces of butter.
**5** Strain the infused cream over the potatoes, pressing the herbs and lemon down well to extract as much flavour as possible. Cover the dish with foil, place on a baking sheet and bake in the oven at 200°C (400°F) Mark 6 for 1 hour. Remove the foil and bake for a further 15-20 minutes until the potatoes are softened and the top is golden brown.

**NOTE** Slice the potatoes as evenly as possible, to ensure that they will cook evenly.

## SAGE HACKLE BACKS

**SERVES 6**
PREPARATION
10 minutes
COOKING TIME
1-1¼ hours
FREEZING
Not suitable
CALS/SERVING
325

6 large baking potatoes, each 300-350 g (10-12 oz)
90 ml (6 tbsp) olive oil
30 ml (2 tbsp) chopped fresh sage
2 garlic cloves, peeled and crushed
grated zest of ½ lemon
salt and pepper

**1** Peel the potatoes and cut a thin slice off one side of each – so they will sit flat. Using a sharp knife, cut vertical slits in each potato at tiny intervals without cutting all the way through. Place in a roasting tin.
**2** Combine the rest of the ingredients in a small bowl. Carefully spoon over the potatoes, allowing some of the garlic and sage to slip down into the slits.
**3** Bake in the oven at 200°C (400°F) Mark 6 for 1-1¼ hours, basting from time to time until the potatoes are well crisped, golden and cooked through.

## NEW POTATOES WITH PEAS AND BROAD BEANS

**SERVES 4**
PREPARATION
5 minutes
COOKING TIME
20 minutes
FREEZING
Not suitable
CALS/SERVING
275
COLOUR INDEX
Page 69

700 g (1½ lb) small new potatoes
salt and pepper
200 g (7 oz) shelled fresh peas
200 g (7 oz) shelled fresh broad beans
40 g (1½ oz) butter
pinch of sugar
75 ml (5 tbsp) water
45 ml (3 tbsp) chopped fresh parsley, preferably flat-leaf

**1** Cook the new potatoes in a large pan of boiling salted water for about 15 minutes until tender, then drain and set aside.
**2** In the meantime, place the peas and broad beans in a large frying pan with the butter, sugar and water. Bring to the boil, cover and simmer for 10 minutes.
**3** Remove the lid from the pan, add the potatoes and simmer until all the liquid has evaporated. Season well and stir in the chopped parsley. Serve at once.

## CREAMY BAKED POTATOES WITH MUSTARD SEEDS

**SERVES 6**
PREPARATION
15-20 minutes
COOKING TIME
1¼ hours
FREEZING
Suitable: Stage 3
CALS/SERVING
330
COLOUR INDEX
Page 69

6 baking potatoes, about 1.4 kg (3 lb) in total
30 ml (2 tbsp) sun-flower oil
15 ml (1 tbsp) coarse sea salt
4-5 large garlic cloves, unpeeled
50 g (2 oz) butter
90 ml (6 tbsp) crème fraîche
30 ml (2 tbsp) mustard seeds, toasted and lightly crushed
salt and pepper
oregano or parsley sprigs, to garnish

**1** Prick the potato skins, rub with oil and sprinkle with salt. Bake in the oven at 200°C (400°F) Mark 6 for 40 minutes. Add the garlic cloves and cook for 20 minutes.
**2** Slice the tops off the potatoes and scoop out the flesh into a warm bowl, leaving 1 cm (½ inch) shells.
**3** Squeeze the garlic out of the skins and add to the potato flesh with the butter, crème fraîche and mustard seeds. Mash together and season generously with salt and pepper. Pile the mixture back into the hollowed-out potato skins.
**4** Return to the oven for 20-25 minutes or until hot through to the centre. Serve garnished with oregano or parsley sprigs.

**NOTE** If frozen, thaw overnight at cool room temperature, then bake at 200°C (400°F) Mark 6 for 20-25 minutes.

## STEAMED BASIL AND MUSTARD SEED RICE

**SERVES 4**
PREPARATION
10 minutes
COOKING TIME
25 minutes
FREEZING
Not suitable
CALS/SERVING
270

225 g (8 oz) basmati rice
12 large basil leaves
30 ml (2 tbsp) sunflower oil
30 ml (2 tbsp) black mustard seeds
5 ml (1 tsp) salt
300 ml (½ pint) water
basil leaves, to garnish

**1** Wash the rice in several changes of cold water or in a sieve under cold running water until the water runs clear. Drain well. Shred the basil leaves or tear into pieces.
**2** Heat the oil in a medium non-stick saucepan and add the mustard seeds. Cook for a few minutes until the seeds start to pop.
**3** Stir in the rice, salt and water. Bring to the boil, stir, then boil rapidly until the water has evaporated and there are steam holes all over the surface.
**4** Stir in all but 15 ml (1 tbsp) of the basil and cover very tightly, so no steam can escape. Set on a simmering mat (see note) over a very low heat for 15 minutes for the rice to swell. Fluff up with a fork, adding the reserved basil. Serve immediately, garnished with basil leaves.

**NOTE** A simmering mat is used here to ensure the heat is very low and evenly distributed. You can obtain one of these mats from a cookshop or hardware store. If you don't have one make sure the heat is kept to a minimum and add a little more water if necessary to prevent the rice sticking.

## SOFT POLENTA WITH SAGE BUTTER

**SERVES 4**
PREPARATION
10 minutes
COOKING TIME
10 minutes
FREEZING
Not suitable
CALS/SERVING
425

POLENTA
750 ml (1¼ pints) water
5 ml (1 tsp) salt
15 g (½ oz) butter
125 g (4 oz) quick-cook polenta
50 g (2 oz) Parmesan cheese, freshly grated

SAGE BUTTER
1 small garlic clove
125 g (4 oz) unsalted butter
15 ml (1 tbsp) roughly chopped fresh sage
pinch of cayenne pepper
TO SERVE
extra Parmesan cheese

**1** First prepare the sage butter. Peel and slice the garlic. Melt the butter in a small saucepan, add the garlic and cook gently for 30 seconds, then remove with a slotted spoon.

**2** Add the chopped sage and cayenne pepper to the butter and fry for about 1 minute until the butter is golden and the sage softened. Keep warm.

**3** To make the polenta, bring the water to a rolling boil in a large saucepan. Add the salt and butter, then gradually whisk in the polenta, making sure that no lumps form. Lower the heat and cook gently for 8-10 minutes, stirring constantly with a wooden spoon.

**4** As soon as the polenta starts to come away from the sides of the pan, remove from the heat and stir in the Parmesan. Spoon into warmed serving bowls and pour a little of the sage butter over each portion. Serve at once, sprinkled with a little extra Parmesan and pepper.

**VARIATION** Turn the cooked polenta into a greased baking tin, smooth the surface and leave until set. Cut the set polenta into slices and fry or grill until golden. Serve drizzled with the sage butter.

## SUMMER VEGETABLE COUSCOUS

**SERVES 8**
PREPARATION
15 minutes
COOKING TIME
10 minutes
FREEZING
Not suitable
CALS/SERVING
370
COLOUR INDEX
Page 69

350 g (12 oz) quick-cook couscous
600 ml (1 pint) boiling water
225 g (8 oz) broccoli
225 g (8 oz) fennel, trimmed
125 g (4 oz) mangetout, trimmed
125 g (4 oz) petit pois
salt and pepper
DRESSING
grated zest of 1 lemon
75 ml (5 tbsp) lemon juice
175 ml (6 fl oz) olive oil
60 ml (4 tbsp) whole-grain mustard
30 ml (2 tbsp) thin honey
1 bunch of spring onions, trimmed
1 bunch of chives, snipped

**1** Place the couscous in a bowl and pour over the boiling water. Cover with foil and leave to stand for about 10 minutes until all of the water is absorbed.
**2** Meanwhile, cut the broccoli into small florets; halve, core and slice the fennel. Blanch the broccoli, fennel, mangetout and petit pois together in boiling salted water for about 2-3minutes.
**3** Meanwhile, prepare the dressing. In a bowl, whisk together the lemon zest and juice, oil, mustard, honey and seasoning. Chop the spring onions and stir into the dressing with the chives.
**4** Drain the blanched vegetables and fold into the warm couscous, together with the dressing. Fork through and serve immediately.

# Desserts

## APPLE FRITTERS WITH HONEY CREAM

**SERVES 4**
PREPARATION
15 minutes, plus resting
COOKING TIME
3-4 minutes
FREEZING
Not suitable
CALS/SERVING
560

1 egg, separated
50 g (2 oz) plain white flour
25 g (1 oz) caster sugar
1.25 ml (¼ tsp) ground cloves
90 ml (3 fl oz) apple juice
4 large eating apples
oil, for deep-frying

HONEY CREAM
200 ml (7 fl oz) double cream
30 ml (2 tbsp) thin honey
15 ml (1 tbsp) lemon juice

TO FINISH
icing sugar, for dusting

**1** Put the egg yolk, flour, sugar, cloves and apple juice in a bowl and beat until smooth. Cover and set aside for 30 minutes.

**2** For the honey cream, whip the cream until it almost holds its shape, then fold in the honey and lemon juice. Chill.

**3** When required, heat a 10 cm (4 inch) depth of oil in a deep saucepan until it registers 180°C (350°F) on a sugar thermometer, or until a cube of bread dropped in the oil turns crisp and golden within 30 seconds.

**4** Quarter, core and thickly slice the apples. Whisk the egg white until stiff and fold into the batter. Dip a few apple slices into the batter to coat, then deep-fry in the oil for up to 1 minute, until crisp and golden brown.

**5** Drain on kitchen paper and keep warm, while cooking the remaining apples in the same way. Serve the hot apple fritters dusted with icing sugar and accompanied by the chilled honey cream.

## TROPICAL FRUITS WITH SABAYON

**SERVES 4**
PREPARATION
25 minutes
COOKING TIME
15 minutes
FREEZING
Not suitable
CALS/SERVING
250
COLOUR INDEX
Page 70

4 passion fruit
125 g (4 oz) fresh lychees, or a 425 g can lychees
1 large mango
1 medium ripe pineapple
2 bananas

SABAYON
1 large egg, plus 2 large egg yolks
50 g (2 oz) caster sugar
90 ml (6 tbsp) sweet white wine or Grand Marnier

**1** Halve the passion fruit and scoop out the flesh into a bowl. Peel and stone fresh lychees; if using canned ones, drain. Peel and slice the mango, from the stone. Peel, core and slice the pineapple. Peel and thickly slice the bananas.
**2** Divide all the fruit between 4 shallow ovenproof dishes, about 12 cm (5 inch) in diameter. Cover with foil and bake in the oven at 200°C (400°F) Mark 6 for 15 minutes.
**3** Meanwhile, make the sabayon. Place the whole egg, egg yolks, sugar and wine or liqueur in a heatproof bowl (preferably ceramic) and whisk until beginning to thicken. Place over a pan of simmering water, so the bowl is just touching the water; whisk for 10-15 minutes until fluffy and thick enough to leave a ribbon trail when the whisk is lifted; don't overheat or the mixture may curdle.
**4** Spoon the sabayon over the baked fruit and place under a hot grill for a few minutes until golden and bubbling.

## FRANGIPANE BAKED PEARS

**SERVES 6**
PREPARATION
40 minutes, plus macerating
COOKING TIME
50 minutes
FREEZING
Suitable: See note
CALS/SERVING
575
COLOUR INDEX
Page 70

25 g (1 oz) blanched almonds
25 g (1 oz) candied peel
25 g (1 oz) raisins
45 ml (3 tbsp) kirsch or rum
75 g (3 oz) flaked almonds
50 g (2 oz) plain white flour
900 ml (1½ pints) water
225 g (8 oz) caster sugar
6 pears
15 ml (1 tbsp) apricot jam
125 g (4 oz) butter
2 eggs, beaten
few drops of almond essence (optional)

**1** Chop the almonds and candied peel and mix with the raisins in a small bowl. Sprinkle with the kirsch or rum, cover and leave to macerate for 6 hours or overnight. Drain the fruits, reserving the liquor.
**2** Place the flaked almonds and flour in a food processor, and process until the nuts are finely ground; set aside.
**3** Pour the water into a large saucepan and add 125 g (4 oz) of the sugar. Slowly bring to the boil, stirring until the sugar is dissolved.
**4** Peel the pears and place in the syrup. Cover with a disc of greaseproof paper and poach gently for 10-15 minutes or until tender. Remove the pears with a slotted spoon and set aside.
**5** Add the apricot jam to the syrup and let bubble for 30 minutes or until reduced and syrupy. Set aside.
**6** Meanwhile, cream the butter and remaining sugar together in a bowl until light and fluffy. Add the eggs a little at a time, beating well. Fold in the flour and almond mixture, the reserved kirsch or rum and almond essence, if using.
**7** Using a teaspoon, scoop out the base of each pear. Stir a spoonful of the creamed mixture into the raisin mixture and use to fill the pears. Place in a 900 ml (1½ pint) shallow ovenproof dish and spoon the remaining creamed mixture around them. Brush the pears with a little of the syrupy glaze.
**8** Bake at 190°C (375°F) Mark 5 for 50 minutes or until the frangipane is golden brown and just firm to the touch; cover with foil during baking if the frangipane appears to be over-browning.
**9** Brush with a little more glaze and serve with cream.

**NOTES**
❑ Roughly processed flaked almonds give the frangipane a good texture, but ground almonds may be used if preferred.
❑ The pudding can be frozen at the end of stage 8. Thaw overnight at room temperature, cover loosely with foil and reheat at 190°C (375°F) Mark 5 for about 30 minutes.

## GOLDEN CROISSANT PUDDING

**SERVES 6**
PREPARATION
15 minutes
COOKING TIME
40-50 minutes
FREEZING
Suitable: Before baking
CALS/SERVING
645

4 large croissants (preferably 1 or 2 days old)
75 g (3 oz) unsalted butter (at room temperature)
50 g (2 oz) sultanas
CUSTARD
300 ml (½ pint) milk (at room temperature)
300 ml (½ pint) double cream (at room temperature)
1 vanilla pod, split
6 egg yolks
125 g (4 oz) caster sugar
TO FINISH
icing sugar, for dusting

**1** Slice the croissants thickly, then spread with the butter. Arrange the croissant slices, butter-side up and overlapping, in a buttered 1.7 litre (3 pint) shallow baking dish, scattering in the sultanas as you do so.
**2** To make the custard, pour the milk and cream into a saucepan. Add the vanilla pod and place over a very low heat for about 5 minutes until the mixture is almost boiling and well flavoured with vanilla.
**3** Meanwhile, in a large bowl, whisk together the egg yolks and caster sugar until light and foamy. Strain the flavoured milk on to the egg mixture, whisking all the time.
**4** Pour the egg mixture evenly over the croissants. Place the dish in a bain-marie or large roasting tin and pour in enough boiling water to come halfway up the sides of the dish. Bake at 180°C (350°F) Mark 4 for 40-50 minutes until the custard is softly set and the top is crisp and golden.
**5** Leave the pudding in the bain-marie to cool slightly. Serve warm, sprinkled with icing sugar and accompanied by cream or creme fraîche.

# INDIVIDUAL STICKY TOFFEE PUDDINGS

**SERVES 4**
PREPARATION
20 minutes
COOKING TIME
25-30 minutes
FREEZING
Not suitable
CALS/SERVING
570

15 ml (1 tbsp) golden syrup
15 ml (1 tbsp) black treacle
150 g (5 oz) butter, softened
25 g (1 oz) pecan nuts or walnuts
75 g (3 oz) self-raising flour
125 g (4 oz) caster sugar
2 eggs, beaten

**1** Put the syrup, treacle and 25 g (1 oz) of the butter in a bowl and beat until smooth. Divide between four 150 ml (¼ pint) timbales or ramekins and set aside.
**2** Finely grind the nuts and place in a bowl. Sift in the flour.
**3** Put the remaining butter and the caster sugar into a food processor and blend briefly. Add the eggs and flour mixture and blend again for 30 seconds.
**4** Spoon the sponge mixture into the timbales or ramekins, covering the syrup mixture on the bottom. Bake at 180°C (350°F) Mark 4 for 25-30 minutes until risen and golden.
**5** Remove from the oven and leave to rest for 5 minutes, then unmould onto warmed serving plates. Serve with custard or cream.

# CHRISTMAS PUDDING

**SERVES 8**
PREPARATION
30 minutes
COOKING TIME
6 hours
FREEZING
Suitable
CALS/SERVING
445
COLOUR INDEX
Page 70

50 g (2 oz) blanched almonds
50 g (2 oz) walnuts
50 g (2 oz) brazil nuts
75 g (3 oz) no-soak pitted dried prunes
25 g (1 oz) candied peel
75 g (3 oz) carrots
125 g (4 oz) butter, softened
125 g (4 oz) soft dark brown sugar
finely grated zest of 1 lemon
2 eggs, beaten
350 g (12 oz) mixed seedless raisins, currants and sultanas
50 g (2 oz) fresh brown breadcrumbs
125 g (4 oz) plain wholemeal flour
50 g (2 oz) plain white flour
15 ml (1 tbsp) ground mixed spice
200 ml (7 fl oz) stout
30 ml (2 tbsp) brandy
30 ml (2 tbsp) black treacle
TO SERVE
60 ml (4 tbsp) brandy
Sabayon Sauce (see page 293), or Crème Anglaise (see page 293)

**1** Roughly chop the nuts, prunes and candied peel. Peel and coarsely grate the carrots.
**2** In a large mixing bowl, cream together the butter, sugar and lemon zest. Gradually beat in the eggs. Add all of the other ingredients and stir well. Cover and leave at cool room temperature overnight.
**3** The next day, lightly grease a 1.4-1.6 litre (2½-2¾ pint) heatproof pudding basin and line the base with non-stick baking parchment. Beat the pudding mixture again and spoon into the basin. Cover the surface with a disc of greaseproof paper. Cover the bowl with a double thickness of greaseproof paper, pleat in the centre and secure under the rim of the bowl with string.
**4** Stand the pudding basin in a large saucepan containing enough boiling water to come halfway up the sides of the basin. Cover tightly and boil for about 4 hours, topping up the pan with boiling water as necessary.
**5** Cool the pudding completely, then re-cover the basin with fresh greaseproof paper and foil. Store in a cool larder or the refrigerator for up to 2 months.
**6** On the day, steam the pudding (as above) for about 2 hours.
**7** Turn out the pudding on to a warmed serving plate. Warm the brandy in a small pan, pour over the pudding and set alight. When the flames have died down, serve cut into wedges, with the sabayon or crème Anglaise.

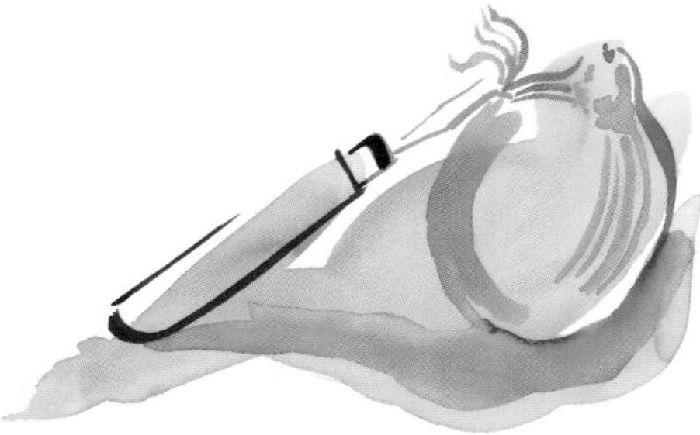

# GLAZED BRANDIED PRUNE TART

**SERVES 8**
PREPARATION
25 minutes, plus macerating and chilling
COOKING TIME
50 minutes
FREEZING
Suitable
CALS/SERVING
450

PASTRY
- 175 g (6 oz) plain white flour
- 75 g (3 oz) lightly salted butter, diced
- 75 g (3 oz) caster sugar
- 3 egg yolks

FILLING
- 250 g (9 oz) no-soak dried prunes
- 75 ml (5 tbsp) brandy
- 1 vanilla pod
- 150 ml (¼ pint) double cream
- 150 ml (¼ pint) single cream
- 25 g (1 oz) caster sugar
- 2 eggs

TO GLAZE
- 60 ml (4 tbsp) apricot jam
- 30 ml (2 tbsp) brandy

**1** For the filling, put the prunes into a small bowl, add the brandy, cover and leave to soak overnight or for several hours, until the brandy is absorbed.

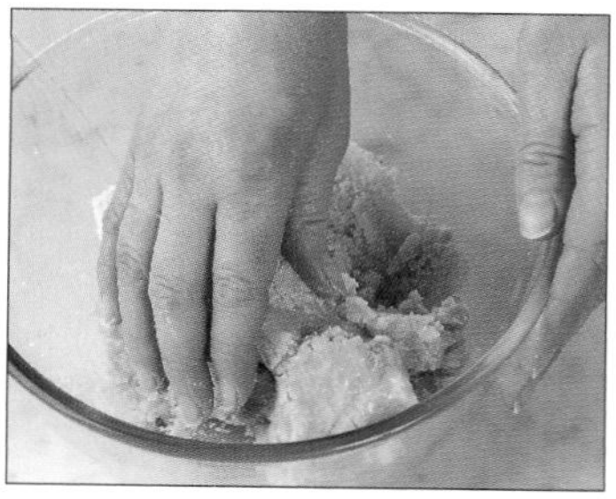

**2** To make the pastry, sift the flour into a bowl, then rub in the butter until the mixture resembles fine breadcrumbs. Stir in the sugar, add the egg yolks and mix to a soft dough. Knead lightly, wrap in cling film and chill for 30 minutes.

**3** Roll out the pastry on a lightly floured surface and use to line a 23-24 cm (9-9½ inch) loose-based flan tin, which is about 2.5 cm (1 inch) deep. Chill in the refrigerator for 20 minutes.

**4** Prick the base with a fork, then line with greaseproof paper and baking beans. Place on a baking sheet and bake blind at 200°C (400°F) Mark 6 for 15 minutes until coloured around the edge. Remove paper and beans and bake for a further 5 minutes until the pastry is golden. Lower the oven setting to 180°C (350°F) Mark 4.

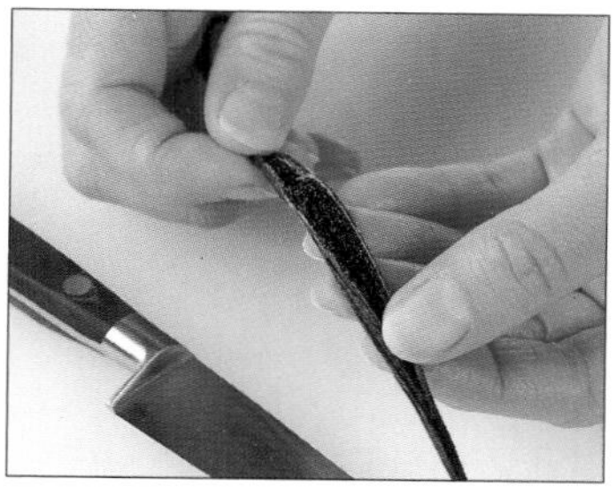

**5** Meanwhile, split the vanilla pod to reveal the seeds and place in a saucepan with the double cream. Bring just to the boil, then remove from the heat and set aside to infuse for 20 minutes.

**6** Discard the vanilla pod. Pour the infused cream into a bowl, add the single cream, sugar and eggs, and beat well.

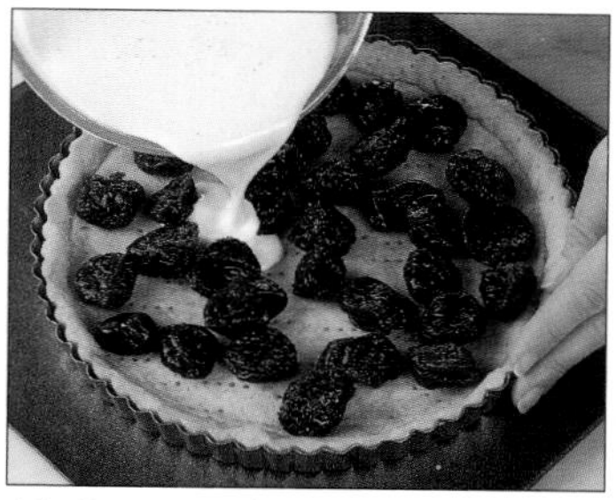

**7** Scatter the prunes in the pastry case, then pour the cream mixture around them. Bake in the oven for about 30 minutes until the custard is turning golden, and is just set in the centre.

**8** Meanwhile, press the jam through a sieve into a saucepan, add the brandy and heat gently until smooth. Brush this glaze over the tart. Serve warm or cold, with crème fraîche.

## APPLE AND PECAN TART WITH SPICED CARAMEL

**SERVES 8**
PREPARATION
40 minutes, plus chilling
COOKING TIME
35 minutes
FREEZING
Not suitable
CALS/SERVING
550

PASTRY
125 g (4 oz) plain white flour
50 g (2 oz) pecan nuts, finely ground
75 g (3 oz) lightly salted butter, diced
50 g (2 oz) caster sugar
3 egg yolks
FILLING
75 g (3 oz) pecan nuts
1.4 kg (3 lb) cooking apples
15 ml (1 tbsp) lemon juice
75 g (3 oz) unsalted butter
50 g (2 oz) light muscovado sugar
CARAMEL
225 g (8 oz) caster sugar
300 ml (½ pint) water
200 ml (7 fl oz) crème fraîche
2.5 ml (½ tsp) ground cinnamon

**1** To make the pastry, mix the flour and ground nuts together in a bowl, then rub in the butter until the mixture resembles fine breadcrumbs. Stir in the sugar, then add the egg yolks and mix to a soft dough. Knead lightly, then wrap in cling film and chill in the refrigerator for 30 minutes.
**2** Roll out the pastry on a lightly floured surface and use to line a 23-24 cm (9-9½ inch) loose-based flan tin, which is about 2.5 cm (1 inch) deep. Chill for 20 minutes.
**3** Prick the base with a fork, then line with greaseproof paper and baking beans. Place on a baking sheet and bake blind at 200°C (400°F) Mark 6 for 15 minutes until coloured around the edge. Remove the paper and beans and bake for a further 5 minutes until the pastry is golden.
**4** Meanwhile, roughly chop the pecans if preferred. Peel, quarter and core the apples; slice thickly and immerse in a bowl of cold water with the lemon juice added.
**5** Melt the butter in a large heavy-based pan, add the sugar and heat gently until the sugar is dissolved. Drain the apples and pat dry on kitchen paper, then add to the pan. Cook gently until slighty softened.
**6** Add the pecan nuts to the apples. Turn the mixture into the pastry case and bake in the oven for 15 minutes.
**7** Meanwhile make the caramel. Put the sugar and water in a heavy-based pan and heat gently until dissolved. Bring to the boil and boil steadily until the syrup is a deep caramel colour. Immediately dip the base of the pan into cold water to prevent further cooking.
**8** Heat the crème fraîche and cinnamon in a separate pan until thin in consistency, then carefully add to the caramel and cook, stirring, until a smooth sauce is formed.
**9** Pour a little of the caramel over the apple filling. Serve at once, with the remaining caramel sauce handed separately.

## PLUM TART WITH CINNAMON CREAM

**SERVES 6**
PREPARATION
40 minutes, plus chilling
COOKING TIME
1-1¼ hours
FREEZING
Not suitable
CALS/SERVING
230
COLOUR INDEX
Page 71

PASTRY
125 g (4 oz) plain white flour
5 ml (1 tsp) ground cinnamon
pinch of salt
75 g (3 oz) butter, diced
1 egg yolk
15 ml (1 tbsp) chilled water
FILLING
450 g (1 lb) plums
30 ml (2 tbsp) caster sugar
TO GLAZE
45 ml (3 tbsp) apricot jam, sieved, or redcurrant jelly
CINNAMON CREAM
300 ml (½ pint) double cream
2.5 ml (½ tsp) ground cinnamon
15 ml (1 tbsp) icing sugar

**1** To make the pastry, put the flour, cinnamon, salt, diced butter and egg yolk in a food processor and process for 30 seconds or until evenly combined. Add the water and process for a further 30 seconds. Turn out onto a lightly floured surface and knead lightly.
**2** Roll out the pastry to a 25 cm (10 inch) circle and place on a baking sheet. Chill in the refrigerator for 15 minutes.
**3** Prick the pastry all over with a fork and bake in the oven at 200°C (400°F) Mark 6 for 20-25 minutes until golden brown. Lower the oven setting to 190°C (375°F) Mark 5.
**4** Meanwhile, halve, stone and slice the plums. Arrange over the cooked pastry and sprinkle with the sugar. Bake for a further 45-50 minutes until the plums are tender.
**5** For the cinnamon cream, whip the cream in a bowl until it forms soft peaks. Sift in the cinnamon and icing sugar, and fold in until evenly incorporated.
**6** For the glaze, heat the jam or redcurrant jelly with 30 ml (2 tbsp) water until melted, then bring to the boil and let bubble for 1 minute. Brush over the warm tart and serve warm, with the cinnamon cream.

# SPICED NUT STRUDEL

**SERVES 8-10**
PREPARATION
20 minutes
COOKING TIME
30 minutes
FREEZING
Suitable
CALS/SERVING
365-290

8 large sheets filo pastry
25 g (1 oz) unsalted butter
FILLING
50 g (2 oz) glacé cherries
200 g (7 oz) mixed chopped nuts, such as walnuts, hazelnuts and almonds
50 g (2 oz) soft white breadcrumbs
25 g (1 oz) dark muscovado sugar
25 g (1 oz) chopped candied peel
50 g (2 oz) raisins
5 ml (1 tsp) ground cinnamon
5 ml (1 tsp) ground ginger
50 g (2 oz) unsalted butter, melted
90 ml (6 tbsp) maple syrup
1 egg
TO FINISH
a little extra maple syrup

**1** For the filling, chop the glacé cherries and place in a bowl with the chopped nuts, breadcrumbs, sugar, candied peel, raisins and spices. Add the melted butter, maple syrup and egg and mix well until evenly combined.

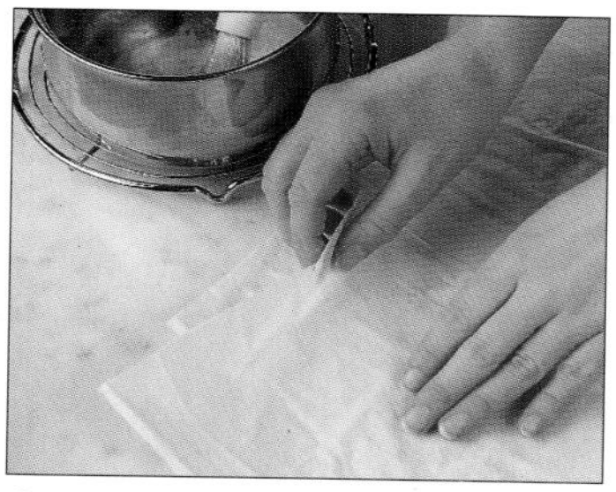

**2** Lay one sheet of filo pastry on a clean surface; brush lightly with melted butter. Take a second sheet of pastry and place it overlapping the first sheet by 5 cm (2 inches). Brush lightly with melted butter.

**3** Spoon half of the filling over the pastry, leaving a 5 cm (2 inch) border free around the edges.

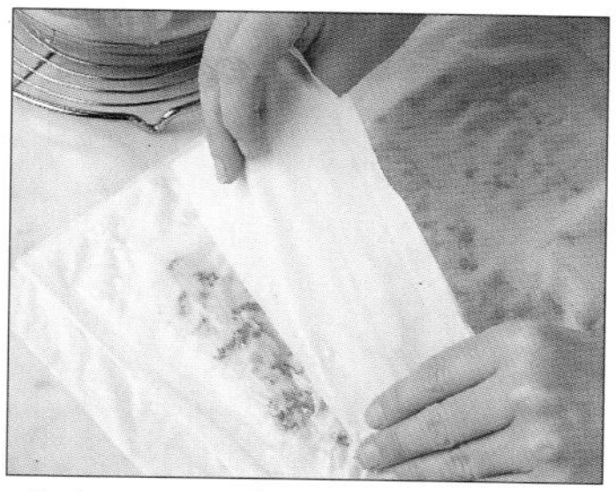

**4** Lay another two sheets of filo pastry over the filling, again overlapping them slightly. Brush lightly with butter.

**5** Spoon the remaining filling on top. Fold the two opposite edges of the pastry over the edge of the filling.

**6** Loosely roll up like a Swiss roll to enclose the filling. Carefully transfer the strudel to a baking sheet, placing it seam-side down. Brush lightly with melted butter. Cut the remaining filo pastry into strips.

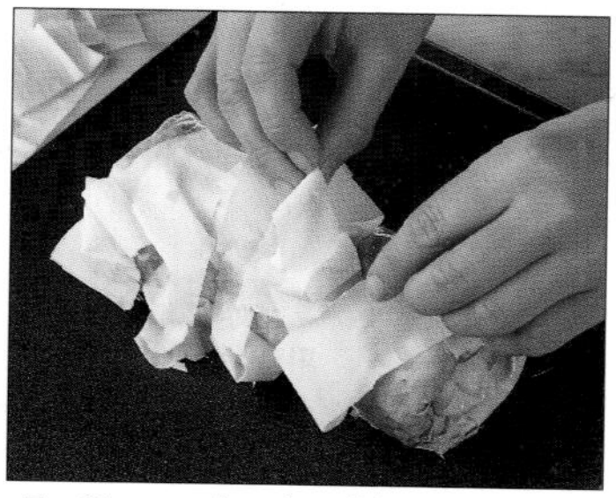

**7** Crumple the filo strips and lay on top of the strudel. Brush with the remaining butter and bake at 190°C (375°F) Mark 5 for about 30 minutes until deep golden brown. Drizzle over a little extra maple syrup and serve warm, with cream or ice cream.

**VARIATIONS**

❑ Replace the glacé cherries with chopped preserved stem ginger in syrup.
❑ Add the grated zest of 1 lemon to the filling.

# APRICOT, PISTACHIO AND HONEY SLICES

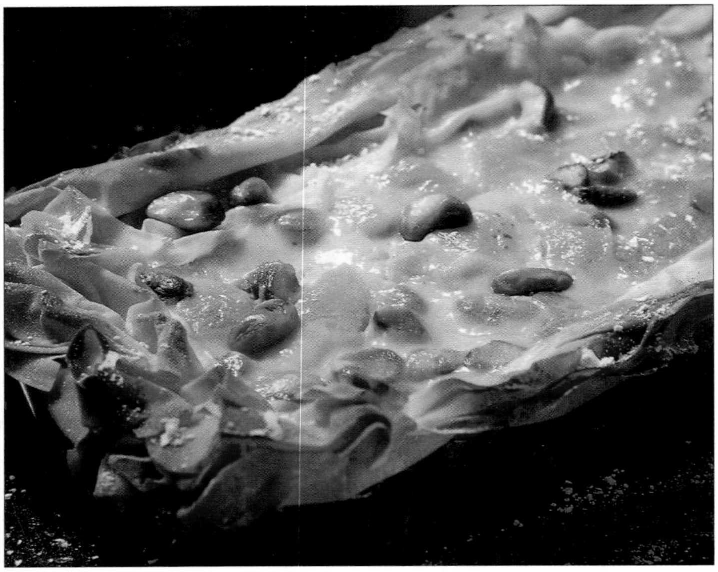

**SERVES 8**
PREPARATION
25 minutes
COOKING TIME
30 minutes
FREEZING
Not suitable
CALS/SERVING
250

100 g (3½ oz) pistachio nuts
175 g (6 oz) no-soak dried apricots
150 ml (¼ pint) fresh orange juice
150 ml (¼ pint) single cream
150 ml (¼ pint) milk
2 eggs
75 ml (5 tbsp) thin honey
5 ml (1 tsp) ground cinnamon
10 ml (2 tsp) icing sugar
20 ml (4 tsp) oil
4 large sheets filo pastry
icing sugar, for dusting

**1** Put the pistachios in a bowl, add boiling water to cover and leave for 1 minute; drain. Place on a clean tea-towel and rub to remove the skins. Set aside 30 ml (2 tbsp) for decoration. Roughly chop the rest of the nuts and apricots.
**2** Place the chopped pistachios in a small pan with the apricots and orange juice. Simmer gently for about 10 minutes until the orange juice is absorbed. Transfer to a bowl.
**3** Add the cream, milk, eggs and 15 ml (1 tbsp) honey to the apricot mixture and mix until evenly combined.
**4** Mix the cinnamon, icing sugar and oil in a bowl. Lay one sheet of filo in a 35 x 10 cm (14 x 4 inch) loose-based flan tin, or a 23 cm (9 inch) round tin, allowing excess pastry to overhang the edges. Brush lightly with the spice mixture.
**5** Cover with another sheet of pastry and brush with more spice mixture. Repeat these layers, finishing with a layer of filo pastry. Pour the filling into the pastry case. Bring the excess pastry up around the edges of the tart and pinch at intervals to secure; brush with any remaining spice mixture.
**6** Bake at 190°C (375°F) Mark 5 for about 30 minutes until the custard is set and the pastry is golden. Check towards the end of the cooking time and cover with foil if the pastry appears to be over-browning. Roughly chop the reserved pistachios and scatter over the filling. Spoon the remaining honey over the nuts. Serve dusted with icing sugar.

# TRADITIONAL MINCE PIES

**MAKES 12**
(See note)
PREPARATION
30 minutes, plus standing
COOKING TIME
20-25 minutes
FREEZING
Suitable: See note
CALS/PIE
260
COLOUR INDEX
Page 71

APRICOT MINCEMEAT
225 g (8 oz) no-soak dried apricots
finely grated zest of 1 orange
45 ml (3 tbsp) orange juice
900 g (2 lb) mixed currants, sultanas and raisins
60 ml (4 tbsp) orange marmalade
450 g (1 lb) demerara sugar
7.5 ml (1½ tsp) ground mixed spice
1.25 ml (¼ tsp) ground nutmeg
300 ml (½ pint) brandy
PASTRY
225 g (8 oz) plain white flour
pinch of salt
150 g (5 oz) butter
30 ml (2 tbsp) caster sugar
1 egg yolk
TO FINISH
1 egg white, lightly beaten
caster sugar, for sprinkling

**1** To prepare the mincemeat, chop the apricots and mix with the other ingredients in a large bowl. Cover and leave in a cool place for 48 hours, stirring occasionally. Pot in sterilised jars, and store in a cool place for up to 2 months.
**2** To make the pastry, sift the flour and salt into a large mixing bowl. Using a round-bladed knife, roughly cut in the butter, then rub in using your fingertips until the mixture resembles coarse breadcrumbs. Stir in the sugar.
**3** Mix the egg yolk with 45 ml (3 tbsp) cold water, then add to the dry ingredients, and mix with a round-bladed knife to a dough. Knead gently until just smooth. Wrap in cling film and chill in the refrigerator for 30 minutes.
**4** On a lightly floured surface, roll out half of the pastry to a 3 mm (⅛ inch) thickness. Using a 7.5 cm (3 inch) fluted cutter, stamp out 12 circles of pastry. Gently press these into patty tins – the pastry should just protrude above the tins to allow for shrinkage when cooked. Spoon about 10-15 ml (2-3 tsp) mincemeat into each tin.
**5** Roll out the remaining pastry and stamp out 12 circles, using a 6 cm (2½ inch) fluted cutter. Dampen the edges of the pastry in the patty tins, then top with the smaller pastry circles. Press the edges together to seal. Brush the tops with egg white, then sprinkle lightly with caster sugar.
**6** Bake in the oven at 190°C (375°F) Mark 5 for 20-25 minutes. Leave in the tins for 5 minutes, then transfer to a wire rack. Serve warm, with pouring cream if desired.

**NOTES**
❑ This recipe makes 1.8 kg (4 lb) mincemeat; you will only need to use about 225 g (8 oz) for this quantity of mince pies. Store the rest in a cool place for future use.
❑ Freeze the uncooked mince pies before brushing with egg white. Glaze and bake from frozen, as above, allowing an extra 10-15 minutes baking.

**VARIATION** At stage 5, use holly leaves and berries cut from the remaining pastry, to form the pastry lids. Arrange, overlapping, over the mincemeat, glaze and bake as above.

## PEACH CINNAMON TARTLETS

**SERVES 4**
PREPARATION
20 minutes
COOKING TIME
12-15 minutes
FREEZING
Not suitable
CALS/SERVING
360

225 g (8 oz) ready-made puff pastry
40 g (1½ oz) unsalted butter
15 g (½ oz) ground almonds
15 ml (1 tbsp) caster sugar
5 ml (1 tsp) ground cinnamon
2 large ripe peaches
EGG GLAZE
1 egg yolk
15 ml (1 tbsp) milk
pinch of sugar
TO FINISH
icing sugar, for dusting

**1** Preheat a baking sheet on the middle shelf of the oven. Divide the pastry into 4 equal pieces. Roll each one out thinly on a lightly floured surface and cut out a 13 cm (5 inch) round, using a fluted pastry cutter. Prick the base leaving a 1 cm (½ inch) border.
**2** Cream the butter, ground almonds, sugar and cinnamon together in a bowl until smooth.
**3** Halve the peaches and carefully cut out the stone. Stand the peach halves rounded-side up and slice each one into 6-8 wedges, holding them in shape.
**4** To make the egg glaze, whisk the egg yolk, milk and sugar together in a small bowl.
**5** Divide the cinnamon butter between the pastry rounds, spreading it evenly to within 1 cm (½ inch) of the edges. Arrange a sliced peach half in the middle of each one, fanning it out slightly if wished.
**6** Brush the pastry edges with the egg glaze and dust the peaches with icing sugar. Transfer the pastries to the hot baking sheet and bake in the oven at 220°C (425°F) Mark 7 for 12-15 minutes until the pastry is puffed and golden and the peaches are tender. Serve hot or warm, with cream.

## PINEAPPLE, DATE AND KUMQUAT SALAD

**SERVES 6**
PREPARATION
35 minutes
COOKING TIME
15 minutes
FREEZING
Not suitable
CALS/SERVING
330
COLOUR INDEX
Page 72

75 ml (5 tbsp) acacia honey
50 g (2 oz) soft brown sugar
300 ml (½ pint) Earl Grey tea, strained
225 g (8 oz) kumquats
2 oranges
1 medium pineapple
12 fresh or dried dates
125 g (4 oz) walnut halves

**1** Put the honey, sugar and tea into a saucepan, bring to the boil and boil for 1 minute. Halve the kumquats, add to the syrup and simmer, uncovered, for about 10 minutes until tender. Leave to cool in the syrup.
**2** Peel the oranges, removing all the rind and white pith. Slice them crosswise and place in a bowl.
**3** Using a sharp knife, cut the top and bottom off the pineapple. Cut away the skin and the brown 'eyes'. Quarter the pineapple lengthwise and cut out the core. Cut the flesh into large chunks. Carefully mix with the oranges.
**3** Halve the dates and remove the stones. Stir into the fruit mixture with the walnuts. Drain the kumquats and set aside; strain the syrup and pour over the fruit in the bowl. Cover and chill in the refrigerator for 1 hour.
**4** Spoon the fruit salad into a serving bowl and scatter the kumquats on top. Serve with whipped cream.

## SYLLABUB WITH POACHED PLUMS

**SERVES 8**
PREPARATION
25 minutes
COOKING TIME
12 minutes
FREEZING
Not suitable
CALS/SERVING
350
COLOUR INDEX
Page 72

700 g (1½ lb) ripe red plums
40-65 g (1½-2½ oz) caster sugar (depending on sweetness of the plums)
175 ml (6 fl oz) dessert wine
450 ml (¾ pint) double cream
2-3 rosemary sprigs

**1** Quarter the plums, removing the stones. Put the sugar and wine in a saucepan and heat gently, stirring until the sugar dissolves. Add the plums, cover and simmer very gently for 5-10 minutes until softened but not pulpy.
**2** Drain the plums, reserving 200 ml (7 fl oz) syrup; if necessary make up to this quantity with a little wine.
**3** Put 150 ml (¼ pint) of the cream in a saucepan with the rosemary and bring almost to the boil. Set aside to infuse for 15 minutes. Spoon the plums into 8 tall serving glasses.
**4** Strain the infused cream into a large bowl and add the rest of the cream. Whip until just holding its shape, then slowly whisk in the reserved syrup, until the mixture is thick enough to leave a trail when the whisk is lifted.
**5** Spoon the cream over the plums. Chill the syllabubs for at least 2 hours before serving.

# CRÈMETS WITH RED FRUIT SAUCE

**SERVES 6**
PREPARATION
20 minutes, plus draining
COOKING TIME
3-5 minutes
FREEZING
Not suitable
CALS/SERVING
370

300 ml (½ pint) crème fraîche
225 g (8 oz) mascarpone or other cream cheese
30 ml (2 tbsp) caster sugar
2 egg whites
RED FRUIT SAUCE
50 g (2 oz) redcurrants
25 g (1 oz) blackcurrants
50 g (2 oz) caster sugar
125 g (4 oz) raspberries
TO DECORATE
4 mint sprigs
icing sugar, for dusting

**1** Line six 150 ml (¼ pint) perforated moulds with muslin. Place the crème fraîche, mascarpone and sugar in a large bowl and beat until smooth. In a clean bowl, whisk the egg whites until holding soft peaks; fold into the crème mixture.

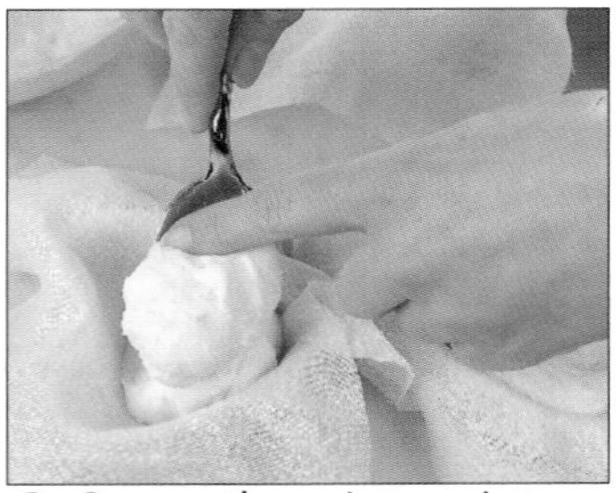

**2** Spoon the mixture into the muslin-lined moulds. Place on a tray and leave to drain in a cool place for at least 8 hours, or better still, overnight.

**3** To make the sauce, place the currants and sugar in a small pan and cook over a low heat for 3-5 minutes until just soft. Press the raspberries through a fine sieve into a bowl, then stir in the black and red currant mixture. Leave to cool.

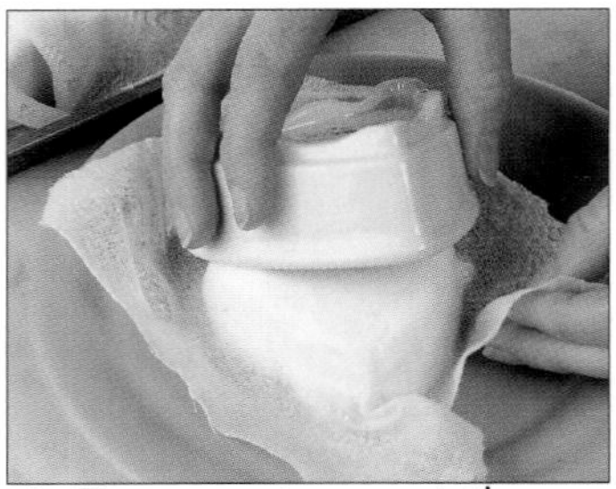

**4** To serve, turn out the crèmets onto individual plates and spoon around the red fruit sauce. Serve at once, decorated with mint sprigs. Dust with a little icing sugar, if desired.

**NOTE** Special heart-shaped moulds with draining holes are available from kitchen shops. Shallow 200 ml (7 fl oz) crème fraîche or yogurt pots make good round substitutes; puncture 8 holes in the base of each one with a skewer.

**VARIATION** Instead of using moulds, you could leave the cream mixture to drain in a large sieve lined with muslin. Serve in small spoonfuls on the fruit sauce.

# PETITS POTS DE CRÈME AU CHOCOLAT

**SERVES 6-8**
PREPARATION
15 minutes, plus chilling
COOKING TIME
1 hour
FREEZING
Not suitable
CALS/SERVING
475-355
COLOUR INDEX
Page 72

600 ml (1 pint) single cream
2.5 ml (½ tsp) vanilla essence
225 g (8 oz) good quality plain dark chocolate, in pieces
1 egg
5 egg yolks
25 g (1 oz) caster sugar
TO DECORATE
90-120 ml (6-8 tbsp) whipped cream
cocoa powder, for dusting

**1** Put the cream, vanilla essence and chocolate into a heavy-based pan over a low heat and heat gently, stirring, until the chocolate melts and the mixture is smooth.
**2** Lightly mix together the whole egg, egg yolks and sugar in a bowl, then stir in the chocolate cream until smooth.
**3** Strain the mixture into eight 90 ml (3 fl oz) custard pots, or six ramekins. Cover with lids or discs of foil.
**4** Stand the custard pots or ramekins in a roasting tin and pour in enough hot water to come halfway up the sides of the dishes. Cook in the oven at 150°C (300°F) Mark 2 for about 1 hour until lightly set; the centres should still be slightly soft. Do not overcook or the texture will be spoilt.
**5** Remove the pots or ramekins from the tin and allow to cool. Chill before serving, topped with a spoonful of cream and a dusting of cocoa powder.

# BERRY TRIFLE WITH PRALINE

**SERVES 10**
PREPARATION
45 minutes, plus chilling
COOKING TIME
40 minutes
FREEZING
Not suitable
CALS/SERVING
610
COLOUR INDEX
Page 73

SPONGE
125 g (4 oz) self-raising flour
1.25 ml (¼ tsp) baking powder
75 g (3 oz) unsalted butter, softened
75 g (3 oz) caster sugar
2 eggs
finely grated zest of 1 orange

CUSTARD
4 egg yolks
15 ml (1 tbsp) cornflour
5 ml (1 tsp) vanilla essence
125 g (4 oz) caster sugar
600 ml (1 pint) milk

PRALINE
125 g (4 oz) caster sugar
75 g (3 oz) blanched almonds, toasted

TO ASSEMBLE
700 g (1½ lb) mixed soft fruits, such as raspberries, redcurrants, blackberries
175 ml (6 fl oz) Muscat or other dessert wine
30 ml (2 tbsp) Grand Marnier
600 ml (1 pint) double cream
extra berries, to decorate

**1** Grease and line an 18 cm (7 inch) cake tin with greaseproof paper. Sift the flour and baking powder into a bowl. Add the butter, sugar, eggs and orange zest and beat, using an electric whisk, until pale and creamy. Turn into the prepared tin and bake at 180°C (350°F) Mark 4 for about 40 minutes until risen and just firm to the touch. Turn out onto a wire rack and leave to cool.
**2** To make the custard, whisk the egg yolks, cornflour, vanilla, sugar and 30 ml (2 tbsp) of the milk together in a bowl until smooth. Put the remaining milk in a saucepan and slowly bring to the boil. Pour onto the egg mixture, whisking constantly. Return to the pan and cook gently, stirring, until thickened enough to coat the back of the wooden spoon; do not boil. Turn into a bowl and cover the surface with greaseproof paper to prevent a skin forming. Leave to cool.
**3** Meanwhile, make the praline. Place the sugar and almonds in a heavy-based pan over a low heat until the sugar melts and turns a nut brown colour. Immediately remove from the heat and pour into a shallow oiled baking tin. Leave to cool until set hard.
**4** Cut the sponge into pieces, arrange over the base of a 2 litre (3½ pint) glass serving bowl and sprinkle with half of the wine. Scatter the berries over the sponge and sprinkle with the remaining wine and liqueur.
**5** Spoon the custard over the fruit. Whip the cream in a bowl until soft peaks form, then spoon on top of the custard. Cover and chill in the refrigerator for 3-4 hours.
**6** When ready to serve, break the praline into pieces and arrange on top of the trifle. Scatter over a few extra berries and serve at once.

**VARIATION** For a quicker alternative, use 350 g (12 oz) ready-made Madeira cake in place of the sponge. Omit the praline topping.

# SUMMER FRUIT BRULÉE

**SERVES 4**
PREPARATION
15 minutes, plus standing
COOKING TIME
3-4 minutes
FREEZING
Not suitable
CALS/SERVING
280

1 ripe nectarine
350 g (12 oz) mixed summer berries, such as strawberries, blackberries, raspberries and redcurrants
30 ml (2 tbsp) ruby port
150 ml (¼ pint) double cream
125 g (4 oz) Greek-style yogurt
few drops of vanilla essence
25 g (1 oz) demerara sugar

**1** Halve and stone the nectarine; thinly slice the flesh. Place in a bowl with the summer berries, add the port and stir to mix. Leave to stand for 1-2 hours if possible. Transfer to a 900 ml (1½ pint) gratin dish.
**2** Whip the cream in a bowl until it holds its shape, then fold in the yogurt, together with the vanilla essence. Spread the cream mixture evenly over the fruit, to cover completely.
**3** Scatter the demerara sugar over the cream and grill under a high heat as close to the heat source as possible for 3-4 minutes until the sugar is golden brown and caramelised. Allow to cool for 5 minutes, then serve.

**VARIATION** Divide the fruit between 4-6 ramekins. Cover with the cream and finish as above.

## SUMMER PUDDING

**SERVES 6-8**
PREPARATION
35 minutes, plus chilling
COOKING TIME
5 minutes
FREEZING
Suitable
CALS/SERVING
180-135

450 g (1 lb) raspberries
225 g (8 oz) redcurrants
225 g (8 oz) blackcurrants
75 g (3 oz) caster sugar
8 large slices white bread, 5 mm (¼ inch) thick (preferably one day old)

TO DECORATE
redcurrant sprigs
lemon balm or mint leaves

**1** Place the raspberries in a saucepan with the currants, sugar and 45 ml (3 tbsp) water. Bring to a gentle simmer over a low heat, then cook gently for 3-4 minutes until the juices begin to run. Remove from the heat; set aside.
**2** Remove the crusts from the bread, then cut a round of bread from one slice to fit the base of a 1.5 litre (2½ pint) pudding basin. Halve the remaining slices.
**3** Arrange the bread slices around the side of the pudding basin, overlapping them slightly at the bottom, so they fit neatly and tightly together. Position the round of bread to cover the hole in the middle.
**4** Spoon about 100 ml (3½ fl oz) of the juice from the fruit into a jug; set aside. Spoon the fruit and remaining juice into the bread-lined pudding basin. Cover completely with the remaining bread slices, trimming to fit as necessary.
**5** Cover the pudding with a saucer, that fits just inside the top of the pudding basin, then set a 2 kg (4 lb) weight on the saucer. Chill the pudding in the refrigerator overnight.
**6** To unmould pudding, remove the weight and saucer. Invert the serving plate over the pudding basin, hold the two firmly together, invert and shake firmly (up and down).
**7** Spoon the reserved juice over the pudding and decorate with redcurrant sprigs and lemon balm or mint sprigs. Serve cut into wedges, with cream.

**VARIATION** Vary the fruits according to availability. Blackberries, blueberries, cherries and plums are all suitable. The total weight of fruit should be 900 g (2 lb).

## PISTACHIO PRALINE FLOATING ISLANDS

**SERVES 4-6**
PREPARATION
30 minutes, plus chilling
COOKING TIME
18-20 minutes
FREEZING
Not suitable
CALS/SERVING
520-350
COLOUR INDEX
Page 73

PRALINE
50 g (2 oz) unskinned pistachio nuts
50 g (2 oz) caster sugar

FLOATING ISLANDS
2 eggs, separated
150 g (5 oz) caster sugar
300 ml (½ pint) single cream
300 ml (½ pint) milk

**1** First make the praline. Lightly oil a baking sheet. Put the pistachios and sugar in a small heavy-based saucepan over a gentle heat and stir until the sugar melts and begins to caramelise. Continue to cook until the mixture is a deep brown colour, then immediately pour onto the oiled baking sheet. Leave to cool completely, then pound to a coarse powder in a food processor or blender.
**2** To make the meringue, whisk the egg whites in a bowl until they form soft peaks. Gradually whisk in 75 g (3 oz) of the sugar until the mixture is very stiff and shiny. Quickly and carefully fold in all but 30 ml (2 tbsp) of the praline.
**3** Place the cream, milk and remaining sugar in a medium saucepan and bring to a gentle simmer. Spoon 5-6 small rounds of meringue mixture into the pan and cook gently for 2-3 minutes, or until they have doubled in size and are quite firm to the touch. Remove with a slotted spoon and drain on kitchen paper. Repeat with the remaining mixture: you should have 12-18 meringues, depending on size.
**4** Whisk the egg yolks into the poaching liquid. Heat gently, stirring all the time, until the custard thickens to the consistency of double cream; do not allow to boil.
**5** Strain the custard into serving dishes, and position the meringues on top. Cool, then chill for 30 minutes. Serve sprinkled with the remaining praline.

**NOTE** The meringues can be made a few hours in advance and kept floating on the custard. Sprinkle with praline just before serving.

**VARIATIONS**
❑ Instead of pistachios, use hazelnuts or almonds.
❑ Add a pinch of cinnamon or nutmeg to the custard.

## CHOCOLATE AND ORANGE CHEESECAKE

**SERVES 8**
PREPARATION
35 minutes, plus cooling
COOKING TIME
About 1 hour
FREEZING
Suitable: Stage 7
CALS/SERVING
630

2 large oranges
125 g (4 oz) plain dark chocolate, in pieces
3 eggs, separated
125 g (4 oz) caster sugar
three 200 ml (7 oz) tubs full-fat soft cheese
90 ml (6 tbsp) crème fraîche

TO DECORATE
orange segments
chocolate caraque (see page 286)
deep-fried orange zest (optional)
icing sugar, for dusting

**1** Grate the zest from the oranges. Grease a 23 cm (9 inch) spring-release cake tin and line the base with non-stick baking parchment.
**2** Melt the chocolate in a heatproof bowl over a pan of simmering water.
**3** Meanwhile, in a bowl, whisk the egg yolks with 50 g (2 oz) of the sugar until pale and thick. Add the soft cheese and crème fraîche; beat until evenly blended. Add one third of this mixture to the melted chocolate; mix until smooth and set aside.
**4** Stir the grated orange zest into the rest of the cheese mixture.
**5** In a separate bowl, whisk the egg whites until stiff. Gradually whisk in the remaining sugar, until the mixture is stiff and shiny.
**6** Using a large metal spoon, fold a third of the egg whites into the chocolate mixture. Turn into the prepared tin and smooth the surface.
**7** Fold the remaining egg whites into the orange cheese mixture, spoon on top of the chocolate mixture and level the surface.
**8** Bake at 180°C (350°F) Mark 4 for 55-60 minutes until the centre is just firm to the touch. Turn off oven and leave the cheesecake to cool in the oven with the door slightly ajar.
**9** Unmould the cheesecake and decorate with orange segments, chocolate curls and deep-fried orange zest, if using. Dust with icing sugar to serve.

**NOTES**
❑ For the orange decoration, thinly pare strips of zest and deep-fry in hot oil until crisp; drain on kitchen paper.
❑ If frozen, the cheesecake can be baked straight from the freezer; allow an extra 10 minutes.

## HAZELNUT MERINGUE GÂTEAU

**SERVES 8-10**
PREPARATION
40 minutes, plus cooling
COOKING TIME
About 1½ hours
FREEZING
Not suitable
CALS/SLICE
785-630
COLOUR INDEX
Page 74

MERINGUE
125 g (4 oz) shelled hazelnuts
75 g (3 oz) plain chocolate
75 g (3 oz) white chocolate
5 egg whites
250 g (9 oz) caster sugar
2.5 cm (½ tsp) ground mixed spice

TO ASSEMBLE
75 g (3 oz) shelled hazelnuts
125 g (4 oz) caster sugar
300 ml (½ pint) double cream
cocoa powder, for dusting

**1** Line 2 baking sheets with non-sticking baking parchment. Draw a 23 cm (9 inch) circle on one sheet, using a plate as a guide. On the other sheet, draw a 17.5 cm (6½ inch) circle. Turn the paper over.
**2** For the meringue, lightly toast the hazelnuts; let cool. Roughly chop the plain and white chocolate, and the nuts.
**3** Whisk the egg whites in a bowl until stiff but not dry. Gradually whisk in the sugar, a tablespoon at a time, whisking well between each addition until the meringue is stiff and very shiny. Whisk in the spice with the last of the sugar. Carefully fold in the chopped chocolate and nuts.
**4** Spoon the meringue onto the prepared baking sheets, to the edges of the marked circles and swirl with a palette knife. Bake at 140°C (275°F) Mark 1 for about 1½ hours until dry and the undersides are firm when tapped. Turn the oven off and leave the meringues to cool in the oven.
**5** For the praline, put the hazelnuts in a small heavy-based pan with the sugar. Place over a gentle heat, stirring until the sugar melts. Continue cooking until the mixture caramelises to a rich golden brown colour, then pour onto an oiled baking sheet. Leave to cool and harden.
**6** Place the praline in a polythene bag and beat with a rolling pin until very coarsely crushed.
**7** Carefully transfer the largest meringue round to a serving plate. Whip the cream until softly peaking, then spread over the meringue. Scatter the praline on top of the cream. Cover with the smaller meringue round and dust the top of the gâteau with cocoa powder.

# ALMOND AND APRICOT ROULADE

**SERVES 8**
PREPARATION
20 minutes, plus standing
COOKING TIME
20 minutes
FREEZING
Not suitable
CALS/SERVING
380

ROULADE
25 g (1 oz) flaked almonds
125 g (4 oz) white almond paste
5 eggs, separated
150 g (5 oz) caster sugar
5 ml (1 tsp) vanilla essence
45 ml (3 tbsp) plain white flour
45 ml (3 tbsp) amaretto liqueur

FILLING
6 ripe apricots
300 g (10 oz) crème fraîche
caster or icing sugar, for dusting

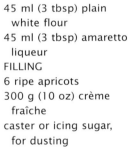

**1** Grease a 33 x 23 cm (13 x 9 inch) Swiss roll tin and line with greased non-stick baking parchment. Scatter the flaked almonds evenly over the paper. Grate the almond paste.

**2** Whisk the egg yolks with 125 g (4 oz) of the sugar until pale and fluffy. Stir in the vanilla essence and grated almond paste. Sift the flour over the mixture, then lightly fold in.

**3** Whisk the egg whites in another bowl, until stiff but not dry. Gradually whisk in the remaining sugar. Using a large metal spoon, fold a quarter of the egg whites into the almond mixture to loosen it, then carefully fold in the remainder.

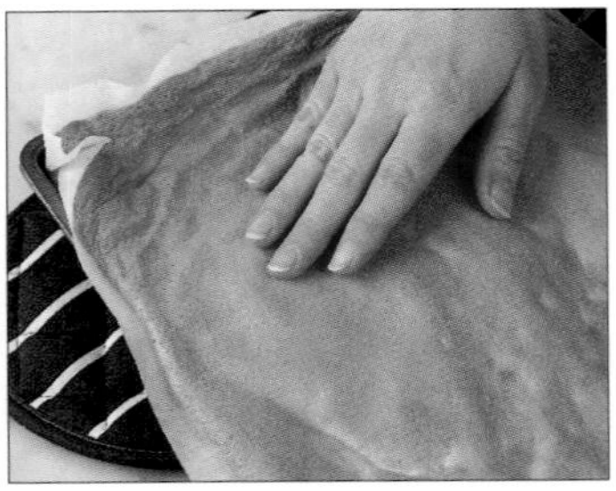

**4** Turn into the prepared tin and gently ease the mixture into the corners. Bake at 180°C (350°F) Mark 4 for about 20 minutes or until well risen and just firm to the touch. Cover with a sheet of non-stick baking parchment and a damp tea-towel. Leave until cool.

**5** Remove the tea-towel and invert the roulade (and paper) onto a baking sheet. Peel off the lining paper. Sprinkle another piece of baking parchment with caster sugar and flip the roulade onto it. Drizzle with the amaretto liqueur.

**6** Halve and stone the apricots; cut into small pieces. Spread the roulade with the crème fraîche and scatter over the apricots. Starting from one of the narrow ends, carefully roll up the roulade, using the paper to help. Transfer to a plate and dust with caster or icing sugar to serve.

**NOTE** The roulade will probably crack during rolling – this is an appealing characteristic!

**VARIATIONS**

❑ For the filling, use 300 ml (½ pint) whipped cream instead of the crème fraîche.
❑ Replace the apricots with strawberries or raspberries. Use kirsch or Grand Marnier instead of amaretto liqueur.

## CHOCOLATE CINNAMON MOUSSE CAKE

**SERVES 8**
PREPARATION
35 minutes, plus cooling
COOKING TIME
30-40 minutes
FREEZING
Not suitable
CALS/SERVING
455

225 g (8 oz) plain chocolate, in pieces
125 g (4 oz) unsalted butter
30 ml (2 tbsp) brandy
5 eggs, separated
125 g (4 oz) caster sugar
5 ml (1 tsp) ground cinnamon

TO DECORATE
50 g (2 oz) plain chocolate, in pieces
125 g (4 oz) strawberries
chocolate caraque (see page 286)
icing sugar, for dusting

**1** Grease and line a 23 cm (9 inch) spring-release cake tin.
**2** Melt the chocolate in a heatproof bowl over a pan of simmering water. Add the butter and leave until melted. Remove from the heat and stir in the brandy.
**3** Place the egg yolks in a bowl with 75 g (3 oz) of the sugar. Whisk until the mixture is pale and thick enough to leave a thin trail on the surface when the whisk is lifted. Stir in the melted chocolate.
**4** In a separate bowl, whisk the egg whites until stiff. Gradually whisk in the remaining sugar, adding the cinnamon with the final addition. Using a large metal spoon, fold a quarter into the chocolate mixture to loosen it, then carefully fold in the remainder.
**5** Turn the mixture into the prepared tin and bake at 160°C (325°F) Mark 3 for 30-40 minutes until well risen and the centre feels just spongy. Leave to cool in the tin.
**6** Transfer the cake to a serving plate, peeling away the lining paper. For the decoration, melt the chocolate in a heatproof bowl set over a pan of simmering water. Dip the strawberries in the chocolate to half-coat. Casually pile the chocolate curls and strawberries onto the cake and dust lightly with icing sugar to serve.

## ORANGE SORBET

**SERVES 4-6**
PREPARATION
20 minutes, plus chilling
FREEZING TIME
3-4 hours
CALS/SERVING
240-160
COLOUR INDEX
Page 74

10 juicy oranges
200 g (7 oz) caster sugar
200 ml (1/3 pint) water
30 ml (2 tbsp) orange flower water
1 egg white

**1** Finely pare the zest from the oranges, using a citrus zester, then squeeze the juice. Place in a saucepan with the sugar and water and heat gently to dissolve the sugar. Increase the heat and boil for 1 minute.
**2** Leave the sugar syrup to cool, then stir in the orange flower water. Cover and chill in the refrigerator for about 30 minutes.
**3** Strain the cooled syrup through a fine sieve into a bowl. In another bowl, beat the egg white until just frothy, then whisk into the orange mixture.
**4** For optimum results, freeze in an ice-cream maker. Alternatively, pour into a shallow freezer tray and freeze until the sorbet is almost frozen; mash well with a fork and refreeze until solid.
**5** Transfer to the refrigerator 30 minutes before serving to soften slightly.

## STRAWBERRY SORBET

**SERVES 4-6**
PREPARATION
20 minutes, plus chilling
FREEZING TIME
3-4 hours
CALS/SERVING
280-185
COLOUR INDEX
Page 74

250 g (9 oz) caster sugar
250 ml (8 fl oz) water
450 g (1 lb) ripe strawberries
15 ml (1 tbsp) balsamic vinegar
1 egg white

**1** Place the sugar and water in a saucepan and heat gently to dissolve the sugar. Increase the heat and boil for 1 minute. Leave the sugar syrup to cool. Cover and chill in the refrigerator for 30 minutes.
**2** Meanwhile, hull the strawberries if necessary. Place in a blender or food processor and process until smooth. Pass through a sieve into a bowl to remove the seeds, if preferred. Cover and chill for 30 minutes.
**3** Stir the syrup and vinegar into the strawberry purée.
**4** In another bowl, beat the egg white until just frothy, then whisk into the strawberry mixture.
**5** For optimum results, freeze in an ice-cream maker. Alternatively, pour into a shallow freezer tray and freeze until the sorbet is almost frozen; mash well with a fork and refreeze until solid.
**6** Transfer to the refrigerator 30 minutes before serving to soften slightly.

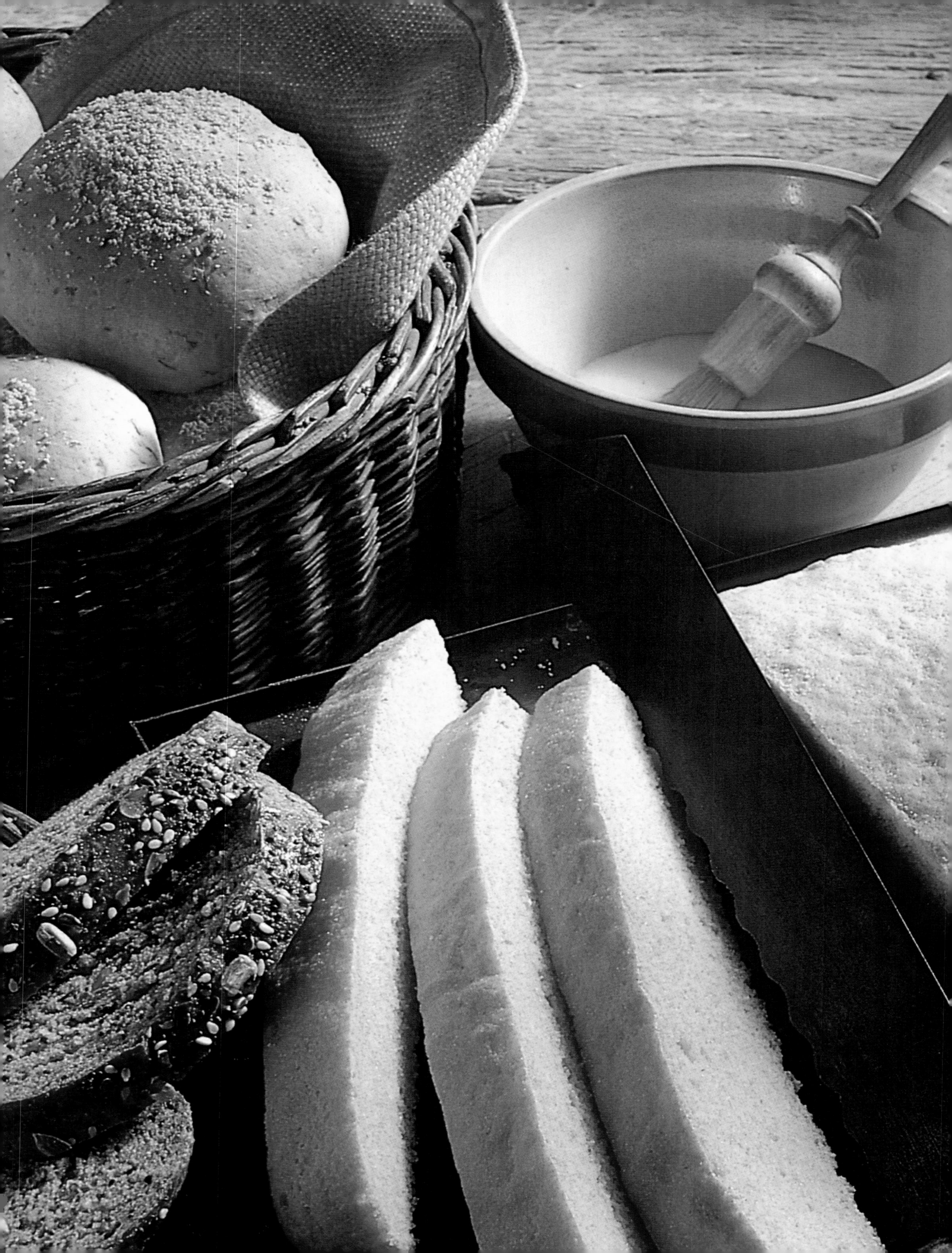

# BREADS, BISCUITS AND CAKES

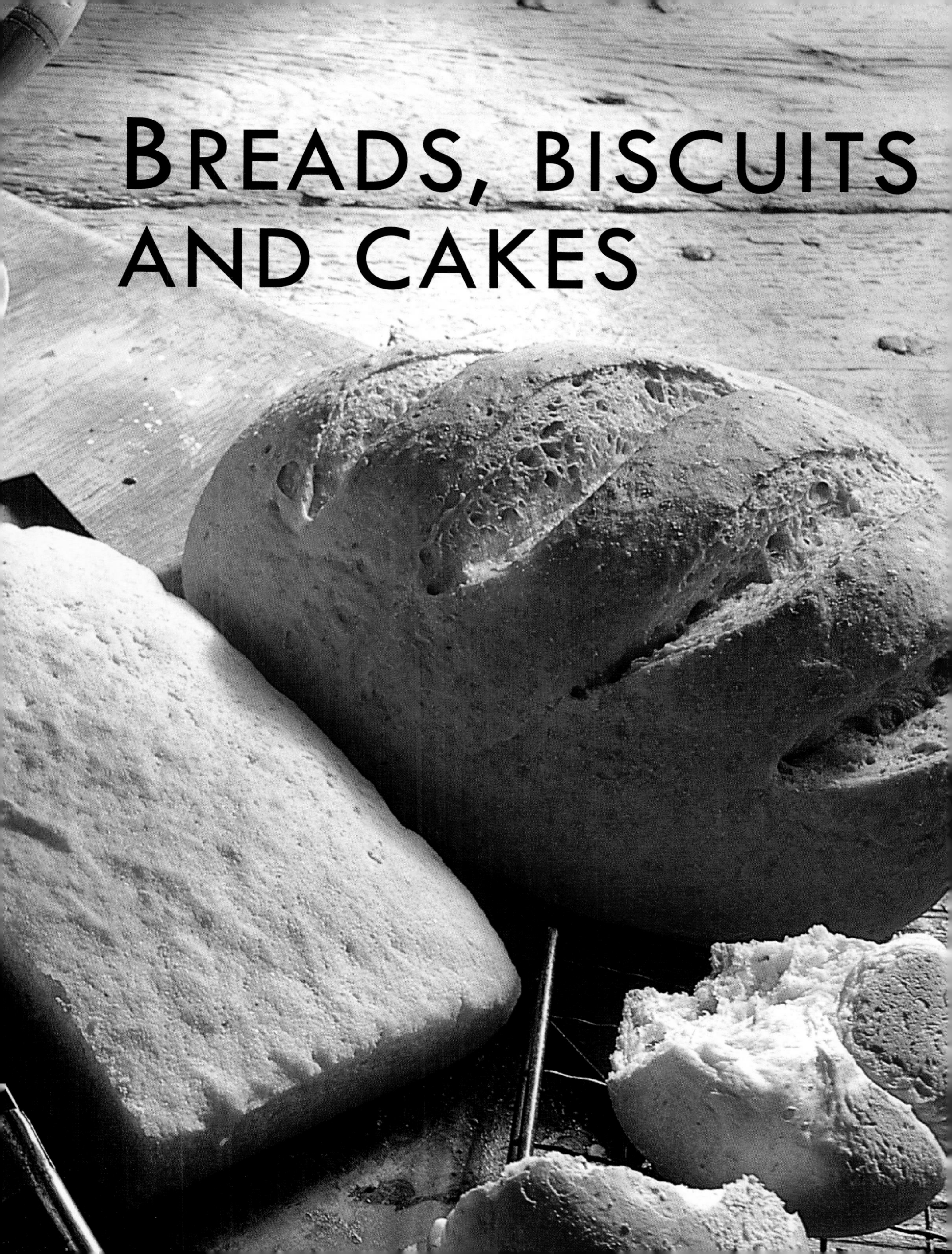

## MULTIGRAIN LOAF

**MAKES 2**
PREPARATION
20 minutes, plus rising
COOKING TIME
30-35 minutes
FREEZING
Suitable
CALS/SLICE
115
COLOUR INDEX
Page 75

225 g (8 oz) wholemeal bread flour
350 g (12 oz) granary flour
125 g (4 oz) rye flour
25 g (1 oz) butter or margarine, diced
10 ml (2 tsp) salt
10 ml (2 tsp) fast-action dried yeast (see note)
5 ml (1 tsp) caster sugar
40 g (1½ oz) rolled oats or barley, or millet flakes
30 ml (2 tbsp) each sesame seeds, poppy seeds, sunflower seeds and linseed
450 ml (¾ pint) warmed water
30 ml (2 tbsp) malt extract

TO FINISH
beaten egg, to glaze
extra seeds (as above)

**1** Mix the flours together in a large bowl. Rub in the butter, then stir in the other dry ingredients. Make a well in the centre, add the warm water and malt and work to form a soft dough.

**2** Knead the dough for 10 minutes, then transfer to a greased bowl, cover and leave to rise in a warm place for 2 hours or until doubled in size.

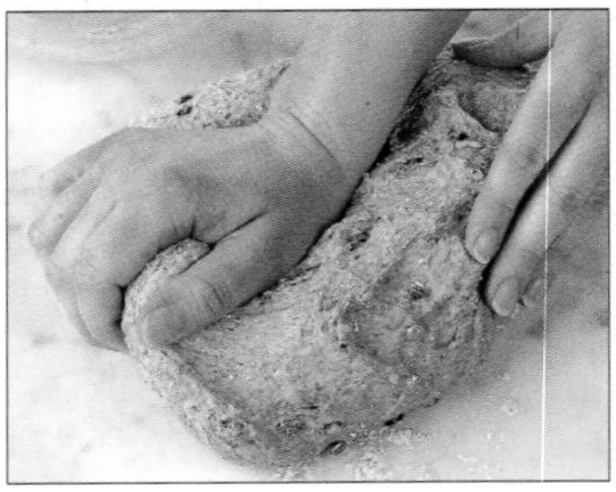

**3** Lightly oil two 900 g (2 lb) loaf tins. Knock back the dough, cut in half and shape each into an oblong.

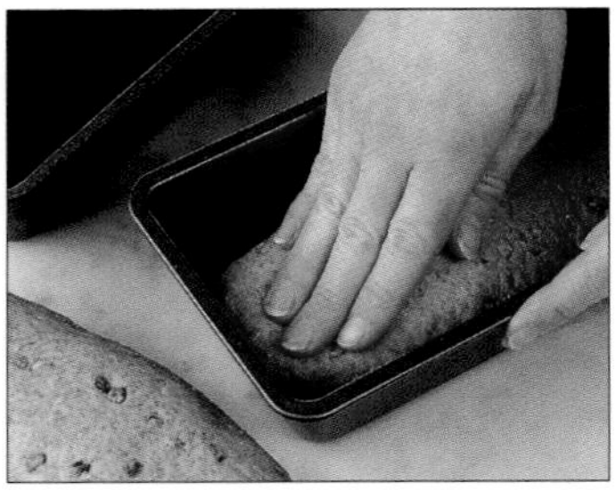

**4** Press into the tins, cover loosely and leave to rise for 30 minutes until the dough reaches the top of the tins.

**5** Carefully brush each loaf with egg glaze and scatter over some extra seeds. Bake in the oven at 220°C (425°F) Mark 7 for 30-35 minutes until the breads are risen and golden brown.

**6** To test whether the bread is cooked, tap the bottom of the loaf – it should sound hollow. Leave in the tins for 10 minutes, than transfer to a wire rack to cool.

**NOTES**

❑ If available, use 25 g (1 oz) fresh yeast instead of dried. Crumble into a bowl, add the sugar, 150 ml (¼ pint) of the warmed water and 60 ml (4 tbsp) of the wholemeal flour. Stir well to dissolve the yeast, then leave to froth in a warm place for 10 minutes. Continue as above, adding the yeast to the dry ingredients with the rest of the water.

❑ As a vegan alternative to the glaze, brush the loaf with olive oil.

## RUSTIC LOAF

**MAKES 1**
PREPARATION
15 minutes, plus overnight 'sponging'
COOKING TIME
35-40 minutes
FREEZING
Suitable
CALS/SLICE
120
COLOUR INDEX
Page 75

STARTER DOUGH
10 ml (2 tsp) fast-action dried yeast
75 ml (5 tbsp) warmed water
1.25 ml (¼ tsp) caster sugar
50 g (2 oz) strong plain white flour

BREAD DOUGH
300 g (10 oz) strong plain white flour
125 g (4 oz) wholemeal bread flour
10 ml (2 tsp) salt
200 ml (7 fl oz) warmed water
30 ml (2 tbsp) olive oil

**1** To make the starter dough, put the yeast in a bowl with the warmed water, sugar and flour and stir well. Cover and leave to 'sponge' in the refrigerator overnight.
**2** The next day remove the starter from the refrigerator 1 hour before required.
**3** Place all the dry ingredients for the bread dough in a bowl. Make a well in the centre and add the starter, warm water and olive oil. Work together to form a soft dough.
**4** Knead for 10 minutes until smooth, then transfer the dough to a greased bowl, cover and leave to rise in a warm place for 2-3 hours until doubled in size.
**5** Preheat a baking sheet on the top shelf and a roasting tin filled with water on the bottom shelf of the oven – set at 230°C (450°F) Mark 8.
**6** Knock back the dough and shape into an oval. Place on a well floured baking sheet, cover loosely and leave to rise for a further 30 minutes.
**7** Using a sharp knife, cut 3-4 deep slashes in the dough, brush with a little water and transfer to the heated baking sheet. Bake for 15 minutes, then reduce the temperature to 190°C (375°F) Mark 5 and bake for a further 20-25 minutes until the bread is risen and golden, and sounds hollow when tapped underneath. Cool on a wire rack.

## CORNBREAD

**MAKES 1**
PREPARATION
15 minutes, plus rising
COOKING TIME
25-30 minutes
FREEZING
Suitable
CALS/SLICE
125
COLOUR INDEX
Page 75

225 g (8 oz) coarse cornmeal
225 g (8 oz) strong plain white flour
7.5 ml (1½ tsp) fast-action dried yeast
5 ml (1 tsp) salt
2.5 ml (½ tsp) caster sugar
400 ml (14 fl oz) milk
15 g (½ oz) butter or margarine

**1** Combine all of the dry ingredients in a large bowl. Heat the milk and butter in a small pan until the butter is melted, cool until tepid, then work into the dry ingredients to form a soft dough.
**2** Knead for 8-10 minutes until smooth, then transfer the dough to a greased bowl. Cover and leave to rise in a warm place for 1-1½ hours until doubled in size.
**3** Oil a 20 cm (8 inch) square cake tin. Knock back the dough and shape into a square a little smaller than the prepared tin. Press into the tin, cover loosely and leave to rise for a further 30 minutes.
**4** Bake at 220°C (425°F) Mark 7 for 25-30 minutes until risen and golden. Leave in the tin for 10 minutes, then transfer to a wire rack to cool. Serve cold, cut into fingers.

## PARMESAN AND CHIVE ROLLS

**MAKES 8**
PREPARATION
20 minutes, plus rising
COOKING TIME
10-15 minutes
FREEZING
Suitable
CALS/ROLL
270
COLOUR INDEX
Page 75

450 g (1 lb) strong plain white flour
5 ml (1 tsp) salt
10 ml (2 tsp) fast-action dried yeast
pinch of sugar
60 ml (4 tbsp) chopped fresh chives (or chervil or parsley)
60 g (2½ oz) Parmesan cheese, freshly grated
300 ml (½ pint) milk
25 g (1 oz) butter

**1** Sift the flour and salt into a bowl and stir in the yeast, sugar, chives, and all but 15 g (½ oz) of the cheese.
**2** Heat the milk and butter in a small pan until the butter is melted, then cool slightly until tepid. Gradually add to the dry ingredients and work together to form a soft dough.
**3** Knead for 8-10 minutes until smooth and elastic, then transfer the dough to a greased bowl. Cover and leave to rise in a warm place for 1 hour.
**4** Knock back the dough and divide into 8 equal pieces. Shape into balls, flatten slightly to form rolls and place on an oiled large baking sheet. Cover loosely and leave to rise for a further 30 minutes.
**5** Sprinkle the remaining Parmesan over the rolls and bake at 220°C (425°F) Mark 7 for 15-20 minutes until risen and golden. Cool on a wire rack.

## SODA BREAD

**MAKES 1**
PREPARATION
15 minutes
COOKING TIME
30-35 minutes
FREEZING
Suitable
CALS/SLICE
125-110

350 g (12 oz) wholemeal flour
125 g (4 oz) pin-head oatmeal
10 ml (2 tsp) bicarbonate of soda
5 ml (1 tsp) salt
5 ml (1 tsp) thin honey
300 ml (½ pint) buttermilk
30-45 ml (2-3 tbsp) milk

**1** Combine all of the dry ingredients in a large bowl. Make a well in the centre and gradually beat in the honey, buttermilk and enough milk to form a soft dough.
**2** Transfer to a lightly floured surface and knead for 5 minutes. Shape the dough into a 20 cm (8 inch) round and place on a lightly oiled baking sheet.
**3** Using a sharp knife, cut a deep cross on top of the dough. Brush with a little extra milk and bake at 200°C (400°F) Mark 6 for 30-35 minutes until the bread is slightly risen and sounds hollow when tapped underneath. Cool on a wire rack and serve the same day.

## GRIDDLED FLAT BREADS

**MAKES 12**
PREPARATION
15 minutes, plus rising
COOKING TIME
2-3 minutes per batch
FREEZING
Suitable
CALS/SERVING
140

300 g (10 oz) strong plain white flour
175 g (6 oz) gram flour
5 ml (1 tsp) salt
10 ml (2 tsp) fast-action dried yeast
10 ml (2 tsp) ground cumin
2.5 ml (½ tsp) caster sugar
250-300 ml (8-10 fl oz) warmed water

**1** Mix the dry ingredients together in a large bowl. Make a well in the centre and gradually work in the warmed water to form a soft dough.
**2** Knead for 8-10 minutes until smooth and elastic, transfer to a greased bowl, cover and leave to rise in a warm place for 1-1½ hours until doubled in size.
**3** Knock back the dough and divide into 12 equal pieces. Roll each one out to a small oval about 7.5 x 15 cm (3 x 6 inches) and place on well floured baking sheets. Spray with a little water, cover loosely and leave to rise for a further 15 minutes.
**4** Preheat a lightly oiled griddle, or the grill. Cook, a few at a time, for about 1-2 minutes until puffed up and golden (see note). Flip the breads over and cook the underside for a further 30 seconds-1 minute. Transfer to a basket, cover with a tea-towel and keep warm while cooking the rest. Serve the breads as soon as possible.

**NOTES**
❑ If grilling the breads, position the grill rack 8-10 cm (3-4 inches) below the heat to allow room for the breads to puff up.
❑ If not serving immediately, place the breads in a polythene bag as they are cooked, to keep them soft.

## FRIED ONION BREAD

**MAKES 2**
**(each serves 4)**
PREPARATION
20 minutes, plus rising
COOKING TIME
25-30 minutes
FREEZING
Not suitable
CALS/SERVING
115
COLOUR INDEX
Page 76

450 g (1 lb) strong plain white flour
5 ml (1 tsp) salt
5 ml (1 tsp) fast-action dried yeast
2.5 ml (½ tsp) caster sugar
300 ml (½ pint) warmed water

TOPPING
1 red onion
10 ml (2 tsp) chopped fresh thyme
50 g (2 oz) Cheddar cheese, grated
pepper
oil, for brushing

**1** Sift the flour and salt into a bowl, stir in the yeast and sugar, then make a well in the centre. Gradually work in the warmed water to form a soft dough.
**2** Knead for 8-10 minutes until smooth and elastic, then transfer the dough to a greased bowl. Cover and leave to rise in a warm place for 1-1½ hours until doubled in size.
**3** Knock back the dough, divide in half and knead briefly. Roll each portion out to a 20 cm (8 inch) flat round, transfer to a well-floured baking sheet or board, cover loosely and leave to rise for a further 30 minutes.
**4** Meanwhile, peel and slice the onion very finely. Place in a bowl and mix with the thyme and cheese; season with pepper and set aside.
**5** Brush a griddle or ovenproof skillet (see note) with oil and heat until starting to smoke. Carefully transfer one dough to the pan, immediately lower the heat and cook for 10 minutes until the base is golden.
**6** Remove from the heat and sprinkle half the onion, thyme and cheese mixture over the top of the bread. Bake in the oven at 200°C (400°F) Mark 6 for about 15 minutes until the dough is risen and firm to the touch. Transfer to a wire rack to cool. Repeat with the remaining dough and topping to make the second loaf. Serve warm.

**NOTE** Best results are obtained if a cast-iron griddle is used. A skillet or ovenproof frying pan with sides prevents the top from browning properly, although you can rectify this by popping the bread under a hot grill for 1 minute.

## PESTO-STUFFED BREADS

**MAKES 4**
**(each serves 2)**
PREPARATION
20 minutes, plus rising
COOKING TIME
10-15 minutes
FREEZING
Suitable
CALS/SERVING
265

450 g (1 lb) strong plain white flour
5 ml (1 tsp) fast-action dried yeast
5 ml (1 tsp) sugar
5 ml (1 tsp) sea salt
15 ml (1 tbsp) olive oil
300 ml (½ pint) warmed milk
75 ml (5 tbsp) Pesto (see page 292) – ½ quantity

**1** Sift the flour into a bowl and stir in the yeast, sugar and salt. Make a well in the centre and gradually work in the oil and warmed milk to form a soft dough.
**2** Knead for 8-10 minutes until smooth, then transfer the dough to a greased bowl. Cover and leave to rise in a warm place for 1-1½ hours.
**3** Knock back the dough and divide into 4 equal pieces. Roll each one out to a long thin rectangle about 30 x 10 cm (12 x 4 inches). Spread a quarter of the pesto over each dough, leaving a 1 cm (½ inch) border free around the edges, then fold each side into the centre to almost enclose the pesto.
**4** Place on a lightly oiled large baking sheet. Cover loosely and leave to rise for a further 20 minutes. Bake in the oven at 220°C (425°F) Mark 7 for 10-15 minutes until the bread is risen and sounds hollow when tapped underneath. Wrap the breads in a clean tea-towel to cool. Serve warm.

## SCHIACCIATA

**MAKES 2**
**(each serves 4)**
PREPARATION
15 minutes, plus rising
COOKING TIME
15-20 minutes
FREEZING
Suitable
CALS/SERVING
265

450 g (1 lb) strong plain white flour
5 ml (1 tsp) fast-action dried yeast
5 ml (1 tsp) sea salt
2.5 ml (½ tsp) caster sugar
30 ml (2 tbsp) extra-virgin olive oil
250-300 ml (8-10 fl oz) warmed water

TOPPING
60 ml (4 tbsp) extra-virgin olive oil
2 garlic cloves, peeled and crushed
15 ml (1 tbsp) chopped sage

**1** Sift the flour into a large bowl and stir in the yeast, salt and sugar. Make a well in the centre and gradually work in the oil and sufficient warmed water to form a soft dough.
**2** Knead for 8-10 minutes until smooth and elastic, then transfer the dough to a greased bowl. Cover and leave to rise in a warm place for 1-1½ hours until doubled in size.
**3** Preheat a large baking sheet on the top shelf of the oven set at 220°C (425°F) Mark 7. Knock back the dough, divide in half and roll each piece out to a 12 x 25 cm (5 x 10 inch) oval. Transfer to a well floured baking sheet, cover loosely and leave to rise for a further 30 minutes.
**4** To prepare the topping, in a small bowl, mix the oil with the garlic, sage and a little salt.
**5** Make 4 deep slashes along each oval and transfer to the preheated baking sheet. Quickly drizzle over the garlic oil and bake for 15-20 minutes until the bread is risen and golden. Transfer to a wire rack to cool. Serve warm.

## PESHWARI NAAN BREAD

**MAKES 4**
PREPARATION
30 minutes, plus rising
COOKING TIME
10-12 minutes
FREEZING
Not suitable
CALS/NAAN
395

350 g (12 oz) strong plain white flour
5 ml (1 tsp) salt
5 ml (1 tsp) fast-action dried yeast
175 ml (6 fl oz) warmed water
15 g (½ oz) butter or margarine, melted

FILLING
1 onion
25 g (1 oz) butter or margarine
2 garlic cloves, peeled and crushed
5 ml (1 tsp) grated fresh root ginger
10 ml (2 tsp) ground coriander
5 ml (1 tsp) ground cumin
5 ml (1 tsp) ground cinnamon
pinch of chilli powder
25 g (1 oz) sultanas
25 g (1 oz) desiccated coconut

TO FINISH
melted butter, for brushing (optional)

**1** Sift the flour and salt into a bowl and stir in the dried yeast. Make a well in the centre and gradually work in the warm water and melted butter to form a soft dough.
**2** Knead for 8-10 minutes until smooth and elastic, then transfer the dough to a greased bowl. Cover and leave to rise in a warm place for 1-1½ hours until doubled in size.
**3** Meanwhile, prepare the filling. Peel and chop the onion very finely. Melt the butter in a frying pan, add the onion, garlic, ginger and spices and fry gently for 10-15 minutes until completely softened. Chop the sultanas and stir into the spiced mixture, together with the coconut and 30 ml (2 tbsp) water. Cover and simmer for 10 minutes. Remove from the heat and set aside to cool.
**4** Knock back the dough and divide into 4 equal pieces. Roll each one out to a 20 cm (8 inch) round. Divide the filling between the rounds, spreading it over one half of each round.
**5** Fold the bread over and carefully reshape, pressing the edges together to seal. Roll out again, to form flat ovals, about 20 cm (8 inch) long. Transfer the breads to a well floured baking sheet, cover loosely and leave to rise for 15 minutes. Meanwhile, preheat a large baking sheet on the top shelf of the oven at 230°C (450°F) Mark 8.
**6** Carefully transfer the breads to the heated baking sheet and bake for 10-12 minutes until puffed up and lightly golden. Brush with melted butter and serve hot.

## FOCACCIA

**MAKES 2 (each serves 6)**
PREPARATION
30 minutes, plus rising
COOKING TIME
20-25 minutes
FREEZING
Suitable
CALS/SERVING
275
COLOUR INDEX
Page 76

700 g (1½ lb) strong plain white flour
15 ml (1 tbsp) fast-action dried yeast
450 ml (¾ pint) warmed water
45 ml (3 tbsp) extra-virgin olive oil

TO FINISH
60 ml (4 tbsp) olive oil
coarse sea or crystal salt, for sprinkling

**1** Sift the flour into a large bowl and stir in the yeast. Make a well in the centre and gradually work in the warmed water and olive oil to form a soft dough.
**2** Knead for 10 minutes until smooth and elastic, then place in a greased bowl. Cover and leave to rise in a warm place for 1½-2 hours until doubled in size.
**3** Lightly oil two shallow 25 cm (10 inch) metal pizza or pie plates. Knock back the dough and divide in half. Roll out each piece to a 25 cm (10 inch) circle. Place in the oiled tins. Cover with a damp tea-towel and leave to rise in a warm place for 30 minutes.
**4** Using your fingertips, make deep dimples all over the surface of the dough. Drizzle with the olive oil, sprinkle generously with salt and spray with water.
**5** Bake in the oven at 200°C (400°F) Mark 6 for 20-25 minutes, spraying with water twice during cooking. Transfer to a wire rack to cool. Serve warm.

**NOTE** Eat focaccia the day it is made, or freeze as soon as it is cool; defrost and warm through in the oven to serve.

**VARIATION**
OLIVE AND SUN-DRIED TOMATO FOCACCIA Drain 50 g (2 oz) sun-dried tomatoes in oil, slice and knead into the dough at stage 2. Scatter 225 g (8 oz) black or green olives over the dough at stage 4.

# STUFFED FOCACCIA

**SERVES 6-8**
PREPARATION
30 minutes, plus rising
COOKING TIME
30-35 minutes
FREEZING
Suitable
CALS/SERVING
420-315

450 g (1 lb) strong plain white flour
10 ml (2 tsp) fast-action dried yeast
300 ml (½ pint) warmed water
45 ml (3 tbsp) extra-virgin olive oil

FILLING
225 g (8 oz) frozen leaf spinach, thawed and drained
225 g (8 oz) fontina or mozzarella cheese
15 ml (1 tbsp) chopped fresh herbs, such as oregano, sage, rosemary and thyme
salt and pepper

TO FINISH
extra-virgin olive oil, for brushing
coarse sea salt, for sprinkling

**1** Sift the flour into a bowl and stir in the dried yeast. Make a well in the centre and gradually work in the warmed water and oil to form a soft dough.

**2** Knead for 10 minutes until smooth and elastic. Place in a greased bowl. Cover and leave to rise in a warm place for 1½-2 hours until doubled in size.

**3** To prepare the filling, squeeze the spinach to remove all excess moisture, then place in a bowl. Dice the cheese and add to the spinach. Add the chopped herbs and season generously with salt and pepper. Mix well.

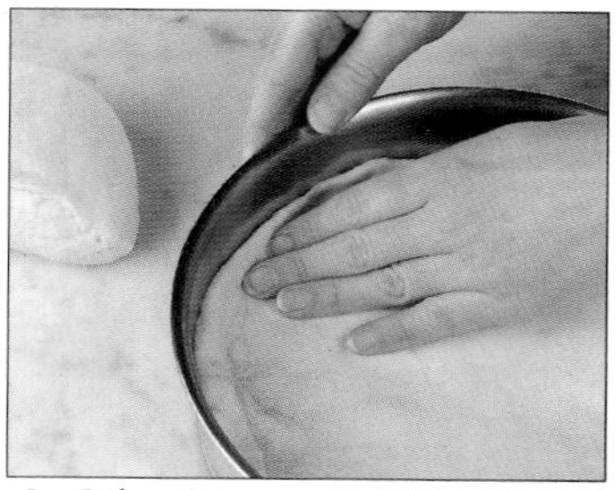

**4** Oil a 25 cm (10 inch) loose-bottomed cake tin. Knock back the dough and divide in half. Roll out one half to a round, a little larger than the tin, then place in the tin, pressing it onto the base and a little way up the side.

**5** Spread the filling over the dough to within 1 cm (½ inch) of the edge. Roll out the remaining dough to a 25 cm (10 inch) round, dampen the edge with a little water and place over the filling. Press the edges together well to seal.

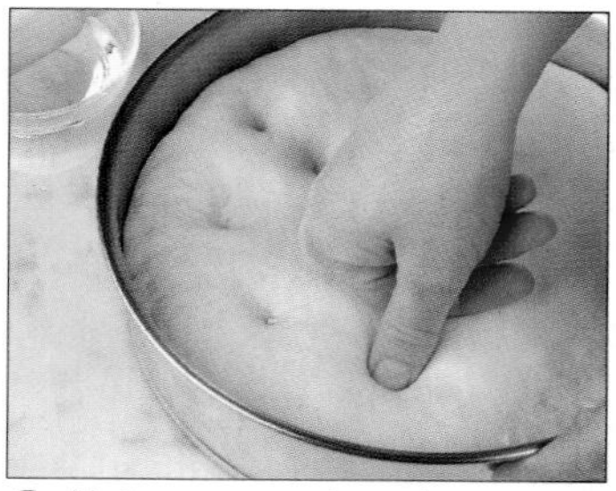

**6** Using your thumb, press indentations all over the surface. Brush the surface with a little olive oil.

**7** Sprinkle generously with sea salt and spray with water. Bake at 220°C (425°F) Mark 7 for 30-35 minutes until risen and firm to the touch. Leave in the tin for 10 minutes, then transfer to a wire rack to cool. Serve warm, cut into wedges.

**NOTE** Eat this stuffed focaccia the day it is made or freeze as soon as it is cool. Defrost at room temperature and warm through in the oven to serve.

## APRICOT AND HAZELNUT BREAD

**MAKES 2**
PREPARATION
20 minutes, plus rising
COOKING TIME
30-35 minutes
FREEZING
Suitable
CALS/SLICE
125-105

450 g (1 lb) granary flour
225 g (8 oz) strong plain white flour
10 ml (2 tsp) salt
25 g (1 oz) butter
75 g (3 oz) hazelnuts, toasted
75 g (3 oz) dried apricots
7.5 ml (1½ tsp) fast-action dried yeast
30 ml (2 tbsp) molasses
350 ml (12 fl oz) warmed water

**1** Put the granary and white flour into a large bowl. Add the salt, then rub in the butter. Chop the hazelnuts and dried apricots; stir into the flour mixture with the yeast.
**2** Make a well in the centre and gradually work in the molasses and warmed water to form a soft dough.
**3** Knead for 8-10 minutes until smooth, then transfer the dough to a greased bowl. Cover and leave to rise in a warm place for 1-1½ hours until doubled in size.
**4** Preheat a large baking sheet on the top shelf of the oven set at 220°C (425°F) Mark 7. Knock back the dough, then divide in half. Shape each portion into a small flattish round and place on a well floured baking sheet. Cover loosely and leave to rise for a further 30 minutes.
**5** Using a sharp knife, cut several slashes on each round, brush with a little milk and transfer to the heated baking sheet. Bake for 15 minutes, then reduce the oven setting to 190°C (375°F) Mark 5 and bake for a further 15-20 minutes or until the bread is risen and sounds hollow when tapped underneath. Cool on a wire rack.

## HINNY CAKES WITH BLUEBERRIES

**MAKES 10**
PREPARATION
10 minutes
COOKING TIME
14-18 minutes
FREEZING
Not suitable
CALS/CAKE
190
COLOUR INDEX
Page 77

175 g (6 oz) self-raising white flour
pinch of salt
5 ml (1 tsp) baking powder
1.25 ml (¼ tsp) ground mace
1.25 ml (¼ tsp) ground cloves
75 g (3 oz) unsalted butter
25 g (1 oz) ground rice
25 g (1 oz) caster sugar
90 ml (3 fl oz) milk
30 ml (2 tbsp) sunflower oil
TO FINISH
225-350 g (8-12 oz) blueberries
40 g (1½ oz) caster sugar

**1** Sift the flour, salt, baking powder, mace and cloves into a bowl. Add 50 g (2 oz) of the butter, in small pieces, and rub in using the fingertips until the mixture resembles fine breadcrumbs. Stir in the ground rice and sugar. Add the milk and mix to a fairly soft dough, using a round-bladed knife.
**2** Turn the dough out onto a lightly floured surface and knead very lightly. Shape into a log, then cut into 10 slices. Shape into small flat cakes, using lightly floured hands.
**3** Melt 15 g (½ oz) of the remaining butter with half the oil in a large heavy-based frying pan or griddle and fry half of the cakes over a low heat for 3-4 minutes until golden underneath. Turn the cakes over and cook for a further 3-4 minutes until cooked through. Transfer to a large baking sheet. Melt the remaining butter with the oil and fry the rest of the cakes in the same way.
**4** Spoon the blueberries onto the cakes, piling them up slightly in the centre. Sprinkle with the sugar. Place on the grill rack and grill for about 2 minutes, watching closely, until the blueberries are bubbling and the cake edges are lightly toasted. Serve immediately, with whipped cream or crème fraîche.

**VARIATIONS** Use cranberries, or a mixture of dessert apples and blackberries instead of blueberries.

## SHORTBREAD

**MAKES 18-20**
PREPARATION
20 minutes, plus chilling
COOKING TIME
15-20 minutes
FREEZING
Not suitable
CALS/SHORTBREAD
270-180
COLOUR INDEX
Page 77

225 g (8 oz) butter
125 g (4 oz) caster sugar
225 g (8 oz) plain white flour
125 g (4 oz) ground rice or rice flour
pinch of salt
TO DECORATE
golden or coloured granulated sugar, for coating
caster sugar, for sprinkling

**1** Make sure all of the ingredients are at room temperature. Cream the butter and sugar together in a bowl until pale and fluffy. Sift the flour, rice flour and salt together onto the

creamed mixture and stir in, using a wooden spoon, until the mixture resembles breadcrumbs.
**2** Gather the dough together with your hand and turn onto a clean work surface. Knead lightly until it forms a ball, then lightly roll into a sausage, about 5 cm (2 inches) thick. Wrap in cling film and chill in the refrigerator until firm.
**3** Unwrap the roll and slice into discs, about 7-10 mm (⅓-½ inch) thick. Pour golden or coloured granulated sugar onto a plate and roll the edge of each disc in the sugar. Place the biscuits, cut-side up, on two baking sheets, lined with greaseproof paper.
**4** Bake at 190°C (375°F) Mark 5 for 15-20 minutes, depending on thickness, until very pale golden. Remove from the oven and sprinkle with caster sugar. Leave on the baking sheet for 10 minutes, then transfer to a wire rack to cool.

**NOTES**
❑ Never overwork shortbread or it will become tough.
❑ Take care to avoid overcooking too – shortbread should never really colour, just set and turn very pale.

**VARIATIONS**
SPICED SHORTBREAD Sift 15 ml (1 tbsp) ground mixed spice with the flours.
GINGER SHORTBREAD Sift 5 ml (1 tsp) ground ginger with the flours. Add 50 g (2 oz) chopped crystallised ginger to the dough.

## DOUBLE CHOCOLATE COOKIES

**MAKES 18**
PREPARATION
15 minutes
COOKING TIME
12-15 minutes
FREEZING
Suitable
CALS/BISCUIT
215
COLOUR INDEX
Page 77

125 g (4 oz) white chocolate
125 g (4 oz) plain dark chocolate
125 g (4 oz) unsalted butter, softened
125 g (4 oz) caster sugar
1 egg
5 ml (1 tsp) vanilla essence
125 g (4 oz) porridge oats
150 g (5 oz) plain white flour
2.5 ml (½ tsp) baking powder

**1** Chop the white and plain chocolate into small chunks, no larger than 1 cm (½ inch) in diameter.
**2** Cream the butter and sugar together in a bowl until pale and creamy. Add the egg, vanilla essence and oats. Sift the flour and baking powder into the bowl and mix until evenly combined. Stir in the chocolate chunks.
**3** Place dessertspoonfuls of the mixture on two lightly greased baking sheets, spacing them well apart to allow room for spreading. Flatten slightly with the back of a fork.
**4** Bake in the oven at 180°C (350°F) Mark 4 for 12-15 minutes until risen and turning golden. Leave on the baking sheets for 5 minutes, then transfer to a wire rack to cool. Store in an airtight tin for up to 1 week.

**NOTE** The cookies will only become firm as they cool. Don't be tempted to bake them until crisp.

## ALMOND FUDGE CRUMBLES

**MAKES 24**
PREPARATION
10 minutes
COOKING TIME
12 minutes
FREEZING
Suitable
CALS/BISCUIT
130

75 g (3 oz) flaked almonds
50 g (2 oz) vanilla fudge
200 g (7 oz) plain white flour
pinch of salt
2.5 ml (½ tsp) bicarbonate of soda
125 g (4 oz) unsalted butter
125 g (4 oz) muscovado sugar
1 egg
5 ml (1 tsp) almond essence

TOPPING
25 g (1 oz) flaked almonds
25 g (1 oz) vanilla fudge
icing sugar, for dusting

**1** Crumble the almonds into small flakes. Finely dice the fudge.
**2** Sift the flour, salt and bicarbonate of soda into a bowl. Add the butter, cut into small pieces, and rub in using the fingertips. Add the sugar, egg, almond essence, flaked almonds and fudge and mix to a fairly firm dough.
**3** Turn onto a lightly floured surface and roll into a cylinder, 23 cm (9 inches) long. Cut the dough into 24 rounds. Place the rounds, slightly apart, on two lightly greased baking sheets.
**4** For the topping, lightly crumble the almonds and chop the fudge. Scatter over the biscuits and press lightly to adhere. Bake in the oven at 190°C (375°F) Mark 5 for about 12 minutes until turning golden around the edges. Leave on the baking sheets for 5 minutes, then transfer to a wire rack to cool. Serve dusted with icing sugar.

## DOUBLE CHOCOLATE MUFFINS

**MAKES 12-15**
PREPARATION
15 minutes
COOKING TIME
25 minutes
FREEZING
Suitable
CALS/MUFFIN
370

- 300 g (10 oz) plain chocolate
- 125 g (4 oz) white chocolate
- 375 g (13 oz) self-raising white flour
- 15 ml (1 tbsp) baking powder
- 65 g (2½ oz) cocoa powder
- 75 g (3 oz) light muscovado sugar
- 1 egg
- 1 egg yolk
- 10 ml (2 tsp) vanilla essence
- 90 ml (6 tbsp) sunflower oil
- 375 ml (13 fl oz) milk

**1** Line 12-15 deep bun tins or muffin tins with paper muffin cases. Break up 175 g (6 oz) of the plain chocolate and melt in a heatproof bowl over a pan of simmering water.

**2** Roughly chop the remaining plain and white chocolate. Sift the flour, baking powder and cocoa powder together into a bowl. Stir in the sugar.

**3** In another bowl, beat together the egg, egg yolk, vanilla essence, oil, milk and melted chocolate. Add to the dry ingredients with the chopped chocolate and stir quickly until the flour is only just incorporated; do not over-mix.

**4** Spoon the mixture into the paper cases, piling it up in the centre. Bake at 220°C (425°F) Mark 7 for 25 minutes until the muffins are well risen and craggy in appearance. Transfer to a wire rack to cool. Serve warm or cold.

## STICKY GINGERBREAD

**12 SLICES**
PREPARATION
20 minutes
COOKING TIME
1 hour 20 minutes
FREEZING
Suitable
CALS/SLICE
350
COLOUR INDEX
Page 77

- 150 g (5 oz) preserved stem ginger in syrup, plus 45 ml (3 tbsp) syrup from jar
- 1 large cooking apple, about 225 g (8 oz)
- 15 ml (1 tbsp) lemon juice
- 125 g (4 oz) black treacle
- 175 g (6 oz) molasses or dark muscovado sugar
- 125 g (4 oz) golden syrup
- 175 g (6 oz) unsalted butter, in pieces
- 225 g (8 oz) plain white flour
- 125 g (4 oz) plain wholemeal flour
- 5 ml (1 tsp) ground mixed spice
- 7.5 ml (1½ tsp) bicarbonate of soda
- 2 eggs

**1** Grease and line a deep 18 cm (7 inch) square cake tin. Thinly slice the stem ginger. Peel, core and quarter the apple; immerse in a bowl of water with the lemon juice added to prevent discolouration.

**2** Put the treacle, molasses or sugar, golden syrup and butter in a saucepan. Heat gently until the butter melts; leave to cool slightly.

**3** Sift the flours, spice and bicarbonate of soda into a bowl. Grate three quarters of the apple into the bowl and toss lightly. Add the melted mixture, eggs and three quarters of the ginger pieces. Beat until thoroughly combined.

**4** Turn the mixture into the prepared tin, spreading it into the corners. Using a potato peeler, pare the remaining apple into thin slices. Scatter the apple slices and remaining ginger over the surface of the gingerbread and press down lightly into the mixture with the tip of a knife. Bake at 160°C (325°F) Mark 3 for 1 hour 20 minutes or until firm to the touch. Leave to cool in the tin.

**5** Turn out the cake and drizzle the ginger syrup over the surface. For optimum flavour, store in an airtight tin for several days before eating.

## SYRUPY SEMOLINA HALVA

**10 SLICES**
PREPARATION
30 minutes
COOKING TIME
30 minutes
FREEZING
Suitable:
Stage 3
CALS/SLICE
485

125 g (4 oz) unsalted butter, softened
125 g (4 oz) light muscovado sugar
grated zest of 1 orange
grated zest of 1 lemon
30 ml (2 tbsp) lemon juice
2 eggs
175 g (6 oz) semolina
5 ml (1 tsp) baking powder
125 g (4 oz) ground almonds
30 ml (2 tbsp) poppy seeds
TO FINISH
2 oranges
2 lemons
300 g (10 oz) caster sugar
300 ml (½ pint) freshly squeezed orange juice
2 cinnamon sticks, halved

**1** Grease and base-line a shallow 23 cm (9 inch) square baking tin.
**2** Cream the butter and sugar together until pale and fluffy. Add the orange and lemon zest, lemon juice, eggs, semolina, baking powder, ground almonds and poppy seeds. Beat well until evenly mixed, then turn into the prepared tin and level the surface.
**3** Bake at 220°C (425°F) Mark 7 for about 20 minutes until slightly risen and turning golden. Let cool in the tin, then peel off the paper and return to the tin.
**4** To finish, finely pare the zest from 1 orange and 1 lemon in strips using a citrus zester. Cut away all the white pith from both oranges and lemons, then thinly slice the fruit. Place the sugar in a heavy-based saucepan with the orange juice, cinnamon sticks and citrus zest. Heat gently, stirring until the sugar dissolves, then bring to the boil and boil for 3 minutes.
**5** Remove the citrus zest and cinnamon from the syrup with a slotted spoon and reserve. Pour just over half of the syrup evenly over the surface of the cake. Scatter the fruit slices, citrus zest and cinnamon sticks on top.
**6** Return the remaining syrup to the heat and boil for a further 5 minutes or until thickened and beginning to caramelise. Pour the syrup evenly over the fruit and leave for several hours before cutting.

**NOTE** This halva can be stored in an airtight plastic container for up to 4-5 days.

## APPLE, SULTANA AND CIDER SLICES

**MAKES 12**
PREPARATION
25 minutes
COOKING TIME
1 hour
FREEZING
Suitable
CALS/SERVING
380
COLOUR INDEX
Page 77

225 g (8 oz) puff pastry
3 dessert apples
15 ml (1 tbsp) lemon juice
175 g (6 oz) unsalted butter, softened
175 g (6 oz) caster sugar
125 g (4 oz) self-raising white flour
75 g (3 oz) self-raising wholemeal flour
2.5 ml (½ tsp) baking powder
3 eggs
45 ml (3 tbsp) medium dry cider
50 g (2 oz) sultanas
10 ml (2 tsp) icing sugar
TO FINISH
icing sugar, for sprinkling

**1** Roll out the pastry thinly on a lightly floured surface to a 28 cm (11 inch) square and place on a dampened baking sheet. Prick all over with a fork and bake at 200°C (400°F) Mark 6 for 10 minutes until risen. Reduce the oven temperature to 180°C (350°F) Mark 4.
**2** Lightly grease a 23 cm (9 inch) square shallow baking tin. Cut the pastry to fit the base of the tin, then carefully press into position.
**3** Peel, core and slice one of the apples. Place in a bowl of water with 5 ml (1 tsp) of the lemon juice. Core and slice the remaining apples, but do not peel; place in a separate bowl with the remaining lemon juice.
**4** Cream the butter and sugar together in a bowl until pale and creamy. Sift the flours and baking powder into the bowl. Add the eggs and cider and beat well until smooth. Drain the peeled apple slices and stir into the mixture with the sultanas. Spoon over the pastry and level the surface.
**5** Drain the unpeeled apple slices thoroughly and arrange over the filling. Sprinkle with the icing sugar and bake for 45-50 minutes until just firm. Leave to cool in the tin for 15 minutes.
**6** Dust the cake with icing sugar and serve warm, cut into squares.

**VARIATION** Instead of dusting with icing sugar, apply a cider-flavoured glaze. Mix 125 g (4 oz) sifted icing sugar with 30 ml (2 tbsp) cider to make a smooth glacé icing. Pour evenly over the warm cake, leaving some of the apple slices exposed.

# STICKY ORANGE FLAPJACKS

**MAKES 18**
PREPARATION
10 minutes
COOKING TIME
25-30 minutes
FREEZING
Suitable
CALS/FLAPJACK
300

- 2 small oranges
- 250 g (9 oz) unsalted butter
- 250 g (9 oz) caster sugar
- 175 g (6 oz) golden syrup
- 425 g (15 oz) porridge oats
- 30 ml (2 tbsp) sunflower seeds
- 45 ml (3 tbsp) fine-shred orange marmalade

**1** Grease a baking tin measuring 22 x 29 cm (8½ x 11 ½ inches) across the top and 19 x 27 cm (7½ x 10 ½ inches) across the base. (Or use a tin with similar dimensions). Using a citrus zester, finely pare the zest from the oranges in fine strips.

**2** Place the orange zest in a heavy-based saucepan. Add the butter, cut into pieces, with the sugar and syrup. Cook over a moderate heat, stirring until the butter has melted. Remove from the heat and stir in the oats, until evenly coated in syrup.

**3** Turn the mixture into the prepared tin, level the surface and sprinkle with the sunflower seeds. Bake at 180°C (350°F) Mark 4 for 25-30 minutes until deep golden around the edges; the mixture will still be very soft in the centre. Leave in the tin until almost cold.

**4** Heat the marmalade in a small saucepan with 15 ml (1 tbsp) water until syrupy. Brush this glaze evenly over the flapjack. Turn out onto a board and cut into 18 bars. Store in an airtight container for up to 1 week.

**NOTE** To weigh syrup, first measure out the sugar quantity and leave it in the scales bowl, making a small well in the centre. Add additional weights for the required quantity of syrup and spoon the syrup into the well. Both sugar and syrup will then slide cleanly into the saucepan.

**VARIATIONS**
FRUIT AND NUT FLAPJACKS Omit the orange zest, sunflower seeds and marmalade. Add 125 g (4 oz) luxury mixed dried fruit and 75 g (3 oz) chopped and toasted mixed nuts with the oats.
PEAR AND CINNAMON FLAPJACKS Omit the orange zest, sunflower seeds and marmalade. Add 5 ml (1 tsp) ground cinnamon with the sugar, and 150 g (5 oz) roughly chopped dried pears with the oats.

## RIPPLED DATE AND BANANA LOAF

**8-10 SLICES**
PREPARATION
20 minutes
COOKING TIME
1¼-1½ hours
FREEZING
Suitable
CALS/SERVING
495-395
COLOUR INDEX
Page 78

250 g (9 oz) pitted dried dates
90 ml (3 fl oz) water
grated zest and juice of 1 lemon
2 ripe bananas
175 g (6 oz) unsalted butter, softened
175 g (6 oz) caster sugar
3 eggs
225 g (8 oz) self-raising white flour
2.5 ml (½ tsp) baking powder
2.5 ml (½ tsp) ground cinnamon (optional)

**1** Grease and line a 1.2 litre (2 pint) loaf tin. Set aside 4 dates; place the rest in a small heavy-based saucepan with the water, lemon zest and juice. Bring to the boil, reduce the heat and simmer gently for 5 minutes until the dates are soft and pulpy. Purée the mixture in a food processor or blender until smooth; alternatively mash together in a bowl, using a fork.
**2** Mash the bananas until completely smooth.
**3** Cream the butter and sugar together in a bowl until pale and fluffy. Add the banana purée and eggs. Sift the flour, baking powder and cinnamon if using, into the bowl and beat until thoroughly combined.
**4** Spoon a third of the banana mixture into the prepared loaf tin and level the surface. Spread half of the date purée over the surface. Repeat these layers, then cover with the remaining banana mixture.
**5** Cut the reserved dates into thin lengths and scatter them over the surface. Bake in the oven at 160°C (325°F) Mark 3 for 1-1¼ hours until well risen and firm to the touch. Leave in the tin for 15 minutes, then transfer to a wire rack to cool. Store in an airtight container for up to 1 week.

**NOTE** The date purée needs to be similar in consistency to the banana mixture. If too thick, beat in a little water.

**VARIATIONS**
❑ Add 25 g (1 oz) toasted sunflower seeds to the banana mixture.
❑ Use other plump dried fruit – such as apricots, figs or prunes – instead of dates.

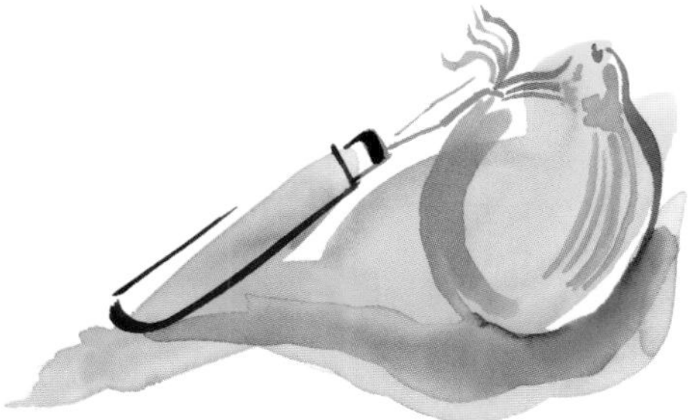

## WHITE CHOCOLATE BROWNIES

**MAKES 12**
PREPARATION
20 minutes
COOKING TIME
30-35 minutes
FREEZING
Suitable
CALS/BROWNIE
490

175 g (6 oz) shelled hazelnuts
500 g (1 lb 2 oz) white chocolate
75 g (3 oz) butter
3 eggs
175 g (6 oz) caster sugar
175 g (6 oz) self-raising white flour
pinch of salt
5 ml (1 tsp) vanilla essence

**1** Grease and line a baking tin measuring 22 x 29 cm (8½ x 11½ inches) across top and 19 x 27 cm (7½ x 10½ inches) across base (or a tin with similar dimensions).
**2** Roughly chop the hazelnuts. Roughly chop 400 g (14 oz) of the chocolate; set aside. Break remaining chocolate into a heatproof bowl, add the butter and place over a pan of simmering water until melted. Leave to cool slightly.
**3** Whisk the eggs and sugar together in a large bowl until smooth, then gradually beat in the melted chocolate. Sift the flour and salt over the mixture, then fold in with the hazelnuts, chopped chocolate and vanilla essence.
**4** Turn the mixture into the prepared tin and level the surface. Bake at 190°C (375°F) Mark 5 for 30-35 minutes until risen and golden, and the centre is just firm to the touch. Leave to cool in the tin. Turn out and cut into 12 squares. Store in an airtight container for up to 1 week.

**NOTE** When cooked, the mixture will still be very soft under the crust; it firms up during cooling.

**VARIATIONS** Use almonds, walnuts, pecans or brazil nuts instead of hazelnuts.

## CHOCOLATE PECAN FUDGE CAKE

**16 SLICES**
PREPARATION
50 minutes, plus cooling
COOKING TIME
25 minutes
FREEZING
Suitable: Without decoration
CALS/SLICE
590

175 g (6 oz) self-raising white flour
50 g (2 oz) cocoa powder
10 ml (2 tsp) baking powder
175 g (6 oz) unsalted butter or margarine, softened
175 g (6 oz) caster sugar
4 eggs
10 ml (2 tsp) vanilla essence
FILLING
300 ml (½ pint) double cream
125 g (4 oz) shelled pecan nuts
90 ml (6 tbsp) maple syrup
ICING
300 g (10 oz) plain dark chocolate
50 g (2 oz) unsalted butter
60 ml (4 tbsp) milk
225 g (8 oz) icing sugar
TO DECORATE
chocolate caraque (see note)
cocoa powder, for dusting

**1** Grease and base-line three 19 cm (7½ inch) sandwich tins. Sift the flour, cocoa and baking powder into a bowl. Add the butter or margarine, sugar, eggs and vanilla essence. Beat, using an electric whisk, for 2 minutes until smooth and paler in colour. Divide the mixture between the prepared tins and level the surfaces. Bake at 180°C (350°F) Mark 4 for 25 minutes until risen and just firm to the touch. Turn out onto a wire rack to cool.
**2** For the filling, whip the cream until just peaking. Roughly chop the pecans. Place one cake on a serving plate and spread with a quarter of the cream. Scatter with half of the nuts, then drizzle with half the maple syrup. Spread carefully with another quarter of the cream and position the second cake on top. Cover with the remaining cream, nuts and syrup, then top with the remaining cake.
**3** To make the icing, break up the chocolate and place in a saucepan with the butter and milk. Heat gently until the chocolate is melted, stirring frequently. Remove from the heat and beat in the icing sugar until smooth. Leave to cool, then swirl over the top and sides of the cake with a palette knife.
**4** Scatter the chocolate caraque over the top of the cake and dust lightly with cocoa powder to serve.

**NOTE** To make the chocolate caraque, melt 150 g (5 oz) plain, dark chocolate in a heatproof bowl over a pan of hot water, then spread evenly onto a marble slab or work surface. When just set draw the blade of a knife, held at a 45° angle, across the chocolate to shave off curls. If the chocolate breaks, it has set too hard and should be left in a warm place for a few minutes before trying again.

To make two-tone caraque use half white and half dark chocolate. Melt separately and swirl together on the marble surface. Continue as above.

## CRUMBLY APPLE AND CHEESE CAKE

**10 SLICES**
PREPARATION
20 minutes
COOKING TIME
About 1 hour
FREEZING
Suitable
CALS/SLICE
345
COLOUR INDEX
Page 78

575 g (1¼ lb) dessert apples
50 g (2 oz) brazil nuts
175 g (6 oz) self-raising white flour
5 ml (1 tsp) baking powder
75 g (3 oz) light muscovado sugar
50 g (2 oz) raisins
50 g (2 oz) sultanas
2 eggs
90 ml (3 fl oz) sunflower oil
225 g (8 oz) Caerphilly cheese
TO FINISH
icing sugar, for dusting

**1** Grease a 5 cm (2 inch) deep, 23 cm (9 inch) round loose-based flan tin. Peel, core and thinly slice the apples. Roughly chop the nuts.
**2** Sift the flour and baking powder into a bowl. Stir in the sugar, raisins, sultanas, nuts and apples, and mix until evenly combined. Beat the eggs with the oil and add to the dry ingredients. Stir until all the flour mixture is moistened and evenly incorporated.
**3** Turn half the mixture into the prepared tin and level the surface. Crumble the cheese over the surface, to within 1 cm (½ inch) of the edge. Cover with the remaining cake mixture, spreading it roughly to give an interesting finish.
**4** Bake at 180°C (350°F) Mark 4 for 50 minutes to 1 hour until golden and just firm. Leave to cool in the tin for 10 minutes, then transfer to a wire rack. Serve warm, sprinkled with icing sugar.

**VARIATION** Replace the Caerphilly with a similar cheese, such as Wensleydale or Lancashire.

# CARROT CAKE WITH MASCARPONE TOPPING

**8-10 SLICES**
PREPARATION 25 minutes, plus cooling
COOKING TIME 35-40 minutes
FREEZING Suitable: Without filling and topping
CALS/SLICE 735-570

350 g (12 oz) carrots
125 g (4 oz) brazil nuts
225 g (8 oz) unsalted butter or margarine, softened
225 g (8 oz) caster sugar
175 g (6 oz) self-raising white flour
5 ml (1 tsp) baking powder
2.5 ml (½ tsp) ground allspice
grated zest of 1 orange
15 ml (1 tbsp) orange juice
4 eggs
50 g (2 oz) ground almonds

FROSTING
250 g (9 oz) mascarpone
5 ml (1 tsp) finely grated orange zest (optional)
30 ml (2 tbsp) orange juice
30 ml (2 tbsp) icing sugar

TO DECORATE
1 large carrot
oil, for shallow-frying
icing sugar, for dusting

**1** Grease and base-line two 18 cm (7 inch) sandwich tins or moule à manque tins. Dust the sides of the tins with flour and shake out excess. Peel and finely grate the carrots. Coarsely chop the brazil nuts and lightly toast them.
**2** Cream the butter and sugar together in a bowl until pale and fluffy. Sift the flour, baking powder and spice into the bowl. Add the orange zest and juice, eggs, and ground almonds; beat well. Stir in the carrots and brazil nuts.
**3** Divide the mixture between the tins and level the surfaces. Bake in the oven at 180°F (350°F) Mark 4 for 35-40 minutes until risen and firm to touch. Transfer to a wire rack to cool.
**4** For the topping, beat the marscapone, orange zest if using, orange juice and icing sugar together in a bowl until smooth. Use half to sandwich the cakes together. Spread the remainder on top of the cake, swirling it attractively.
**5** For the decoration, peel the carrot and pare into long thin ribbons, using a swivel vegetable peeler. Pat dry with kitchen paper. Heat a 1 cm (½ inch) depth of oil in a frying pan until a piece of carrot added to the hot oil sizzles on the surface. Fry the carrot ribbons, in two batches, until they shrink and turn golden. Drain with a slotted spoon and dry on kitchen paper.
**6** Scatter the carrot ribbons over the top of the cake and dust with icing sugar. Chill until ready to serve.

# RASPBERRY AND PISTACHIO CAKE

**8-10 SLICES**
PREPARATION 20 minutes, plus cooling
COOKING TIME 30 minutes
FREEZING Suitable: Sponge only
CALS/SLICE 635-510
COLOUR INDEX Page 78

65 g (2½ oz) shelled pistachio nuts
225 g (8 oz) self-raising white flour
10 ml (2 tsp) baking powder
4 eggs
225 g (8 oz) caster sugar
225 g (8 oz) unsalted butter, softened
5 ml (1 tsp) vanilla essence

FILLING
125 g (4 oz) raspberries
150 ml (¼ pint) double cream, or half yogurt and half cream
75 ml (5 tbsp) raspberry jam, warmed

TO DECORATE
225 g (8 oz) raspberries
25 g (1 oz) pistachio nuts
icing sugar, for dusting (optional)

**1** Grease and base-line two 20 cm (8 inch) sandwich tins. Put the pistachio nuts in a bowl, pour on boiling water to cover, leave for 1 minute, then drain and remove the skins. Finely chop the nuts.
**2** Sift the flour and baking powder into a bowl. Add the eggs, sugar, butter and vanilla essence and beat, using an electric whisk, until pale and creamy. Stir in the chopped nuts. The mixture should be a soft dropping consistency; if a little stiff, stir in a dash of milk or water.
**3** Divide the mixture evenly between the tins and level the surfaces. Bake at 160°C (325°F) Mark 3 for about 30 minutes until well risen and firm to the touch. Turn out of the tins and leave to cool on a wire rack.
**4** Place one cake layer on a serving plate. Whip the cream until just peaking and spread over the cake. Scatter with the raspberries, then spoon over the melted jam. Top with the second cake layer.
**5** To decorate, scatter the raspberries on top of the cake. Skin the pistachios (as above) and sprinkle over the top. Dust with icing sugar if desired, and keep in a cool place until ready to serve.

# CHRISTMAS CAKE

**16-24 SLICES**
PREPARATION
1 hour, plus standing
COOKING TIME
About 2 hours
FREEZING
Not suitable
CALS/SLICE
745-560

- 225 g (8 oz) plain white flour
- 2.5 ml (½ tsp) ground cinnamon
- 2.5 ml (½ tsp) ground nutmeg
- pinch of salt
- 125 g (4 oz) dried mango
- 125 g (4 oz) dried pineapple
- 125 g (4 oz) pecan nuts
- 350 g (12 oz) raisins
- 450 g (1 lb) sultanas
- 175 g (6 oz) butter, softened
- grated zest of 1 orange
- 175 g (6 oz) muscovado or soft light brown sugar
- 4 eggs
- 60 ml (4 tbsp) dark rum

TO FINISH

- 45 ml (3 tbsp) sieved apricot jam, warmed
- 450 g (1 lb) white almond paste
- 700 g (1½ lb) ready-to-roll fondant icing
- green food colouring
- icing sugar, for dusting

**1** Grease and line a deep 23 cm (9 inch) round cake tin with a double thickness of greaseproof paper. Sift flour with spices and salt. Chop mango, pineapple and nuts. Mix all fruit and nuts together in a bowl with half of the flour mixture.

**2** In a large bowl, beat the butter with the orange zest until soft. Beat in the sugar until well mixed, then beat in the eggs, one at a time.

**3** Fold in the flour, using a metal spoon, then the fruit/flour mixture, and finally the rum. Spoon into the cake tin and level the surface.

**4** Tie a brown paper band around tin. Bake at 150°C (300°F) Mark 2 for 2 hours, or until a fine skewer inserted in centre comes out clean. Leave in tin for 30 minutes, then turn out and cool on a wire rack. When cold, wrap tightly in fresh greaseproof paper and foil. Store in a cool, dry place for at least 1 week.

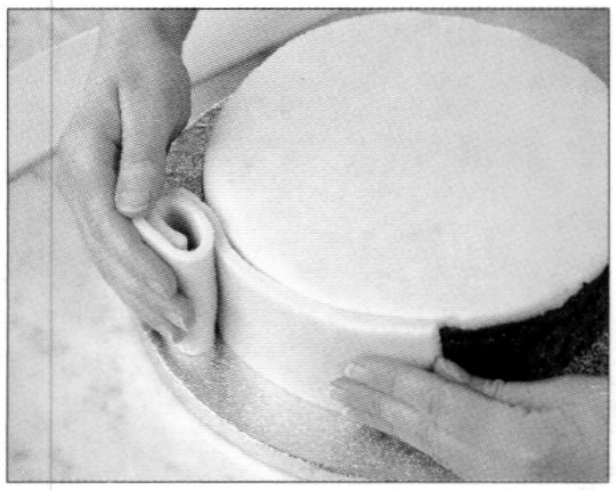

**5** Place cake on a board and brush with jam. On a surface dusted with icing sugar, roll out half the almond paste to a round and use to cover top of cake. Roll out remaining marzipan into 2 strips; use to cover side. Press gently; trim to neaten. Leave in a cool dry place for 2 days before applying icing.

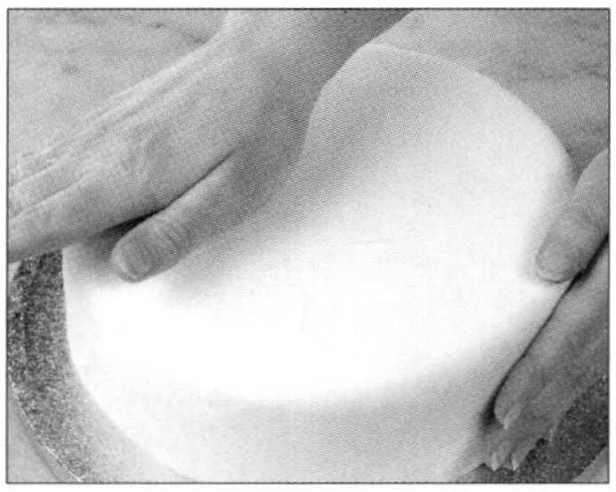

**6** On a surface dusted with cornflour, roll out 450 g (1 lb) fondant icing to a round, 12 cm (5 inches) larger than top of cake. Using a rolling pin, lift on top of cake. Dust hands with cornflour and press icing onto side of cake; trim off excess at base. Buff icing by rubbing gently in a circular movement.

**7** Colour three quarters of remaining icing green. Roll out and cut out Xmas trees. Stick onto side of cake using icing sugar mixed with a little water. Skewer 2 trees onto cocktail sticks; position on top of cake. Shape remaining white icing into snowballs; stick onto cake. Dust with icing sugar.

# Basic Reference

The following recipes are cross-referred to throughout the book. Most are available ready-made from supermarkets, but you will find that the homemade version is far superior.

## VEGETABLE STOCK

**MAKES 1.5 LITRES (2½ PINTS)**
PREPARATION 15 minutes
COOKING TIME 1½ hours
FREEZING Suitable

- 2 large leeks
- 4 carrots, peeled
- 2 celery sticks
- 2 onions, peeled
- 2 large potatoes, peeled
- 125 g (4 oz) mushrooms
- 4 ripe tomatoes
- 60 ml (4 tbsp) olive oil
- 2 garlic cloves, peeled
- 150 ml (¼ pint) dry white wine
- 50 g (2 oz) red lentils
- 1 bouquet garni
- 10 ml (2 tsp) sea salt
- 1.75 litres (3 pints) cold water

**1** Slice the leeks, carrots and celery; roughly chop the onions, potatoes, mushrooms and tomatoes.
**2** Heat the oil in a large saucepan and fry the garlic, onions and leeks for 10 minutes. Add the carrots, potatoes and celery and fry for a further 10 minutes until softened but not coloured.
**3** Add the wine and boil rapidly for 5 minutes until almost completely reduced. Add the remaining ingredients. Bring to the boil, partially cover the pan and simmer for 1 hour.
**4** Strain the stock through a fine sieve into a bowl, or return to the pan and reduce by further boiling if a concentrated stock with a more intense flavour is required.
**5** Let cool. Refrigerate for up to 3 days. Use as required.

## VEGETABLE STOCK (ALTERNATIVE)

**MAKES 1.1 LITRES (2 PINTS)**
PREPARATION 15 minutes
COOKING TIME 1¾ hours
FREEZING Suitable

- large handful of vegetable trimmings, such as celery tops, cabbage or brussels sprout leaves, mushroom peelings, tomato skins
- 1 onion, peeled
- 4 celery sticks
- 1 carrot
- 50 g (2 oz) turnip
- 50 g (2 oz) parsnip
- 30 ml (2 tbsp) oil
- few onion skins (optional)
- 1.75 litres (3 pints) cold water
- 1 bouquet garni
- 6 black peppercorns
- 7.5 ml (1½ tsp) sea salt

**1** Wash the vegetable trimmings thoroughly. Finely chop the onion; roughly chop the celery; dice the carrot, turnip and parsnip.
**2** Heat the oil in a large saucepan, add the onion and fry gently for 5 minutes or until soft and lightly coloured. Add the other vegetables to the pan, with the trimmings.
**3** Add the remaining ingredients. Bring to the boil, partially cover the pan and simmer for 1 hour.
**4** Strain the stock through a fine sieve into a bowl, or return to the pan and reduce by further boiling if a concentrated stock with a more intense flavour is required.
**5** Let cool. Refrigerate for up to 2 days. Use as required.

## MUSHROOM STOCK

**MAKES 1.5 LITRES (2½ PINTS)**
PREPARATION 15 minutes
COOKING TIME 1 hour
FREEZING Suitable

- 1 onion, peeled
- 2 carrots, peeled
- ½ head of fennel
- 125 g (4 oz) open-cup mushrooms
- 15 ml (1 tbsp) oil
- 10 g (⅓ oz) dried porcini mushrooms
- few fresh herb sprigs, such as thyme, rosemary, parsley
- 1.75 litres (3 pints) cold water
- salt and pepper

**1** Roughly chop the onion, carrots, fennel and fresh mushrooms. Heat the oil in a large saucepan, add the chopped vegetables and fry gently for 5 minutes, or until softened.
**2** Add the dried mushrooms, herbs, water and seasoning. Bring to the boil, partially cover the pan and simmer for 45-50 minutes.
**4** Strain the stock through a fine sieve into a bowl, or return to the pan and reduce by boiling if a concentrated stock with a more intense flavour is required.
**5** Allow to cool and refrigerate for up to 3 days. Use the stock as required.

## BROWN ONION STOCK

**MAKES 900 ML (1½ PINTS)**
PREPARATION 15 minutes
COOKING TIME 45 minutes
FREEZING Suitable

- 2 large onions, peeled
- 2 carrots, peeled
- 2 celery sticks
- 2 garlic cloves, peeled
- 30 ml (2 tbsp) oil
- 2 bay leaves
- few fresh herbs, such as thyme stalks, parsley stalks, sage leaves
- 5 ml (1 tsp) yeast extract (optional)
- 1.1 litres (2 pints) cold water
- salt and pepper

**1** Roughly chop the onions, carrots and celery; halve the garlic cloves.
**2** Heat the oil in a large heavy-based saucepan, add the onions and cook, stirring, over a moderate heat for 10 minutes, or until they turn dark golden brown; do not allow them to burn.
**2** Add the remaining vegetables, herbs and yeast extract, if using. Cook for 4-5 minutes or until the vegetables are lightly browned.
**3** Add the water and bring to the boil. Season with salt, partially cover the pan and simmer for 30 minutes.
**4** Strain the stock through a fine sieve into a bowl and check the seasoning; or return to the pan and reduce by boiling if a concentrated stock with a more intense flavour is required.
**5** Allow to cool and refrigerate for up to 3 days. Use the stock as required.

## BÉCHAMEL SAUCE

**MAKES 300 ML (½ PINT)**
PREPARATION
5 minutes, plus infusing
COOKING TIME
5 minutes
FREEZING
Suitable
CALS/SERVING
90

300 ml (½ pint) milk
1 slice onion
6 peppercorns
1 mace blade
1 bay leaf
15 g (½ oz) butter
15 g (½ oz) plain flour
salt and pepper
freshly grated nutmeg

**1** Pour the milk into a saucepan. Add the onion slice, peppercorns, mace and bay leaf. Bring almost to the boil, remove from the heat, cover and leave to infuse for about 20 minutes. Strain.
**2** To make the roux, melt the butter in a saucepan, stir in the flour and cook, stirring, for 1 minute.
**3** Remove from the heat and gradually pour on the milk, whisking constantly. Season lightly with salt, pepper and nutmeg.
**4** Return to the heat and cook, stirring, until the sauce is thickened and smooth. Simmer gently for 2 minutes.

**VARIATIONS**
THICK BÉCHAMEL SAUCE Increase the butter and flour to 25 g (1 oz) each.

SIMPLE WHITE SAUCE Omit the flavouring ingredients and infusing stage, simply stirring the cold milk into the roux.

CHEESE SAUCE Off the heat, stir in 50 g (2 oz) finely grated gruyère or mature Cheddar and a pinch of mustard powder.

## HOLLANDAISE

**SERVES 6**
PREPARATION
20 minutes
COOKING TIME
2-3 minutes
FREEZING
Not suitable
CALS/SERVING
230

60 ml (4 tbsp) white wine vinegar
6 black peppercorns
1 mace blade
1 slice onion
1 bay leaf
3 egg yolks
150 g (5 oz) unsalted butter, at room temperature
salt and pepper
30 ml (2 tbsp) single cream
lemon juice, to taste

**1** Put the vinegar in a small saucepan with the peppercorns, mace, onion slice and bay leaf. Bring to the boil and reduce to 15 ml (1 tbsp) liquid. Dip the base of the pan in cold water to stop further evaporation. Set aside.
**2** Beat the egg yolks in a heatproof bowl with 15 g (½ oz) butter and a pinch of salt. Strain in the reduced vinegar.
**3** Place the bowl over a pan of barely simmering water. Stir until beginning to thicken, then beat in the remaining soft butter a piece at a time, until the mixture begins to thicken and emulsify. Ensure each addition of butter is incorporated before adding the next. Do not allow the mixture to overheat or the eggs will scramble and split.
**4** Remove from the heat and whisk in the cream. Season with salt and pepper, and add lemon juice to taste. Serve at once, with freshly cooked vegetables, such as asparagus and globe artichokes.

**NOTE** If the sauce shows signs of curdling, add an ice cube and whisk thoroughly to combine.

## FRESH TOMATO SAUCE

**SERVES 4**
PREPARATION
10 minutes
COOKING TIME
About 1 hour
FREEZING
Suitable
CALS/SERVING
105

900 g (2 lb) vine-ripened tomatoes
30 ml (2 tbsp) extra-virgin olive oil
2 garlic cloves, peeled and crushed
grated zest of 1 lemon
5 ml (1 tsp) dried oregano
30 ml (2 tbsp) chopped fresh basil
salt and pepper
pinch of sugar, or to taste (optional)

**1** Roughly chop the tomatoes and place in a saucepan with the olive oil, garlic, lemon zest and oregano. Bring to the boil, cover and simmer gently for 30 minutes.
**2** Add the basil, salt and pepper to taste and a little sugar if required. Simmer, uncovered, for a further 20-30 minutes until the sauce is thickened. If a smooth sauce is preferred, pass through a sieve.

## RICH TOMATO SAUCE

**SERVES 4-6**
PREPARATION
10-20 minutes
COOKING TIME
25-30 minutes
FREEZING
Suitable
CALS/SERVING
175-115

1 onion
2 garlic cloves
50 g (2 oz) butter
1 kg (2 lb) ripe tomatoes, preferably plum, or two 400 g (14 oz) cans plum tomatoes with juice
45 ml (3 tbsp) sun-dried tomato paste (see note)
2 oregano sprigs
salt and pepper

**1** Peel and finely chop the onion and garlic. Melt the butter in a saucepan, add the onion and garlic and cook over a medium-low heat for about 8 minutes.
**2** Skin fresh tomatoes, if using: immerse in a bowl of boiling water for 30 seconds; drain, refresh under cold running water and peel away the skins. Quarter the tomatoes, discard the seeds, then roughly chop the flesh. If using canned plum tomatoes, chop them roughly.
**3** Add the tomatoes to the onion and garlic mixture, together with the sun-dried tomato paste and oregano sprigs. Simmer, uncovered, over a low heat for 25-30 minutes, stirring occasionally, until the sauce is thick and pulpy. Discard the oregano sprigs and season with salt and pepper to taste.

**NOTE** Full-flavoured ripe, fresh tomatoes give the best result but canned plum tomatoes are a better choice than under-ripe or flavourless fresh ones.

## CLASSIC PESTO

**SERVES 4**
PREPARATION
10 minutes
FREEZING
Not suitable
CALS/SERVING
310

50 g (2 oz) fresh basil leaves
1 garlic clove, peeled
25 g (1 oz) pine nuts, toasted
90 ml (6 tbsp) extra-virgin olive oil
salt and pepper
30 ml (2 tbsp) freshly grated Parmesan cheese
squeeze of lemon juice (optional)

**1** Roughly chop the basil and place in a mortar with the garlic, pine nuts and a little of the oil. Pound with a pestle to a paste. Alternatively, work in a food processor to a fairly smooth paste.
**2** Work in the rest of the oil and season with salt and pepper to taste.
**3** Transfer to a bowl and stir in the cheese. Check the seasoning and add a squeeze of lemon juice if desired.
**4** Store in a screw-topped jar, covered with a thin layer of oil, in the refrigerator for up to 2 weeks.

**VARIATION**
CORIANDER PESTO Replace the basil with coriander. Add 1-2 seeded, chopped chillies at stage 1. Omit the cheese.

## ROCKET PESTO

**SERVES 4**
PREPARATION
10 minutes
FREEZING
Not suitable
CALS/SERVING
215

50 g (2 oz) rocket leaves
1 garlic clove, peeled
15 ml (1 tbsp) capers, rinsed and drained
15 g (½ oz) pecorino or Parmesan cheese, freshly grated
15 ml (1 tbsp) chopped fresh parsley
15 g (½ oz) pine nuts, toasted
75 ml (5 tbsp) extra-virgin olive oil
salt and pepper

**1** Roughly chop the rocket and place in a mortar, blender or food processor with the garlic, capers, cheese, parsley and pine nuts. Work to a fairly smooth paste.
**2** Stir in the oil and season with salt and pepper to serve.

## OLIVE PESTO

**SERVES 4**
PREPARATION
10 minutes
FREEZING
Not suitable
CALS/SERVING
85

125 g (4 oz) pitted black olives
2 garlic cloves, peeled
25 g (1 oz) capers, drained and rinsed
15 ml (1 tbsp) chopped fresh parsley
5 ml (1 tsp) chopped fresh thyme
pinch of mustard powder
30 ml (2 tbsp) extra-virgin olive oil
pepper

**1** Place all the ingredients in a blender or food processor and work until fairly smooth.
**2** Transfer to a screw-topped jar, seal and store in the refrigerator for up to 2 weeks.

## SUN-DRIED TOMATO PESTO

**SERVES 4**
PREPARATION
10 minutes
FREEZING
Not suitable
CALS/SERVING
290

1 garlic clove, peeled
2.5 ml (½ tsp) sea salt
50 g (2 oz) drained sun-dried tomatoes in oil, chopped
25 g (1 oz) basil leaves
25 g (1 oz) pine nuts
90 ml (6 tbsp) extra-virgin olive oil
30 ml (2 tbsp) freshly grated Parmesan cheese

**1** Place all the ingredients, except the Parmesan, in a blender or food processor and work until fairly smooth.
**2** Transfer to a screw-topped jar and stir in the cheese. Seal and store in the refrigerator for up to 2 weeks.

## MAYONNAISE

**MAKES 300 ML (½ PINT)**
PREPARATION
10 minutes
FREEZING
Not suitable
CALS/SERVING
150-200

2 egg yolks
10 ml (2 tsp) lemon juice or white wine vinegar
5 ml (1 tsp) Dijon mustard
salt and pepper
pinch of sugar
300 ml (½ pint) light olive oil

**1** Place all the ingredients except the oil in a food processor and blend briefly until pale and creamy.
**2** With the blade motor running, pour in the oil through the feeder tube, in a steady stream, until the mayonnaise is thick. Thin to the required consistency with a little boiling water if necessary.

## FRENCH DRESSING

**MAKES 100 ML (3½ FL OZ)**
PREPARATION
10 minutes
FREEZING
Not suitable
CALS/SERVING
110-80

5 ml (1 tsp) Dijon mustard
pinch of sugar
15 ml (1 tbsp) white or red wine vinegar
salt and pepper
90 ml (6 tbsp) extra-virgin olive oil

**1** Whisk the mustard, sugar, vinegar and seasoning together in a bowl until evenly blended.
**2** Gradually whisk in the olive oil until amalgamated.

**NOTE** Alternatively, put all of the ingredients into a screw-topped jar and shake vigorously to combine.

**VARIATIONS**
HERB DRESSING Omit the mustard. Replace the vinegar with lemon juice and add 30 ml (2 tbsp) chopped mixed fresh herbs, such as parsley, chervil and chives.

BALSAMIC DRESSING Omit the mustard and sugar. Use balsamic vinegar instead of wine vinegar.

## CRÈME ANGLAISE

**SERVES 4**
PREPARATION
20 minutes, plus infusing
COOKING TIME
15 minutes
FREEZING
Not suitable
CALS/SERVING
115

1 vanilla pod
300 ml (½ pint) milk
3 egg yolks, beaten
15 ml (1 tbsp) caster sugar

**1** Split the vanilla pod to reveal the seeds. Pour the milk into a heavy-based saucepan, add the vanilla pod and heat slowly until almost boiling. Take off the heat, then leave to infuse for about 20 minutes. Remove the vanilla pod.
**2** Whisk the egg yolks and sugar together in a bowl until thick and creamy. Gradually whisk in the hot milk, then strain back into the pan. Cook over a low heat, stirring constantly, until the custard thickens enough to lightly coat the back of the wooden spoon; do not allow to boil or the custard may curdle.
**3** Serve hot or, if serving cold, pour into a chilled bowl, cover with dampened greaseproof paper to prevent a skin forming and allow to cool.

**NOTES**
❑ If preferred, omit the vanilla pod and stir in 2.5 ml (½ tsp) vanilla essence with the cream.
❑ To reduce the risk of curdling, add 5 ml (1 tsp) cornflour to the egg yolks at stage 2. Once the custard is thickened, cook gently for a little longer to ensure the taste of cornflour has disappeared.
❑ To rescue a custard which is beginning to separate and curdle, strain into a cold bowl, add a few ice cubes and whisk vigorously to reduce the temperature; the custard should smooth out again.

## SABAYON SAUCE

**SERVES 8**
PREPARATION
15 minutes
COOKING TIME
About 5 minutes
FREEZING
Not suitable
CALS/SERVING
115

75 g (3 oz) caster sugar
120 ml (4 fl oz) water
3 egg yolks
120 ml (4 fl oz) double cream
grated zest and juice of 1 lemon

**1** Place the sugar and water in a small saucepan over a low heat until dissolved. Increase the heat to high and boil for 7-8 minutes, until the syrup registers 105°C (225°F) on a sugar thermometer (and looks very syrupy with large pea-size bubbles).
**2** Meanwhile, lightly whisk the egg yolks in a small bowl. Gradually pour on the hot syrup in a thin stream, whisking all the time. Continue to whisk until the mixture is thick, mousse-like and cool.
**3** In a separate bowl, whisk the cream until it forms stiff peaks, then add the lemon zest and juice and whip again to soft peaks. Fold into the mousse mixture.
**4** Cover and chill in the refrigerator until required. Whisk well before serving.

## VANILLA ICE CREAM

**SERVES 4-6**
PREPARATION
20 minutes, plus infusing
COOKING TIME
15 minutes
CALS/SERVING
480-320

1 vanilla pod, split
300 ml (½ pint) milk
3 egg yolks
50-75 g (2-3 oz) caster sugar
300 ml (½ pint) double cream

**1** Split the vanilla pod to reveal the seeds. Pour the milk into a heavy-based saucepan, add the vanilla pod and heat slowly until almost boiling. Take off the heat, then leave to infuse for about 20 minutes. Remove the vanilla pod.
**2** Whisk the egg yolks and sugar together in a bowl until thick and creamy. Gradually whisk in the hot milk, then strain back into the pan. Cook over a low heat, stirring constantly, until thickened enough to coat the back of the wooden spoon; do not allow to boil. Pour into a chilled bowl and allow to cool.
**3** Whisk the cream into the cold custard. Pour into an ice-cream maker and churn until frozen. Alternatively freeze in a shallow container, whisking 2 or 3 times during freezing to break down the ice crystals and ensure an even-textured result.
**4** Allow the ice cream to soften slightly at cool room temperature before serving.

**VARIATIONS**
FRUIT ICE CREAM Add 300 ml (½ pint) fruit purée, sweetened to taste, to the cooled custard.

CHOCOLATE ICE CREAM Omit the vanilla pod. Add 125 g (4 oz) plain chocolate to the milk, heat gently until melted, then bring almost to the boil and continue as above.

COFFEE ICE CREAM Omit the vanilla pod. Add 150 ml (¼ pint) freshly made strong cooled coffee to the cooled custard, or 10 ml (2 tsp) instant coffee granules to the hot milk, stirring to dissolve.

# GLOSSARY

A brief guide to cooking methods, terms and ingredients used in the recipes featured in this book.

**Acidulated water** Water to which lemon juice or vinegar has been added in which fruit or vegetables, such as pears or Jerusalem artichokes, are immersed to prevent dis-colouration.
**Agar-agar** Obtained from various types of seaweed, this is a useful vegetarian alternative to gelatine. It is available in powdered form and in long white strands.
**Al dente** Italian term used to describe food, especially pasta and vegetables, which are cooked until tender but still firm to the bite.
**Arrowroot** Fine, white powder used as a thickening agent for sauces. Unlike cornflour, arrowroot gives a sauce a clear gloss.
**Au gratin** Describes a dish which has been coated with sauce, sprinkled with breadcrumbs or cheese and browned under the grill or in the oven. Low-sided gratin dishes are used.
**Bain-marie** Literally, a water bath, used to keep foods, such as delicate custards and sauces, at a constant low temperature during cooking. On the hob a double saucepan or heatproof bowl placed over a pan of simmering water is used; for oven cooking, the baking dish(es) is placed in a roasting tin containing enough hot water to come halfway up the sides.
**Baking blind** Pre-baking a pastry case partially or totally before filling. The pastry case is lined with greaseproof paper and weighted down with dried pulses or ceramic baking beans.
**Baking powder** A raising agent consisting of an acid, usually cream of tartar and an alkali, such as bicarbonate of soda, which react to produce carbon dioxide. This expands during baking and makes cakes and breads rise.
**Balsamic vinegar** Italian oak-aged vinegar, dark brown in colour with a superior sweet, mellow flavour.
**Baste** To spoon the juices and melted fat over vegetables during roasting to keep them moist. The term is also used to describe spooning over a marinade.
**Beat** Method of incorporating air into an ingredient or mixture by agitating it vigorously with a spoon, fork, whisk or electric mixer. The technique is also used to soften ingredients.
**Béchamel** Classic French white sauce, used as the basis for other sauces and savoury dishes.
**Beurre manié** Equal parts of flour and butter kneaded together to form a paste. Used for thickening soups, stews and casseroles. It is whisked into the hot liquid a little at a time at the end of cooking.
**Bind** To mix beaten egg or other liquid into a dry mixture to hold it together.
**Blanch** To immerse food briefly in fast-boiling water to loosen skins, such as peaches or tomatoes, or to remove bitterness, or to destroy enzymes and preserve the colour, flavour and texture of vegetables (especially prior to freezing).
**Bouquet garni** Small bunch of herbs – usually a mixture of parsley stems, thyme and a bay leaf – tied in muslin and used to flavour stocks, soups and stews.
**Braise** To cook vegetables slowly in a small amount of liquid in a pan or casserole with a tight-fitting lid. The food is usually first browned in oil or fat.
**Brochette** Food cooked on a skewer or spit.
**Brûlée** A French term, literally meaning 'burnt' used to refer to a dish with a crisp coating of caramelised sugar.
**Bulghar wheat** Partially processed cracked wheat which readily absorbs moisture and therefore cooks quickly. It is used extensively in Middle Eastern cooking, as an alternative to rice. Also known as pourgouri, bulghul and cracked wheat.
**Calorie** Strictly a kilocalorie, this is used in dietetics to measure the energy value of foods.
**Caper** Small bud of a flowering Mediterranean shrub, usually packed in brine. Small French capers in balsamic vinegar are the best variety.
**Caramelise** To heat sugar or sugar syrup slowly until it is brown in colour; ie forms a caramel.
**Casserole** Strictly speaking, a dish with a tight-fitting lid used for slow-cooking vegetables. Now applied to the food cooked in this way.
**Chill** To cool food in the refrigerator.
**Clarify** To remove sediment or impurities from a liquid. Butter which is clarified will withstand a higher frying temperature.

To clarify butter, heat until melted and all bubbling stops. Remove from the heat and let stand until the sediment has sunk to the bottom, then gently pour off the fat, straining it through muslin.
**Coconut milk** Used in curries and other ethnic dishes. Available in cans from larger supermarkets and ethnic stores. Alternatively creamed coconut, sold compressed in blocks, can be reconstituted to make coconut milk.
**Compote** Mixture of fresh or dried fruit stewed in sugar syrup. Served hot or cold.
**Concassé** Diced ingredient; the term is most often applied to skinned, seeded tomatoes.
**Coulis** A smooth fruit or vegetable purée, thinned if necessary to a pouring consistency.
**Couscous** Processed semolina grains; a staple food in North African countries.

**Cream of tartar** (tartaric acid) A raising agent which is an ingredient of baking powder and self-raising flour.
**Cream** To beat together fat and sugar until the mixture is pale and fluffy, and resembles whipped cream in texture and colour. Used in cakes and puddings which contain a high proportion of fat and require the incorporation of a lot of air.
**Crêpe** French term for a pancake.
**Crimp** To decorate the edge of a pie, tart or shortbread by pinching it at regular intervals to give a fluted effect.
**Croûtons** Small pieces of fried or toasted bread, served with soups and salads.
**Crudités** Raw vegetables, usually cut into slices or sticks, typically served with a dipping sauce as an appetiser.
**Crystallise** To preserve fruit in sugar syrup.
**Curdle** To cause sauces or creamed mixtures to separate once the egg is added, usually by overheating or over-beating.
**Deglaze** To heat stock, wine or other liquid with the cooking juices left in the pan after roasting or sautéing, stirring to dissolve the sediment.
**Dégorge** To draw out moisture from a food, eg salting aubergines to remove bitter juices.
**Dredge** To sprinkle food generously with flour, sugar, icing sugar etc.
**Dropping consistency** Term used to describe the required texture of a cake or pudding mixture just before cooking. Test for it by taking a spoonful of the mixture and holding the spoon on its side above the bowl. The mixture should fall of its own accord within 5 seconds.
**Dust** To sprinkle lightly with flour, cornflour, caster sugar, icing sugar etc.
**E numbers** Used on food packaging to denote the additives in the product, including any preservatives, flavourings and colourings. E120 and E542 are of animal origin. A large number of others may be derived from vegetarian or non-vegetarian sources (see list on page 9).
**Emulsifier** A substance added to foods to create a stable emulsion (see below). Emulsifing agents may not necessarily be of vegetable origin.
**Emulsion** A mixture of two liquids which do not dissolve into one another, eg oil and vinegar. Vigorous shaking or heating will emulsify them, as for a vinaigrette.
**Extract** Concentrated flavouring which is used in small quantities, eg yeast extract, vanilla extract.
**Fermentation** Term used to denote chemical changes deliberately or accidentally brought about by fermenting agents, such as yeast or bacteria. The process is utilised for making bread, yogurt and wine.
**Filo Pastry** A type of Greek pastry manufactured in wafer-thin sheets and sold in packets or boxes. It must be kept covered to prevent it drying out.
**Fines herbes** Classic French mixture of chopped herbs, ie parsley, tarragon, chives and chervil.
**Flambé** Flavouring a dish with alcohol, usually brandy or rum, which is then ignited so that the actual alcohol content is burnt off.
**Folding in** Method of combining a whisked or creamed mixture with other ingredients by cutting and folding so that the mixture retains its lightness. A large metal spoon is generally used.
**Fry** To cook food in hot fat or oil. There are various methods: shallow-frying in a little fat in a shallow pan; deep-frying where the food is totally immersed in oil; dry-frying in which fatty foods are cooked in a non-stick pan without extra fat; see also Stir-frying.
**Galette** Cooked savoury or sweet mixture shaped into a round.
**Garnish** A decoration, usually edible, such as parsley or lemon, which is added to a savoury dish to enhance its appearance.
**Gelozone** A vegetarian gelling agent sold in powdered form in sachets, and used as a substitute for gelatine.
**Ghee** Clarified butter widely used in Indian cookery.
**Glaze** A glossy coating given to sweet and savoury dishes to improve their appearance and sometimes flavour. Ingredients for glazes include beaten egg, egg white, milk and syrup.
**Gluten** A protein constituent of grains, such as wheat and rye, which develops when the flour is mixed with water giving the dough elasticity.
**Griddle** A flat, heavy, metal plate used on the hob for cooking scones or for searing savoury ingredients.
**Grind** To reduce foods such as nuts and spices to small particles in a food mill, pestle and mortar, electric grinder or food processor.
**Herb Salt** Sea salt mixed with chopped fresh herbs, such as thyme, rosemary, sage and oregano, used to impart extra seasoning to savoury dishes. Use 15 ml (1 tbsp) mixed chopped fresh herbs to 225 g (8 oz) sea salt and store in a screw-topped jar in a dry place.
**Hull** To remove the stalk and calyx from soft fruits, such as strawberries.
**Infuse** To impart flavour to a liquid by immersing flavourings, such as aromatic vegetables, herbs and spices, usually bringing to the boil, then leaving to stand for a while.
**Julienne** Fine 'matchstick' strips of vegetables or citrus zest, sometimes used as a garnish.
**Knead** To work dough by pummelling with the heel of the hand.
**Knock back** To knead a yeast dough for a second time after rising, to ensure an even texture.
**Macerate** To soften and flavour raw or dried foods by soaking in a liquid, eg soaking fruit in alcohol.
**Mandolin(e)** A flat wooden or metal frame with adjustable cutting blades for cutting vegetables.
**Marinate** To soak raw vegetables – usually in a mixture of oil, wine, vinegar and flavourings – to soften and impart flavour. The mixture, which is known as a marinade, may also be used to baste the food during cooking.
**Mayonnaise** Classic salad dressing made from an emulsion of oil and vinegar, combined with egg yolk and flavouring ingredients. Commercially produced mayonnaise

is widely available, but strict vegetarians should scrutinize labels for the V symbol, as many brands contain eggs from battery hens.
**Mocha** A term which has come to mean a blend of chocolate and coffee.
**Monosodium Glutamate** Common food additive of vegetable origin – used as a flavour enhancer.
**Parboil** To boil a vegetable or other food for part of its cooking time before finishing it by another method.
**Passata** A purée of plum tomatoes, used in many Italian dishes. Available ready-made from supermarkets.
**Pâte** The French word for pastry, familiar in pâte sucrée, a sweet flan pastry.
**Pâté** A savoury mixture of finely chopped or minced pulses and/or vegetables, usually served as a starter with bread or toast and crudités.
**Patty tin** Tray of cup-shaped moulds for cooking small cakes and deep tartlets. Also called a bun tin.
**Pectin** A naturally occurring substance found in most fruit and some vegetables which is necessary for setting jams and jellies.
**Pestle and mortar** Heavy marble or porcelain bowl with a heavy grinding tool for grinding herbs, spices etc.
**Pesto** A paste-like sauce made from puréed herbs and oil, used to add flavour to pasta and vegetables. A classic pesto is made from basil, pine nuts, garlic and olive oil.
**Pith** The bitter white skin under the thin zest of citrus fruit.
**Poach** To cook food gently in liquid at or just below simmering point, so that the surface of the liquid is just trembling.
**Purée** Fruit or vegetable pounded, sieved or liquidised to a smooth pulp. Purées often form the basis for soups and sauces.
**Reduce** To fast-boil stock or other liquid in an uncovered pan to evaporate water and concentrate the flavour.
**Refresh** To cool hot vegetables very quickly and stop the cooking process – by plunging into ice-cold water or holding under running water.
**Rennet** Unsuitable for vegetarians, this enzyme is extracted from the lining of calves' stomachs and is used in the manufacture of cheese. A vegetarian alternative is available and is being increasingly utilized. The VR symbol denotes that a cheese has been manufactured using vegetarian rennet.
**Rub-in** Method of incorporating fat into flour when a short texture is required. It is used for pastry, cakes, scones and biscuits.
**Salsa** Piquant sauce made from chopped fresh vegetables and sometimes fruit.
**Sauté** To cook food in a small quantity of fat over a high heat, shaking the pan constantly – usually in a sauté pan (a frying pan with straight sides and a wide base).
**Scald** To pour boiling water over food to clean it, or loosen skin, eg tomatoes. Also used to describe heating milk to just below boiling point.
**Score** To cut parallel lines in the surface of food to improve its appearance or help it cook more quickly.
**Sear** To brown vegetables quickly in a little hot fat before grilling or roasting.
**Seasoned flour** Flour mixed with a little salt and pepper, used for dusting vegetables etc before frying.
**Shred** To grate cheese or slice vegetables into very fine pieces or strips.
**Sieve** To press food through a perforated sieve to obtain a smooth texture.
**Sift** To shake dry ingredients through a sieve to remove lumps.
**Simmer** To keep a liquid just below boiling point.
**Skim** To remove froth, scum or fat from the surface of stock, stews, jam etc. Use either a skimmer, a spoon or absorbent kitchen paper.
**Stabilizer** Food additive which may or may not be of vegetable origin.
**Steam** To cook food in the steam of rapidly boiling water.
**Sterilise** To destroy bacteria in foods by heating.
**Stew** To cook food such as vegetables slowly in flavoured liquid which is kept at simmering point.
**Stir-fry** To cook small even-sized pieces of food rapidly in a little fat, tossing constantly over a high heat, usually in a wok.
**Suet** Hard fat of animal origin used in pastry and steamed puddings. A vegetarian alternative is available.
**Sweat** To cook chopped or sliced vegetables in a little fat without liquid in a covered pan over a low heat.
**Tepid** The term used to describe temperature at approximately blood heat, ie 37°C (98.7°F).
**Thermometer, Sugar/Fat** Used for accurately checking the temperature of boiling sugar syrups, and fat for deep-frying respectively. Dual purpose thermometers are obtainable.
**Whipping (whisking)** Beating air rapidly into a mixture either with a manual or electric whisk.
**Worcestershire sauce** A pungent flavouring sauce. Most brands contains anchovies but a vegetarian version is available.
**Wok** Large Chinese pan with a rounded base and sloping sides, used for stir-frying.
**Zest** The thin coloured outer layer of citrus fruit which contains essential oil.
**Zester** Small bevelled tool with five holes drawn across citrus fruit to remove the zest in fine strips.

# Food Safety

Correct food storage and hygenic preparation is important to ensure that food remains as nutritious and flavourful as possible, and to prevent food poisoning.

## FOOD POISONING

As the majority of food poisoning cases are caused by contaminated meat or fish, vegetarians are far less likely to suffer from this very unpleasant illness than others. Food poisoning resulting from vegetarian foods is highly unlikely to cause serious or life-threatening illness, but the following 'at risk' groups should take precautions:

- Children under 2 years old
- Pregnant women
- Elderly people
- Anyone who is already ill or convalescing
- Those with an impaired immune system
- Anyone taking drugs which suppress their body's natural defences, such as transplant patients, people receiving chemotherapy or taking large doses of steroids.

❑ To avoid the slight risk of salmonella poisoning from raw or lightly cooked eggs, at-risk groups are advised to avoid the following: all soft-cooked eggs, mayonnaise, egg custard, Hollandaise sauce, meringues, ice creams and sorbets (unless they are made with pasteurised egg).

❑ To reduce the risk of listeria poisoning, at-risk groups should avoid the following: goat's cheeses, sheep's milk cheeses, soft-ripened cheeses, such as Brie and Camembert, all unpasteurised milk products.

## KITCHEN HYGIENE

Following a few simple guidelines will help make your kitchen a safer place for preparing food.

❑ Always wash your hands before handling food and again between handling different types of food. Keep any cuts or grazes covered with a waterproof plaster.

❑ Wash down work surfaces regularly with a mild detergent solution or multi-surface cleaner.

❑ Use rubber gloves for washing up, so that the water can be hotter than hands can bear. Leaving dishes to drain is more hygienic than drying them with a tea-towel.

❑ Keep raw and cooked foods separate. Wash kitchen utensils in between preparing raw and cooked foods. Never put cooked or ready-to-eat foods onto a surface which has just had raw food on it.

❑ Keep pets out of the kitchen if possible; at least make sure they keep away from work surfaces.

## BUYING FOOD

Always shop at a reliable source with a regular turnover. Foods with a longer shelf life have a best-before date; more perishable items have a use-by date. Make sure items are well within either date.

❑ Pack frozen and chilled items in an insulated cool bag at the check-out and put them into the freezer or refrigerator as soon as you get home.

❑ During warm weather buy perishable items just before returning home, as these foods will deteriorate quickly if left in a warm car for any length of time.

## STORAGE

❑ Always check packaging for storage advice – even with familiar foods. As manufacturers have removed some of the additives from foods and reduced sugar and salt, storage requirements may have changed.

❑ Never keep goods beyond their use-by date.

❑ Keep your cupboards, refrigerator and freezer scrupulously clean.

❑ Once opened, canned foods should be treated as though fresh. Transfer the contents to a clean container, cover and keep in the refrigerator.

❑ Transfer dry goods such as sugar, rice and pasta to moisture-proof containers. Old supplies should be used up before new ones are started and containers washed out and dried thoroughly before refilling.

## REFRIGERATOR STORAGE

❑ Use a refrigerator thermometer to check that your refrigerator is operating at the correct temperature, between 1-5°C (34-41°F).

❑ Always store cooked and raw foods on separate shelves in the refrigerator.

❑ Never put hot food into the refrigerator as this will cause the internal temperature to rise.

❑ Avoid overfilling the refrigerator as this restricts the circulation of air and prevents it from working properly.

❑ Do not leave the refrigerator door open any longer than necessary.

❑ Clean the refrigerator regularly, using one of the specially formulated germicidal 'fridge cleaners'.

❑ Defrost your refrigerator regularly.

## COOKING AND REHEATING FOOD

❑ Remember that to kill any food poisoning bacteria present food needs to reach a temperature of 70°C (158°F) for at least 2 minutes.

❑ Always reheat food until it is 'piping hot'. Never reheat food more than once.

❑ Cooked food should be cooled as quickly as possible before placing it in the refrigerator or freezer. Small quantities will cool quite quickly but larger quantities should be either divided into smaller portions, or transferred to a container with a large surface area. During warm weather place the container in a bowl of iced water. Do not cover the food while it is cooling.

# Freezing

Many of the recipes in this book are suitable for freezing and, of course, freezing is ideal for preserving seasonal fresh fruit and vegetables. The following guidelines apply:-

❑ Only freeze food that is in prime condition.

❑ Handle the food as little as possible.

❑ Never put any foods that are still slightly warm into the freezer, as this will cause a rise in temperature and may result in deterioration of other foods in the freezer.

❑ Never freeze more than one tenth of your freezer's capacity in any 24 hours, as this will also cause the internal temperature to rise.

❑ When freezing relatively large quantities, use the fast-freeze option.

❑ Pack and seal food with care. If moisture or cold air is allowed to come into contact with the food it will begin to deteriorate. Cross-flavouring might also occur.

❑ Be sure to wrap non-packaged foods well before freezing. Solid foods must be packaged tightly, with as little air as possible. Wrap items in foil or freezer film; ordinary cling film is not suitable for the freezer. Freezer film can also be used as a lining for acidic foods which should then be over-wrapped in foil.

❑ Where possible use square containers to store food in the freezer; they stack better than round ones and therefore waste less space.

❑ Interleave any items of food that might otherwise stick together with pieces of greaseproof paper, polythene, foil or freezer film.

❑ When freezing liquids always leave room for expansion, as frozen liquid expands by about one-tenth of its volume and will push the lids off containers that have been over-filled.

❑ Freeze single and double portions for versatility and faster thawing.

❑ Do not re-freeze food once it is thawed

❑ Keep your freezer as full as possible. If necessary add loaves of bread to fill up spaces. Empty spaces require more energy to keep cool.

❑ Label and date containers clearly. This helps ensure items are used in rotation – within recommended maximum storage times.

❑ Use a freezer thermometer to check that your freezer is operating at the correct temperature which is -18°C (0°F).

FREEZER STORAGE TIMES

Where applicable for ready-prepared foods, follow the manufacturer's instructions. Otherwise use the following recommended maximum times:-

FRUIT

*fruit in syrup* 9-12 months
*open frozen fruit* 6-8 months
*fruit purées* 6-8 months
*fruit juice* 4-6 months

VEGETABLES

*blanched vegetables* 10-12 months
*mushrooms and tomatoes* 6-8 months
*vegetable purées* 6-8 months

DAIRY PRODUCE

*cream* 6-8 months
*butter (salted)* 3-4 months
*cheese (hard)* 4-6 months
*cheese (soft)* 3-4 months
*ice cream, mousses etc* 3-4 months

PREPARED FOOD

*soups and sauces* 3 months
*stock* 6 months
*prepared meals* 4-6 months
  *if highly seasoned* 2-3 months
*bread* 2-3 months
*pastries* 3-4 months
*cakes* 4-6 months

FREEZER EMERGENCIES

The most common freezer emergency is loss of power. This can be as a result of a power cut or someone inadvertently turning the freezer off. If there is a power cut, don't panic; if you leave the freezer door closed the food should stay frozen for about 30 hours (48 hours in a chest freezer).

❑ If possible, wrap the freezer with a blanket to increase insulation, but do not cover the condenser and pipes.

❑ If you have advance warning of a power cut, turn on the fast-freeze switch, making sure the freezer is full to capacity. Towels or rolled newspaper can be used to fill any gaps.

❑ Do not re-freeze any food you suspect may have begun to thaw.

THAWING FROZEN FOOD

Thawing must be done thoroughly and efficiently to ensure food is safe to eat.

❑ Never leave food to thaw in a warm environment; this is the ideal breeding ground for harmful bacteria. Instead, let the food thaw gradually in the refrigerator or in a cool larder.

❑ Cover food loosely while thawing.

❑ Make sure large items are thoroughly thawed before cooking.

❑ Cook food as soon as possible after it is thawed.

❑ If thawing ready-prepared frozen meals in a microwave, follow the manufacturer's instructions.

# INDEX

Should you require any specific information on vegetarianism, contact:
**The Vegetarian Society**
Parkdale, Dunham Road, Altrincham, Cheshire, WA14 4QG TEL: 0161 928 0793